An Introduction to the Science of Deception and Lie Detection

This accessible book provides a foundational understanding of the science of deception and lie detection. Focusing on core issues for the field, it discusses classic and current psychological research into lying as well as theoretical approaches to understanding human lie detection.

This book explores engaging questions around how people lie, how people make decisions about believing others, and how we can detect deception. Each chapter is clearly structured to support students of all levels by summarising content, presenting key research, and systematically evaluating findings. Chapters explore topics including some of the most promising current lie detection techniques, how and why people lie, how lying develops in children, and whether unconscious thinking can boost lie detection accuracy.

Providing an overview of key issues in deception, this book will be of great interest to students and lecturers in the field of deception and lie detection, as well as anyone generally interested in this fascinating field of research.

Chris N. H. Street is Senior Lecturer in Cognitive Psychology at the University of Keele, UK. His research explores the cognition of how people make lie or truth judgements. He is a recipient of the Association for Psychological Science award recognising him as a Rising Star in psychological research.

An Introduction to the Science of Deception and Lie Detection

Chris N. H. Street

LONDON AND NEW YORK

Designed cover image: © Getty Images

First published 2023
by Routledge
4 Park Square, Milton Park, Abingdon, Oxon OX14 4RN

and by Routledge
605 Third Avenue, New York, NY 10158

Routledge is an imprint of the Taylor & Francis Group, an informa business

© 2023 Chris N. H. Street

The right of Chris N. H. Street to be identified as author of this work has been asserted in accordance with sections 77 and 78 of the Copyright, Designs and Patents Act 1988.

All rights reserved. No part of this book may be reprinted or reproduced or utilised in any form or by any electronic, mechanical, or other means, now known or hereafter invented, including photocopying and recording, or in any information storage or retrieval system, without permission in writing from the publishers.

Trademark notice: Product or corporate names may be trademarks or registered trademarks, and are used only for identification and explanation without intent to infringe.

British Library Cataloguing-in-Publication Data
A catalogue record for this book is available from the British Library

Library of Congress Cataloging-in-Publication Data
Names: Street, Chris N. H., author.
Title: An introduction to the science of deception and lie detection / Chris N.H. Street.
Description: Milton Park, Abingdon, Oxon ; New York, NY : Routledge, 2023. | Includes bibliographical references and index. |
Identifiers: LCCN 2022054676 (print) | LCCN 2022054677 (ebook) | ISBN 9780367492441 (paperback) | ISBN 9780367492434 (hardback) | ISBN 9781003045298 (ebook)
Subjects: LCSH: Lie detectors and detection. | Truthfulness and falsehood—Psychological aspects. | Deception—Psychological aspects.
Classification: LCC HV8078 .S77 2023 (print) | LCC HV8078 (ebook) | DDC 363.25/4—dc23/eng/20221115
LC record available at https://lccn.loc.gov/2022054676
LC ebook record available at https://lccn.loc.gov/2022054677

ISBN: 978-0-367-49243-4 (hbk)
ISBN: 978-0-367-49244-1 (pbk)
ISBN: 978-1-003-04529-8 (ebk)

DOI: 10.4324/9781003045298

Typeset in Bembo
by codeMantra

To Molly, Coby, and Alesha.

Contents

	Acknowledgements	ix
1	Introduction: Becoming an Evaluative Reasoner	1
2	The Process of Honesty and Deception	21
3	Cues to Deception	59
4	Making Lie-Truth Judgements	83
5	Accurate Lie Detection	115
6	Developmental Factors in Deception and Lie Detection	147
7	Unconscious Lie Detection	173
8	Challenges for Deception and Lie Detection Research	196
	Glossary	213
	Index	231

Acknowledgements

I am grateful to all the people who have had to listen to me complain about not having enough time to write this book. Thanks always to my undergraduate and postgraduate supervisors who put their faith in me: Prof. Ben Tatler and Prof. Daniel Richardson. To my friends and family who have always supported me. Thank you for your love mam, dad, Mel, and my brother, sister, nieces, and nephew. My dear friends with whom I have played board games through COVID, a much-needed respite from researching this book: Jayne, Ruth, Richard and Michelle, David and Sara, Jack and Will. My wonderful new friends and fellow gamers: Jens, Robin, May, Kym, Krystian, Emma. I love you all very much. Alex, thank you for always being there for me. I would also like to thank each of my collaborators, especially Jaume Masip who took a risk on collaborating with a naive PhD student. Ching-Yu Huang has listened to me talk about this book for a long time: thank you for your patience. And finally, thank you to my friends and colleagues at the University of Huddersfield and Keele University.

1 Introduction

Becoming an Evaluative Reasoner

> **Box 1.1 Donald Trump and an Attempt to Overturn a Presidential Election**
>
> Donald Trump lost the US presidential election in 2020. He attempted to stop the democratic process of certifying the next elected president, Joe Biden. The 'Big Lie' was that Donald Trump was the legitimate winner of the presidential election. Ahead of the results, Trump claimed that the vote should be treated as fraudulent if it did not show him winning the election. When the results did not come out in his favour, Trump and his supporters turned to conspiracy theories such as claims that voting machines were rigged against him. He filed lawsuits to undermine the democratic election and tweeted "THE DEMOCRATS DUMPED HUNDREDS OF THOUSANDS OF BALLOTS IN THE SWING STATES LATE IN THE EVENING. IT WAS A RIGGED ELECTION!!!" (Brown, 2016). For an analysis of the impact of Trump's lies on US democracy, see Pfiffner (2020). For those interested in reviewing Trump's tweets since September 2016, visit www.thetrumparchive.com.

One question I often get asked at parties is "why would you study deception? Aren't there more important issues facing the world?". Or rather, I probably would get asked that at parties if I were invited to them. And I think it is a fair question. Is it a sensible use of resources to find ways of detecting if our friends and family are lying to us? Is it really worthwhile accruing a list of behaviours that might give a liar away? I hope I can convince you that lie detection research has far more value than that. Let us think about that for a moment.

Box 1.2 The Impact of Our Research

Is it worthwhile spending time researching deception and its detection? With very broadly defined issues like this, it can often be helpful breaking it down into something more manageable and tangible. Let's give that a go. I recognise that not everyone enjoys active learning, but I would ask that as a minimum you read these questions and think about each for at least five seconds. I would hope for more, but I'll take five seconds if that is all you will give me.

1. List (mentally or in writing) up to five situations where deception may have an important role to play. To do that, consider:

    a   professions where deception or lie detection would be helpful,
    b   news items where deception was involved, and
    c   how deception and lie detection can help or harm (i) industry, (ii) society, and (iii) sovereignty.

2. Now list up to three areas of study within Psychology that you enjoy studying, such as developmental psychology.

    a   How might deception have a role to play in each discipline you listed?

After you have given a little thought to the above questions, keep reading. I will offer some thoughts after each Box so that you can see an example of someone engaging in the evaluative process. But you will best develop your own capacity by doing it yourself.

The purpose of this exercise was to encourage you to describe and explore how broad an impact deception can have on society and on our academic understanding of human thought and behaviour. Understanding the importance of your research area is a useful skill and thinking about the further impact of your work can helps us look beyond what is right in front of us. It allows you to understand the broader context in which your research sits. It is easy to lose sight of the bigger picture. Don't be afraid to be creative and allow yourself to explore areas outside of your comfort zone.

In this Box, we aimed to describe something about the field. As we progress through the chapter, we will slowly shift from description (which demonstrates your knowledge of the field) to evaluation (which demonstrates an independent intellectual capacity).

As we saw in Box 1.2, deception has a broad impact on society and touches on many aspects of human thought and behaviour. You may have considered the role of lie detection in the courts and law enforcement, the act of 'social engineering' or gaining unauthorised access to an organisation's sensitive data and assets, or the deceptive claims of abusive or neglectful caregivers are interviewed by social workers. Then, there are examples of business negotiation tactics, political deception, and employment interviews. The list goes on. A broad range of economic and societal issues are affected by deception and its detection, and it is studied by researchers in a broad range of areas such as communication, anthropology, philosophy and ethics, marketing, and management, to name but a few.

Consider the issue of online safety. Cyber security training organisations develop training materials to teach companies how to avoid becoming a victim of a 'phishing' email (an email that looks as though it was sent from someone trustworthy to trick people into giving up sensitive information like credit card details and passwords). Training organisations need a firm understanding of the psychology of deception to offer appropriate and effective advice. Should they train clients to become ever sceptical and reduce their willingness to trust (the 'truth bias', see Chapter 4) or would it be more effective to teach organisations a set of clues that indicate that the email is fraudulent (see Chapter 3 for cues to deception)? Do people become victims of phishing attacks because they are unable to withhold some built-in cognitive bias to believe, and so perhaps need a technological intervention to regularly flag the possibility of deception? Or are they actively considering deception already, but need to spend more time looking for indicators, or spend more time reflecting on their confidence in their judgement? Our theoretical understanding of the psychology of deception and how people try to detect it provides an evidence base on which we can advise cyber security training firms.

Box 1.2 asked you to also consider the role of deception in psychological theory. When thinking about the subdisciplines within psychology, you may have considered the role of deception in social psychology, such as its positive and negative influences on maintaining intimate relationships. Or you may have thought about the cognitive processes involved in deciding whether someone is lying. Or perhaps you thought of the development of the ability to deceive in children and how this may be a marker of more sophisticated reasoning. If you recognised some of these connections or others, then great job! Finding these connections allows us to draw on related work in separate subdisciplines to develop a well-rounded understanding of deception and its detection. Perhaps more practically relevant for you right now is that it helps you demonstrate (e.g., in an assessment) an independence of thought and ability to collate and synthesise relevant information about a scientific question from a number of perspectives. Trust me, we lecturers are easily impressed.

A Brief Modern History of Deception and Its Detection

As you might imagine, it is not possible for me to provide comprehensive coverage of a whole field of research in a brief subsection like this. For those areas that I have neglected, I have done so either because of a lack of space or through my own ignorance. There are many exciting research streams that I will miss, and to those working in those areas please accept my apologies.

In this section, I will highlight what I consider to be broad approaches and research questions that have and/or continue to be important questions for deception and lie detection. Many of these are explored in greater detail in future chapters. This very brief section serves to provide a quick entry point into deception and lie detection, and also signposts how future chapters fit into the broader context of understanding deception and lie detection.

In the 1960s, lie detection research began from the assumption that liars would experience emotions such as guilt and fear and that these emotions may 'leak' from the liar despite their attempts to conceal them. This 'leakage hypothesis' (Ekman & Friesen, 1969) proposed that emotion would leak more readily from bodily movements than from the face. Over time, researchers shifted focus towards understanding the thinking process, or 'cognition', of the liar as one who has to think harder than truth-tellers because they have to inhibit the truth and invent a story that is consistent and does not contradict what the person listening to the lie may be aware of already (Zuckerman et al., 1981; see also Hartwig et al., 2014; Kassin, 2012).

At around this time, the 'heuristics and biases' programme of research (rules of thumb that people use to make satisfactorily useful judgements with their limited mental resources to make sense of the wealth of information in the environment) was taking hold across psychology and behavioural economics (Kahneman et al., 1982). In the lie detection field, researchers started to take an interest in systematic biases in making a lie or truth judgement. It turns out that people tend to judge others are telling the truth more often than they are actually telling the truth (see Bond & DePaulo, 2006, for a 'meta-analysis'; that is, a study that combines multiple past studies and analyses them together to see what can be learnt from the collection of past research). It is perhaps no surprise that this became known as the 'truth bias', given the rapid proliferation of biases that were discovered across psychology as a result of the heuristic and biases programme of research (e.g., Gilovich et al., 2002). An early account of how people make lie-truth judgements suggested that people cannot help but automatically believe information is true initially, and this may be causing the truth bias (Gilbert, 1991). This 'Spinozan mind' account still influences the field today. Another account has recently been proposed that is conceptually similar to the Spinozan mind: Truth-Default Theory (Levine, 2014). However, the Adaptive Lie Detector (Street, 2015) takes a rather different perspective of the truth bias. It argues that the truth bias results from functional, sensible, and informed decision-making.

Alongside this research, the search for a useful cue to deception (either from the emotional leakage or a sign of mental effort) fails to generate anything that is 'diagnostic' (i.e., a cue that is present more often when people lie than tell the truth or vice versa; see DePaulo et al., 2003, for a meta-analysis). It is perhaps not surprising, then, that people make for poor lie detectors. They score marginally, but reliably, above chance, with an accuracy rate of 54% where 50% would be chance (Bond & DePaulo, 2006). Training, expertise, or other factors that one may imagine would increase accuracy (such as confidence or profession) do little to increase accuracy (Aamodt & Custer, 2006). In more recent years, researchers have shifted towards trying to develop techniques that actively prompt these cues in the liars and truth-tellers (e.g., Nahari, 2019; Vrij & Granhag, 2012).

This very brief review of the field is, of course, *my* personal view of the field. Other researchers who are more interested in, say, the emotional cues to deception (such as the concept of 'micro-expressions', emotions that supposedly briefly expose the true emotional feelings of a liar; see Chapter 3) or in the use of the polygraph (known colloquially as the 'lie detector', a device that measures the bodily reactions of a potential liar to assess whether they are lying; see Chapter 5) may offer quite a different modern history. Don't worry, we will touch on these topics later in the book.

Aims of the Book

This book is intended as an introduction into some core issues in deception and its detection by considering the historical and cultural context in which the research sits. Regarding the historical context, we will cover 'seminal' work (i.e., work that is important to understand and has influenced researchers, leading to streams of future research) which provides the background and context to the current state of the field. But we will also discuss the latest findings and even engage in some stargazing (i.e., speculation and as-yet untested suggestions). Regarding the cultural context, while it is an understudied area of deception (George et al., 2018), cross-cultural findings are explored alongside discussion of the findings using Westernised samples.

The book is primarily written for students new to the field of deception and lie detection. I strongly encourage you to engage with the Boxes in each chapter and take just a few seconds to reflect on the questions I ask there. Truly, this need not be more than a few seconds in many cases, and even where more time is seemingly required, I would ask for a minimum of five seconds thought. I hope you will at least spare me that small amount of time so that you can practice and build your evaluative reasoning. Hopefully, of course, you will engage for longer than this, but any time I can secure that helps you build your evaluative capacities is a win for me. Lecturers and educators may find these Boxes to be useful in helping them reflect on possible formative tasks.

While this book is intended as a student textbook, there may be something to be gleaned by practitioners too. But I caution that the book should not be used as a sole reference source for translating psychological research directly into practice. The book is a wayfinder, helping guide you towards the relevant questions and issues being explored in this field. Your primary source of reading should be academic articles. These can be a little daunting for the practitioner, and so you may find it beneficial to team with academics who are experts in the area you aim to learn more about.

Finally, you may be reading this book for general interest. If so, read just the first few sentences of the Boxes to see if they may be of interest. I think you will find yourself pleasantly surprised at how easy it can be to build your evaluative and creative reasoning, which is very important if you are to be a consumer of science. We should not blindly accept what anyone says—not even academics. You will find mentions of authors followed by a year throughout the book. This is a reference to a full research article that has been reviewed by two or more independent academics before it was published. This 'peer review' process helps ensure that what is published in scientific journals is credible and robust. That I cite evidence alongside my claims should help you feel at ease in believing the contents of this book. Always look out for the author names and year of publication. This should not only add some veridicality to the claims being made here, but if you find a particular topic of interest, you have a set of journal articles that you could look up to learn more (that you can often find, sometimes for free, by running an internet search for the title and author names. I recommend using the Google Scholar search engine, http://scholar.google.com). You should also look out for these references in other sources too, whether that is an online video or popular psychology book. If there are no or few references given in those videos or books, it is appropriate to have a healthy scepticism of the claims and to keep in mind that they may not reflect the science.

This book is not intended as an exhaustive resource of the contemporary and historical literature. The aim is to provide an overview of key issues in deception and offer a starting point from which you can discover more about this fascinating field of research. Among some of the topics that do not appear in this book (or appear only in passing) are the evolution of lying, the moral and ethical implications of deception, animal and plant deception, military deception, medical malingering (appearing to show signs of an ailment the person does not have or concealing signs of an ailment the person does actually have), fake news, social engineering, a compilation of cues that give away the liar (sorry, but highly diagnostic cues to deception do not exist! More of this in Chapter 3), and a psychodynamic perspective on deception and juror decision-making, to name but a few topics. This book is not a definitive guide to the whole field. No book (that can be feasibly carried by a human) ever could be. It is an up-to-date introduction to core research themes and questions that have been and are being tackled in universities and research institutions today. It is for you to discover the particular rabbit holes that most appeal to you and to burrow deeper.

The Author's Perspective

As already alluded to, each of us has our own perspective. This will become clear as we begin to unpick the debates we will see in future chapters. We need to be able to challenge our own perspectives[1] and check that they are the result of sound reasoning built on a solid base of scientific evidence. One difficulty I have in writing this book is that I cannot negate my own perspective. The best I can do is to offer you a sense of where I come from as a researcher. Also, as we progress through the chapters, I will encourage you to evaluate alternative viewpoints and to actively challenge any particular perspective in the book. But ultimately, any textbook will be written by an author or authors that have a viewpoint that will influence its content and direction, and it is worthwhile understanding what that perspective is.

My first interest in Psychology began when I learnt about behaviourism. What a truly wonderful, deterministic, and elegant explanation of the complexities of human behaviour: there is an input into the human system, and it triggers an output. Ring a bell, and the dog salivates.[2] How anyone could first hear of behaviourism and not be moved by its elegance as a simple explanation of human behaviour is beyond my imagination. Ever since, I have been driven by finding simplifying explanations of that complex and messy system that is human thought. But it has taken a few twists and turns.

During my undergraduate degree at the University of Dundee, Scotland, I was lucky enough to have the opportunity to work in a lab for three years exploring how the human mind represents visual information. I thought for sure that my academic career lay in the direction of understanding the visual system. And that was the plan: I joined a lab at UCL in London as a research assistant on the social and cognitive aspects of visual perception. But then an undergraduate wanted to do a project on deception. Knowing nothing about it, I began reading on the subject and found the research fascinating: both for what it was doing and for what it was not doing. That then became a PhD project in the same lab (a degree where the student carries out their own research agenda over a period of three or more years), followed by a post-doctoral fellowship (similar to a PhD, except the duration varies considerably and this is a salaried, non-student post) continuing that work in a cognition lab at UBC in Vancouver, Canada. I then went on to the University of Huddersfield, England, and finally to Keele University, England, where at the time of writing I continue to work on deception.

I tell you all this because my approach to the field of deception has not begun by asking "how do liars give themselves away?", or "how can we help practitioners detect a liar?". Instead, my training in vision and cognition leads me to wonder "how do people reach a lie or truth decision—rightly or wrongly?" That is, what are the processes at work when people lie and when people try to detect a lie? What goes through their mind when making the decision? I am a cognitive psychologist and not a forensic psychologist, or a social psychologist, or a communication researcher. Ultimately, the approach of this book is going to be somewhat influenced by an understanding of the underlying cognitive mechanisms, but it will not be wholly and solely driven by that perspective. You will also find discussions of the social, developmental, applied, and other approaches to understanding deception and lie detection, and we will draw on research from forensic psychologists, social psychologists, and communication researchers, among others.

Box 1.3 Influences on Your Reasoning

By understanding your own interests and approach, you will have a sense of the biases that may come into play when interpreting literature and conducting your own research. We cannot become detached robots with a purely unadulterated view of the world. Let's reflect on your view for a moment:

1. Where in the world did you grow up? How might your socio-economic background, culture, and political views affect your willingness to accept evidence or to consider an argument contrary to your lived experience? Might you be inclined to give less weighting to research in cultures other than your own or that comes from more or less financially secure parts of the world?
2. If you are reading this book, you will likely have some understanding of psychology, sociology, or a related discipline. Are there some areas that interest you or some that bore you? How do you feel about developmental explanations, evolutionary accounts, and cognitive models of behaviour? Are you quick to dismiss work suggesting personality causes behaviour or work that suggests situational influences are more important than personality in determining behaviour? Are these judgements truly supported by an evidence base or driven more by a preference to interpret human behaviour in a particular light?
3. Imagine a scientist (let's call them Julie) publishes a study finding that a sample of 50 people eating 400g (five portions) of fruit and veg had an increased risk of a heart attack compared to a sample of 50 people who ate 400g of chocolate (I know which condition I would have wanted to be in if I had taken part in this study):
    a. How convinced are you that eating fruit and vegetables is bad for your health (or that substituting it for chocolate is good for your health)? Why?
    b. Assuming Julie's study did not convince you that you should eat less fruit and veg, what evidence would lead you to start believing that you should eat less fruit and veg?

I cannot answer these questions for you. But I hope on reflection that you have realised that you may be coming to the situation with some preformed opinions that may affect how you seek out and evaluate evidence (see Brady et al., 2018). As students, scientists, or practitioners, we should be aware of our own particular lens and understand how it influences the questions we ask, the data we collect and the interpretations we make.

> Notice that I have not suggested that you try to become a detached, objective robot. One cannot simply abandon one's belief system. However, we must nonetheless be careful not to dismiss others' views simply because they are inconsistent with our beliefs (see Garland et al., 1990; Harrison & Harrell, 1993; Staw, 1976, for some evidence that we are motivated to maintain our current beliefs and actions rather than change them). We should take the time to reflect on why we hold our beliefs, consider the evidence, and be willing to update our beliefs—*if* the evidence is sufficiently demonstrative. That is, we do not abandon our prior beliefs simply because one study with questionable methods contradicts our views, but rather we should change our views as the data becomes sufficiently evidential that we need to reflect on our beliefs. That word 'sufficient' is defined by you and your academic training.[3]

Introducing Evaluative Reasoning

You may have noticed the intermingling of research content and evaluative reasoning. Research in deception (or any field, for that matter) requires not only a knowledge of past work, but also an evaluative eye and a capacity to meaningfully interpret it. Regardless of your discipline and regardless of whether you are a scientist or a consumer of science, being able to critically evaluate information is a core skill that you should learn to form rational interpretations and is a desirable skill for further study or starting a career beyond academia (Gabennesch, 2006; Jeevanantham, 2005). Brookfield (as cited in Garrison, 1991) claimed that "learning to think critically is one of the most significant activities of adult life". In this section, I hope to show you some tricks and tips for improving your evaluative game.[4]

You may already be thinking of skipping this subsection. Students tend to rate evaluative reasoning as rather unimportant on the list of skills needed to be effective at university and seem to have a limited view of what it actually entails (Buckist et al., 2002; Tapper, 2004). But the World Economic Forum (2018) placed problem-solving and evaluative reasoning at the top of their ten most needed skills in the labour market (see Indrašienė et al., 2020), and educators value it highly in their students (Buckist et al., 2002). It is certainly worth more than a few minutes of your time. Stick with me for a moment.

Each chapter will explore the field while pitching you a question or two in Boxes like the one we saw earlier (see Box 1.2). Towards the start of the book, the Boxes will check your understanding of what has been covered and reflect on your ability to summarise what you have learnt. As we progress through the book and through a given chapter, there will be a shift towards more evaluative reasoning. Sometimes you will be dealing with concrete, tangible examples and at other times you will be tackling more abstract, nebulous concepts, which will give you experience of evaluative reasoning from different perspectives. You may have already noticed how the questions in each of the Boxes we have seen so far have shifted from description to evaluation, and from concrete issues about the applicability of deception research to more abstracted and broader questions about how we form and update our beliefs about the world. The questions that are posed are optional, but they offer an opportunity to dig deeper into the subject matter while also developing your reasoning abilities. Naturally, I will not be sticking rigidly to this formula: the questions that arise at a given point in a chapter may require us to take a deeper intellectual dive from the outset of the chapter or we may find more descriptive reflections useful in later sections of the chapter.

There are many books that you can source for developing your evaluative reasoning, each with their own definition of what evaluative reasoning entails. We do not need to get too consumed by this: for our purposes, I will consider evaluative reasoning to involve:

1 developing novel and original arguments,
2 considering the relative merits of alternative viewpoints,
3 reflecting on the strengths and limitations of evidence and arguments, especially one's own arguments, and
4 arriving at sound conclusions that can be cogently communicated to others.

Evaluative Reasoning Practices

Alternative viewpoints. At the end of the previous section a broad definition of evaluative reasoning was given. One element of this definition was to develop novel and original arguments. Developing such arguments will, to some degree, mean challenging your preconceived notions of what is accepted as the truth. Mason (2008) argues that "a strong critical thinker is able to understand the bigger picture holistically, to see different worldviews in perspective, rather than just to critique the individual steps in a particular argument". Achieving this involves speaking with people who have different cultural and socio-economic backgrounds and viewpoints. Engaging with others around you, especially if they have a different outlook on the issue, can be fruitful. Hearing an alternative viewpoint gives you an opportunity to compare against your own views and begin to identify what assumptions you may have been making, whether you have a credible base of evidence to base your argument on, whether your position is logical and coherent, and whether there is any strength to a viewpoint that contradicts your own. And equally, of course, one can evaluate the arguments of others, too. But self-reflection is critical for deeper evaluative reasoning, especially as we have a tendency to prefer ideas that we have come up with compared to the ideas of others (Tiehen, 2022).

If you are at a university, your department may have seminars where invited speakers discuss their research. Attending these seminars gives an insight into how other scientists view the world and how they evaluate evidence and gives you that opportunity to see the world from another viewpoint—possibly one that contradicts yours. If possible, take a friend and afterwards discuss whether you agree or disagree with the speaker's arguments and why. Try finding alternative psychological explanations of the speaker's findings. If you go to the seminar alone, then take some time afterwards to think about these same points. If your university does not have a seminar series, try creating a journal club with some friends or some people on your course. If you are not at a university, try emailing the head of the psychology department of your local university and ask if you can attend the seminar series. You might be surprised by how welcoming they are, and if not, the worst that can happen is that they tell you that you cannot attend.

Take this same open-mindedness with you into your reading of the research literature. When you read about data supporting a particular argument or perspective, consider whether it might also be supporting other perspectives. Is the perspective under consideration the only possible perspective? How could other perspectives be made to fit this data? Are other perspectives ruled out by this data? Having a good understanding of the research area you are working in will help you here: knowing what contrasting perspectives exist out there will allow you to assess whether they can explain the data. However, you are by no means limited if you are not an expert in a particular field. Bring your knowledge from other psychological subdisciplines (or from other fields) to bear: are the claims consistent with accounts and perspectives found in other research areas? Are there other possible explanations that have not been considered that might be worthwhile exploring in future research? The aim is to generate alternate explanations of phenomena, alternative interpretations of data, and so on. Once they are generated, their plausibility can be evaluated: we can worry about that later. Try to be liberal in the generation process and allow yourself the freedom to consider a whole host of different interpretations, regardless of how silly they may at first seem. You can always dismiss options when you begin evaluating your alternatives.

As you generate these alternatives, what you are actually doing is formulating meaningful future research questions that push the field of psychology forward (tip: these are likely the sorts of future research questions that lecturers are hoping to see in the discussion section of a lab report). However, be careful not to fall into the trap of jumping to conclusions. At this stage, you are formulating *possible* explanations and do not yet have data to determine whether those explanations are correct.

Consider an example by Butterworth and Thwaites (2013): you hold two bank notes that have the same serial number. Which of these conclusions are safe and fair conclusions to reach? (i) At least one of the notes is a forgery, (ii) at least one cannot be legally spent, and (iii) at least one was made by terrorists. Try to answer that before continuing. Also see if you can find the assumptions associated with the conclusions. An assumption common to all three is that genuine bank notes have serial numbers and that they are different. Are these assumptions true? As it turns out, they are both true in my country (the UK) at the time of writing, but it is worth checking the assumptions. Given the assumptions, the first and second conclusions are safe: at least one of the notes cannot be genuine. Because it is not legal to spend forgeries, the second conclusion is also safe. But the third conclusion is not safe. There are a variety of possible explanations for the bank notes having come into existence, and the information given (what we can think of as 'data') do not allow us to reach this conclusion safely. We can often find it tempting to jump to conclusions when those conclusions match our existing beliefs about the world. This is where interacting with others who have different viewpoints will come in useful. That interaction might be through attendance at seminars, reading articles by researchers who have different views to you, or through self-reflection and challenging your own ideas.

Considering alternative viewpoints will involve taking a step back and considering how the current study fits within the broader field of research. While it can certainly be helpful to dive deep into the minutiae of the experimental procedure in a given study, also remember to take a mental step back and view the core aims and conclusions of the work in light of what is already known about the field (the 'field' may be the field of deception research, cognition, psychology, societal issues, practical application and more).

You will gain hands-on experience of considering alternative viewpoints, and the other practical tips in this section, as we progress through the book. For now, try Box 1.4.

Box 1.4 Considering All Available Options

I happen to be an avid board gamer, so let us jump to that topic for a moment. There is a game called Cockroach Poker. The core rules are very straightforward: someone takes one of eight insect cards from their hand, places it face down, and passes it to you, telling you what the insect is. But they are allowed to lie. You have to decide whether you believe them or not. If you are correct, they take the card in front of them as a punishment. If you are incorrect, you gain the card in front of you as a punishment. You lose if you gain four insects of the same kind in front of you. Imagine a situation where you already have three cockroaches in front of you—one more will make you lose the game. But you have no other insects in front of you, just the three cockroaches. I pass you a card and say "it's, umm … a cockroach" as I shuffle in my seat and avoid making eye contact. What do you do? Have a quick think about this before reading further.

Table 1.1 The possible outcomes of each action you could take (in the columns) after an opponent passes you a card and claims "this is a cockroach". The cells indicate the outcome of those actions depending on whether the opponent was telling the truth (i.e., it is a cockroach card) or lying

Claim: "This is a cockroach"		Belief judgement	
		"I believe you"	"I do not believe you"
Actual value of card	Cockroach (telling the truth)	Opponent gains a cockroach card	You gain your final cockroach, losing the game
	Not a cockroach (lying)	You gain a non-cockroach card	Opponent gains a non-cockroach card

You could try to rely on my signs of nervousness to decide if I am lying. But let's break down the possibilities. *Think of all the alternatives,* depicted in Table 1.1. You could choose to say you believe me (left column) or disbelieve me (right column). And the card could be a cockroach (top row) or not a cockroach (bottom row).

If you say that you believe me and you are correct (the card actually is a cockroach: top-left cell of Table 1.1), the cockroach will be placed in front of me (good news for you). If you believe me and you are incorrect (it actually is not a cockroach, maybe it is a leaf bug: bottom-left cell), the card will go to you. But it is not a cockroach, so you have not lost the game: this is your first leaf bug. If you choose to say you believe me (left column), you cannot lose the game regardless of whether the card is or is not a cockroach.

What happens if you choose to disbelieve me (right column)? If it actually is a cockroach but you didn't believe my claim that it is a cockroach (top-right cell), you would be incorrect and you would gain your fourth cockroach card, losing the whole game. If the card is not a cockroach (bottom-right cell), it is placed in front of me, and I have to take a non-cockroach card. When you claim you do not believe me (right column), you risk losing the whole game. You cannot lose the game on this turn by saying you believe me (left column). It might be a good idea, in the short term at least, to say you will believe me about it being a cockroach on this occasion. Working through all the possible outcomes gives us a more informed view of the situation.

Challenging the assumptions. Research typically begins from the statement of a research question. This question will be built on a set of assumptions. Many of these assumptions will be supported with data from past research, but that does not make them infallible. Reflecting on whether the assumptions are sound is critical because the logical soundness of the conclusions reached will rest upon those starting assumptions. One practical approach to rooting out the assumptions in our reasoning (or others' reasoning) is to ask yourself, "how do you know that?" each time a statement of fact is made or when an answer to a question is provided (Halpern, 1998). Try to abandon the idea that we can rely on agreed upon facts and knowledge and instead challenge and question those base assumptions. The theory of evolution challenges the assumption that species of animals are fundamentally distinct from one another. Einstein's theory of relativity challenges the assumption that space and time are two separate constructs. Embodiment theory challenges the assumption that processing meaning is solely an act of the mind independent of the body it inhabits. These assumptions seem reasonable, and yet challenging them has led to some of our biggest breakthroughs in science. For more on challenging assumptions, see Thomson (2013), Chapter 1.

Deconstructing the issue. Having assessed the assumptions, it is important to deconstruct the research question, problem, theory, or whatever it is that you are evaluating. What is meant here is that you should be able to simplify the matter to a point where it is clear to someone with no expertise in psychology. This simplification should not change or remove details, but rather expand the explanation to be well-defined and testable. For example, when we offer explanations such as "the unconscious improves lie detection because it can automatically process information", what exactly is meant here? What does it mean to *process* information? What does *automatic* processing look like in a biological organism? What is the *unconscious*? Breaking down these constituent parts and having a clearly defined and testable explanation both improves our own understanding of the problem and enhances the testability and applicability of our science. Deconstructing the problem is rather similar to assumption challenging, insofar as the assumption here is that we understand what these words mean and that we all agree on a definition of these words. Similarly, if we propose a question such as "Do children develop an ability to lie because of nature or nurture?", we need to ask what it is we mean by *nature* and *nurture*, how do we define both *children* and *lying*, and how we are defining *develop* in this context (e.g., does develop mean to learn?). If we are using the word *develop* to mean learning, *nature* to mean born with a skill, and *nurture* to mean a learnt skill, the question answers itself: developing only fits the definition of nurture (to learn) and does not fit with the tight definition of nature we are using here (to be born with the skill and so requires no learning). In deconstructing the question, we may come to realise that the question is not all that meaningful after all. Deconstructing a problem is certainly worthwhile and can lead to self-discovery and unearthing some interesting problems with the object of our evaluations.

Source credibility. Evaluating the credibility of the sources that are being used to support an argument or develop a research question will help create an understanding of the logical soundness of the conclusions being reached or the questions being asked. Are the authors making appeals to authority, common sense, or anecdotes, or are they using more credible sources such as peer-reviewed journal articles? If the arguments rely on peer-reviewed articles, do the methods allow the research question to be answered? Do the methods follow robust standards for effective scientific investigation (e.g., following 'open science' principles of making the data and resources available and transparent for others to openly review and assess, or preregistering the hypotheses and methods in an online, immutable repository that can be readily checked by others *before* the data is collected so that there is less room for adjusting hypotheses after the data have been analysed)? Assessing the rigour of research methods is too big an issue to tackle here, and is more the domain of a research methods course, for which you will readily find many research articles and books on the subject.

Evaluating conclusions. Once one has developed a sound conclusion on the basis of evaluative reasoning, a natural question is whether the conclusion is true. I find this sort of thinking unhelpful. Scientific theories are regularly incorrect (factually untrue), with one theory being overthrown by another (see Kuhn, 1962, on the scientific revolution).[5] Many of us still learn of Newton's theory of gravitation at high school, despite Einstein's conception of gravity having displaced it and with Einstein's conception being able to explain phenomena that Newton's theory could not (e.g., Do et al., 2019). The Einsteinian universe too may be displaced someday.

What is the purpose of science if it is not pulling us closer towards being correct? This is a big question. I cannot possibly hope to answer it in such a brief chapter as this. Broadly speaking, I subscribe to the position that accounts need not be definitively True with a capital 'T', but it does need to have 'explanatory power'. This power to explain phenomena comes from making predictions that could falsify the account. That is, the account explains the conditions that would be necessary for the account to be shown to be wrong.

This may seem rather odd: surely accounts should be trying to tell us what they *can* explain, not what they fail to. Let us take an example to see what I mean. Consider Newton's theory: it predicted that a body of a particular mass existed in space moving with a particular trajectory, even though at the time telescopes were not powerful enough to observe the planet's existence. All it would take is for the body to be of a different mass or travelling on a different trajectory, or not existing at all, and the theory could have been challenged. However, it survived the attempt to be falsified and we now know that planet as Neptune (see Bamford, 1996).

Thus, the strength of an account is not merely gained from explaining what phenomena are already known (although, of course, any account with explanatory power must be able to do this), but from being able to generate *new* predictions that are as-yet largely untested and specify the conditions that would show the account to be wrong. When we reflect on the strength of an account, then we should ask ourselves not only whether it can explain past phenomena (which it almost surely will), but whether it generates clear, testable predictions about new phenomena and allows the *possibility* for the data to show that the account could be wrong. Being able to determine this will require deconstructing the problem in order to identify what is testable and what is not. Indeed, we may discover that the account is not testable at all or that the predictions it puts forward are not testing the core claims of the account. This may all feel a little abstracted at this point, but we will try this out with more concrete examples in the deception and detection field later in the book.

Practical implications. We should also take some time to reflect on the practical implications of the conclusions reached. Might a conclusion have practical significance that could benefit people? Or perhaps it pushes forward our theoretical understanding of psychology. Could the conclusion have negative implications for certain groups, such as stigmatising those groups? Reflect on what the findings would mean for both practice and theory as you evaluate your outcomes. However, ensure that you are being realistic, too. For example, is it realistic to suggest that police forces should only hire cisgender females on the basis of one study finding that cisgender females achieve 2% higher detection rates compared to cisgender males (that is, people who identify as male and their birth sex was determined as male)? Aside from the enormous change to the structure of the police force on the basis of a rather small effect in a single study, we might also need to think about the implications this would have in terms of discrimination, the impact such a change would have on the other functions that police force is required to do beyond detecting lies, and so on.

Summary. In this section we have reflected on how we may evaluate information in a meaningful way. The purpose is to reach sound conclusions about deception and lie detection. The techniques that we have discussed are not definitive and not without limitation. You may decide that the techniques do not fit with how you are developing or have developed your evaluative reasoning. You may see flaws in the evaluative tips suggested—and if so, excellent! These points of guidance come from a combination of published work on evaluative reasoning and critical thinking as well as a reflection on the approach I take in my own thinking. If you find that the guidance is not helpful for you, then take a moment to pause and consider why, because you are on a tipping point of developing your own evaluative reasoning approach, which can be the difference between being able to describe psychology to being an evaluative consumer and practitioner of psychology.

Perhaps the most critical element of deeper reasoning is to explore the alternative interpretations. Take time to imagine what the data may have told us had they come out differently, what might cause such a difference, and whether there are other explanations of observed phenomena than the ones being put forward. Importantly, a strong evaluative reasoner is able to turn this critical eye back on their own thoughts and conclusions. As you do so, explore the assumptions you may be basing your reasoning on. Ensure that you can clearly define the problem and are testing ideas that are in principle falsifiable. As you read research, consider whether they are basing their inferences on credible sources, whether the conclusions they reach logically follow from the data, and what the broader societal and practical implications of those conclusions may be.

Keep in mind that the purpose of evaluative reasoning is not to win the argument, but to try to learn something meaningful about deception or lie detection. While it can certainly be helpful to be critical of the work of others, one must also be willing to be charitable to the claims of others too. Hughes et al. (2015) refer to this latter point as the Principle of Charity. If a claim by a researcher is ambiguous or unclear, for instance, but you could provide an interpretation that is favourable to the researcher's claims, the Principle of Charity encourages us to offer that favourable opinion. This helps us not only generate a collegiate discussion in our writing, but also forces us to be more critical of our own perspective, which is a truly useful skill to have as both a consumer and producer of scientific research. However, there is nothing wrong with noting that the argument is vague or ambiguous and so requires redefining.

Chapter Summary

Deception and its detection have broad reach across our lives and societies. They inform (and can be informed by) the spectrum of psychological subdisciplines and beyond reaching into issues of morality, ethics, and philosophy, to name but a few. We have seen that the modern history of deception is one of cue-seeking (such as looking for behaviours that reflect the unique emotional or cognitive elements of deception that may give the liar away), although this has been largely unsuccessful: liars do not seem to give themselves away so easily. It is perhaps unsurprising, then, that lie detection accuracy tends to be rather low and that neither training nor individual differences (such as expertise or confidence) do much to increase accuracy. This may also explain why the field has now taken a turn towards more active methods of detecting deception, with a view to eliciting cues from liars (or truth-tellers) about the veracity of their claims. Alongside this, in recent years we have seen researchers becoming more concerned with the core theoretical issues of how people decide to deceive and how they decide who is lying.

But I hope you finish this book feeling that the journey has been more than a recounting of 'facts' that you need to learn. Far from it! Your job as a scientist in training is to evaluate the information, to assess its credibility and cogency. Evaluative reasoning involves developing novel, robust arguments that reflect on the strengths and limitations of multiple alternative viewpoints to arrive at a logically and/or empirically defensible conclusion. This chapter has offered some reflections on how you may engage in evaluative reasoning. We will revisit these as we progress through the chapters.

To further develop your evaluative reasoning, I recommend Chapter 4 of Butterworth and Thwaites (2013). For a concise, contemporary overview of the field of lie detection, check out Masip (2017).

Notes

1 I am referring solely to one's academic perspective. I am also a white male from a western developed society, a member of the LGBTQIA+ community, from a working-class background, financially stable, trained as a quantitative scientist, and so on. These influences will also affect my assumptions and interpretations.
2 For anyone not familiar with Pavlov's dog, a quick internet search of the term will return many relevant results on 'classical conditioning'.
3 Bayesian analysis formalises this belief updating process. For a gentle introduction to what Bayesian analysis is, I strongly recommend checking out the Bayesian chapter in Dienes's (2008) book.
4 I will use the terms evaluative reasoning and critical thinking synonymously. I prefer the term evaluative reasoning because, in my experience, students tend to confuse critical thinking to mean that they must find fault with any argument put forward, which can lead to a neglect of evidence that may support that same argument. That is, some students equate critical thinking with taking a negative view of the argument being evaluated. Critical thinking or evaluative reasoning can, of course, lead us to believe an argument is grounded, consistent, backed with supporting data and theory, and has the potential to change the practitioner's approach for the better.
5 To be clear, I am not stating that science is unhelpful. Far from it. If you have ever taken medication, used some form of transport, or worn a pair of glasses, you are benefiting from the scientific process. What I mean by 'wrong' in this context is a more philosophical matter of whether we can fully understand the universe from the perspective of human experience rather than a more practical 'wrong' in terms of whether the account makes predictions that turn out to be supported with the data.

References

Aamodt, M. G., & Custer, H. (2006). Who can best catch a liar? A meta-analysis of individual differences in detecting deception. *The Forensic Examiner, 15*(1), 6–11.

Bamford, G. (1996). Popper and his commentators on the discovery of Neptune: A close shave for the law of gravitation? *Studies in History and Philosophy of Science Part A, 27*(2), 207–232. https://doi.org/10.1016/0039-3681(95)00045-3

Bond, C. F., & DePaulo, B. M. (2006). Accuracy of deception judgments. *Personality and Social Psychology Review, 10*(3), 214–234. https://doi.org/10.1207/s15327957pspr1003_2

Brady, L. M., Fryberg, S. A., & Shoda, Y. (2018). Expanding the interpretive power of psychological science by attending to culture. *Proceedings of the National Academy of Sciences, 115*(45), 11406–11413. https://doi.org/10.1073/pnas.1803526115

Brown, B. (2016). *Trump Twitter Archive.* www.thetrumparchive.com

Buckist, W., Sikorski, J., Buckley, T., & Saville, B. K. (2002). Elements of master teaching. In S. F. Davis & W. Buckist (Eds.), *The teaching of psychology: Essays in Honor of Wilbert J. McKeachie and Charles L. Brewer* (pp. 27–39). Erlbaum.

Butterworth, J., & Thwaites, G. (2013). *Thinking skills: Critical thinking and problem solving* (2nd edn). Cambridge University Press.

DePaulo, B. M., Lindsay, J. J., Malone, B. E., Muhlenbruck, L., Charlton, K., & Cooper, H. (2003). Cues to deception. *Psychological Bulletin, 129*(1), 74–118.

Dienes, Z. (2008). *Understanding psychology as a science: An introduction to scientific and statistical inference*. Palgrave Macmillan. https://www.bloomsbury.com/uk/understanding-psychology-as-a-science-9780230542310/

Do, T., Hees, A., Ghez, A., Martinez, G. D., Chu, D. S., Jia, S., Sakai, S., Lu, J. R., Gautam, A. K., O'Neil, K. K., Becklin, E. E., Morris, M. R., Matthews, K., Nishiyama, S., Campbell, R., Chappell, S., Chen, Z., Ciurlo, A., Dehghanfar, A., … Wizinowich, P. (2019). Relativistic redshift of the star S0-2 orbiting the Galactic Center supermassive black hole. *Science, 365*(6454), 664–668. https://doi.org/10.1126/science.aav8137

Ekman, P., & Friesen, W. V. (1969). Nonverbal leakage and clues to deception. *Psychiatry, 32*(1), 88–106. https://doi.org/10.1080/00332747.1969.11023575

Gabennesch, H. (2006). Critical thinking: What is it good for (in fact, what is it?). *Skeptical Inquirer, 30*(2), 36–41.

Garland, H., Sandefur, C. A., & Rogers, A. C. (1990). De-escalation of commitment in oil exploration: When sunk costs and negative feedback coincide. *Journal of Applied Psychology, 75*(6), 721–727. https://doi.org/10.1037/0021-9010.75.6.721

Garrison, D. R. (1991). Critical thinking and adult education: A conceptual model for developing critical thinking in adult learners. *International Journal of Lifelong Education, 10*(4), 287–303. https://doi.org/10.1080/0260137910100403

George, J. F., Gupta, M., Giordano, G., Mills, A. M., Tennant, V. M., & Lewis, C. C. (2018). The effects of communication media and culture on deception detection accuracy. *MIS Quarterly, 42*(2), 551–575. https://doi.org/10.25300/MISQ/2018/13215

Gilbert, D. T. (1991). How mental systems believe. *American Psychologist, 46*(2), 107–119. https://doi.org/10.1037/0003-066X.46.2.107

Gilovich, T., Griffin, D., Kahneman, D., & Press, C. U. (2002). *Heuristics and Biases: The Psychology of Intuitive Judgment*. Cambridge University Press.

Halpern, D. F. (1998). Teaching critical thinking for transfer across domains. *American Psychologist, 53*, 449–455.

Harrison, P. D., & Harrell, A. (1993). Impact of "adverse selection" on managers' project evaluation decisions. *Academy of Management Journal, 36*(3), 635–643. https://doi.org/10.5465/256596

Hartwig, M., Granhag, P. A., & Luke, T. (2014). Strategic use of evidence during investigative interviews: The state of the science. In D. C. Raskin, C. R. Honts, & J. C. Kircher (Eds.), *Credibility assessment: Scientific research and applications* (pp. 1–36). Academic Press. https://doi.org/10.1016/B978-0-12-394433-7.00001-4

Hughes, W., Lavery, J., & Doran, K. (2015). *Critical thinking: An introduction to the basic skills* (7th ed.). Broadview Press.

Indrašienė, V., Jegelevičienė, V., Merfeldaite, O., Penkauskiene, D., Pivoriene, J., Railienė, A., Sadauskas, J., & Valavičienė, N. (2020). The critically thinking employee: Employers' point of view. *Entrepreneurship and Sustainability Issues, 7*, 2590–2603. https://doi.org/10.9770/jesi.2020.7.4(2)

Jeevanantham, L. S. (2005). Why teach critical thinking? *Africa Education Review, 2*(1), 118–129. https://doi.org/10.1080/18146620508566295

Kahneman, D., Slovic, P., & Tversky, A. (Eds.). (1982). *Judgment under uncertainty: Heuristics and biases*. Cambridge University Press. https://doi.org/10.1017/CBO9780511809477

Kassin, S. M. (2012). Paradigm shift in the study of human lie-detection: Bridging the gap between science and practice. *Journal of Applied Research in Memory and Cognition*, *1*(2), 118–119. https://doi.org/10.1016/j.jarmac.2012.04.009

Kuhn, T. S. (1962). Historical structure of scientific discovery. *Science*, *136*(3518), 760–764.

Levine, T. R. (2014). Truth-default theory (TDT): A theory of human deception and deception detection. *Journal of Language and Social Psychology*, *33*(4), 378–392. https://doi.org/10.1177/0261927X14535916

Masip, J. (2017). Deception detection: State of the art and future prospects. *Psicothema*, *29*(2), 149–159. https://doi.org/10.7334/psicothema2017.34

Mason, M. (2008). *Critical thinking and learning*. Blackwell Publishing.

Nahari, G. (2019). Verifiability approach: Applications in different judgmental settings. In T. Docan-Morgan (Ed.), *The Palgrave handbook of deceptive communication* (pp. 213–225). Springer International Publishing. https://doi.org/10.1007/978-3-319-96334-1_11

Pfiffner, J. P. (2020). The lies of Donald Trump: A taxonomy. In C. M. Lamb & J. R. Neiheisel (Eds.), *Presidential leadership and the trump presidency: Executive power and democratic government* (pp. 17–40). Springer International Publishing. https://doi.org/10.1007/978-3-030-18979-2_2

Staw, B. M. (1976). Knee-deep in the big muddy: A study of escalating commitment to a chosen course of action. *Organizational Behavior and Human Performance*, *16*(1), 27–44. https://doi.org/10.1016/0030-5073(76)90005-2

Street, C. N. H. (2015). ALIED: Humans as adaptive lie detectors. *Journal of Applied Research in Memory and Cognition*, *4*(4), 335–343. https://doi.org/10.1016/j.jarmac.2015.06.002

Tapper, J. (2004). Student perceptions of how critical thinking is embedded in a degree program. *Higher Education Research & Development*, *23*(2), 199–222. https://doi.org/10.1080/0729436042000206663

Thomson, A. (2013). *Critical reasoning: A practical introduction*. Routledge.

Tiehen, J. (2022). The IKEA effect and the production of epistemic goods. *Philosophical Studies*, 1–20. https://doi.org/10.1007/s11098-022-01840-3

Vrij, A., & Granhag, P. A. (2012). Eliciting cues to deception and truth: What matters are the questions asked. *Journal of Applied Research in Memory and Cognition*, *1*(2), 110–117. https://doi.org/10.1016/j.jarmac.2012.02.004

World Economic Forum. (2018). *10 skills you'll need to survive the rise of automation*. https://www.weforum.org/agenda/2018/07/the-skills-needed-to-survive-the-robot-invasion-of-the-workplace/

Zuckerman, M., DePaulo, B. M., & Rosenthal, R. (1981). Verbal and nonverbal communication of deception. In L. Berkowitz (Ed.), *Advances in experimental social psychology* (Vol. 14, pp. 1–59). Academic Press. https://doi.org/10.1016/S0065-2601(08)60369-X

2 The Process of Honesty and Deception

> **Box 2.1 Belle Gibson**
>
> As an Australian wellness guru, Instagrammer Belle Gibson pushed beyond the frontiers of Western medicine in search of an effective treatment for multiple cancers. Or at least, this was her claim. Supposedly, she had discovered a way to manage her multiple cancers through appropriate diet and alternative therapy, advocated in a mobile phone app and cookbook. In her book, she says "I was empowering myself to save my own life through nutrition, patience, determination and love". A journalistic investigation uncovered that she did not have cancer. Belle admitted in 2015 that "none of it's true". The story has been explored in a BBC documentary *Bad Influencer: The Great Insta Con*. She was fined $410,000 in 2017.

Before we start, let us very quickly define what we mean by lying. In a philosophical exploration, Mahon (2008) considers two defensible definitions of lying. Let us take the simplest of these as our definition: "to make a believed-false statement (to another person) with the intention that that statement be believed to be true (by the other person)" (p. 221). While different cultures have different conceptions of what may be considered a lie (see Giles et al., 2021), hopefully this reads like a reasonable definition to you, and so we will not belabour the definition. But let us quickly explore three points about this definition. First, you will notice that the statement is delivered and received by people (and not animals, plants, or other beings). While there is certainly scope for discussing animal and plant deception, the scope of this book is to focus on human lying, which shall be treated synonymously with the concept of deception herein. Second, the definition focuses on statements rather than, say, the deceptive appearance of the camouflaged cuttlefish or the deceptive illuminated lure used by the anglerfish. Finally, an intention to mislead is critical: if we tell falsehoods but do not intend for the listener to believe them, we may be telling a joke or a fairy tale. It is perhaps not surprising that the concept of intention appears in many definitions of lying in both the psychological and philosophical literatures (e.g., Chisholm & Feehan, 1977; DePaulo et al., 2003; Fallis, 2012; Masip et al., 2004; Miller & Stiff, 1993; Vrij, 2008; Zuckerman et al., 1981).

Intentionality may seem to be a requirement for lying, but not all agree on that point. For example, the philosopher David Smith (2007) considers it sufficient to prevent others obtaining true information (without the intention to mislead, e.g., keeping a secret) for the person to be considered as lying. However, it is broadly considered that intentionality is a necessary element of lying (see Peterson, 1995). And this broad definition gives us scope to explore deception and lying in different contexts. You may wish to evaluate the strengths and limitations of this definition of lying, and I encourage you to do so. In Chapter 3, we will briefly engage in some evaluation of what we mean by deception and lying. But I suspect that in developing your own definition of lying you will come to find that the contents of this book will still hold meaning for you.

Why Do People Lie or Tell the Truth?

In their daily lives, people tend to tell the truth rather than lie. DePaulo et al. (1996) asked 147 university students across two studies to record all of the lies they told over a period of one week in a diary, no matter how big or small, with the exception of being told not to record statements such as "fine" in response to "How are you?". Participants typically reported that deceptions were casual and of relatively little consequence. They also reported lying twice per day on average, with between 20% and 31% of all interactions involving deception. Similar frequencies of deception are seen in studies exploring online interactions. Caspi and Gorsky (2006) invited people on topic-specific discussion forums (e.g., internet culture forums) and broader general forums (e.g., university student forums) to respond to a questionnaire asking, among other questions, whether they have ever deceived online. Of the 257 respondents, 29% reported that they sometimes, often, or always deceive online while the remaining 71% reported that they never or hardly ever deceive online (see George & Robb, 2008; Hancock et al., 2004 for similar findings).

Box 2.2 The Importance of Dispersion

Does the average number of lies told per day seem very high (or low) to you? Reflect on your statistics knowledge and consider which one of the following is true:

1 The average can be a poor representation of the central tendency when the data is normally distributed.

> 2 The average can be a poor representation of the central tendency of the data when the distribution is skewed.
> 3 The average is always the best representation of the central tendency.
>
> If you have completed any statistics classes, you will likely see that only one of those options is reasonable. Option 2, the correct option, tells us that when we have a small number of extremely large (or small) values in our data, the average (or 'mean') will not be a reliable summary of the centre of the data. For instance, if 20 people tell zero lies per day and three people tell 15 lies per day, this would average to 1.96 lies per day. Yet the value of 1.96 is not a terribly good representation of the 20 people who never lie nor of those three people who lie very frequently. In this case, the mean is providing a rather poor description of the central tendency of the data.

As implied by Box 2.2, this is not the end of the story. Relying on the average can be misleading. In a number of studies, the prevalence of deception has been shown to be heavily skewed. In replications of DePaulo et al.'s (1996) diary study, approximately 40%–50% of participants told zero lies over a 24-hour period and around 5% of people in these studies are telling about 50% of all the lies being told (Halevy et al., 2014; T. R. Levine et al., 2013; Serota et al., 2010, 2021). That is, a lot of lies are told by a small number of people: most people tell the truth most of the time (see Abeler et al., 2019, for a similar conclusion when reviewing research in economics, psychology, and sociology). Note, though, that those telling a lot of lies are not always the same people from day to day: while some do consistently lie a lot, about 42% of the variance in the frequency of deception can be explained as a given person's day-to-day variability in their willingness to lie (Serota et al., 2021). Put another way, it is not always the case that the people who are lying a lot are the same people: tomorrow people may lie more or less than they did today.

One possible concern in these studies is that liars can choose to self-report how often they lie in the diary. Can the participants' accounts of their own honesty be believed? In their diary study, DePaulo et al. (1996) attempted to minimise this potential issue multiple ways. Among other steps taken, they explained to their participants that they see lying as having no particular moral implications, ensured that participants knew that their diaries were entirely anonymous, and explained that they need not report all of their social lies if they did not feel comfortable. Participants reported that they recorded 89% (Study 1) and 92% (Study 2) of their lies told during the study. However, it is unknown to what degree lies were not recorded due to momentary lapses in their astuteness to their own interactions, for example. Halevy et al.'s

(2014) work may further strengthen our confidence in the diary studies. They found that participants who self-reported a higher frequency of deception on a questionnaire also scored higher on measures that capture a pathological tendency to compulsively lie. Such a finding may lend credence to the notion that self-reports of the frequency of deception are capable of capturing the distribution of how often people tend to lie, which is to say that they do not lie very often.

That people lie so infrequently is somewhat counterintuitive: strategically lying when it is in the person's own best interest will provide the better outcomes. Classic economic theory has taken just such a position (Crawford & Sobel, 1982). For instance, Akerlof (1978) suggests that if a seller has an unreliable car to sell, they should lie to a prospective buyer in order to benefit themselves. Indeed, there is an increased reluctance to provide honest information to a listener as the goals and desires of the two people increasingly diverge (Cai & Wang, 2006). And yet, people seem to choose to lie infrequently (e.g., DePaulo et al., 1996), and while Cai and Wang (2006) found that people provide less information to a listener as the desires of the two people in the interaction diverge, they also found that people offer more information than would be expected if people were maximising their potential for personal gains (called the 'overcommunication phenomenon'), suggesting a tendency towards delivering truthful information and minimising their lying. So why do people lie so infrequently?

A prominent explanation is pure lie aversion: a preference to avoid lying (e.g., Abeler et al., 2012, 2019; Cappelen et al., 2013; Gneezy, 2005; Gneezy et al., 2016; López-Pérez & Spiegelman, 2013). A German telephone survey of 658 people at their home address asked participants to flip a coin and report whether it showed heads or tails, knowing in advance that reporting 'tails' would pay €15 while reporting 'heads' would pay nothing (Abeler et al., 2012). Even though participants would have gained financially from lying, knew that they could not be detected in their lie and that they were lying to a stranger (and so concerns for their reputation were minimised), only 44.4% of respondents reported tails while 55.6% of participants, or a slim majority, reported heads and so received no payout. Gneezy (2005) has similarly shown that people will more often choose not to achieve maximal gains for themselves in a situation where it involves having to lie compared to situations where deception is not required, again suggesting an aversion to lying.[1]

The aversion may result from an intrinsic desire to be honest (Kartik, 2009; T. R. Levine et al., 2010; Sánchez-Pagés & Vorsatz, 2007; Vanberg, 2008), wanting to avoid feelings of guilt that may be associated with lying (Battigalli et al., 2013; Dufwenberg & Gneezy, 2000), and/or from wanting to avoid damaging their own reputation and social identity (Bénabou & Tirole, 2006; Gneezy et al., 2016). Consistent with the guilt and reputational damage perspectives, people tell fewer liars to those with whom they feel closer (DePaulo & Kashy, 1998; Van Swol et al., 2012), and the lie aversion is more important in deciding whether to be honest in a personal context compared to the context of buying and selling goods (Cappelen et al., 2013). Even when people know that their lies cannot be detected (by choosing to report the result of a fair die roll under a cup), it is estimated that participants tell the truth up to 39% of the time and do so even when the payout for claiming a value higher than what was rolled is tripled (Fischbacher & Föllmi-Heusi, 2013).

But people do lie, and sometimes (albeit somewhat rarely) they lie rather frequently. Why do people lie? One simple explanation is that people lie because telling the truth will not succeed in achieving what the person wants to achieve. At first glance this may seem obvious. Indeed, you may even think that this is circular, as though it is being claimed that people lie because they do not want to tell the truth. There may be a seed of truth to that. But try reflecting on that statement and see if you can find the hidden assumption: 'People lie because they do not want to tell the truth'. It is hard to see the assumption here, but training your eye to pick out assumptions is going to be critical to improving your evaluative reasoning skills.

The assumption is that people would choose to tell the truth first and only resort to deception if they must. It may be easier to see this assumption by comparing it with a contradictory assumption: 'people tell the truth because they ordinarily want to lie but lying will not achieve what they are setting out to achieve'. Thus, the truth-preference assumption is that there is some form of primacy or priority given to truth-telling. We have seen above that people show an aversion to lying, and so this point need not be developed further. What is important for our purposes is to understand that people lie as an alternative to one's preferred approach of truth-telling in order to achieve a goal. Levine et al. (2016) found that this was true of participants in Egypt, Guatemala, Pakistan, Saudi Arabia, and the US, potentially hinting at a pan-cultural motive for lying. However, Kim et al. (2008) found that the motivation to deceive for self and other benefit was culturally dependent, with more collectivistic cultures that value interdependence and personal relationships having a greater motivation to lie for the benefit of others compared to more individualistic cultures.

What someone may seek to achieve by lying can be as varied as any form of desire (except a desire to be honest). It would not serve psychologists well to produce a long list of all the possible types of lies that a person may tell or situations in which a person may lie. This would be an impossible task. However, we will consider some situations under which people deceive with an aim to give a sense of the motivations one may have for deceiving.

Lies can offer benefits for the self or for others, and a lie can allow for an advantage to be gained or a loss to be avoided (DePaulo et al., 1996; Vrij, 2008). This taxonomy (of self versus other lies and advantage gaining versus loss avoiding lies) seems to imply that people deceive based on what can be achieved in a given *situation* rather than being driven by inherent characteristics of the person lying. Consistent with the position that situation more so than disposition drives the decision to lie, Drouin et al. (2016) found that a participant's beliefs about whether others would lie in a particular online situation was a better predictor of the participant's own lying compared to personality traits such as psychopathy, Machiavellianism, or extraversion. Similarly, while a disposition to low attachment security (i.e., holding fears of rejection, doubt about one's own value, and/or a disliking of close relationships) has been found to be related to lying, experimentally inducing feelings of more secure attachment reduces the likelihood of lying (Gillath et al., 2010), suggesting that while there may be dispositional drivers of the decision to lie, momentary situational changes can moderate this.

The self-other/gain-loss taxonomy is consistent with the findings of Ganis et al. (2009), who used functional magnetic resonance imaging (fMRI) to show that brain regions critical to creating of lies about oneself are partially distinct (but also partially overlapping) with regions critical to creating lies about others. The taxonomy can also readily categorise the many reasons why people lie. For example, people are more inclined to lie to appear unprejudiced when they are more aware that experimenters are measuring their prejudice (Walker & Jussim, 2002), an example of lying to avoid (reputational or self-image) costs to the self. Similarly, the so-called 'butler lie', used as a way of maintaining positive relationships (e.g., by deceptively claiming that one is busy via instant messenger in order to avoid a new conversation), can be seen as an example of lying to avoid loss of a friendship (Hancock et al., 2009).

In another example, a study exploring the motives behind why people lie surveyed participants in Egypt, Guatemala, Pakistan, Saudi Arabia, and the US (T. R. Levine et al., 2016). From the responses obtained, the authors develop ten motives for deception. The three most frequently reported lie motives were recorded collectively across 51.8% of the lies told, and all were for self-interested gains, while lies intended for the purposes of being polite were reported in no more than 10.3% of lies told in any given country. One may be surprised by how relatively rarely people lie for polite compared to selfish reasons (more on this in Chapter 6). However, participants were asked to "think of a recent situation (in the last week if possible) where someone lied to you" (p. 6). It is unclear whether participants would consider polite lies as deceptive and so may not reflect on those, may not remember them, or may have difficulty detecting them relative to selfish lies.

There are reasons to believe that altruistic lying may be more frequent (or at least more favourably viewed) than the preceding study may suggest. DePaulo et al. (1996, p. 980) were proponents of the view put forward by a social interaction theorist, Goffman (1959), namely that people lie in their everyday lives to "avoid tension and conflict and to minimize hurt feelings and ill-will". A neuroimaging study by Yin et al. (2017) had a computer randomly choose between two options: either (i) the participant and their partner would each receive €6 or (ii) the participant would receive €10 and the partner would receive just €6. The participant had to decide whether to lie about which option was chosen by the computer or not. Note that if the receiving partner thought that the participant was lying, the participant would receive no money. This setup is referred to as the sender-receiver game. The 'self-interest' condition was experienced as just described, where lying could result in better payouts for themselves. In a second 'charity' condition, the payouts were the same, but rather than the money being paid to the participant, that money would be paid to a charity. People were more inclined to lie for the altruistic reason of getting more money to the charity than they were to lie for their own personal gain. The anterior insular, a location where greater activation has been associated with a lower willingness to lie (Baumgartner et al., 2013), was less active in the charity condition compared to the self-interest condition, potentially indicating that this region plays a role in deciding to lie or tell the truth depending on whether the lie is for altruistic or selfish purposes.

Naturally, other taxonomies have been proposed. For instance, in a cross-cultural study of 1,345 participants across seven countries, Cantarero et al. (2018) found a taxonomy that separates between self versus other and private life versus professional domains to be a useful way to evaluate attitudes towards lying.

Finally, one form of lying that may seem difficult to categorise under either taxonomy is that intended to cause a loss for others. For example, in romantic relationships, people lie to avoid being punished, in response to the partner lying to them, and to hide their fear of intimacy (Cole, 2001; see also Guthrie & Kunkel, 2013). Similarly, military deception frequently uses deception to mislead the enemy and create misinformation to disrupt or destabilise the enemy (e.g., The British Army, 2017). However, these may be reframed in terms of emotional or strategic gains for the liar, respectively, and thus fitting existing taxonomies.

In summary, there appears to be a preference towards truth-telling, as demonstrated in diary studies recording the frequency of deception. The tendency to not lie has been exhibited in a lie aversion, where people will forgo potential economic or non-financial gains that could be achieved by lying in order to avoid having to tell the lie. A self-other/gain-loss taxonomy can categorise a variety of lie types, although other taxonomies have been proposed.

Individual Influences on the Decision to Lie

We have been aiming to understand the situations in which people lie and why they choose to do so. But there are personality and dispositional factors that may also need to be accounted for. Pathological lying has been defined by Healy and Healy (1926, p. 1) as "falsification entirely disproportionate to any discernible end in view, may be extensive and very complicated, manifesting over a period of years or even a lifetime, in the absence of definite insanity, feeble-mindedness or epilepsy". More succinctly, pathological lying is considered to be repeated and potentially compulsive in nature, told not as a means to some other goal but as a goal in its own right. Pathological lying, then, is distinct from how we use the term day-to-day to refer to people who frequently lie.

To pathologically lie is to do so without clear motivation to achieve some other end and may result from an irresistible urge to lie. There remains debate about whether pathological lying can be considered a clinical diagnosis in its own right or whether it is part of another psychiatric disorder (Dike et al., 2005), but the concept of pathological lying is one that is still discussed today. One view is that pathological liars develop because of low self-esteem and develop a false idealised characterisation of oneself with feelings of grandiosity and pride (Muzinic et al., 2016). Another view is that it reflects a neurocognitive deficit in the prefrontal cortex (Poletti et al., 2011; Yang et al., 2005), an area associated with higher level reasoning and 'theory of mind' (i.e., the capacity to reason about the mental state of others: Baron-Cohen et al., 2000. For more on theory of mind, see Chapter 6).

Naturally, we are not all pathological liars, but nonetheless many people do lie. Serota et al. (2010; see also Markowitz, 2022) have argued that there are a few 'prolific liars' who tell most of the lies (see also Daiku et al., 2021; Park et al., 2021, for claims of a few prolific liars in Japan and South Korea, respectively). Those who lie more frequently may exhibit particular tell-tale traits. Those who frequently lie are able to better remember who they have lied to (compared to those who lie infrequently), potentially in order to keep track of their lies and maintain consistency in their claims (El Haj et al., 2017, 2018). Reflecting on matters of personality in their two studies, Kashy and DePaulo (1996) had participants record all of their social interactions and lies told in a diary over a week. Those who score high on measures of Machiavellianism (a personality trait associated with manipulating and cunning), those who are sociable, and those who have concerns about how they appear to others have been found to have higher rates of deception (Kashy & DePaulo, 1996). They also found that those with longer lasting and positive same-sex friendships told other-centred lies while those with poorer same-sex friendships told more self-interested lies.

One may wonder if this means that those who lie frequently lack a moral compass. Halevy et al. (2014, Study 2) found that participants' decisions to lie on the value of a fair rolled die did not correlate with their responses on a test that assesses participants responses to moral dilemmas and an index of moral development, which the researchers take as evidence that frequent liars do not lack morality.

There may also be cultural influences on the willingness to lie. For example, while American participants in two studies by Park et al. (2018) tended towards rewarding honesty and would be less willing to lie to their boss for a friend who was running late for work, Korean participants indicated a willingness to lie to their boss and consider the deception beneficial for maintaining relationships. These differences may reflect what is considered socially desirable or acceptable: protecting one's integrity in more individualistic cultures (cultures that value independence and individuality) compared with maintaining relationships in collectivistic cultures (cultures that value relationship and group goals) (see also Choi et al., 2011; Dmytro et al., 2014; Fu et al., 2007; Wang & Leung, 2010, for similar findings in other countries with adults and children; although see Seiter et al., 2002, for a more complex effect of culture on the acceptability of deception). These findings converge with research by Bessarabova (2014), who found that 88% of Russian participants (i.e., from a collectivistic culture) chose to lie to cover up for a member of their social group compared to just 30% of American participants (i.e., from an individualistic culture) who were prepared to lie for their group member. These results suggest discrepancies in how dishonesty is perceived between cultures, and this can affect their willingness to lie for the sake of others.

We may also wish to consider whether there are traits that make people more willing to tell the truth. Sánchez-Páges and Vorsatz (2007) made use of the sender-receiver game. They engaged 66 participants (referred to as 'senders') how much both they and the partner they were working with (referred to as 'receivers') would be paid, totalling a sample size of 132 participants.[2] Sometimes, the payout would be for equal amounts to both parties, but sometimes the payout favoured the sender with more money than the receiver. The sender had to decide what to tell their receivers about the payout structure that was selected. If the receiver disbelieved the sender, neither party would receive any money. The researchers found that 15 out of 66 receivers chose to disbelieve the sender and withheld payment on 81% of future trials after they had been lied to by the sender. When the roles were swapped, the same participants acting now as senders told the truth on 70.6% of trials compared with the rest of the participants who told the truth on 52% of trials. This suggests that certain individuals hold strong to the notion of 'procedural justice': that is, that procedures should be fair and show this in both their punishment of others when they are lied to as well as telling the truth more frequently than others.

Finally, there may also be more neurobiological causes. People with Parkinson's disease can have difficulty with 'executive function' (what Gilbert & Burgess, 2008, p.R110, describe as 'the high-level cognitive processes that facilitate new ways of behaving, and optimise one's approach to unfamiliar circumstances'), a function that may be important to deceive (more on this later). A neuroimaging technique known as positron emission tomography (PET for short) found that such patients have difficult lying as a result of this pathological condition, and that this difficulty is associated with lower metabolic rates in prefrontal regions of the brain that may be linked to executive function (Abe et al., 2009).

In summary, pathological lying is a compulsion to lie for its own sake and may result from low self-esteem or have more neurobiological causes. Even among the non-pathological population, there are a 'few prolific liars' who tell more lies than most others. These people do not lack a moral compass but have been found to score high on a personality trait associated with manipulation and cunning. Finally, we have seen that there are cultural influences on the acceptance of deception, which will be important to keep in mind as we progress into chapters considering how people make lie-truth judgements (Chapter 4) and how children develop an understanding of deception (Chapter 6).

Meso Level Accounts of How People Lie

The term 'meso level' account is used here to categorise accounts that aim to describe or explain human behaviour at a relatively high level of abstraction. In our case, this will refer to the interaction of both the liar and the recipient of the lie. Naturally, this categorisation is somewhat arbitrary and is intended more to aid the organisation of this book than as a meaningful construct that ties these accounts together. A recent review of deception accounts conducted by Vrij et al. (2019; see also Vrij, 2008) report on three such accounts: a moral psychology account (Bond & DePaulo, 2006), self-presentational theory (DePaulo, 1992; see also Ekman & Friesen, 1969; Zuckerman et al., 1981), and interpersonal deception theory (IDT; Buller & Burgoon, 1996).

The moral psychology account (Bond & DePaulo, 2006) bears similarities to discussions observed in the field of cheating research. The position is that people judge others' deceptions as morally deficient but view their own deceptions as a result of circumstance or as relatively innocuous. Exploring how people cheat, Shu et al. (2011) showed across four studies that people actively try to forget moral rules and justify their actions (and only their own actions, not those of other people) when they engage in dishonesty. People may provide justifications before or after they cheat to excuse themselves (Shalvi et al., 2015). For a review of the research on why people cheat, see Jacobsen et al. (2018). In another review, Vrij et al. (2019) note that more research is needed to explore this account.

The self-presentational perspective (DePaulo, 1992) has already been discussed in passing: this is the perspective that, following Goffman (1959), both liars and truth-tellers are strategically presenting themselves to appear credible and honest. That is, even honest people may aim to convey a particular impression to the listener, and this may involve strategic presentation. For example, in job interviews honest applicants may use smiling and eye contact to convey a positive impression to the interview panel (Bolino et al., 2008). But it is not just the truth-tellers who present a particular image of themselves: liars will also manage their impression to appear honest. For example, Toma and Hancock (2010) find that less physically attractive online daters are more likely to lie, but elect to lie only about their physical characteristics, suggesting that deception is used as an attempt to manage how they are perceived by others rather than a blanket rule to lie frequently when online.

Given that liars and truth-tellers are thought to manage their social impressions, it may be difficult to distinguish the two (see also DeAndrea et al., 2012). Consistent with this notion, both guilty and innocent suspects in a mock crime appear calm before a supposed police interview and then deny any accusations of wrongdoing (Hartwig et al., 2007). However, in order to present these behaviours, liars describe more strategies for presenting themselves than did truth-tellers, suggesting a discrepancy in *how* they come to achieve their self-presentation.

Self-deception (i.e., deceiving oneself about the truth) may be the ultimate form of impression management: lying to oneself may be a useful strategy to better convince others and removes the need to intentionally mislead others, given that they have misled themselves (Trivers, 2011; von Hippel & Trivers, 2011). However, lying to someone from another culture may require an understanding of their cultural perspective (see Giles et al., 2021), and so self-presentation may not benefit from self-deception in cross-cultural settings. For evidence that self-presentational goals affect the willingness to lie, see Tyler and Feldman (2004) and Feldman et al. (2002), both of which are briefly discussed in Chapter 3.

The matter of self-presentation and impression management is also important for understanding IDT (Buller & Burgoon, 1996). Critically, this account proposes that to understand deception one must understand the dynamics of the interaction between the liar and the receiver of that lie. Each person monitors the behaviours of the other (along with their understanding of the situation and past experiences) over the course of the interaction to adjust their behaviours in real time, and so deception in interactive settings can be considered distinct from deception that occurs in a passive setting (e.g., watching a video of someone telling a lie or using a scripted interviewing method).

In one study, 126 participants took part in pairs as partners and had to reach joint agreement about which of 12 items would be most useful to their survival if their jeep had crashed in the Kuwaiti desert (Burgoon et al., 2010). One member of the pair was instructed by the experimenters to deceive their partner as to what would be the most valuable items to salvage for their survival. The partners communicated either in real time via a computer-based instant messenger or asynchronously via an online message board. Discussing in real time led to greater trust between partners compared to asynchronous discussion, and deceivers were more successful in presenting themselves as credible compared to truth-tellers. The authors argue that understanding how the interaction dynamics unfold in real time is important for understanding person-to-person discourse.

In other work, Burgoon et al. (2014) found that liars try to take control of the conversation and guide the group's discussion. Neuroscientific evidence also suggests that deceivers may attend to the environment to understand when deception is needed and respond appropriately, monitoring the social situation and engaging in theory of mind (Abe et al., 2007; Christ et al., 2009; Langleben et al., 2005; Lisofsky et al., 2014). For other work on IDT, see Burgoon et al. (1999, 2001), Derrick et al. (2013), and Dunbar et al. (2015).

In summary, a moral psychology perspective holds that people distance themselves from the moral implications of lying. The self-presentational perspective suggests that both liars and truth-tellers manage the impressions that they form in the minds of others. IDT places focus on the importance of the dynamics that exist between two people (hence the first initial I for 'interpersonal') and contends that deception in an interactive environment may be quite different to deception observed in more static environments. This final point is worth keeping in mind as we reflect what cues to deception have been found in research studies (Chapter 3), how it is that people come to decide who is lying or telling the truth (Chapter 4), and how people may accurately detect deception (Chapter 5).

The Psychological Costs of Lying

The leakage hypothesis. Ekman and Friesen (1969) subscribed to the Freudian perspective that while people attempt to conceal their deceptions, the emotions that accompany those deceptions (e.g., fear or anxiety) may not be possible to fully conceal. This perspective has become known as the 'leakage hypothesis', which spotlights the unique emotional experience of deceivers. In particular, the face is considered to be more controlled than the rest of the body because senders are more aware of their facial displays and are more visible to others for detecting cues, and so leakage will be more readily detected in non-facial displays. There is one notable exception to this rule, so-called 'micro-expressions' (Ekman, 1985; Ekman & Matsumoto, 2011) that leak from the face. We shall return to these in Chapter 3.

The leakage hypothesis has been met with scepticism in the field for some time (e.g., Brennen & Magnussen, 2020; Nortje & Tredoux, 2019; Vrij et al., 2006, 2010; but see Ekman, 2003, for an argument in favour of the leakage hypothesis). This is because truth-tellers may equally experience these emotions under scrutiny. It is possible that the nonverbal expressions that are supposedly indicating deception may instead be arising from an emotional response (e.g., anxiety) that is not being caused by deceiving (e.g., social anxiety; see Leo & Ofshe, 2008; Nortje & Tredoux, 2019).

Deception as cognitively effortful. Zuckerman et al. (1981) were possibly the first to note that deceiving may entail different cognitive implications associated with the difficulty of generating and producing a lie, namely ensuring it is logically consistent and does not contradict what the listener already knows. They speculated that there may be resulting observable differences such as pauses in speech and a longer time taken to respond to a question or statement. This view of deception became known as the four-factor theory because it also proposes three additional factors that may be different between liars and truth-tellers: emotional experience, attempts to control behaviour (akin to the perspective of Ekman & Friesen, 1969), and physiological arousal. We shall not discuss those further here, but instead explore the cognitive approach to understanding how people lie because it has become a predominant area for research.

It is often claimed that deception is an effortful process (e.g., Buller & Burgoon, 1996; J. Lane & Wegner, 1995; Vrij, 2008; Vrij et al., 2008; Walczyk et al., 2014; Zuckerman et al., 1981) because it requires inhibiting or suppressing the memory of the truth and fabricating a new coherent story that does not contradict what the listener knows. However, such claims tend not to attempt to explain what cognitive processes are at work (see Blandón-Gitlin et al., 2014; S. M. Lane & Vieira, 2012; Tabatabaeian et al., 2015). Naturally, accounts of cognitive load will be somewhat limited in scope if they are unable to explain the cognitive processes that are supposedly being loaded onto. However, neuroimaging and behavioural research can provide insights in this regard.

A meta-analytic approach to examining a variety of neuroimaging studies aimed to understand what past fMRI studies are able to tell us about the processing of deception (Christ et al., 2009). Comparisons between brain activity for processes involving executive function and deception found similarities between the two, with similar activation in the prefrontal cortex (ventrolateral and dorsolateral), anterior insular and anterior cingulate cortex, areas which are associated with inhibitory control, task switching, and working memory. Working memory may have a more important function than task switching and inhibitory control, given that brain activity in these latter two functions did not show strict overlap with areas involved in deception (Christ et al., 2009). Importantly, a separate review of the evidence found that while deception is associated with greater activation of areas linked to executive function, truth-telling is not associated with increased activation of any brain regions in comparison to deception (Spence et al., 2004), suggesting that deception may be more effortful than truth-telling.[3]

Electroencephalography (EEG) measures brain electrical activity by recording from the scalp of the participant. As a result, it has difficulty localising activity to particular brain regions because the electrical signal conducts across the scalp, but the method can offer more precise timings of activity compared to fMRI, which measures the relatively slow changes in blood oxygenation level in the brain. EEG studies have found evidence of a greater 'contingent negative variation', a signal reflecting a preparation to respond, in liars compared to truth-tellers (Dong & Wu, 2010; Sun et al., 2011), again suggesting a difference in the cognitive load of deceiving compared to truth-telling.

Behavioural studies have similarly found that deception can be more cognitively effortful than truth-telling. Debey et al. (2012, Study 1) presented 69 participants with the Sheffield lie test, which consists of a number of autobiographical questions (e.g., "In the course of today, have you made your bed?"). Participants were instructed to lie or tell the truth on different trials and either had 200 ms or 5000 ms between the end of their response and the next question appearing. They reasoned that the longer duration would lead to 'goal neglect', whereby a participant does not carry out the task because of a lapse in their attention, and so requires more cognitive effort to keep their goal of deceiving in mind. Consistent with this position, they found that participants took longer to respond and more frequently gave the wrong response when having longer trial delays (5000 ms) compared to shorter trial delays (200 ms), the latter of which would be less prone to attentional slips. Other work has shown that the time taken to begin telling a lie (or 'response latency') compared to the response latency for telling a truth is longer (see Suchotzki et al., 2017, for a meta-analysis and Verschuere & De Houwer, 2011, for a review), and that time pressure to respond increases the likelihood of being honest. It is argued that this reflects that lying requires inhibiting memory for the truth (Farrow et al., 2010). Together, these findings suggest that deception is cognitively more taxing than truth-telling.

> ### Box 2.3 Can Lying Be Cognitively *Less* Effortful?
>
> When reading any claim that I or others put forward, be sure to ask yourself whether the opposite or alternative viewpoints could be true. Take a few moments to reflect on whether there may be situations in which people might find truth-telling harder than lying. Can you think of any situations where or reasons why this would be the case? For example, might you find it less effortful to lie if you have regularly rehearsed the deceptive story and so remember it more clearly than the truth? Could there be other situations like this one?
>
> Consideration of alternative explanations demonstrates a high level of evaluative reasoning. However, be careful not to assume that your reflections are an accurate and true representation of reality, especially if you have no data or evidence on which you are basing those reflections. This might make you wonder why we would even bother engaging in this exercise. First, that you do not have the evidence to hand does not mean that there is no past research that is consistent with that view. Second, these introspective reflections can be a fruitful ground for conducting or suggesting future research. For example, the phenomenon of 'joint perception', that the way people distribute their gaze around a scene is affected by whether they believe others are also looking at the same scene (Richardson et al., 2012), was inspired by the experience of reading a newspaper on the London Underground when another person is looking over one's shoulder compared to when there is no one peering over one's shoulder.
>
> However, keep in mind that relying too heavily on one's own view of the world may lead you to reframe or misinterpret data through your particular preferred lens (whether that is a preferred psychological subdiscipline such as cognitive psychology, linguistics, or sociology, or through more personal lenses such as your cultural background) and may lead to a biased view of the research. But reflecting on these alternative viewpoints will help you find potential flaws in the logic of arguments that are presented, or at least provide insights into how predictions and assumptions of an account may be tested.

> For now, all I ask is that you read what is claimed in this book and always ask yourself "might a viewpoint that contradicts the one that is being claimed here be true?". Do not assume that just because I have presented a number of studies supporting a position that the position must be true. Always remember that while evidence may be *consistent* with a particular position, it does not mean that the same evidence may not also be consistent with other positions.

The Cognitive Process of Lying

While we may like to think of deception as an invention and truth-telling as memory recall, this may be somewhat misleading. In *An Enquiry Concerning Human Understanding*, the 18th-century Scottish philosopher David Hume (1748/2007) argued that to use our imagination and invent details is to take our memory of experiences and combine them in new ways, such as combining the memories of seeing hills, countryside, and sheep to imagine having taken a trip to the rural parts of Wales. That is, invention is not truly novel inspiration but a recombination of memories of and knowledge about reality. And so while truth-telling will require a recollection of memory, so too will deceiving in order to retrieve past experiences and knowledge from long-term memory from which the deception can be generated (Sporer & Schwandt, 2007). Sporer (2016) argues that the working memory model (Baddeley, 2007, 2012) offers opportunities for understanding the processes of honesty and deception.[4] The concept of working memory, in contrast to the concept of short-term memory which it has come to replace, refers not only to temporary storage of visual and auditory information but also active manipulation of that information.

Sporer (2016) contends that liars can retrieve memories of their personal experiences of similar situations to generate their lies or, if liars do not have a personal experience of the situation that their lie is about, they will retrieve more generalised 'schema' or broad prototypes generated from multiple pieces of information that lack specific details but provide the gist of the situation (e.g., the schema for 'a restaurant' may include tables, chairs, mood lighting, and so on, even though this is not a memory of a specific restaurant).[5] As a result, liars will tend to include schema-consistent details (e.g., a waiter served the table) and fewer schema-inconsistent details (e.g., the restaurant required people to stand at tables rather than sit at them) should be included. Truth-tellers are expected to include schema-inconsistent details because they are drawing on a specific memory of the events. They should also remember information that is irrelevant to the schema soon after the event (e.g., the floor of the restaurant was carpeted), but memory for this information should decay with time.

Box 2.4 What Makes an Account a 'Good' Account?

This question is trickier than it may seem on first glance. It might be tempting to want to conclude that a theory that is consistent with all the available evidence is performing rather well. But this may not be the case. Consider the following hypothetical: imagine we have a phenomenon that we have measured (perhaps lie detection accuracy) and the observable values are limited to a finite range (e.g., you may only score somewhere between 0% and 100% accuracy, inclusive, but no other value is possible to observe). Now imagine two accounts that can explain this phenomenon. The first account predicts that the range of possible values that would be consistent with it is smaller than the range of possible values that would be consistent with the second account. If this highly abstracted situation seems tricky to imagine, try to make it more concrete for yourself by placing some arbitrary numbers on it. For the sake of argument, let us say Account 40–60 predicts that when the phenomenon occurs, lie detection accuracy will be between 40% and 60% while Account 30–80 predicts 30%–80% lie detection accuracy. Which of these two is more likely to find evidence consistent with the account?

Hopefully you can see that the second account is more likely to have data to be found consistent with it: all of the predictions of Account 40–60 are consistent with those of Account 30–80, and Account 30–80 has some additional values that can be consistent with it. Let us extend this a little further with Account 0–100: it results in a prediction of somewhere between 0% and 100% lie detection accuracy. Naturally, any observed data *must* be consistent with this account: the only possible values that can be observed are in this range. How useful does this account feel?

I suspect you can start to see the issue here: an account that allows for all possible data to be consistent with its claims fails to inform us of anything. The reason for this is the same as the reason that the following account is also not a 'good' account. See if you can pick out the issue. Working in your office, you want to find out if any of your colleagues are also in the building. You step out of your office and see that the motion-activated lights are on. You reason that someone is in their office because someone must have triggered the lights to enter their office. This may seem intuitively plausible, but hold that thought. A little later, you step out into the corridor and see that the motion lights are off. You reason that someone must be in their office because no one has triggered the motion sensors as they would have done if they were leaving their office. In this case, the account ('someone is in their office') is supported by all the data that could ever possibly be observed (i.e., the lights are on—with the interpretation that they triggered them upon entering—and the lights are off—with the interpretation that no one triggered them when leaving). Consider another account. The planets spin because invisible space giants, undetectable by scientific instruments, are spinning them. This may sound ludicrous, but how would you show it to be wrong? You may argue for photograph evidence, but I could then claim that these particular giants can't be detected with observable light. I can keep bending my account like this to 'explain away' all the data you bring to critique my account, and in doing so, I can make every possible data point consistent with my account. The problem we are facing is that when an account does not allow for any observation that could show it to be *potentially* wrong, then it is untestable or unfalsifiable, and so we have no means by which we can determine if this is an accurate and useful account of reality. I am sure you could come up with 100 other accounts of how the planets spin if you are allowed to bend all the data to fit them. In short, accounts like these are unscientific because they are not subject to testing.

Account 40–60 is a more predictive account insofar as any observation below 40 and above 60 could show the account to be wrong. Thus, when we observe values that are between 40% and 60% accuracy (let us say 50% accuracy results from a particular experiment where the phenomenon is present), the account gains credibility. An even more predictive Account 49–51, which predicts between 49% and 51% accuracy, would have even more opportunity to be falsified: almost all observable values would falsify the account, and so if the values are observed in the predicted range, the account can be considered to be highly credible. By contrast, the same data offers no credibility to Account 0–100 because no possible data could have falsified the account. This leads to a rather surprising conclusion: the strength of evidence that results from the data is not purely determined by the data, but also by the predictions that are made by the account.

When evaluating accounts of deception (or any account, for that matter), always reflect on what *could* falsify the account, in principle. If an account adopts the constraints and predictions of a tightly defined theory (with clearly testable and in principle falsifiable predictions), this gives the account credibility. Naturally, one can conduct the research to then determine whether those predictions hold. But being open to the possibility of being falsified is critical for us to be able to consider an account a 'good' account.

It is important to bear in mind that the examples given above may have seemed patently problematic in their reasoning. Take the motion light example where both the lights on and off 'supported' the account that someone was in their office. We would likely notice the problem

(*Continued*)

> in this logic when all possible data points (lights on, lights off) are explicitly shown to lead to the same conclusion. The difficulty arises when we do not reflect on all the possible data interpretations and their conclusions. For example, it may be relatively easy to fool ourselves into believing that there is someone in their office because the motion lights are on if we did not also consider other interpretations (e.g., the lights are on because they were triggered as someone left the building). A critical aspect of evaluative reasoning (and determining falsifiability), then, will involve you reflecting on all the *possible* data that could be observed (not just those that were observed) and considering whether those possible data would also be consistent with the account. The more observations that could be consistent with the account, the less predictive the account is. In extremis, an account that is consistent with *all* possible outcomes is entirely useless to us as scientists.

The benefit of building on an established theoretical perspective is that it can make testable predictions. Some of these predictions are consistent with past data, although it is not clear whether one can truly call these 'predictions' given that the data for them are already known (in much the same way as one would not be suitably impressed by a fortune teller predicting what you plan to do next week after you had already told them what you plan to do next week: see Box 2.4). Nonetheless, the perspective does account for existing phenomena, for example, that lying is more cognitively difficult than truth-telling (Debey et al., 2012; Spence et al., 2004). It also predicts that lying will take longer to respond than truth-telling (e.g., Kaylor-Hughes et al., 2011; Verschuere et al., 2011) due to the need to actively manipulate information in working memory, although the findings here are somewhat mixed (Suchotzki et al., 2017) and tend to use highly controlled and thus somewhat simple lies that require only a 'yes' or 'no' response (Sporer, 2016). Other predictions can be developed by reviewing the research into the working memory model (Baddeley, 2007, 2012) and understanding the predictions that arise from that model (e.g., that the frequency of recalling or encoding information via repeated exposure or rehearsal should result in faster recall times for that information, whether that information is to be used to tell the truth or generate a lie. As another example, that when there is no useful schematic information in long-term memory, working memory will carry a heavier processing load to develop the lie).

A more elaborate account of the deception process is offered by the Activation-Decision-Construction-Action Theory (ADCAT) (Walczyk et al., 2014). It provides an explanation of how people lie in high-stakes situations, where 'high stakes' refers to a situation where telling the truth could be very costly to the person telling the lie, such as may be found when a guilty suspect is cross-examined in the courtroom. As with the working memory model, truth-telling and lying are seen to arise from the same underlying cognitive processes. In the case of ADCAT, those processes are memory, theory of mind, problem-solving, and decision-making. Initially, a situation arises such that the potential liar understands that they are being asked to provide an honest statement. While each component of ADCAT is presented sequentially below, the researchers note that these processes may occur in parallel.

The first A in ADCAT is the activation component. It is suggested that truths are activated automatically. For example, an fMRI study (Greene & Paxton, 2009) asked participants to predict the outcome of a coin and either had to make the prediction in advance (and so could not cheat) or self-report how many predictions they achieved correctly at the end of the study (and so could lie to inflate their accuracy and achieve more money). Those who chose to lie showed higher activity in prefrontal regions associated with cognitive control. Those who chose not to lie showed no additional control processing compared to those who were forced to make a prediction in advance (and so could not lie). The researchers interpret these findings as evidence that choosing to tell the truth does not require any additional control beyond situations where one does not get to decide whether to lie or tell the truth. This would suggest that truth-telling comes easily and relatively effortlessly.

In a behavioural study by Duran et al. (2010), 26 participants held a Nintendo Wii video console remote (similar to a laser pointer or virtual reality handset) and were asked autobiographical questions such as "Have you ever been to Asia?". After reading the question, the screen showed a circle at the bottom-centre of the screen, whose colour determined if the participant should lie or tell the truth. In the top-left and top-right corners of the screen were the words 'YES' and 'NO', respectively. Participants had to move the cursor from the starting position of the circle to the appropriate response at the top-corner of the screen. The trajectory of the cursor was captured, and it was found that when participants told the truth, the cursor took a somewhat straight trajectory to the correct response option, but when they lied the cursor path was more arced, suggesting that the truthful response presented in the other corner of the screen was actively competing with the deceptive response that participants were intending to select. The arcing was thus taken as evidence of online, real-time competition of truthful information in memory during the production of a lie. These findings are further evidence that truth-telling can be relatively effortless. However, it should be noted that if the truth is infrequently accessed and so has a weak memory trace, ADCAT predicts that it will take effort to retrieve the truth.

After a solicitation of the truth, the person must decide whether to tell the truth or lie. This is the decision component of ADCAT. It is proposed that people use 'quasi-rational' decision-making approaches, meaning that they choose to lie or tell the truth by evaluating the pros and cons that most readily come to mind and making the response that is *perceived* to be the best to achieve their goal. To achieve this, the person determines the 'expected value' of both lying and telling the truth and selects the action that provides the higher expected value. Expected value is the anticipated gain or loss as a result of an action (e.g., lying may persuade the jury to give a not-guilty verdict, which may have a relatively high value to the person. In contrast, lying may result in being caught and create a lengthier sentencing, which may have lower value) weighted by how likely that event is to occur (e.g., how likely it is the jury will give a not-guilty verdict as a result of lying or how likely the lie will be detected). Weighting is achieved rather simply by multiplying, and so the expected value of lying in this example would be ([value of not-guilty verdict] × [probability of not-guilty verdict]) + ([value of being caught in a lie] × [probability of being caught]). This can be repeated for truth-telling, and the option with the higher value is selected as the course of action to take. A consequence of this calculation is that the person should be willing to invest more resources in preparing their statement and managing their impression when the expected value for one option far exceeds the expected value for the other option, meaning that the preferred option has relatively high value and so deserves greater investment.

Having decided the course of action, the lie or truth is to be constructed (the C in ADCAT). If the person decides to lie, they are thought to first attempt to adapt the truth or other autobiographical memories from long-term memory to create a plausible lie in working memory, noting that the more recently encoded or retrieved memories will be preferred because they will have had less time to decay from memory. This burying of the lie in a truth is often referred to as an 'embedded lie' (Vrij, 2008). Leins et al. (2013) found in two studies totalling 57 participants that approximately 75% of lies told involved reporting an actually experienced memory from their past (see also DePaulo et al., 2003; Strömwall & Willén, 2011, for evidence that people with and without criminal experience will stick close to the truth as one of their deception strategies). Similarly, heavily rehearsed stories should entail lower cognitive load because of its ready accessibility, and this may even be more accessible than the truth (which requires recall and reconstruction to take place in working memory) as some studies have found (Van Bockstaele et al., 2015; Verschuere et al., 2011). Both ADCAT (Walczyk et al., 2014) and the working memory model of deception (Sporer, 2016) propose that schema will be relied upon when there are no relevant past experiences in memory from which to draw information.

Departing somewhat from the self-presentational perspective (DePaulo, 1992), ADCAT argues that liars will feel a greater need to manage how they portray themselves compared to truth-tellers in the action of producing the lie (the final A of ADCAT). This is in part because truth-telling comes naturally and does not require additional processing effort (Greene & Paxton, 2009; T. R. Levine et al., 2010).

As can be seen, ADCAT is a relatively detailed account of deception, and as such offers a number of explicit opportunities to test and falsify the account. This is a core strength of the account: if the account has the potential for data to show it to be wrong and yet subsequent data fails to produce data showing the account to be wrong, this lends a sense of robustness to the claims of the account. There is, in fact, evidence that challenges one of ADCAT's claims. The truth may not be automatically activated, and deception can be faster and more accurately produced than truth-telling (e.g., Shalvi et al., 2012). Indeed, an EEG study found that the truth can be cognitively more effortful to produce than a lie when the truth is told with the intention to deceive (Carrión et al., 2010). Rather than the truth being automatically activated, then, it may be that truthful communicative intentions are what come first with a tendency to then seek out truthful information (even though sometimes the truth can be told with deceptive information, such as when being sarcastic).[6]

On a final note, both the working memory model of deception (Sporer, 2016) and ADCAT (Walczyk et al., 2014) highlight the fundamental role that memory plays not only in truth-telling but also in deceiving. While these accounts focus on utilising long-term memory in order to construct lies, there is also evidence that the act of deceiving can subsequently affect what is remembered (Colwell et al., 2011; Li et al., 2022). In a study of children and adults (Otgaar et al., 2014), it was found that repeating a (false) denial that they had talked to the experimenter about particular details led them to forget that they had ever talked to the experimenter at all. At a subsequent meeting one week later, despite being under instruction to be honest, they denied having ever talked about those details, suggesting that they had forgotten the truth. This 'denial-induced forgetting' phenomenon has been found across a number of studies (e.g., Battista et al., 2020, 2021; Otgaar et al., 2016, 2020; Riesthuis et al., 2022; Vieira & Lane, 2013). Such a result is consistent with the previously discussed findings that rehearsing a lie may lead it to being more accessible than a less-rehearsed truth (Van Bockstaele et al., 2015; Verschuere et al., 2011), a point that was considered in Box 2.3 and one that we will return to later.

In summary, the working memory model and ADCAT both contend that memory processes are involved in lying as well as truth-telling. While truthful information may come readily to mind, rehearsed lies can sometimes be easier to retrieve than the truth.

The Process of Lying: A Communication Perspective

The above accounts provide cognitive explanations of how people lie. Information Manipulation Theory 2 (IMT2; McCornack et al., 2014)[7] is a communication account of deceptive discourse. Building on the claim that people take the path of least effort to achieve their goals (Zipf, 1949), IMT2 proposes that people monitor and adapt their communication in-the-moment and on-the-fly in order to achieve the desired conversational goal. This means that people need not necessarily start with an intention to deceive at the onset of their utterance: it may be that the potential liar recognises that their discourse is not achieving the desired effect and so adapt and edit as they are producing their speech with an aim to better align their speech with their conversational goal. That is, the intention to deceive may only become apparent after the sender recognises that there is a perceived gap between the desired end goal of the conversation and where the conversation is currently at. As a result, the discourse may fluidly shift between honesty and deception across the duration of the utterance. This is consistent with findings that liars embed their deceptions in amongst truthful detail (Leins et al., 2013) and with work showing that collectivistic cultures may be willing to deviate from the truth if it serves the goal of preserving social relationships (Kim et al., 2008).

This leads to an interesting prediction: because lying follows the road of least resistance, lying should sometimes be cognitively more efficient than telling the truth. People lie because telling the truth will make achieving the conversational goal easier, following the principle of least effort. This is a tantalising prediction, given our previous discussions that the truth appears to be automatic and requires inhibiting it in order to tell the truth (Debey et al., 2012; Duran et al., 2010; Farrow et al., 2010; Greene & Paxton, 2009; Kaylor-Hughes et al., 2011; Spence et al., 2004, 2008; Suchotzki et al., 2017; although see Van Bockstaele et al., 2015; Verschuere et al., 2011). We will return to this point shortly (as I keep promising!), but for now, let us continue to describe IMT2.

To achieve the conversational goal, IMT2 argues that people draw from the available (and easily accessible) information in memory that in the past has helped them solve situations such as the one they are currently experiencing. This may be the truth, but it may instead be deceptive information that has been successful for the person in similar situations in the past. As with the working memory model of deception (Sporer, 2016) and ADCAT (Walczyk et al., 2014), then, IMT2 recognises the important role that memory has to play in the deception process. If there is no relevant information that is easy to draw upon in working memory, it is argued that people may falter as they have to engage in the cognitive work of retrieving additional information to construct a story on the fly. This may exhibit itself through measures of cognitive load or longer latencies in beginning the utterance, or even simply confessing the truth.

It has been noted by the authors of both the working memory model of deception and ADCAT that a core distinction between their own accounts and IMT2 is that their accounts are intended to explain high-stakes and complex lies while IMT2 is better equipped to explain how low-stakes lies may naturally unfold in daily discourse (Sporer, 2016; Walczyk et al., 2014), which McCornack (the first author of IMT2) has also stated in a personal communication to Walczyk et al. (2014; the authors of ADCAT). Thus, IMT2 need not be seen as a competitor theory to those discussed previously but may instead serve to complement our understanding of deceptive discourse in daily life. You may also see links to Buller and Burgoon's (1996) IDT, given the focus of both accounts on the dynamics of the discourse.

A particular strength of the account is that it makes defined predictions about the nature of deception. As an example, it predicts that the most common form of deception will be deceit that involves withholding information and editing out details (rather than inventing or adding new details). Other such predictions can be found in the original theory paper. One prediction that may be at the forefront of your mind at this point, though, is whether lying can be cognitively more efficient than telling the truth, which seems to stand in contrast to what has been discussed thus far. However, I hope you have engaged with Box 2.3 and already reflected on this possibility, which we can now evaluate with substantive evidence in the next section.

Deception is sometimes *cognitively effortful*. While it is typically claimed that deceiving is more effortful and truth-telling is supposedly automatic, psychological accounts and research findings indicate that there are situations where deception can be less effortful and truth-telling can require active deliberation (e.g., Burgoon, 2015; Hu et al., 2015; S. M. Lane & Vieira, 2012; McCornack et al., 2014). One such situation is when the gains for lying are relatively high and so the desire to be dishonest is rather tempting (Bereby-Meyer & Shalvi, 2015; Burgoon, 2015; Verschuere & Shalvi, 2014). When the incentives to lie become sufficiently high, people switch from telling the truth to lying (Kajackaite & Gneezy, 2015). In a study where participants had to report the value of a die rolled under a cup, with certain values providing a greater monetary payout, people lied more frequently if they were given relatively little time in which to decide whether to be honest or deceptive compared to people who were given longer to make a decision (Shalvi et al., 2012; see also Gunia et al., 2012). Similarly, Tabatabaeian et al. (2015) using a methodology similar to Duran et al. (2010) recorded the path that a mouse cursor took from the bottom-centre of the screen to either a truthful or deceptive response option, each located in the top corners of the screen. They found that self-serving lies that gained a monetary bonus resulted in faster responses than truth-telling and showed a relatively straight mouse trajectory towards the deceptive response option and away from the honest response option. Such a finding suggests that the honest response located in the opposite corner had relatively little interference with the decision. That is, people's deceptive responses showed relatively little hesitation.

It is worth considering that the lies considered thus far have been not only highly tempting, but also self-serving. While disentangling these variables is difficult, Burgoon (2015) observed that a study by Shalvi and De Dreu (2014) found lies that serve one's social group are more quickly provided than lies that serve oneself after oxytocin (a neuropeptide promoting group affiliation) was taken, suggesting that the ease with which lies are told may be driven more by the temptation of benefits rather than strictly because they are directly self-serving. Given that the decision component of ADCAT (Walczyk et al., 2014) proposes that people will choose to lie when the expected value of lying is higher than truth-telling and that IMT2 (McCornack et al., 2014) similarly proposes that people lie in order to more easily achieve their desires and goals, this increased motivation or temptation to lie facilitates the cognitive ease of deception which is consistent with these positions.

The activation level of information stored in memory may also be an important moderator. When deceptions are repeated, liars not only make fewer errors in their deceptions and show shorter response latencies (Van Bockstaele et al., 2015; Verschuere et al., 2011), they have also been shown to negatively impact the ability to correctly recall truthful information from memory (e.g., Battista et al., 2020; Colwell et al., 2011; Li et al., 2022; Otgaar et al., 2014; Vieira & Lane, 2013). Relatedly, when liars are given more time to prepare their statement, the time taken to begin delivering the lie reduces (see Sporer & Schwandt, 2007, for a meta-analysis).

Findings such as these support S. M. Lane and Vieira's (2012) suggestion that those capable of holding and manipulating more information in their working memory may find that they can better inhibit the truth. In a study where 36 participants had to lie about the colour of a Box, if the number of possible colours it could take on was only two, the response latency for deception was shorter than if the number of possible colours the Box could take on was three (Williams et al., 2013). This is consistent with the notion that lies which create less cognitive load on working memory (in this case, two rather than three possible options to decide amongst) are easier to generate.

In summary, IMT2 claims that lies and truths can be created in the moment to most fluently achieve the conversational goal. As such, it is expected that in some situations, telling a lie can be cognitively less effortful than telling the truth. We have seen that lying can be less cognitively effortful when there are temptations to lie (i.e., the benefits of deceiving substantially outweigh the benefits of telling the truth) and when telling a lie involves a reduced cognitive load (e.g., because of the complexity of the lie to be told or the degree to which the lie is active in memory through rehearsal or preparation). For further evaluation of IMT2, see Walczyk (2014).

Being an Effective Liar

As will be seen in the following chapters, in one sense we are all effective liars: people do not produce clear and reliable indicators of their deception (DePaulo et al., 2003; Luke, 2019), and others are only marginally more accurate than chance accuracy when deciding if people are lying or telling the truth (Bond & DePaulo, 2006). While the self-presentational perspective suggests that being a highly motivated liar would result in more effective strategic control of the lie given their desire to provide more plausible tales (Hauch et al., 2016), the motivational impairment effect (DePaulo et al., 1988) argues that highly motivated liars fail to do so. Consistent with this latter claim, highly motivated liars produce more cues to deceit compared to when motivations are not so high (DePaulo et al., 2003; Sporer & Schwandt, 2006) and are slightly easier to detect than truth-tellers as a result (Bond

& DePaulo, 2006). Motivational impairment may be the result of a greater emotional burden or the truthful information becoming more salient to the liar. For instance, liars have been shown to have a slower heart rate and larger skin conductance compared to truth-tellers, but these effects are even larger for highly motivated liars (Meijer et al., 2016; Suchotzki & Gamer, 2019).

However, Burgoon et al. (Burgoon, 2015; Burgoon & Floyd, 2000) have been critical of the evidence for the motivational impairment effect, arguing that the findings of a meta-analysis (Hartwig & Bond, 2014) suggest that highly motivated liars are no easier to detect than low-motivated liars. Burgoon and Floyd (2000) further argue that there are multiple ways in which motivation may be defined and show in an experiment that different definitions of motivation typically improved the liar's performance rather than impairing it.

So how might people become more effective liars? As seen in the preceding section, reducing the cognitive load of the lie (by reducing the complexity of the lie or taking time to prepare the lie) can facilitate faster and more accurate deception (e.g., Sporer & Schwandt, 2007; Verschuere et al., 2011; Williams et al., 2013). Liars report using a strategy in preparation for being questioned and that these strategies typically involved streamlining their story (Hartwig et al., 2007) and preparing for possible questions (Vrij et al., 2015). One means of simplifying the account is to embed the lie inside truthful information, another strategy that is used by liars (Hartwig et al., 2007; Leins et al., 2013; Nahari, 2018). Perhaps the ultimate embedding of a lie is to convince oneself that the lie being prepared is actually the truth (von Hippel & Trivers, 2011), a strategy that is argued to reduce the cognitive demand of deception (Butterworth et al., 2022). Consistent with this position, when people are given a chance to check some of the answers they have given on a general knowledge test, those given a goal of trying to persuade others of their ability (compared to those given a goal to be as accurate as possible) were more likely to check the answers only of those questions they answered correctly (Schwardmann & van der Weele, 2019; see also Soldà et al., 2020). This finding suggests that people seek out information that confirms a world view to themselves so that they can better deceive others.

Deception is not purely a decision-making act. There can be a moral component to deception (see Chapter 6). There is some work showing that modulating brain activity by applying a small electrical signal to the scalp (using transcranial direct current stimulation [tDCS]) in the region of the prefrontal cortex improves deceptive ability (Fecteau et al., 2013; Karim et al., 2010; Mameli et al., 2010). For instance, Karim et al. (2010) applied tDCS to inhibit activation of the anterior prefrontal cortex, an area that has been associated with moral cognition, and found that deceptive performance improved in terms of reduced feelings of guilt and shorter response latencies.

As discussed previously, people with more a Machiavellian manipulative personality trait tend to lie more frequently (Drouin et al., 2016; Kashy & DePaulo, 1996). A review of the personality traits associated with being an effective liar concludes that while the number of studies exploring manipulative personality traits such as Machiavellianism is rather sparse, there may be some merit to the suggestion that people exhibiting these traits may make for less detectable liars (Semrad et al., 2019). For instance, Daiku et al. (2021) found that people with Machiavellian and psychopathic traits lie more frequently because they have less guilt about lying (see also Neville et al., 2020).

In summary, while it has been argued that motivation may impair an ability to lie, others contend that the research does not support this claim. Preparing ones lie, embedding them in the truth, and inhibiting moral cognition may produce more convincing lies.

Chapter Summary

People lie relatively infrequently, although there are a few 'prolific liars' whose lies far outnumber most other people. These are not to be confused with pathological liars who lie compulsively with no other goal to achieve other than to lie (for more on pathological lying, see Curtis & Hart, 2022). This chapter considered one taxonomy of why we lie, contrasting lies in favour of oneself with those in favour of others and contrasting lies that are told to achieve a gain compared with those avoiding a cost. A moral psychology account of deception (Bond & DePaulo, 2006) contends that we view others' lies as egregious but our own as morally acceptable.

The self-presentational perspective (DePaulo, 1992) argues that both liars and truth-tellers aim to present a 'face' to the receiver that appears credible and believable. However, the leakage hypothesis (Ekman & Friesen, 1969) contends that people unintentionally produce behaviours that show their true emotions. As we shall see in Chapter 3, such cues to deception have not been found. Research has, broadly speaking, shifted away from exploring the emotional experiences of liars and towards accounting for the cognitive impact of deception. The working memory model of deception (Sporer, 2016) and ADCAT (Walczyk et al., 2014) rely on cognitive psychological research on memory to explain how deceiving and truth-telling is produced. Broadly speaking, these accounts see deception as cognitively more effortful than truth-telling. However, IMT2 (McCornack et al., 2014) argues that sometimes deceiving is cognitively less effortful than truth-telling and is a decision that is made in the moment as the conversation unfolds. Similarly, IDT (Buller & Burgoon, 1996) contends that in order to understand deception, researchers must consider the interaction between the sender and the receiver of the statement.

Notes

1 People are more willing to lie and overcome this aversion if they are able to delegate the act of lying to another person (Erat, 2013; Gawn & Innes, 2019; Kandul & Kirchkamp, 2016) or at least are able to pretend that they delegated the deceptive act to another person (Sutan & Vranceanu, 2016).

2 The terms of sender and receiver are sometimes used in the deception literature to indicate the person who is lying or telling the truth and the person who is told the lie or truth, respectively. These terms will be used throughout the book.
3 These findings are replicated when participants get to choose when to lie rather than being artificially instructed by the experimenter (Spence et al., 2008).
4 It is worth noting here that Baddeley's (2007, 2012) working memory model is by no means the only model of memory. For other approaches to understanding memory, see Barnard and Teasdale (1991), Cowan (2005), Engle and Kane (2004), Jonides et al. (2008), and Nairne (1990), which are discussed in Baddeley's (2012) review of working memory.
5 Those who have read Chapter 4 may note the similarity between this account and the Adaptive Lie Detector account of lie-truth judgements.
6 Lies that deceive the receiver but are intended to benefit the receiver, so-called prosocial lies, can be the basis of developing trust (E. E. Levine & Schweitzer, 2015), again highlighting the important role that intention has to play above and beyond the categorisation of the discourse as honest or deceptive.
7 The number 2 in IMT2 reflects that this is a revision of the original IMT put forward by McCornack (1992).

References

Abe, N., Fujii, T., Hirayama, K., Takeda, A., Hosokai, Y., Ishioka, T., Nishio, Y., Suzuki, K., Itoyama, Y., Takahashi, S., Fukuda, H., & Mori, E. (2009). Do parkinsonian patients have trouble telling lies? The neurobiological basis of deceptive behaviour. *Brain: A Journal of Neurology, 132*(Pt 5), 1386–1395. https://doi.org/10.1093/brain/awp052

Abe, N., Suzuki, M., Mori, E., Itoh, M., & Fujii, T. (2007). Deceiving others: Distinct neural responses of the prefrontal cortex and amygdala in simple fabrication and deception with social interactions. *Journal of Cognitive Neuroscience, 19*(2), 287–295. https://doi.org/10.1162/jocn.2007.19.2.287

Abeler, J., Becker, A., & Falk, A. (2012). Truth-telling: A representative assessment. *Instruction Study Labor, 6919*. https://doi.org/10.2139/ssrn.2164648

Abeler, J., Nosenzo, D., & Raymond, C. (2019). Preferences for truth-telling. *Econometrica, 87*(4), 1115–1153. https://doi.org/10.3982/ECTA14673

Akerlof, G. A. (1978). The market for 'lemons': Quality uncertainty and the market mechanism. In P. Diamond & M. Rothschild (Eds.), *Uncertainty in Economics* (pp. 235–251). Academic Press. https://doi.org/10.1016/B978-0-12-214850-7.50022-X

Baddeley, A. (2007). *Working memory, thought and action*. Oxford University Press.

Baddeley, A. (2012). Working memory: Theories, models, and controversies. *Annual Review of Psychology, 63*, 1–29. https://doi.org/10.1146/annurev-psych-120710-100422

Barnard, P. J., & Teasdale, J. D. (1991). Interacting cognitive subsystems: A systemic approach to cognitive-affective interaction and change. *Cognition and Emotion, 5*(1), 1–39. https://doi.org/10.1080/02699939108411021

Baron-Cohen, S., Tager-Flusberg, H., & Cohen, D. J. (2000). *Understanding other minds: Perspectives from developmental cognitive neuroscience*. Oxford University Press.

Battigalli, P., Charness, G., & Dufwenberg, M. (2013). Deception: The role of guilt. *Journal of Economic Behavior & Organization, 93*, 227–232. https://doi.org/10.1016/j.jebo.2013.03.033

Battista, F., Curci, A., Mangiulli, I., & Otgaar, H. (2021). What can we remember after complex denials? The impact of different false denials on memory. *Psychology, Crime & Law*, *27*(9), 914–931. https://doi.org/10.1080/1068316X.2020.1865956

Battista, F., Mangiulli, I., Herter, J., Curci, A., & Otgaar, H. (2020). The effects of repeated denials and fabrication on memory. *Journal of Cognitive Psychology*, *32*(4), 369–381. https://doi.org/10.1080/20445911.2020.1767626

Baumgartner, T., Gianotti, L. R. R., & Knoch, D. (2013). Who is honest and why: Baseline activation in anterior insula predicts inter-individual differences in deceptive behavior. *Biological Psychology*, *94*(1), 192–197. https://doi.org/10.1016/j.biopsycho.2013.05.018

Bénabou, R., & Tirole, J. (2006). Incentives and prosocial behavior. *American Economic Review*, *96*(5), 1652–1678. https://doi.org/10.1257/aer.96.5.1652

Bereby-Meyer, Y., & Shalvi, S. (2015). Deliberate honesty. *Current Opinion in Psychology*, *6*, 195–198. https://doi.org/10.1016/j.copsyc.2015.09.004

Bessarabova, E. (2014). The effects of culture and situational features on in-group favoritism manifested as deception. *International Journal of Intercultural Relations*, *39*, 9–21. https://doi.org/10.1016/j.ijintrel.2013.09.001

Blandón-Gitlin, I., Fenn, E., Masip, J., & Yoo, A. H. (2014). Cognitive-load approaches to detect deception: Searching for cognitive mechanisms. *Trends in Cognitive Sciences*, *18*(9), 441–444. https://doi.org/10.1016/j.tics.2014.05.004

Bolino, M. C., Kacmar, K. M., Turnley, W. H., & Gilstrap, J. B. (2008). A multi-level review of impression management motives and behaviors. *Journal of Management*, *34*(6), 1080–1109. https://doi.org/10.1177/0149206308324325

Bond, C. F., & DePaulo, B. M. (2006). Accuracy of deception judgments. *Personality and Social Psychology Review*, *10*(3), 214–234. https://doi.org/10.1207/s15327957pspr1003_2

Brennen, T., & Magnussen, S. (2020). Research on non-verbal signs of lies and deceit: A blind alley. *Frontiers in Psychology*, *11*. https://www.frontiersin.org/articles/10.3389/fpsyg.2020.613410

Buller, D. B., & Burgoon, J. K. (1996). Interpersonal deception theory. *Communication Theory*, *6*(3), 203–242. https://doi.org/10.1111/j.1468-2885.1996.tb00127.x

Burgoon, J. K. (2015). When is deceptive message production more effortful than truth-telling? A baker's dozen of moderators. *Frontiers in Psychology*, *6*. https://www.frontiersin.org/articles/10.3389/fpsyg.2015.01965

Burgoon, J. K., Buller, D. B., & Floyd, K. (2001). Does participation affect deception success? *Human Communication Research*, *27*(4), 503–534. https://doi.org/10.1111/j.1468-2958.2001.tb00791.x

Burgoon, J. K., Buller, D. B., White, C. H., Afifi, W., & Buslig, A. L. S. (1999). The role of conversational involvement in deceptive interpersonal interactions. *Personality and Social Psychology Bulletin*, *25*(6), 669–686. https://doi.org/10.1177/0146167299025006003

Burgoon, J. K., Chen, F., & Twitchell, D. (2010). Deception and its detection under synchronous and asynchronous computer-mediated communication. *Group Decision and Negotiation*, *19*, 345–366. https://doi.org/10.1007/s10726-009-9168-8

Burgoon, J. K., & Floyd, K. (2000). Testing for the motivation impairment effect during deceptive and truthful interaction. *Western Journal of Communication*, *64*(3), 243–267. https://doi.org/10.1080/10570310009374675

Burgoon, J. K., Proudfoot, J. G., Schuetzler, R., & Wilson, D. (2014). Patterns of nonverbal behavior associated with truth and deception: Illustrations from three experiments. *Journal of Nonverbal Behavior, 38*(3), 325–354. https://doi.org/10.1007/s10919-014-0181-5

Butterworth, J., Trivers, R., & von Hippel, W. (2022). The better to fool you with: Deception and self-deception. *Current Opinion in Psychology*, 101385. https://doi.org/10.1016/j.copsyc.2022.101385

Cai, H., & Wang, J. T.-Y. (2006). Overcommunication in strategic information transmission games. *Games and Economic Behavior, 56*(1), 7–36. https://doi.org/10.1016/j.geb.2005.04.001

Cantarero, K., Szarota, P., Stamkou, E., Navas, M., & Dominguez Espinosa, A. del C. (2018). When is a lie acceptable? Work and private life lying acceptance depends on its beneficiary. *The Journal of Social Psychology, 158*(2), 220–235. https://doi.org/10.1080/00224545.2017.1327404

Cappelen, A. W., Sørensen, E. Ø., & Tungodden, B. (2013). When do we lie? *Journal of Economic Behavior & Organization, 93*, 258–265. https://doi.org/10.1016/j.jebo.2013.03.037

Carrión, R. E., Keenan, J. P., & Sebanz, N. (2010). A truth that's told with bad intent: An ERP study of deception. *Cognition, 114*(1), 105–110. https://doi.org/10.1016/j.cognition.2009.05.014

Caspi, A., & Gorsky, P. (2006). Online deception: Prevalence, motivation, and emotion. *CyberPsychology & Behavior, 9*(1), 54–59. https://doi.org/10.1089/cpb.2006.9.54

Chisholm, R. M., & Feehan, T. D. (1977). The intent to deceive. *The Journal of Philosophy, 74*(3), 143–159. https://doi.org/10.2307/2025605

Choi, H. J., Park, H. S., & Oh, J. Y. (2011). Cultural differences in how individuals explain their lying and truth-telling tendencies. *International Journal of Intercultural Relations, 35*(6), 749–766. https://doi.org/10.1016/j.ijintrel.2011.08.001

Christ, S. E., Van Essen, D. C., Watson, J. M., Brubaker, L. E., & McDermott, K. B. (2009). The contributions of prefrontal cortex and executive control to deception: Evidence from activation likelihood estimate meta-analyses. *Cerebral Cortex, 19*(7), 1557–1566. https://doi.org/10.1093/cercor/bhn189

Cole, T. (2001). Lying to the one you love: The use of deception in romantic relationships. *Journal of Social and Personal Relationships, 18*(1), 107–129. https://doi.org/10.1177/0265407501181005

Colwell, K., Hiscock-Anisman, C., Corbett, L., Memon, A., Hauselt, W., & Bonilla, Y. (2011). Change in suspect's memory as a result of deception. *American Journal of Forensic Psychology, 29*(4), 1–9.

Cowan, N. (2005). *Working memory capacity*. Psychology Press.

Crawford, V. P., & Sobel, J. (1982). Strategic information transmission. *Econometrica, 50*(6), 1431–1451. https://doi.org/10.2307/1913390

Curtis, D. A., & Hart, C. L. (2022). *Pathological lying: Theory, research, and practice* (1st edition). American Psychological Association.

Daiku, Y., Serota, K. B., & Levine, T. R. (2021). A few prolific liars in Japan: Replication and the effects of Dark Triad personality traits. *PLOS One, 16*(4), e0249815. https://doi.org/10.1371/journal.pone.0249815

DeAndrea, D. C., Tom Tong, S., Liang, Y. J., Levine, T. R., & Walther, J. B. (2012). When do people misrepresent themselves to others? The effects of social desirability, ground truth, and accountability on deceptive self-presentations. *Journal of Communication, 62*(3), 400–417. https://doi.org/10.1111/j.1460-2466.2012.01646.x

Debey, E., Verschuere, B., & Crombez, G. (2012). Lying and executive control: An experimental investigation using ego depletion and goal neglect. *Acta Psychologica, 140*(2), 133–141. https://doi.org/10.1016/j.actpsy.2012.03.004

DePaulo, B. M. (1992). Nonverbal behavior and self-presentation. *Psychological Bulletin*, *111*(2), 203–243. https://doi.org/10.1037/0033-2909.111.2.203

DePaulo, B. M., & Kashy, D. A. (1998). Everyday lies in close and casual relationships. *Journal of Personality and Social Psychology*, *74*(1), 63–79. https://doi.org/10.1037/0022-3514.74.1.63

DePaulo, B. M., Kashy, D. A., Kirkendol, S. E., Wyer, M. M., & Epstein, J. A. (1996). Lying in everyday life. *Journal of Personality and Social Psychology*, *70*(5), 979–995. https://doi.org/10.1037/0022-3514.70.5.979

DePaulo, B. M., Kirkendol, S. E., Tang, J., & O'Brien, T. P. (1988). The motivational impairment effect in the communication of deception: Replications and extensions. *Journal of Nonverbal Behavior*, *12*(3), 177–202. https://doi.org/10.1007/BF00987487

DePaulo, B. M., Lindsay, J. J., Malone, B. E., Muhlenbruck, L., Charlton, K., & Cooper, H. (2003). Cues to deception. *Psychological Bulletin*, *129*(1), 74–118.

Derrick, D. C., Meservy, T. O., jenkins, j. L., Burgoon, J. K., & Nunamaker, J. F. (2013). Detecting deceptive chat-based communication using typing behavior and message cues. *ACM Transactions on Management Information Systems (TMIS)*. https://doi.org/10.1145/2499962.2499967

Dike, C. C., Baranoski, M., & Griffith, E. E. H. (2005). Pathological lying revisited. *The Journal of the American Academy of Psychiatry and the Law*, *33*(3), 342–349.

Dmytro, D., Lo, J., O'Leary, J., Fu, G., Lee, K., & Cameron, C. A. (2014). Development of cultural perspectives on verbal deception in competitive contexts. *Journal of Cross-Cultural Psychology*, *45*(8), 1196–1214. https://doi.org/10.1177/0022022114535485

Dong, G., & Wu, H. (2010). Attempting to hide our real thoughts: Electrophysiological evidence from truthful and deceptive responses during evaluation. *Neuroscience Letters*, *479*(1), 1–5. https://doi.org/10.1016/j.neulet.2010.05.014

Drouin, M., Miller, D., Wehle, S. M. J., & Hernandez, E. (2016). Why do people lie online? "Because everyone lies on the internet". *Computers in Human Behavior*, *64*, 134–142. https://doi.org/10.1016/j.chb.2016.06.052

Dufwenberg, M., & Gneezy, U. (2000). Measuring beliefs in an experimental lost wallet game. *Games and Economic Behavior*, *30*(2), 163–182. https://doi.org/10.1006/game.1999.0715

Dunbar, N. E., Jensen, M. L., Burgoon, J. K., Kelley, K. M., Harrison, K. J., Adame, B. J., & Bernard, D. R. (2015). Effects of veracity, modality, and sanctioning on credibility assessment during mediated and unmediated interviews. *Communication Research*, *42*(5), 649–674. https://doi.org/10.1177/0093650213480175

Duran, N. D., Dale, R., & McNamara, D. S. (2010). The action dynamics of overcoming the truth. *Psychonomic Bulletin & Review*, *17*(4), 486–491. https://doi.org/10.3758/PBR.17.4.486

Ekman, P. (1985). *Telling lies: Clues to deceit in the marketplace, politics, and marriage*. Norton. https://www.amazon.co.uk/Telling-Lies-Marketplace-Politics-Marriage/dp/0393337456

Ekman, P. (2003). Darwin, deception, and facial expression. *Annals of the New York Academy of Sciences*, *1000*(1), 205–221. https://doi.org/10.1196/annals.1280.010

Ekman, P., & Friesen, W. V. (1969). Nonverbal leakage and clues to deception. *Psychiatry*, *32*(1), 88–106. https://doi.org/10.1080/00332747.1969.11023575

Ekman, P., & Matsumoto, D. (2011). Reading faces: The universality of emotional expression. In M. Gernsbacher, R. W. Pew, L. M. Hough, & J. R. Pomerantz

(Eds.), *Psychology and the real world: Essays illustrating fundamental contributions to society* (pp. 140–146). Worth Publishers.

El Haj, M., Antoine, P., & Nandrino, J. L. (2017). When deception influences memory: The implication of theory of mind. *Quarterly Journal of Experimental Psychology, 70*(7), 1166–1173. https://doi.org/10.1080/17470218.2016.1173079

El Haj, M., Saloppé, X., & Nandrino, J. L. (2018). Destination memory and deception: When I lie to Barack Obama about the moon. *Psychological Research, 82*(3), 600–606. https://doi.org/10.1007/s00426-016-0840-8

Engle, R. W., & Kane, M. J. (2004). Executive attention, working memory capacity, and a two-factor theory of cognitive control. In B. H. Ross (Ed.), *The psychology of learning and motivation: Advances in research and theory* (Vol. 44, pp. 145–199). Elsevier Science.

Erat, S. (2013). Avoiding lying: The case of delegated deception. *Journal of Economic Behavior & Organization, 93*, 273–278. https://doi.org/10.1016/j.jebo.2013.03.035

Fallis, D. (2012). Davidson was almost right about lying. *Australasian Journal of Philosophy, 91*(2), 337–353.

Farrow, T. F. D., Hopwood, M.-C., Parks, R. W., Hunter, M. D., & Spence, S. A. (2010). Evidence of mnemonic ability selectively affecting truthful and deceptive response dynamics. *The American Journal of Psychology, 123*(4), 447–453. https://doi.org/10.5406/amerjpsyc.123.4.0447

Fecteau, S., Boggio, P., Fregni, F., & Pascual-Leone, A. (2013). Modulation of untruthful responses with non-invasive brain stimulation. *Frontiers in Psychiatry, 3*(97), 1–9.

Feldman, R. S., Forrest, J. A., & Happ, B. R. (2002). Self-presentation and verbal deception: Do self-presenters lie more? *Basic and Applied Social Psychology, 24*(2), 163–170. https://doi.org/10.1207/S15324834BASP2402_8

Fischbacher, U., & Föllmi-Heusi, F. (2013). Lies in disguise—an experimental study on cheating. *Journal of the European Economic Association, 11*(3), 525–547. https://doi.org/10.1111/jeea.12014

Fu, G., Xu, F., Cameron, C. A., Heyman, G., & Lee, K. (2007). Cross-cultural differences in children's choices, categorizations, and evaluations of truths and lies. *Developmental Psychology, 43*(2), 278–293. https://doi.org/10.1037/0012-1649.43.2.278

Ganis, G., Morris, R. R., & Kosslyn, S. M. (2009). Neural processes underlying self- and other-related lies: An individual difference approach using fMRI. *Social Neuroscience, 4*(6), 539–553. https://doi.org/10.1080/17470910801928271

Gawn, G., & Innes, R. (2019). Lying through others: Does delegation promote deception? *Journal of Economic Psychology, 71*, 59–73. https://doi.org/10.1016/j.joep.2018.08.005

George, J. F., & Robb, A. (2008). Deception and computer-mediated communication in daily life. *Communication Reports, 21*(2), 92–103. https://doi.org/10.1080/08934210802298108

Gilbert, S. J., & Burgess, P. W. (2008). Executive function. *Current Biology, 18*(3), R110–R114. https://doi.org/10.1016/j.cub.2007.12.014

Giles, M., Hansia, M., Metzger, M., & Dunbar, N. E. (2021). The impact of culture in deception and deception detection. In V. S. Subrahmanian, J. K. Burgoon & N. E. Dunbar (Eds.), *Detecting trust and deception in group interaction* (pp. 35–54). Springer.

Gillath, O., Sesko, A. K., Shaver, P. R., & Chun, D. S. (2010). Attachment, authenticity, and honesty: Dispositional and experimentally induced security can reduce self- and other-deception. *Journal of Personality and Social Psychology, 98*(5), 841–855. https://doi.org/10.1037/a0019206

Gneezy, U. (2005). Deception: The role of consequences. *American Economic Review, 95*(1), 384–394. https://doi.org/10.1257/0002828053828662

Gneezy, U., Kajackaite, A., & Sobel, J. (2016). Lying aversion and the size of the lie. *American Economic Review, 108*(2), 419–453. https://doi.org/10.1257/aer.20161553

Goffman, E. (1959). *The presentation of self in everyday life.* Anchor Books.

Greene, J. D., & Paxton, J. M. (2009). Patterns of neural activity associated with honest and dishonest moral decisions. *Proceedings of the National Academy of Sciences, 106*(30), 12506–12511. https://doi.org/10.1073/pnas.0900152106

Gunia, B. C., Wang, L., Huang, L., Wang, J., & Murnighan, J. K. (2012). Contemplation and conversation: Subtle influences on moral decision making. *Academy of Management Journal, 55*(1), 13–33. https://doi.org/10.5465/amj.2009.0873

Guthrie, J., & Kunkel, A. (2013). Tell me sweet (and not-so-sweet) little lies: Deception in romantic relationships. *Communication Studies, 64*(2), 141–157. https://doi.org/10.1080/10510974.2012.755637

Halevy, R., Shalvi, S., & Verschuere, B. (2014). Being honest about dishonesty: Correlating self-reports and actual lying. *Human Communication Research, 40*(1), 54–72. https://doi.org/10.1111/hcre.12019

Hancock, J., Birnholtz, J., Bazarova, N., Guillory, J., Perlin, J., & Amos, B. (2009). Butler lies: Awareness, deception and design. *Proceedings of the SIGCHI Conference on Human Factors in Computing Systems*, 517–526. https://doi.org/10.1145/1518701.1518782

Hancock, J., Thom-Santelli, J., & Ritchie, T. (2004). Deception and design: The impact of communication technology on lying behavior. In *Proceedings, Conference on Computer Human Interaction* (Vol. 6, p. 134). https://doi.org/10.1145/985692.985709

Hartwig, M., & Bond, C. F. (2014). Lie detection from multiple cues: A meta-analysis. *Applied Cognitive Psychology, 28*(5), 661–676. https://doi.org/10.1002/acp.3052

Hartwig, M., Granhag, P. A., & Strömwall, L. A. (2007). Guilty and innocent suspects' strategies during police interrogations. *Psychology, Crime & Law, 13*(2), 213–227.

Hauch, V., Sporer, S. L., Michael, S. W., & Meissner, C. A. (2016). Does training improve the detection of deception? A meta-analysis. *Communication Research, 43*(3), 283–343. https://doi.org/10.1177/0093650214534974

Healy, W., & Healy, M. T. (1926). *Pathological lying, accusation, and swindling.* Little Brown.

Hu, C., Huang, K., Hu, X., Liu, Y., Yuan, F., Wang, Q., & Fu, G. (2015). Measuring the cognitive resources consumed per second for real-time lie-production and recollection: A dual-tasking paradigm. *Frontiers in Psychology, 6.* https://www.frontiersin.org/articles/10.3389/fpsyg.2015.00596

Hume, D. (2007). *An enquiry concerning human understanding.* Oxford University Press; Original work published 1748.

Jacobsen, C., Fosgaard, T. R., & Pascual-Ezama, D. (2018). Why do we lie? A practical guide to the dishonesty literature. *Journal of Economic Surveys, 32*(2), 357–387. https://doi.org/10.1111/joes.12204

Jonides, J., Lewis, R. L., Nee, D. E., Lustig, C. A., Berman, M. G., & Moore, K. S. (2008). The mind and brain of short-term memory. *Annual Review of Psychology, 59*, 193–224. https://doi.org/10.1146/annurev.psych.59.103006.093615

Kajackaite, A., & Gneezy, U. (2015). Lying costs and incentives. *UC San Diego Discussion Paper*.

Kandul, S., & Kirchkamp, O. (2016). *Do I care if others lie? Current and future effects of delegation of lying* (Working Paper No. 2016–011). Jena Economic Research Papers. https://www.econstor.eu/handle/10419/162484

Karim, A. A., Schneider, M., Lotze, M., Veit, R., Sauseng, P., Braun, C., & Birbaumer, N. (2010). The truth about lying: Inhibition of the anterior prefrontal cortex improves deceptive behavior. *Cerebral Cortex, 20*(1), 205–213. https://doi.org/10.1093/cercor/bhp090

Kartik, N. (2009). Strategic communication with lying costs. *The Review of Economic Studies, 76*(4), 1359–1395.

Kashy, D. A., & DePaulo, B. M. (1996). Who lies? *Journal of Personality and Social Psychology, 70*(5), 1037–1051. https://doi.org/10.1037/0022-3514.70.5.1037

Kaylor-Hughes, C., Lankapa, S. T., Fung, R., Hope-Urwin, A. E., Wilkinson, I. D., & Spence, Sean A. (2011). The functional anatomical distinction between truth telling and deception is preserved among people with schizophrenia. *Criminal Behaviour and Mental Health, 21*(1), 8–20.

Kim, M.-S., Kam, K. Y., Sharkey, W. F., & Singelis, T. M. (2008). "Deception: Moral transgression or social necessity?": Cultural-relativity of deception motivations and perceptions of deceptive communication. *Journal of International and Intercultural Communication, 1*(1), 23–50. https://doi.org/10.1080/17513050701621228

Lane, J., & Wegner, D. (1995). *The cognitive consequences of secrecy*. https://doi.org/10.1037/0022-3514.69.2.237

Lane, S. M., & Vieira, K. M. (2012). Steering a new course for deception detection research. *Journal of Applied Research in Memory and Cognition, 1*(2), 136–138. https://doi.org/10.1016/j.jarmac.2012.04.001

Langleben, D. D., Loughead, J. W., Bilker, W. B., Ruparel, K., Childress, A. R., Busch, S. I., & Gur, R. C. (2005). Telling truth from lie in individual subjects with fast event-related fMRI. *Human Brain Mapping, 26*(4), 262–272. https://doi.org/10.1002/hbm.20191

Leins, D. A., Fisher, R. P., & Ross, S. J. (2013). Exploring liars' strategies for creating deceptive reports. *Legal and Criminological Psychology, 18*(1), 141–151. https://doi.org/10.1111/j.2044-8333.2011.02041.x

Leo, R. A., & Ofshe, R. J. (2008). *The Decision to Confess Falsely: Rational Choice and Irrational Action* (SSRN Scholarly Paper No. 1134046). https://papers.ssrn.com/abstract=1134046

Levine, E. E., & Schweitzer, M. E. (2015). Prosocial lies: When deception breeds trust. *Organizational Behavior and Human Decision Processes, 126*, 88–106. https://doi.org/10.1016/j.obhdp.2014.10.007

Levine, T. R., Ali, M. V., Dean, M., Abdulla, R. A., & Garcia-Ruano, K. (2016). Toward a pan-cultural typology of deception motives. *Journal of Intercultural Communication Research, 45*(1), 1–12. https://doi.org/10.1080/17475759.2015.1137079

Levine, T. R., Kim, R. K., & Hamel, L. M. (2010). People lie for a reason: Three experiments documenting the principle of veracity. *Communication Research Reports, 27*(4), 271–285. https://doi.org/10.1080/08824096.2010.496334

Levine, T. R., Serota, K. B., Carey, F., & Messer, D. (2013). Teenagers lie a lot: A further investigation into the prevalence of lying. *Communication Research Reports, 30*(3), 211–220. https://doi.org/10.1080/08824096.2013.806254

Li, Y., Liu, Z., & Liu, X. (2022). Who did I lie to that day? Deception impairs memory in daily life. *Psychological Research*. https://doi.org/10.1007/s00426-021-01619-x

Lisofsky, N., Kazzer, P., Heekeren, H. R., & Prehn, K. (2014). Investigating socio-cognitive processes in deception: A quantitative meta-analysis of neuroimaging studies. *Neuropsychologia, 61*, 113–122. https://doi.org/10.1016/j.neuropsychologia.2014.06.001

López-Pérez, R., & Spiegelman, E. (2013). Why do people tell the truth? Experimental evidence for pure lie aversion. *Experimental Economics, 16*(3), 233–247. https://doi.org/10.1007/s10683-012-9324-x

Luke, T. J. (2019). Lessons from Pinocchio: Cues to deception may be highly exaggerated. *Perspectives on Psychological Science, 14*(4), 646–671. https://doi.org/10.1177/1745691619838258

Mahon, J. (2008). Two definitions of lying. *International Journal of Applied Philosophy, 22*. https://doi.org/10.5840/ijap200822216

Mameli, F., Mrakic-Sposta, S., Vergari, M., Fumagalli, M., Macis, M., Ferrucci, R., Nordio, F., Consonni, D., Sartori, G., & Priori, A. (2010). Dorsolateral prefrontal cortex specifically processes general – but not personal – knowledge deception: Multiple brain networks for lying. *Behavioural Brain Research, 211*(2), 164–168. https://doi.org/10.1016/j.bbr.2010.03.024

Markowitz, D. M. (2022). Toward a deeper understanding of prolific lying: Building a profile of situation-level and individual-level characteristics. *Communication Research*, 00936502221097041. https://doi.org/10.1177/00936502221097041

Masip, J., Garrido, E., & Herrero, C. (2004). Defining deception. *Anales de Psicología, 20*(1), 147–171.

McCornack, S. A. (1992). Information manipulation theory. *Communication Monographs, 59*(1), 1–16. https://doi.org/10.1080/03637759209376245

McCornack, S. A., Morrison, K., Paik, J. E., Wisner, A. M., & Zhu, X. (2014). Information manipulation theory 2: A propositional theory of deceptive discourse production. *Journal of Language and Social Psychology, 33*(4), 348–377.

Meijer, E. H., Verschuere, B., Gamer, M., Merckelbach, H., & Ben-Shakhar, G. (2016). Deception detection with behavioral, autonomic, and neural measures: Conceptual and methodological considerations that warrant modesty. *Psychophysiology, 53*(5), 593–604. https://doi.org/10.1111/psyp.12609

Miller, G. R., & Stiff, J. B. (1993). *Deceptive communication*. SAGE.

Muzinic, L., Kozaric-Kovacic, D., & Marinic, I. (2016). Psychiatric aspects of normal and pathological lying. *International Journal of Law and Psychiatry, 46*, 88–93. https://doi.org/10.1016/j.ijlp.2016.02.036

Nahari, G. (2018). Reality monitoring in the forensic context: Digging deeper into the speech of liars. *Journal of Applied Research in Memory and Cognition, 7*(3), 432–440. https://doi.org/10.1016/j.jarmac.2018.04.003

Nairne, J. S. (1990). A feature model of immediate memory. *Memory & Cognition, 18*(3), 251–269. https://doi.org/10.3758/BF03213879

Neville, K., Gore, J., & Lawson, A. (2020). Personality factors that influence truthfulness and deception. *Kentucky Journal of Undergraduate Scholarship (KJUS), 4*(1). https://encompass.eku.edu/kjus/vol4/iss1/4

Nortje, A., & Tredoux, C. (2019). How good are we at detecting deception? A review of current techniques and theories. *South African Journal of Psychology, 49*(4), 491–504. https://doi.org/10.1177/0081246318822953

Otgaar, H., Howe, M. L., Mangiulli, I., & Bücken, C. (2020). The impact of false denials on forgetting and false memory. *Cognition, 202*, 104322. https://doi.org/10.1016/j.cognition.2020.104322

Otgaar, H., Howe, M. L., Memon, A., & Wang, J. (2014). The development of differential mnemonic effects of false denials and forced confabulations. *Behavioral Sciences & the Law, 32*(6), 718–731. https://doi.org/10.1002/bsl.2148

Otgaar, H., Howe, M. L., Smeets, T., & Wang, J. (2016). Denial-induced forgetting: False denials undermine memory, but external denials undermine belief. *Journal of Applied Research in Memory and Cognition, 5*(2), 168–175. https://doi.org/10.1016/j.jarmac.2016.04.002

Park, H. S., Choi, H. J., Oh, J. Y., & Levine, T. R. (2018). Differences and similarities between Koreans and Americans in lying and truth-telling. *Journal of Language and Social Psychology, 37*(5), 562–577. https://doi.org/10.1177/0261927X18760081

Park, H. S., Serota, K. B., & Levine, T. R. (2021). In search of Korean Outliars: "A few prolific liars" in South Korea. *Communication Research Reports, 38*(3), 206–215. https://doi.org/10.1080/08824096.2021.1922374

Peterson, C. C. (1995). The role of perceived intention to deceive in children's and adults' concepts of lying. *British Journal of Developmental Psychology, 13*(3), 237–260. https://doi.org/10.1111/j.2044-835X.1995.tb00677.x

Poletti, M., Borelli, P., & Bonuccelli, U. (2011). The neuropsychological correlates of pathological lying: Evidence from behavioral variant frontotemporal dementia. *Journal of Neurology, 258*(11), 2009–2013. https://doi.org/10.1007/s00415-011-6058-1

Richardson, D. C., Street, C. N. H., Tan, J. Y. M., Kirkham, N. Z., Hoover, M. A., & Ghane Cavanaugh, A. (2012). Joint perception: Gaze and social context. *Frontiers in Human Neuroscience, 6*, 194. https://doi.org/10.3389/fnhum.2012.00194

Riesthuis, P., Otgaar, H., De Cort, A., Bogaard, G., & Mangiulli, I. (2022). Creating a false alibi leads to errors of commission and omission. *Applied Cognitive Psychology, Advance Online Publication.* https://doi.org/10.1002/acp.3982

Sánchez-Pagés, S., & Vorsatz, M. (2007). An experimental study of truth-telling in a sender–receiver game. *Games and Economic Behavior, 61*(1), 86–112. https://doi.org/10.1016/j.geb.2006.10.014

Schwardmann, P., & van der Weele, J. (2019). Deception and self-deception. *Nature Human Behaviour, 3*(10), Article 10. https://doi.org/10.1038/s41562-019-0666-7

Seiter, J. S., Bruschke, J., & Bai, C. (2002). The acceptability of deception as a function of perceivers' culture, deceiver's intention, and deceiver-deceived relationship. *Western Journal of Communication, 66*(2), 158–180. https://doi.org/10.1080/10570310209374731

Semrad, M., Scott-Parker, B., & Nagel, M. (2019). Personality traits of a good liar: A systematic review of the literature. *Personality and Individual Differences, 147*, 306–316. https://doi.org/10.1016/j.paid.2019.05.007

Serota, K. B., Levine, T. R., & Boster, F. J. (2010). The prevalence of lying in America: Three studies of self-reported lies. *Human Communication Research, 36*(1), 2–25. https://doi.org/10.1111/j.1468-2958.2009.01366.x

Serota, K. B., Levine, T. R., & Docan-Morgan, T. (2021). Unpacking variation in lie prevalence: Prolific liars, bad lie days, or both? *Communication Monographs, 89*(3), 1–25.

Shalvi, S., & De Dreu, C. K. W. (2014). Oxytocin promotes group-serving dishonesty. *Proceedings of the National Academy of Sciences, 111*(15), 5503–5507. https://doi.org/10.1073/pnas.1400724111

Shalvi, S., Eldar, O., & Bereby-Meyer, Y. (2012). Honesty requires time (and lack of justifications). *Psychological Science, 23*(10), 1264–1270. https://doi.org/10.1177/0956797612443835

Shalvi, S., Gino, F., Barkan, R., & Ayal, S. (2015). Self-serving justifications: Doing wrong and feeling moral. *Current Directions in Psychological Science, 24*(2), 125–130. https://doi.org/10.1177/0963721414553264

Shu, L. L., Gino, F., & Bazerman, M. H. (2011). Dishonest deed, clear conscience: When cheating leads to moral disengagement and motivated forgetting. *Personality and Social Psychology Bulletin, 37*(3), 330–349. https://doi.org/10.1177/0146167211398138

Smith, D. L. (2007). *Why we lie: The evolutionary roots of deception and the unconscious mind* (Reprint edition). St. Martin's Press.

Soldà, A., Ke, C., Page, L., & von Hippel, W. (2020). Strategically delusional. *Experimental Economics, 23*(3), 604–631. https://doi.org/10.1007/s10683-019-09636-9

Spence, S. A., Hunter, M. D., Farrow, T. F. D., Green, R. D., Leung, D. H., Hughes, C. J., & Ganesan, V. (2004). A cognitive neurobiological account of deception: Evidence from functional neuroimaging. *Philosophical Transactions of the Royal Society B: Biological Sciences, 359*(1451), 1755–1762. https://doi.org/10.1098/rstb.2004.1555

Spence, S. A., Kaylor-Hughes, C., Farrow, T. F. D., & Wilkinson, I. D. (2008). Speaking of secrets and lies: The contribution of ventrolateral prefrontal cortex to vocal deception. *NeuroImage, 40*(3), 1411–1418. https://doi.org/10.1016/j.neuroimage.2008.01.035

Sporer, S. L. (2016). Deception and cognitive load: Expanding our horizon with a working memory model. *Frontiers in Psychology, 7*. https://www.frontiersin.org/article/10.3389/fpsyg.2016.00420

Sporer, S. L., & Schwandt, B. (2006). Paraverbal indicators of deception: A meta-analytic synthesis. *Applied Cognitive Psychology, 20*(4), 421–446. https://doi.org/10.1002/acp.1190

Sporer, S. L., & Schwandt, B. (2007). Moderators of nonverbal indicators of deception: A meta-analytic synthesis. *Psychology, Public Policy, and Law, 13*(1), 1–34. https://doi.org/10.1037/1076-8971.13.1.1

Strömwall, L. A., & Willén, R. M. (2011). Inside criminal minds: Offenders' strategies when lying. *Journal of Investigative Psychology and Offender Profiling, 8*(3), 271–281. https://doi.org/10.1002/jip.148

Suchotzki, K., & Gamer, M. (2019). Effect of negative motivation on the behavioral and autonomic correlates of deception. *Psychophysiology, 56*(1), e13284. https://doi.org/10.1111/psyp.13284

Suchotzki, K., Verschuere, B., Van Bockstaele, B., Ben-Shakhar, G., & Crombez, G. (2017). Lying takes time: A meta-analysis on reaction time measures of deception. *Psychological Bulletin, 143*(4), 428–453. https://doi.org/10.1037/bul0000087

Sun, S.-Y., Mai, X., Liu, C., Liu, J.-Y., & Luo, Y.-J. (2011). The processes leading to deception: ERP spatiotemporal principal component analysis and source analysis. *Social Neuroscience, 6*(4), 348–359. https://doi.org/10.1080/17470919.2010.544135

Sutan, A., & Vranceanu, R. (2016). Lying about delegation. *Journal of Economic Behavior & Organization, 121*, 29–40. https://doi.org/10.1016/j.jebo.2015.10.023

Tabatabaeian, M., Dale, R., & Duran, N. D. (2015). Self-serving dishonest decisions can show facilitated cognitive dynamics. *Cognitive Processing, 16*(3), 291–300. https://doi.org/10.1007/s10339-015-0660-6

The British Army. (2017). *Land operations*. Land Warfare Development Centre. https://www.gov.uk/government/publications/army-doctrine-publication-operations

Toma, C. L., & Hancock, J. T. (2010). Looks and lies: The role of physical attractiveness in online dating self-presentation and deception. *Communication Research, 37*(3), 335–351. https://doi.org/10.1177/0093650209356437

Trivers, R. (2011). *The folly of fools: The logic of deceit and self-deception in human life.* Basic Books.

Tyler, J. M., & Feldman, R. S. (2004). Truth, lies, and self-presentation: How gender and anticipated future interaction relate to deceptive behavior. *Journal of Applied Social Psychology, 34*(12), 2602–2615. https://doi.org/10.1111/j.1559-1816.2004.tb01994.x

Van Bockstaele, B., Wilhelm, C., Meijer, E. H., Debey, E., & Verschuere, B. (2015). When deception becomes easy: The effects of task switching and goal neglect on the truth proportion effect. *Frontiers in Psychology, 6*(1666), 1–9.

Van Swol, L. M., Malhotra, D., & Braun, M. T. (2012). Deception and its detection: Effects of monetary incentives and personal relationship history. *Communication Research, 39*(2), 217–238. https://doi.org/10.1177/0093650210396868

Vanberg, C. (2008). Why do people keep their promises? An experimental test of two explanations1. *Econometrica, 76*(6), 1467–1480. https://doi.org/10.3982/ECTA7673

Verschuere, B., & De Houwer, J. (2011). Detecting concealed information in less than a second: Response latency-based measures. In *Memory detection: Theory and application of the Concealed Information Test* (pp. 46–62). Cambridge University Press. https://doi.org/10.1017/CBO9780511975196.004

Verschuere, B., & Shalvi, S. (2014). The truth comes naturally! Does it? *Journal of Language and Social Psychology, 33*(4), 417–423. https://doi.org/10.1177/0261927X14535394

Verschuere, B., Spruyt, A., Meijer, E. H., & Otgaar, H. (2011). The ease of lying. *Consciousness and Cognition, 20*(3), 908–911. https://doi.org/10.1016/j.concog.2010.10.023

Vieira, K. M., & Lane, S. M. (2013). How you lie affects what you remember. *Journal of Applied Research in Memory and Cognition, 2*(3), 173–178. https://doi.org/10.1016/j.jarmac.2013.05.005

von Hippel, W., & Trivers, R. (2011). The evolution and psychology of self-deception. *Behavioral and Brain Sciences, 34*(1), 1–16. https://doi.org/10.1017/S0140525X10001354

Vrij, A. (2008). *Detecting Lies and Deceit: Pitfalls and Opportunities*, 2nd ed (pp. xiii, 488). John Wiley & Sons Ltd.

Vrij, A., Fisher, R., Mann, S. A., & Leal, S. (2006). Detecting deception by manipulating cognitive load. *Trends in Cognitive Sciences, 10*(4), 141–142. https://doi.org/10.1016/j.tics.2006.02.003

Vrij, A., Fisher, R., Mann, S. A., & Leal, S. (2008). A cognitive load approach to lie detection. *Journal of Investigative Psychology and Offender Profiling, 5*(1–2), 39–43. https://doi.org/10.1002/jip.82

Vrij, A., Granhag, P. A., & Porter, S. (2010). Pitfalls and opportunities in nonverbal and verbal lie detection. *Psychological Science in the Public Interest, 11*(3), 89–121. https://doi.org/10.1177/1529100610390861

Vrij, A., Hartwig, M., & Granhag, P. A. (2019). Reading lies: Nonverbal communication and deception. *Annual Review of Psychology, 70*, 295–317. https://doi.org/10.1146/annurev-psych-010418-103135

Vrij, A., Leal, S., Mann, S. A., Vernham, Z., & Brankaert, F. (2015). Translating theory into practice: Evaluating a cognitive lie detection training workshop. *Journal of Applied Research in Memory and Cognition, 4*(2), 110–120. https://doi.org/10.1016/j.jarmac.2015.02.002

Walczyk, J. J. (2014). A commentary on information manipulation theory 2: Its place in deception research and suggestions for elaboration. *Journal of Language and Social Psychology, 33*(4), 424–430. https://doi.org/10.1177/0261927X14535395

Walczyk, J. J., Harris, L. L., Duck, T. K., & Mulay, D. (2014). A social-cognitive framework for understanding serious lies: Activation-decision-construction-action theory. *New Ideas in Psychology, 34*, 22–36. https://doi.org/10.1016/j.newideapsych.2014.03.001

Walker, R., & Jussim, L. (2002). Do people lie to appear unprejudiced. *The Rutger Scholar, 4*. https://rutgersscholar.libraries.rutgers.edu/index.php/scholar/article/view/61

Wang, C. S., & Leung, A. K. -y. (2010). The cultural dynamics of rewarding honesty and punishing deception. *Personality and Social Psychology Bulletin, 36*(11), 1529–1542. https://doi.org/10.1177/0146167210385921

Williams, E. J., Bott, L. A., Patrick, J., & Lewis, M. B. (2013). Telling lies: The irrepressible truth? *PLOS One, 8*(4), e60713. https://doi.org/10.1371/journal.pone.0060713

Yang, Y., Raine, A., Lencz, T., Bihrle, S., Lacasse, L., & Colletti, P. (2005). Prefrontal white matter in pathological liars. *The British Journal of Psychiatry, 187*(4), 320–325. https://doi.org/10.1192/bjp.187.4.320

Yin, L., Hu, Y., Dynowski, D., Li, J., & Weber, B. (2017). The good lies: Altruistic goals modulate processing of deception in the anterior insula. *Human Brain Mapping, 38*(7), 3675–3690. https://doi.org/10.1002/hbm.23623

Zipf, G. K. (1949). *Human behaviour and the principle of least effort: An introduction to human ecology*. Martino Fine Books.

Zuckerman, M., DePaulo, B. M., & Rosenthal, R. (1981). Verbal and Nonverbal Communication of Deception. In L. Berkowitz (Ed.), *Advances in experimental social psychology* (Vol. 14, pp. 1–59). Academic Press. https://doi.org/10.1016/S0065-2601(08)60369-X

3 Cues to Deception

Box 3.1 An Extreme Emotional Reaction to Deception

A 51-year-old man working as a European Economic Community (EEC) negotiator was reported by Sellal et al. (1993) to have experienced seizures that involved hot flushes, auditory and visual hallucinations, bodily convulsions, and eventually a loss of consciousness. More than a third of these seizures occurred while the negotiator was lying as part of his job (the remaining seizures occurred without any obvious deception triggering them). The researchers called this a 'Pinocchio syndrome', given its rather evident behavioural manifestation of a lie. The seizures were a result of a 3 cm tumour in the medial area of the right temporal lobe in the approximate region of the limbic system, a deep brain structure believed to be associated with emotional responses (e.g., Rolls, 2015). Treatment was successful, and with the Pinocchio syndrome now gone, the negotiator was able to return to his work.

In Chapter 2, we considered a number of accounts of how people decide to lie and engage in lying. We will couch our understanding of the behaviours of liars and truth-tellers in those accounts to provide a conceptual hook on which to hang our potential list of behaviours. This will help both mentally organise the information and help us assess how the accounts of how people engage in the process of deception are reflected in the behaviours of liars. The accounts of the deception process that were discussed in Chapter 2 are briefly refreshed first.

Accounts of Deception Processes: A Brief Reminder

The leakage hypothesis (Ekman & Friesen, 1969) claims that liars may experience emotions such as fear or guilt. These emotions may 'leak' in the form of bodily behaviours. The leakage occurs less so from facial behaviours because the face is readily observable and salient and so will be the subject of

DOI: 10.4324/9781003045298-3

greater control. One exception to this is the presence of micro-expressions (Ekman, 1985; Ekman & Matsumoto, 2011), a very fleeting emotion that may be unwittingly displayed despite attempts to inhibit true facial expressions of emotion. However, the evidence supporting leakage accounts is limited (Brennen & Magnussen, 2020; Nortje & Tredoux, 2019).

Cognitive accounts similarly argue that there may be differences between liars and truth-tellers, but focus instead on how liars and truth-tellers think (e.g., Lane & Wegner, 1995; Vrij et al., 2006; Zuckerman et al., 1981). Both the activation-decision-construction-action theory (ADCAT; Walczyk et al., 2014) and the working memory model of deception (Sporer, 2016; Sporer & Schwandt, 2006, 2007) contend that working memory plays a fundamental role in the construction of deceptive (and honest) statements. A liar needs to generate an invented state of the world that hopefully does not contradict itself or what the receiver knows to be true. This process may be cognitively more effortful, involving a manipulation of information in working memory. Consistent with this position, functional magnetic resonance imaging (fMRI) studies show that deception involves activation of brain regions associated with inhibitory control and working memory (Christ et al., 2009).

In Chapter 2, we also saw that the process of deception has been considered to be dynamic in nature. Interpersonal deception theory (IDT; Buller & Burgoon, 1996), proposes that both the liar and lie receiver monitor the behaviours of the other and adapt on the fly. Neuropsychological evidence (Abe et al., 2007; Christ et al., 2009; Langleben et al., 2005; Lisofsky et al., 2014) suggests that liars do indeed monitor the social situation and engage in 'theory of mind' (i.e., the capacity to reason about the mental state of others; Baron-Cohen et al., 2000). At the level of discourse, information manipulation theory 2 (IMT2; McCornack et al., 2014) argues that as a person produces their statement, they monitor the conversation and actively manage their statement moment-to-moment, potentially fluctuating between honesty and deception, in order to meet their goal in an efficient manner. Despite evidence suggesting truth-telling is typically less cognitively effortful than deception (e.g., Greene & Paxton, 2009; Spence et al., 2004), IMT2 leads to the prediction that honesty can be as cognitively effortful or even more so than deceiving because honesty and deception result from the same underlying processes. There is evidence to support this prediction (e.g., Li et al., 2022; Shalvi et al., 2012).

In short, IDT and IMT2 consider deception to fundamentally involve an element of adaptive behavioural control. The self-presentational perspective (DePaulo, 1992) similarly argues that both liars and truth-tellers aim to present themselves as credible and honest. When people have self-presentational goals, deception increases (Feldman et al., 2002). And females[1] lied more when they expected to interact with the person they were speaking to at some point in the future compared to when they thought they would not speak to them again, suggesting a desire to tactically control how they present themselves (Tyler & Feldman, 2004; see also Peng, 2020).

For more detail on any of these accounts, see Chapter 2. Having now refreshed ourselves, let us consider whether the behaviours of the liar and truth-teller are reflective of these accounts.

Cues to Deception

Overview. Box 3.1 presents a rather surprising and unique cue to deception. A 'cue' to deception or honesty refers to any indicator that may be useful in determining whether a person is lying or telling the truth, respectively. While we often tend to think of nonverbal behaviours such as avoiding eye contact and fidgeting as potential indicators of deception (more on this later), the definition of a cue is broader in its scope and refers also to verbal (the content of speech) and paraverbal behaviours (those that accompany speech, but are not the content of speech themselves, e.g., response latency, pitch of voice) of the potential liar. Indeed, a meta-analysis suggests that the content of speech is more diagnostic[2] than nonverbal behaviours (DePaulo et al., 2003).

The cue to deception presented in Box 3.1 is rather unusual and unique. In our daily lives, we do not seem to be presented with such salient and readily observable cues to deception that act as a sort of Pinocchio's nose,[3] allowing us to easily and readily tell when someone is lying. The research bears out this view: there has been no discovery of a Pinocchio's nose, that is, an extremely diagnostic cue to deception (DePaulo et al., 2003; Hauch et al., 2015; Kraut, 1980; Luke, 2019; Sporer & Schwandt, 2006, 2007). In fact, the situation is rather bleak for those who want to detect deception through such cues. A meta-analysis by DePaulo et al. (2003) explored 1,338 measurements of 158 cues to deception across 116 research papers. They developed five categories of cues to deception to be explored: (i) forthrightness (e.g., length of statement, amount of detail, complexity of the statement), (ii) how compelling the statement is (e.g., plausibility, engaging, lack of certainty in statement), (iii) pleasantness (e.g., cooperative and helpful statement, head nods, smiling), (iv) tenseness (e.g., vocal pleasantness, relaxed posture, fidgeting), and (v) unusualness of the statement (e.g., spontaneous corrections, superfluous details).

Most of the examined behavioural cues to deception were not diagnostic: that is, the behaviours were not found significantly more or less often in liars' behaviours compared to truth-tellers' behaviours. As Sternglanz et al. (2019) note in their recent review of meta-analyses, if one only considers cues that have at least a small effect size (Cohen's $d \geq 0.20$), that are statistically significant, and that have been explored across at least six studies, only 11 of the examined cues distinguished liars from truth-tellers. Among these cues were that liars appear less emotionally invested in their statement and more ambivalent. To put into context the size of the differences being observed, Cohen (1988) described an effect size of $d = 0.20$ as akin to how diagnostic it would be to use only a person's height to determine if they are a 15- or 16-year-old girl in the US in 1988. In the context of deception, if a random person was chosen from among a set of liars, there would be a 55.6% chance that the selected person will present the cue more often than truth-tellers tend to and a 44.4% chance that they will present the cue *less* often than truth-tellers tend to.

If we consider all the cues to deception that were statistically significant indicators in DePaulo et al.'s (2003) meta-analysis, the effect size shrinks to a median of $d = 0.10$. A randomly selected liar now has only a 52.8% chance of presenting the behaviour more often than truth-tellers or 47.2% chance of presenting the behaviour less often than truth-tellers. These cues to deception have very poor diagnostic value. It would be difficult to judge whether a given person presenting this behaviour is a liar or truth-teller. Perhaps it is not surprising that Brennen and Magnussen (2020) entitled their recent commentary of nonverbal cues to deception, *Research on non-verbal signs of lies and deceit: A blind alley* (see Vrij & Fisher, 2020, for a counterargument that this may prove a fruitful line of enquiry if some as-yet undiscovered cue or combination of cues is unearthed).

Box 3.2 Concrete Reasoning: What Is a 'Cue' to Deception?

The provided definition of cues to deception at the start of this chapter included the vocal and visual cues that a sender produces during their statement. This may seem a rather innocuous statement, but let us evaluate it further.

One useful way to engage in evaluative reasoning is to carry out what I call 'concrete reasoning'. By this, I mean that it is often useful to imagine the details and processes that would be involved in carrying out the action and imagining oneself actually carrying out those actions. We saw an example of this in Chapter 1 (Box 1.4). This can help you recognise where parts of the process are unclear, ambiguous, or undefined, as well as the variety of possible outcomes could result from carrying out those actions. This may all sound a little nebulous, so let us work through the definition of a cue to deception as an example.

Imagine yourself running a study to find a cue to deception. What might be your first step on that journey? Take a moment to think about that before reading on. Mine would likely be trying to decide what cue I would want to explore. If you were in this position, how would you determine what cues might be worthwhile exploring? We could explore the past literature, but this just moves the issue back: we would know what cues to explore because past research tells us what cues to explore. How did the researchers in those previous studies make that decision? One approach would be to engage in trial and error: pick a random behaviour that one has observed in people (e.g., tapping one's foot). Such an approach would be rather time-consuming, requiring us to run through a whole gamut of possible behaviours that we could imagine. If we got lucky, this might produce a list of cues to deception, but it might not. That would be a lot of effort for potentially little pay-off. Indeed, current thinking is such that the research into nonverbal cues to deception to date has failed to result in diagnostic cues to deception (Brennen & Magnussen, 2020; Nortje & Tredoux, 2019).

Despite this, imagine that you have selected a cue to deception that you wish to explore. I will pick one for you, but feel free to choose your own and substitute that into this text: the cue will be foot tapping, which I have chosen somewhat arbitrarily with the proviso that it has promise for being easy to measure. Let us now try to imagine your experiment and how we will detect whether this cue will be present or absent. If a person lifts their foot once and places it down again, is that a 'foot tap'? Would walking, which involves lifting and placing a foot, be counted? Does a foot tap require multiple lifts and replacements to be counted or would each lift and replacement be considered a separate 'tap'? Does the foot have to come clean off the floor or can it be only partly raised (e.g., tapping one's toes)? Does any gap between the floor and the foot, regardless of how small and fleeting, count, or is a certain distance from the floor or duration of action required? Perhaps you can start to see the difficulties in defining a cue to deception. The issue may become even more difficult with more abstracted cues such as hand gesturing (e.g., does any hand movement count?) or nervousness (e.g., what combination of physical movements would be needed to be able to label the behaviour as nervousness?).

This may all seem a little harmless. Surely, if we are rigorous and take the time to define or our measures appropriately, all will be well, and these definitional issues will go away. The issue is that researchers may define them in different ways from one another, which may increase the noise and imprecision in our estimates. Perhaps worse than this, though, a single researcher may hold multiple definitions. Under one definition, they may code the cues and find that liars present more of them than truth-tellers. Under a different definition, the effect may disappear or reverse. This flexibility is problematic because it offers temptation for the researcher to find an effect that is actually little more than noise in the data. Researchers have a strong code of ethics, which should help mitigate intentionally manipulating the results to achieve a desired effect. But because the flexibility exists, researchers can unintentionally come to post-hoc rationalise their analytical decisions in a way that favours their position. If one has flexibility with data, one of the ways in which the data can be interpreted is likely to return a desirable, statistically significant result even if there is no effect that exists in the wider population (see Box 7.4, Chapter 7).

(Continued)

> Concrete reasoning can seem daunting. But it can take as little as a handful of seconds to engage with, and it can provide truly interesting and useful evaluations that may offer promising long-term insights for your assessments, your exams, your degree, your Masters or PhD research plans, and beyond.

Unfortunately, the situation may be worse than it appears. Luke (2019) provides a chilling prospect: using computational simulations, he showed that the diagnostic cues to deception observed in the DePaulo et al. (2003) meta-analysis could have been statistically significant even if there are no cues that exist in the population (i.e., a Cohen's *d* of zero)! This could be the case if one assumes that researchers are flexible in their choice of analyses, that small sample sizes are used in studies, and if only the statistically significant cues to deception are published while the non-significant ones remain unpublished.[4] Unfortunately, as deception studies do tend to use small sample sizes, scientific research is not replicating as often as one would expect because (in part) researchers have been flexible in their choice of analyses, and non-significant findings do tend to go unpublished (more on these issues in Chapter 8). And while DePaulo et al. (2003) explored many different cues to deception, Vrij (2008) noted that most of these cues had only been explored in a small number of studies, potentially limiting the strength of the evidence obtained in that meta-analysis.

Naturally, DePaulo et al.'s (2003) findings may be a true reflection of the population. If so, there may be some diagnostic cues to deception, albeit rather weakly diagnostic. But the recent simulations (Luke, 2019) tell us that we cannot rule out the possibility that no reliable diagnostic cues have been found so far, and that the supposed 'cues' that some studies are finding could result from less than ideal research methodology and practice or reflect the probabilistic nature of science (i.e., in a world where no cues to deception exist, once in a while we should see studies that find differences in how often the cue is presented between the small set of liars and truth-tellers in that particular study, in much the same way as one might expect to see that a handful of flipped coins may show heads ten times in a row when there are thousands of coins being flipped).

Leakage. It may be argued that the lack of leakage cues seen so far may result from using paradigms that involve laboratory-generated lies that hold low stakes for the liar: it may not particularly matter to the liar whether or not they are convincing or get caught, and the lack of a goal to be achieved may fundamentally change the nature of the deception being studied in laboratory research. In an exploration of real-life televised appeals for the return of missing children, ten Brinke et al. (2012) found that those who made genuine, truthful appeals for the return of their child showed emotional expressions that used muscles hypothesised to be involved in grief more so than people who made deceptive appeals for the return of the child but were later found guilty of murdering the child. Liars have also been found to use more negative statements and more negative emotion words in their statements (DePaulo et al., 2003; Newman et al., 2003) and report feeling somewhat more uncomfortable while lying (DePaulo et al., 1996; Kashy & DePaulo, 1996).

However, that emotional states may be detected through nonverbal leakage has recently been critiqued by Burgoon (2018). She argues that, based on the review by Barrett (2006), felt emotion and the expression of emotion do not have a one-to-one mapping: a given felt emotion may have multiple expressions and a given emotional expression may have result from multiple felt emotions. As such, even genuinely expressed emotions may not be highly diagnostic of the emotion being felt.

Empirical evidence against the leakage hypothesis comes from meta-analyses on verbal and paraverbal cues to deception. If liars attempt to exert control over their behaviours to avoid leakage, Sporer and Schwandt (2006) have argued that liars will have a shorter response latency (the time taken to begin uttering the deceptive statement) and a decrease in pitch of voice compared to truth-tellers, but these were both found to be *increased* in liars compared to truth-tellers. They also contend in a subsequent meta-analysis (Sporer & Schwandt, 2007) that the emotion perspective would predict reduced eye contact and smiling and increased bodily movements indicating fear and guilt, but such behaviours are not typically observed (DePaulo et al., 2003; Sporer & Schwandt, 2007).

The leakage hypothesis argues that people are aware that their faces are a social cue to others more so than their bodies, and so can better control their face to avoid leaking cues to deception (Ekman & Friesen, 1969). However, one exception to this is the so-called micro-expression. A micro-expression is a fleeting emotional expression that unwittingly expresses the emotion that the sender is trying to conceal (Ekman, 1985). The expression is said to last between 1/25th and 1/5th of a second. However, there is limited research exploring whether liars exhibit these involuntary expressions. Porter and ten Brinke (2008) asked participants to produce a convincing display of an emotion (e.g., happiness) in response to a range of positive, negative, and neutral emotive images. They found no full micro-expressions, but found partial expressions (i.e., displayed either in the upper or lower half of the face rather than the whole face) in 14 out of 697 analysed expressions, of which six (or 0.9%) were committed when the emotive image matched the emotional display participants were asked to show, and eight (or 1.1%) while producing a deceptive expression. They concluded that micro-expressions appear rarely, and when they do appear they are approximately equally present in honest and deceptive expressions (see Porter et al., 2012; ten Brinke et al., 2012, for similar conclusions).

If micro-expressions are diagnostic of deception, as has been claimed by proponents of the leakage hypothesis (Ekman, 2009; Paul Ekman Group, 2022), training people to detect micro-expressions ought to increase lie detection accuracy. A recent study made use of the Micro-Expression Training Toolkit (METT), a training package for helping people detect micro-expressions, to determine whether training on this toolkit could improve lie detection accuracy (Jordan et al., 2019). Ninety participants were trained either on the METT or else were given 'bogus training' with the intention of ensuring that this comparison group also experienced a training regime. This is needed because it may be that, for example, just training alone, even uninformative training, results in more thoughtful effort given to making the judgement. In such a case, it would be the effect of training more generally rather than METT training specifically that may be increasing accuracy. The bogus trained participants were trained on how to recognise social interactions (e.g., training to identify who in a scene is the employer and who is the employee). Using a range of video stimuli from laboratory-generated deceptions to real-world public appeals, the researchers found that METT training improved micro-expression recognition in a test at the end of the METT. This is to be expected: the training is designed to improve performance on the final METT test. However, the training did not improve lie detection accuracy (Jordan et al., 2019).

Impression management. Whether lying or telling the truth, the self-presentational perspective argues that people will manage their presentation so as to appear honest (DePaulo, 1992). DePaulo et al. (2003) have suggested that the self-presentational perspective would predict that feelings of guilt would generally be mild because lies are typically intended to present a better image of oneself rather than for more nefarious purposes. But more self-serving lies should generate more cues to deception. The meta-analysis of DePaulo et al. (2003, p. 102) found that lies for self-gain created 'more plentiful' cues to deception, while those that were not for self-gain generated cues that were 'barely discriminable from truths'. They also argue that Buller and Burgoon's (1996) IDT predicts that greater interactivity between the sender and receiver should increase signs of greater composure and greater immediacy. In contrast, DePaulo et al. (2003) found that a higher pitched voice (indicating low composure) was a cue to deception in interactive contexts but not in non-interactive contexts. They also found that liars provided fewer details than truth-tellers in interactive contexts, had less vocal involvement, and indicated more uncertainty in their statements, suggesting less immediacy and exhibiting strategic attempts to manage their impression.

A more recent meta-analysis by Hauch et al. (2015) also found support for a self-presentational perspective. Liars may be expected to distance themselves from the statement because the lie is less convincingly embraced compared to truths, possibly due to having less personal investment in the deception. Liars did indeed use fewer first-person references and used more second- and third-person references, suggesting a distancing of oneself from the statement. While they also found evidence that liars produced fewer tentative words than truth-tellers—contradicting a self-presentational perspective that liars want to distance themselves from their statements—the researchers note that there was limited data available to fully test this prediction.

The self-presentation perspective suggests that liars do not assume others will believe they are being honest, and so will engage in greater effort in their communications. This takes greater cognitive effort (Hauch et al., 2015; see the following subsection for more on cognitive effort). As we have seen, the definition of the self-presentational perspective is somewhat loose. As such, multiple phenomena have been argued to be consistent with the perspective, but these phenomena overlap with other, more precise accounts such as IDT or the working memory model (see Box 2.4. in Chapter 2 for more on the precision of psychological accounts).

> **Box 3.3 Defining Deception Again: Does It Exist?**
>
> The meta-analysis by Hauch et al. (2015) also explored a range of potential moderators or factors that might affect the relationship between the cue's presence and veracity. These moderators included personal involvement in the lie, the type of event being discussed, the degree of interaction between sender and receiver, and the level of motivation. Similarly, other meta-analyses on the cues to deception find that there may be important moderators that affect how behaviours relate to deception (DePaulo et al., 2003; Sporer & Schwandt, 2006, 2007) such as preparation and rehearsal, whether the lies were about facts, the experimental design, the relationship between the sender and receiver, and the motivation to succeed.
>
> Recall from Chapter 1 that one of the approaches to evaluative reasoning is to find the hidden assumptions. Throughout the book, we have assumed that there is a phenomenon called deception—it is in the title of the book. This may seem mundane, but assumptions often appear that way. Consider the following statements and what they have to tell us about the existence of the phenomena:
>
> - Illness can be treated with penicillin.
> - Cars have five doors.
> - Sport requires a field to play on.
>
> Perhaps you can see an issue with the above. Sure, some illnesses may be treated with penicillin, but others are not. Some cars have five doors, but others do not. Some sports do not need a field (e.g., table tennis, darts). Contrast them with the following statements, and ask yourself why they differ to the above statements:
>
> - Pneumonia can be treated with penicillin.
> - A Suzuki Swift 2013 has five doors.
> - Rugby requires a field to play on.
>
> *(Continued)*

Why do these statements feel less controversial than the ones preceding them? The answer is that the former statements made use of a broader categorising that is intended to represent an *abstracted* quality. Illness does not tangibly exist, but types of illnesses do (e.g., one can provide treatment for pneumonia, but not for 'illness'). Similarly, while you can teach the rules of rugby, you could not teach the rules of sport. These categories are useful for providing abstract representations, but do not themselves exist as concrete entities. Now consider the following statement: lying is associated with distancing oneself from the statement. How might you apply the same reasoning?

We may ask whether lying does exist as a tangible entity or whether it is an abstracted concept that may refer to different forms of lying. Perhaps 'lying' as a phenomenon does not exist. Instead, it may be important to distinguish 'lies about facts' from 'lies about opinions' from 'lies about family members' and so on, each having a unique cognitive, affective, and behavioural profile. This may lead us to wonder whether seeking out 'cues to lying' is a meaningful exercise, given the issue with defining cues (Box 3.2) and now the issue with defining lying. We may even be so bold as to extend this to questions about how people detect *lying* (Chapter 5) or whether they hold unconscious knowledge about *lying* (Chapter 7). I leave that as an exercise for you as you read those chapters.

Cognitive effort. ADCAT (Walczyk et al., 2014) and the working memory model of deception (Sporer, 2016) propose that lying creates greater cognitive load compared to truth-telling. Before we go any further, this is your interim reminder that cues to deception are largely non-diagnostic and there is an argument to be made that they do not exist at all (see the start of this chapter). Keep in mind that the cues we have been talking about so far are faint and unreliable indicators. Now let us get back on track.

Consistent with a cognitive effort view, liars tend to produce statements with fewer details and words and with less complexity in the words chosen (DePaulo et al., 2003; Hauch et al., 2015). For example, in a set of five studies, Newman et al. (2003) asked participants to lie or tell the truth about a variety of topics in different contexts, such as views on abortion via videotape, typing, or handwriting, feelings about friends and about a mock crime. They applied the Linguistic Inquiry and Word Count (LIWC) text analysis programme to the statements to determine the frequency of a variety of word categories, such as referring to oneself, negative emotions, or cognitive complexity (e.g., 'exclusive' words such as except, but, or without; statements of evaluation and judgement; stating both what did and did not happen). They found that liars' statements tended to be less cognitively complex than truth-tellers' statements, which is consistent with the view that truth-tellers may have greater cognitive resource available to them when generating their statements. Other work has also found that liars use fewer total words and choose less complex words (Hauch et al., 2015). DePaulo et al. (2003) found that liars tell less compelling tales as determined by how logical, plausible, and direct their speech was, potentially indicating the cognitive effort that liars experience.

Van Der Zee et al. (2022) sought to develop a model of a particular individual's potential deceptions, namely those of Donald Trump, the 45th President of the US. The researchers used a variety of fact-checking websites to determine whether Trump's 605 statements made on Twitter between February and April 2018 were true or false. Had the false statements been a result of deception, it would be predicted that the use of language would differ from those of honest and factually correct statements. Specifically, the lies should demonstrate language that reflects the higher cognitive effort involved in deception alongside other potential indicators of deception such as the use of language that distances the speaker from the statement. Had they been merely mistakes, there would be no reason to expect differences between factually accurate and inaccurate statements delivered with an intent to tell the truth. The findings reflect a deception explanation: there was a tendency to use more words associated with cognitive processing, shorter words, and more third-person words (that distance the speaker from the statement) compared to first-person words.[5] Such findings are consistent with the position that deception is cognitively effortful.

While deception may be cognitively effortful, it may be anticipated that people will seek to compensate for this cognitive load. Such a position would suggest that liars do not exhibit signs of cognitive load (what Repke et al., 2018, call a 'cognitive strain' model), but rather show behaviours that indicate their compensatory or behavioural management strategies to conceal the experience of cognitive load (what Repke et al., 2018, call a 'strategic' model). A study conducted by Eapen et al. (2010) was reanalysed by Duran et al. (2013) to assess whether the bodily movements of liars could indicate the cognitive effort of deception. Eapen et al. (2010) had 32 participants wear a body motion tracking suit while taking part in a study supposedly about math performance and bodily sway. During the study, participants had two opportunities to lie or tell the truth: once to protect a younger, cheerful researcher from reprimand by their immediate superior and once to selfishly gain payment by claiming to have performed better on the maths task than they actually did.

Duran et al. (2013) applied dynamical systems theory to analyse liars' and truth-tellers' bodily motion from the tracking suit. They found that truth-tellers' behaviours were more recurring and patterned, while liars' behaviours showed greater flexibility and complexity in their movement. This led the authors to suggest that people adapt to the changing moment-to-moment situational demands. They suggest their results are consistent with the cognitive demands of deception, but that they challenge the position that liars' cognitive resources are always simply depleted as a result of having to deceive. This interpretation is consistent with the more dynamic and situationally positioned IMT2.

Both IMT2 (McCornack et al., 2014) and IDT (Buller & Burgoon, 1996) contend that deception is a dynamic and strategic event and that the situation and temporal unfolding of the behaviour are critical to understanding deception. When people lie in order to appear likable to as much of an audience as possible, how they choose to lie depends on who sits in the audience (Repke et al., 2018). These researchers found in three studies that when the people in the audience held a number of varying views on an issue, liars produce more complex and elaborate responses compared to when the whole audience shared a single uniform view on the issue. The findings suggest that liars adaptively engaged in cognitive effort to produce an appropriate account that met the expectations of the audience rather than being overwhelmed by the cognitive strain of deception. We also saw in Chapter 2 that when the incentives to lie become sufficiently high, people switch from telling the truth to lying (Kajackaite & Gneezy, 2015), suggesting that people are prepared to engage in the cognitive effort of deception if the benefits are thought to be worth it.

The cognitive strain and strategic models need not be contradictory, however. See if you can find a way of allowing both accounts to be correct. This is a very useful exercise any time you find yourself dealing with two (or more) competing accounts, because it can lead to new insights that allow you to marry two apparently contradictory perspectives to suggest a new account and generate new predictions. I will assume you have now attempted it. If not, give it a go. A relatively simple way to allow both accounts to be true is to posit that cognitive strain may only be observed for specific types of lies (e.g., those questions that require a long narrative answer compared to those that require a simple yes/no binary response), as Repke et al. (2018) speculated. Or it may be that liars overcome the cognitive strain when their lies are rehearsed. Or maybe the deleterious effects of cognitive strain are compensated for by the strategic effort to overcome it, and so both are being experienced by the liar simultaneously. Our purpose here is not to provide answers: these are all *speculations* that may or may not be true. Developing these speculations is often the hard part of science. Determining whether they are correct is often relatively easy: we apply the scientific method to collect data and test the predictions of your possible explanations.

Summary. Research has sought to uncover leaked cues from the deceiver that may be diagnostic of deception. Unfortunately for the lie detector, the data appear to suggest that there are no highly diagnostic cues (DePaulo et al., 2003), and indeed there may be none at all (Brennen & Magnussen, 2020; Luke, 2019). It may be for this reason that, as we will see in Chapter 5, lie detection strategies have moved away from seeking out ways of passively observing the liar and shifted towards the receiver actively attempting to create cues to deception in the sender. However, some suggest that there may still be some hope of detecting deception through passive observation—if only the right combination of nonverbal cues can be found (Vrij & Fisher, 2020).

Beliefs About Cues to Deception

In a seminal study by 73 academics in 58 countries, over 2,000 participants were asked "How can you tell when people are lying?" (The Global Deception Research Team, 2006, Study 1). It was found that 63.66% of the participants reported that averting gaze was a cue to deception. Approximately one-quarter of participants also mentioned that liars can be detected by their nervousness, nonverbal behaviour, and incoherence. Interestingly, beliefs reported across the 58 countries were remarkably consistent, with a median correlation in the frequency of beliefs being reported across countries of $r = 0.80$ and an extremely high agreement demonstrated by a Cronbach's alpha of 0.98. In Study 2, a multiple-choice questionnaire was administered in 63 countries, directly probing whether cues such as eye contact and shifting posture reflect deception. Akin to the results of Study 1, 71.5% of participants endorsed the belief that liars avert gaze and 65.2% endorsed the belief that liars shift their posture. This study has been more recently replicated in Japan and China and similarly found that eye contact was commonly believed to be a cue to deception (Yeh et al., 2013). Other work has also found that people hold these beliefs (Akehurst et al., 1996; Al-Simadi, 2000). Collectively, these findings suggest that people tend to believe that liars appear nervous (see Strömwall et al., 2004, for a review).

These beliefs about cues to deception do not line up with actual cues to deception. We have seen that averting gaze is a frequently mentioned cue to deception. However, research shows that gaze aversion is not a cue that separates liars from truth-tellers (DePaulo et al., 2003; Sporer & Schwandt, 2007). Claims that people may look up and to the left when they are lying, as proponents of neurolinguistic programming (NLP) argue (see Gordon et al., 2002; Gray, 1991; Heap, 2008), are also not supported by the data.[6] A study coding the frequency with which people look up and to the left (or right) per second found no differences between liars and truth-tellers (Wiseman et al., 2012, Study 1; see also Mann et al., 2012). Judges informed of the NLP claim also perform no better at detecting deception compared to those who are not informed of the claim (Wiseman et al., 2012, Study 2).[7] Other signs of nervousness such as shifting one's posture and touching of oneself with the intent to manage nervousness (called 'self-adaptors') also bear no relationship to deception (DePaulo et al., 2003; see also Vrij & Fisher, 2020, for a dismantling of the myth that nervousness is a sign of deception).

Unfortunately, police officers hold as many inaccurate stereotypic beliefs about deception as lay people (e.g., Akehurst et al., 1996; Bogaard et al., 2016; Vrij & Semin, 1996). For example, police officers report cues such as nervousness, stress, discomfort, and eye contact as possible indicators to deception (Strömwall et al., 2004; Strömwall & Granhag, 2003). Strömwall and

Granhag (2003, p. 19) concluded that "experts' beliefs about deception were remarkably inconsistent with the general pattern resulting from studies mapping actual cues to deception". Other professionals such as managers (Hart et al., 2006), nurses (Curtis, 2015), therapists (Curtis & Hart, 2015; Dickens & Curtis, 2019), customs agents (T. R. Levine & Daiku, 2019; Vrij & Semin, 1996), and prison officers (Lakhani & Taylor, 2003; Masip & Herrero, 2015; Vrij & Semin, 1996) also hold inaccurate beliefs about deception.

> **Box 3.4 Considering Multiple Causes for a Given Effect**
>
> Schooling can lead us to believe that academic thinking is about learning the right answer and being able to recall that back in one's own words. An important difference between high school- and university-level study is a shift from being a recipient of others' thinking to becoming an independent thinker.
>
> We will start to reflect on the possible causes of these misbeliefs about deception in a moment. In my opinion, one of the most valuable activities you can engage with for developing your evaluative reasoning is to consider the broad range of possible alternative explanations. This is the role of an academic and evaluative thinker. Finding out which of the possibilities is 'correct' is relatively easy: we apply the scientific method for data collection and analysis and form conclusions. One of the most difficult parts of the task is finding the possible explanations in the first place.
>
> You may be wondering how you should go about doing this if you do not already have a foothold in the scientific literature on misbeliefs. Surely your judgement should be based on what is already known, right? Well, to some degree, yes. We cannot ignore what has gone before and having that deeper understanding of past work will certainly help you *evaluate* your own ideas. But try not to be constrained by what others have said when you are *generating* your ideas—at least, not at first. It is acceptable, and perhaps some would argue that it is essential, that you generate your ideas constrained by the current evidence, but I think there is a unique opportunity for you to bring your own views to bear on an issue if you first develop your own possible explanations.
>
> Once you have a range of possible alternative explanations, you can then use data (from past research and/or developing your own research) to whittle these down. This approach might sound like you are wasting your time ("why bother developing alternatives that can be shown to be wrong?"), but past research and evidence can be interpreted in more than one way. Applying your academic evaluative skills to determine whether the past evidence could be made to fit your generated alternatives (even if on the surface those generated alternatives seem evidently

false) gives you the potential to generate some deeply meaningful discoveries and insights.

For now, try to generate at least two different explanations for why you think people may report inaccurate beliefs about cues to deception. Pause here before reading on. Now that you have done that, here are some possibilities that came to my mind as I was writing:

i   Some people may earn financial benefit or pseudo-celebrity status by peddling these popular, tantalising, but ultimately wrong beliefs to the wider population.

ii Parents lie to their children by claiming that their lies are detectable, with a view to deter deception in children. This instils misbeliefs in the child which continue into adulthood.

iii When participants respond on surveys showing that they have the wrong beliefs, they are not saying that this is how *they* detect deception, but rather they are reporting what the societal and public opinion is on how *other people* detect deception.

iv People interpret the question as 'what *behavioural* cues do you rely on', but maybe they do not use behavioural cues at all when they try to detect deception. Nonetheless, they attempt to provide a response to the question they believe is being asked and generate false suggestions in the process that do not match how they actually try to detect deception.

v   Asking people to report on a questionnaire how it is they detect deception is a poor way to capture their beliefs. Perhaps they are unable to recall what cues they use because it has been some time since they have had to detect a lie, or maybe the information they use in their decision-making process is not easily mentally translated by the participant from a decision-making process into a written questionnaire response. By analogy, it may be difficult to verbally explain how to ride a bike even if you are able to ride a bike.

There are likely more possibilities than these. But hopefully you can see how reflecting on that question is developing important psychological research questions that require further testing to assess whether they may or may not be supported. This is how the field of psychology moves forward: through academic evaluation and testing of these ideas. Let us now review the evidence in the main body of the chapter.

Where do these beliefs come from if they are not genuine indicators of deception? A hint may be found in the US Transportation Security Administration's Screening of Passengers by Observation Technique (SPOT) deployed in US airports. Officers were trained to detect security threats by using cues that have no bearing on deception such as avoiding eye contact and covering the mouth with one's hand (Denault et al., 2020). That is, explicit training may be generating false beliefs about deception. This can also be seen in the context of police interviewing. Police manuals such as the Behavioural Analysis Interview of Inbau et al. (1986, 2001) promote the use of nonverbal behaviours such as eye contact and posture to detect deception (see Vrij & Fisher, 2020, for other unuseful nonverbal cues mentioned in police manuals). Supporting the position that false beliefs result from explicit training, Dutch police officers (who are told not to use behavioural indicators to detect deception; van Amelsvoort et al., 2015) mention more verbal cues to deception than students and report fewer believed cues to deception overall (Bogaard et al., 2016), suggesting that they may have fewer false beliefs about cues to deception. For consideration of other possible explanations such as a confirmation bias and post-hoc rationalisations, see Strömwall et al. (2004) or Hurley et al. (2014).

It is difficult to see how explicit training could account for the misguided beliefs of lay people who likely do not read police manuals. But learning may still occur more indirectly by the media perpetuating myths about deception. While this argument may seem prima facie reasonable and is an argument that has been put forward by scholars (e.g., Hurley et al., 2014; Vrij et al., 2019; see also T. R. Levine, 2018), there is a lack of research testing this claim.

Another view, the 'normative hypothesis' (The Global Deception Research Team, 2006), posits that these stereotypes may be perpetuated by ourselves and the society we live in. The younger generations are taught that their lies are detectable in order to discourage lying. Indeed, lying for one's own interest is considered not to be acceptable (Backbier et al., 1997; Inglehart et al., 1998).[8] One other view is that inaccurate beliefs about cues to deception may be internally generated by ourselves rather than communicated to us by others. Strömwall et al. (2004) speculated that the 'representativeness heuristic' (Kahneman et al., 1982; Tversky & Kahneman, 2002) may lead us to erroneously learn that certain behaviours such as eye contact indicate deception. The representativeness heuristic is a mental shortcut or rule of thumb that people use to estimate how likely an event occurs generally (e.g., nervousness is associated with deception across the population) by drawing on one's memory of past representative experiences (e.g., how often nervousness has been seen to occur with deception in one's limited experience). Having observed some liars exhibiting nervousness in the past, this may be overgeneralised as a belief about all liars. Consistent with the notion that people draw on limited representative information and overgeneralise to wider beliefs about deception, people trying to generate many (compared to few) reasons why someone is lying may lead to fewer deception judgements. This is because trying to generate many reasons that someone is lying is rather difficult compared to generating one or two reasons. This experience of difficulty to find enough representative reasons that the person is lying can lead to an interpretation that the sender is telling the truth (this argument also holds for truth-telling and truth judgements; Ask et al., 2012; see also Koch & Forgas, 2012).

If this suggestion about the origin of the inaccurate beliefs is true, it may be difficult to overcome because people rarely have the opportunity to learn whether someone actually did lie—lies are difficult to detect (see Chapter 5), so we often do not know when we have been lied to. Testing the relationship between deception and the cue is thus rather difficult. If such a position were correct, providing explicit feedback about deception through training should increase lie detection accuracy. Deception detection training that offers feedback can improve lie detection accuracy with small to medium effect sizes (Driskell, 2012; Hauch et al., 2016), suggesting people may be able to overcome these beliefs through training (see a meta-analysis by Hartwig & Bond, 2011, discussed in Chapter 4, for a view that the inaccurate beliefs about deception cues are not the cause of people's lie-truth judgements).

In summary, both lay people and professionals appear to hold inaccurate stereotypical beliefs about deception such as gaze aversion and nervousness. However, these cues are not useful in distinguishing liars from truth-tellers. These beliefs may come about through explicit training given to law enforcement. As for lay people, it is speculated that they may arise from media perpetuating the myths, a societal preference to prevent deception through warnings that lies are detectable, and/or from relying on simplified rules of thumb that the observations of a cue (e.g., nervousness) appearing in a small number of one's personal experiences with deception can be generalised to all deceptions.

Chapter Summary

Cues to deception are infrequent and barely detectable at best. At worst, cues that unwittingly 'leak' from the deceiver do not exist at all. While offering a unique perspective at the inception of the field of deception detection, the leakage hypothesis is controversial today. Researchers have, broadly speaking, moved away from this perspective and now explore cues that may result from the dynamics of the interaction or the cognitive effort that may be associated with deceiving. As we shall see in Chapter 5, there has also been a shift away from passively observing the behaviours of the potential liar and towards finding means of actively interacting with the potential liar to generate cues to their honesty or deception.

People seem to hold inaccurate beliefs about cues that indicate when people are lying, mentioning cues such as averting gaze and appearing nervous. This is true for both police officers and lay people. These beliefs may come from explicit training in police manuals, media representations of how deception can be spotted, or even from societal attempts to encourage honesty through promoting the idea that deception is detectable and so should be avoided (the normative hypothesis). Overcoming these inaccurate beliefs may be difficult because people rarely have an opportunity to learn who is lying and who is telling the truth, and so may not be able to distinguish which cues are truly diagnostic of deception and honesty.

As we progress into future chapters where we consider how people decide who is lying or not (Chapter 4), how accurate people are at detecting deception (Chapter 5), and whether people may have unconscious knowledge that improves their detection accuracy (Chapter 7), keep in mind that there may be no clear verbal or nonverbal cues that give away the liar.

Notes

1 But not males. The study only explored binary sex.
2 'Diagnostic' refers to how accurately the cue is able to indicate or 'diagnose' when someone is lying or telling the truth. Pinocchio's nose is perfectly diagnostic of deception: it always grows when he lies. It appears 100% of the time and is absent 0% of the time when lying. A perfectly non-diagnostic cue to deception would appear 50% of the time when the person lies and would be absent 50% of the time when they lie.
3 The story of Pinocchio by Carlo Collodi tells the tale of a wooden puppet who wishes to one day be a real boy. Pinocchio is most famous for his nose that grows when he lies, which offers anyone speaking to Pinocchio a tell-tale sign of his deception (when it grows) and honesty (when it does not grow).
4 The field of psychology has long lamented the problem that journals are less interested in publishing statistically non-significant effects, which languish in the metaphorical file drawer (Rosenthal, 1979) to never be read by others. A meta-analysis of these studies hidden in the file drawer may allow us to learn that there is strong evidence that cues to deception are non-diagnostic, for example.
5 For more work exploring the use of personal pronouns in honest statements versus more distanced language in deceptive statements, see Hancock et al. (2008) or Newman et al. (2003). Note, however, that DePaulo et al.'s (2003) meta-analysis contained 12 studies on the use of self-references and found no differences between liars and truth-tellers.
6 Broader critiques of NLP as unscientific can be found in Witkowski (2010).
7 Synergology, a practice that mimics the tenets of science but is unscientific in its practices, has made similar claims to eye direction being a cue to deception (Denault et al., 2020).
8 People see white lies and altruistic lies (which are intended to be kind to others) as more morally acceptable and may serve to build trust (e.g., Cui et al., 2018; Dunbar et al., 2016; E. E. Levine & Schweitzer, 2015). And while people do not wish to be told white lies by their romantic partners, they are more willing to tell white lies to those partners (Hart et al., 2014; see also Boon & McLeod, 2001). More on children's perception of the appropriateness of lying can be found in Chapter 6.

References

Abe, N., Suzuki, M., Mori, E., Itoh, M., & Fujii, T. (2007). Deceiving others: Distinct neural responses of the prefrontal cortex and amygdala in simple fabrication and deception with social interactions. *Journal of Cognitive Neuroscience, 19*(2), 287–295. https://doi.org/10.1162/jocn.2007.19.2.287

Akehurst, L., Köhnken, G., Vrij, A., & Bull, R. (1996). Lay persons' and police officers' beliefs regarding deceptive behaviour. *Applied Cognitive Psychology, 10*(6), 461–471. https://doi.org/10.1002/(SICI)1099-0720(199612)10:6<461::AID-ACP413>3.0.CO;2-2

Al-Simadi, F. A. (2000). Jordanian students' beliefs about nonverbal behaviors associated with deception in Jordan. *Social Behavior and Personality, 28*(5), 437. https://doi.org/10.2224/sbp.2000.28.5.437

Ask, K., Greifeneder, R., & Reinhard, M.-A. (2012). On the ease of (dis)believing: The role of accessibility experiences in credibility judgments. *Applied Cognitive Psychology, 26*(5), 779–784. https://doi.org/10.1002/acp.2859

Backbier, E., Hoogstraten, J., & Terwogt-Kouwenhoven, K. M. (1997). Situational determinants of the acceptability of telling lies. *Journal of Applied Social Psychology, 27*(12), 1048–1062. https://doi.org/10.1111/j.1559-1816.1997.tb00286.x

Baron-Cohen, S., Tager-Flusberg, H., & Cohen, D. J. (2000). *Understanding other minds: Perspectives from developmental cognitive neuroscience.* Oxford University Press.

Barrett, L. F. (2006). Solving the emotion paradox: Categorization and the experience of emotion. *Personality and Social Psychology Review, 10*(1), 20–46. https://doi.org/10.1207/s15327957pspr1001_2

Bogaard, G., Meijer, E. H., Vrij, A., & Merckelbach, H. (2016). Strong, but wrong: Lay people's and police officers' beliefs about verbal and nonverbal cues to deception. *PLOS One, 11*(6), e0156615. https://doi.org/10.1371/journal.pone.0156615

Boon, S. D., & McLeod, B. A. (2001). Deception in romantic relationships: Subjective estimates of success at deceiving and attitudes toward deception. *Journal of Social and Personal Relationships, 18*(4), 463–476. https://doi.org/10.1177/0265407501184002

Brennen, T., & Magnussen, S. (2020). Research on non-verbal signs of lies and deceit: A blind alley. *Frontiers in Psychology, 11.* https://www.frontiersin.org/articles/10.3389/fpsyg.2020.613410

Buller, D. B., & Burgoon, J. K. (1996). Interpersonal deception theory. *Communication Theory, 6*(3), 203–242. https://doi.org/10.1111/j.1468-2885.1996.tb00127.x

Burgoon, J. K. (2018). Microexpressions are not the best way to catch a liar. *Frontiers in Psychology, 9.* https://www.frontiersin.org/articles/10.3389/fpsyg.2018.01672

Christ, S. E., Van Essen, D. C., Watson, J. M., Brubaker, L. E., & McDermott, K. B. (2009). The contributions of prefrontal cortex and executive control to deception: Evidence from activation likelihood estimate meta-analyses. *Cerebral Cortex, 19*(7), 1557–1566. https://doi.org/10.1093/cercor/bhn189

Cohen, J. (1988). *Statistical power for the behavioral sciences.* Routledge.

Cui, F., Wu, S., Wu, H., Wang, C., Jiao, C., & Luo, Y. (2018). Altruistic and self-serving goals modulate behavioral and neural responses in deception. *Social Cognitive and Affective Neuroscience, 13*(1), 63–71. https://doi.org/10.1093/scan/nsx138

Curtis, D. A. (2015). Patient deception: Nursing students' beliefs and attitudes. *Nurse Educator, 40*(5), 254–257. https://doi.org/10.1097/NNE.0000000000000157

Curtis, D. A., & Hart, C. L. (2015). Pinocchio's nose in therapy: Therapists' beliefs and attitudes toward client deception. *International Journal for the Advancement of Counselling, 37*(3), 279–292. https://doi.org/10.1007/s10447-015-9243-6

Denault, V., Plusquellec, P., Jupe, L. M., St-Yves, M., Dunbar, N. E., Hartwig, M., Sporer, S. L., Rioux-Turcotte, J., Jarry, J., Walsh, D., Otgaar, H., Viziteu, A., Talwar, V., Keatley, D. A., Blandón-Gitlin, I., Townson, C., Deslauriers-Varin, N., Lilienfeld, S. O., Patterson, M. L., ... Koppen, P. J. van. (2020). The analysis of nonverbal communication: The dangers of pseudoscience in security and justice contexts. *Anuario de Psicologia Juridica, 30*(1), 1–12. https://doi.org/10.5093/apj2019a9

DePaulo, B. M. (1992). Nonverbal behavior and self-presentation. *Psychological Bulletin, 111*(2), 203–243. https://doi.org/10.1037/0033-2909.111.2.203

DePaulo, B. M., Kashy, D. A., Kirkendol, S. E., Wyer, M. M., & Epstein, J. A. (1996). Lying in everyday life. *Journal of Personality and Social Psychology, 70*(5), 979–995. https://doi.org/10.1037/0022-3514.70.5.979

DePaulo, B. M., Lindsay, J. J., Malone, B. E., Muhlenbruck, L., Charlton, K., & Cooper, H. (2003). Cues to deception. *Psychological Bulletin, 129*(1), 74–118.

Dickens, C. R., & Curtis, D. A. (2019). Lies within the law: Therapist' beliefs and attitudes about deception. *Journal of Forensic Psychology Research and Practice, 19*(5), 359–375. https://doi.org/10.1080/24732850.2019.1666604

Driskell, J. E. (2012). Effectiveness of deception detection training: A meta-analysis. *Psychology, Crime & Law, 18*(8), 713–731. https://doi.org/10.1080/1068316X.2010.535820

Dunbar, N. E., Gangi, K., Coveleski, S., Adams, A., Bernhold, Q., & Giles, H. (2016). When is it acceptable to lie? Interpersonal and intergroup perspectives on deception. *Communication Studies, 67*(2), 129–146. https://doi.org/10.1080/10510974.2016.1146911

Duran, N. D., Dale, R., Kello, C. T., Street, C. N. H., & Richardson, D. C. (2013). Exploring the movement dynamics of deception. *Frontiers in Psychology, 4*. https://doi.org/10.3389/fpsyg.2013.00140

Eapen, N. M., Baron, S., Street, C. N. H., & Richardson, D. C. (2010). The bodily movement of liars. In L. Carlson, C. Hölscher, & T. Shipley (Eds.), *33rd Annual Conference of the Cognitive Science Society*. Cognitive Science Society.

Ekman, P. (1985). *Telling Lies: Clues to Deceit in the Marketplace, Politics, and Marriage*. Norton.

Ekman, P. (2009). *Lie Catching and Microexpressions*. https://doi.org/10.1093/acprof:oso/9780195327939.003.0008

Ekman, P., & Friesen, W. V. (1969). Nonverbal leakage and clues to deception. *Psychiatry, 32*(1), 88–106. https://doi.org/10.1080/00332747.1969.11023575

Ekman, P., & Matsumoto, D. (2011). Reading faces: The universality of emotional expression. In M. Gernsbacher, R. W. Pew, L. M. Hough, & J. R. Pomerantz (Eds.), *Psychology and the real world: Essays illustrating fundamental contributions to society* (pp. 140–146). Worth Publishers.

Feldman, R. S., Forrest, J. A., & Happ, B. R. (2002). Self-presentation and verbal deception: Do self-presenters lie more? *Basic and Applied Social Psychology, 24*(2), 163–170. https://doi.org/10.1207/S15324834BASP2402_8

Gordon, N. J., Felisher, W. L., & Weinberg, C. D. (2002). *Effective interviewing and interrogation techniques*. Academic Press.

Gray, R. (1991). Tools for the trade: Neuro-linguistic programming and the art of communication. *Federal Probation, 55*(1), 11–16.

Greene, J. D., & Paxton, J. M. (2009). Patterns of neural activity associated with honest and dishonest moral decisions. *Proceedings of the National Academy of Sciences, 106*(30), 12506–12511. https://doi.org/10.1073/pnas.0900152106

Hancock, J. T., Curry, L. E., Goorha, S., & Woodworth, M. (2008). On lying and being lied to: A linguistic analysis of deception in computer-mediated communication. *Discourse Processes, 45*(1), 1–23. https://doi.org/10.1080/01638530701739181

Hart, C. L., Curtis, D. A., Williams, N. M., Hathaway, M. D., & Griffith, J. D. (2014). Do as I say, not as I do: Benevolent deception in romantic relationships. *Journal of Relationships Research, 5*. https://doi.org/10.1017/jrr.2014.8

Hart, C. L., Hudson, L. P., Fillmore, D. G., & Griffith, J. D. (2006). Managerial beliefs about the behavioral cues of deception. *Individual Differences Research, 4*(3), 176–184.

Hartwig, M., & Bond, C. F. (2011). Why do lie-catchers fail? A lens model meta-analysis of human lie judgments. *Psychological Bulletin, 137*(4), 643–659. https://doi.org/10.1037/a0023589

Hauch, V., Blandón-Gitlin, I., Masip, J., & Sporer, S. L. (2015). Are computers effective lie detectors? A meta-analysis of linguistic cues to deception. *Personality and Social Psychology Review, 19*(4), 307–342. https://doi.org/10.1177/1088868314556539

Hauch, V., Sporer, S. L., Michael, S. W., & Meissner, C. A. (2016). Does training improve the detection of deception? A meta-analysis. *Communication Research, 43*(3), 283–343. https://doi.org/10.1177/0093650214534974

Heap, M. (2008). The validity of some early claims of neuro-linguistic programming. *Skeptical Intelligencer, 11*, 6–13.

Hurley, C., Griffin, D., & Stefanone, M. (2014). Who told you that? Uncovering the source of believed cues to deception. *International Journal of Psychological Studies, 6*(1), Article 1. https://doi.org/10.5539/ijps.v6n1p19

Inbau, F. E., Reid, J. E., & Buckley, J. P. (1986). *Criminal interrogation and confessions*. Williams and Wilkins.

Inbau, F. E., Reid, J. E., Buckley, J. P., & Jayne, B. C. (2001). *Criminial interogation and confessions*. Aspen Publishers.

Inglehart, R., Basañez, M., & Moreno, A. (1998). *Human values and beliefs: A cross-cultural sourcebook*. University of Michigan Press.

Jordan, S., Brimbal, L., Wallace, D. B., Kassin, S. M., Hartwig, M., & Street, C. N. H. (2019). A test of the micro-expressions training tool: Does it improve lie detection? *Journal of Investigative Psychology and Offender Profiling, 16*(3), 222–235. https://doi.org/10.1002/jip.1532

Kahneman, D., Slovic, P., & Tversky, A. (Eds.). (1982). *Judgment under uncertainty: Heuristics and biases*. Cambridge University Press. https://doi.org/10.1017/CBO9780511809477

Kajackaite, A., & Gneezy, U. (2015). Lying costs and incentives. *UC San Diego Discussion Paper*.

Kashy, D. A., & DePaulo, B. M. (1996). Who lies? *Journal of Personality and Social Psychology, 70*(5), 1037–1051. https://doi.org/10.1037/0022-3514.70.5.1037

Koch, A. S., & Forgas, J. P. (2012). Feeling good and feeling truth: The interactive effects of mood and processing fluency on truth judgments. *Journal of Experimental Social Psychology, 48*(2), 481–485.

Kraut, R. (1980). Humans as lie detectors. *Journal of Communication, 30*(4), 209–218. https://doi.org/10.1111/j.1460-2466.1980.tb02030.x

Lakhani, M., & Taylor, R. (2003). Beliefs about the cues to deception in high- and low-stake situations. *Psychology, Crime & Law, 9*(4), 357–368. https://doi.org/10.1080/1068316031000093441

Lane, J., & Wegner, D. (1995). *The cognitive consequences of secrecy*. https://doi.org/10.1037/0022-3514.69.2.237

Langleben, D. D., Loughead, J. W., Bilker, W. B., Ruparel, K., Childress, A. R., Busch, S. I., & Gur, R. C. (2005). Telling truth from lie in individual subjects with fast event-related fMRI. *Human Brain Mapping, 26*(4), 262–272. https://doi.org/10.1002/hbm.20191

Levine, E. E., & Schweitzer, M. E. (2015). Prosocial lies: When deception breeds trust. *Organizational Behavior and Human Decision Processes, 126*, 88–106. https://doi.org/10.1016/j.obhdp.2014.10.007

Levine, T. R. (2018). Scientific Evidence and cue theories in deception research: Reconciling findings from meta-analyses and primary experiments. *International Journal of Communication, 12*(0), Article 0.

Levine, T. R., & Daiku, Y. (2019). How custom agents really detect lies. *Communication Research Reports, 36*(1), 84–92. https://doi.org/10.1080/08824096.2018.1555523

Li, Y., Liu, Z., & Liu, X. (2022). Who did I lie to that day? Deception impairs memory in daily life. *Psychological Research*. https://doi.org/10.1007/s00426-021-01619-x

Lisofsky, N., Kazzer, P., Heekeren, H. R., & Prehn, K. (2014). Investigating socio-cognitive processes in deception: A quantitative meta-analysis of neuroimaging studies. *Neuropsychologia, 61*, 113–122. https://doi.org/10.1016/j.neuropsychologia.2014.06.001

Luke, T. J. (2019). Lessons from Pinocchio: Cues to deception may be highly exaggerated. *Perspectives on Psychological Science, 14*(4), 646–671. https://doi.org/10.1177/1745691619838258

Mann, S. A., Vrij, A., Nasholm, E., Warmelink, L., Leal, S., & Forrester, D. (2012). The direction of deception: Neuro-linguistic programming as a lie detection tool. *Journal of Police and Criminal Psychology, 27*(2), 160–166. https://doi.org/10.1007/s11896-011-9097-8

Masip, J., & Herrero, C. (2015). Police detection of deception: Beliefs about behavioral cues to deception are strong even though contextual evidence is more useful. *Journal of Communication, 65*(1), 125–145. https://doi.org/10.1111/jcom.12135

McCornack, S. A., Morrison, K., Paik, J. E., Wisner, A. M., & Zhu, X. (2014). Information manipulation theory 2: A propositional theory of deceptive discourse production. *Journal of Language and Social Psychology, 33*(4), 348–377.

Newman, M. L., Pennebaker, J. W., Berry, D. S., & Richards, J. M. (2003). Lying words: Predicting deception from linguistic styles. *Personality and Social Psychology Bulletin, 29*(5), 665–675. https://doi.org/10.1177/0146167203029005010

Nortje, A., & Tredoux, C. (2019). How good are we at detecting deception? A review of current techniques and theories. *South African Journal of Psychology, 49*(4), 491–504. https://doi.org/10.1177/0081246318822953

Paul Ekman Group. (2022). *Micro expressions training tools*. Paul Ekman Group. https://www.paulekman.com/micro-expressions-training-tools/

Peng, K. (2020). To be attractive or to be authentic? How two competing motivations influence self-presentation in online dating. *Internet Research, 30*(4), 1143–1165. https://doi.org/10.1108/INTR-03-2019-0095

Porter, S., & ten Brinke, L. (2008). Reading between the lies: Identifying concealed and falsified emotions in universal facial expressions. *Psychological Science, 19*(5), 508–514. https://doi.org/10.1111/j.1467-9280.2008.02116.x

Porter, S., ten Brinke, L., & Wallace, B. (2012). Secrets and lies: Involuntary leakage in deceptive facial expressions as a function of emotional intensity. *Journal of Nonverbal Behavior, 36*(1), 23–37. https://doi.org/10.1007/s10919-011-0120-7

Repke, M. A., Conway, L. G., & Houck, S. C. (2018). The strategic manipulation of linguistic complexity: A test of two models of lying. *Journal of Language and Social Psychology, 37*(1), 74–92. https://doi.org/10.1177/0261927X17706943

Rolls, E. T. (2015). Limbic systems for emotion and for memory, but no single limbic system. *Cortex, 62*, 119–157. https://doi.org/10.1016/j.cortex.2013.12.005

Rosenthal, R. (1979). The file drawer problem and tolerance for null results. *Psychological Bulletin, 86*(3), 638–641. https://doi.org/10.1037/0033-2909.86.3.638

Sellal, F., Chevalier, Y., & Collard, M. (1993). 'Pinocchio syndrome': A peculiar form of reflex epilepsy? *Journal of Neurology, Neurosurgery & Psychiatry, 56*(8), 936.

Shalvi, S., Eldar, O., & Bereby-Meyer, Y. (2012). Honesty requires time (and lack of justifications). *Psychological Science, 23*(10), 1264–1270. https://doi.org/10.1177/0956797612443835

Spence, S. A., Hunter, M. D., Farrow, T. F. D., Green, R. D., Leung, D. H., Hughes, C. J., & Ganesan, V. (2004). A cognitive neurobiological account of deception: Evidence from functional neuroimaging. *Philosophical Transactions of the Royal Society B: Biological Sciences, 359*(1451), 1755–1762. https://doi.org/10.1098/rstb.2004.1555

Sporer, S. L. (2016). Deception and cognitive load: Expanding our horizon with a working memory model. *Frontiers in Psychology, 7.* https://www.frontiersin.org/article/10.3389/fpsyg.2016.00420

Sporer, S. L., & Schwandt, B. (2006). Paraverbal indicators of deception: A meta-analytic synthesis. *Applied Cognitive Psychology, 20*(4), 421–446. https://doi.org/10.1002/acp.1190

Sporer, S. L., & Schwandt, B. (2007). Moderators of nonverbal indicators of deception: A meta-analytic synthesis. *Psychology, Public Policy, and Law, 13*(1), 1–34. https://doi.org/10.1037/1076-8971.13.1.1

Sternglanz, R. W., Morris, W. L., Morrow, M., & Braverman, J. (2019). A review of meta-analyses about deception detection. In T. Docan-Morgan (Ed.), *The Palgrave Handbook of Deceptive Communication* (pp. 303–326). Springer International Publishing. https://doi.org/10.1007/978-3-319-96334-1_16

Strömwall, L. A., & Granhag, P. A. (2003). How to detect deception? Arresting the beliefs of police officers, prosecutors and judges. *Psychology, Crime & Law, 9*(1), 19–36. https://doi.org/10.1080/10683160308138

Strömwall, L. A., Granhag, P. A., & Hartwig, M. (2004). Practitioners' beliefs about deception. In P. A. Granhag & L. A. Strömwall (Eds.), *The detection of deception in forensic contexts* (pp. 229–250). Cambridge University Press. https://doi.org/10.1017/CBO9780511490071.010[

ten Brinke, L., Porter, S., & Baker, A. (2012). Darwin the detective: Observable facial muscle contractions reveal emotional high-stakes lies. *Evolution and Human Behavior, 33*(4), 411–416. https://doi.org/10.1016/j.evolhumbehav.2011.12.003

The Global Deception Research Team. (2006). A world of lies. *Journal of Cross-Cultural Psychology, 37*(1), 60–74.

Tversky, A., & Kahneman, D. (2002). Extensional versus intuitive reasoning: The conjunction fallacy in probability judgment. In *Heuristics and biases: The psychology of intuitive judgment* (pp. 19–48). Cambridge University Press. https://doi.org/10.1017/CBO9780511808098.003

Tyler, J. M., & Feldman, R. S. (2004). Truth, lies, and self-presentation: How gender and anticipated future interaction relate to deceptive behavior1. *Journal of Applied Social Psychology, 34*(12), 2602–2615. https://doi.org/10.1111/j.1559-1816.2004.tb01994.x

van Amelsvoort, A., Rispens, I., & Grolman, H. (2015). *Handleiding verhoor [Manual interrogations]*. Reed Business.

Van Der Zee, S., Poppe, R., Havrileck, A., & Baillon, A. (2022). A personal model of trumpery: Linguistic deception detection in a real-world high-stakes setting. *Psychological Science, 33*(1), 3–17. https://doi.org/10.1177/09567976211015941

Vrij, A. (2008). Nonverbal dominance versus verbal accuracy in lie detection: A plea to change police practice. *Criminal Justice and Behavior, 35*(10), 1323–1336. https://doi.org/10.1177/0093854808321530

Vrij, A., Fisher, R., Mann, S. A., & Leal, S. (2006). Detecting deception by manipulating cognitive load. *Trends in Cognitive Sciences*, *10*(4), 141–142. https://doi.org/10.1016/j.tics.2006.02.003

Vrij, A., & Fisher, R. P. (2020). Unraveling the misconception about deception and nervous behavior. *Frontiers in Psychology*, *11*. https://www.frontiersin.org/articles/10.3389/fpsyg.2020.01377

Vrij, A., Hartwig, M., & Granhag, P. A. (2019). Reading lies: Nonverbal communication and deception. *Annual Review of Psychology*, *70*, 295–317. https://doi.org/10.1146/annurev-psych-010418-103135

Vrij, A., & Semin, G. R. (1996). Lie experts' beliefs about nonverbal indicators of deception. *Journal of Nonverbal Behavior*, *20*(1), 65–80. https://doi.org/10.1007/BF02248715

Walczyk, J. J., Harris, L. L., Duck, T. K., & Mulay, D. (2014). A social-cognitive framework for understanding serious lies: Activation-decision-construction-action theory. *New Ideas in Psychology*, *34*, 22–36. https://doi.org/10.1016/j.newideapsych.2014.03.001

Wiseman, R., Watt, C., Brinke, L. ten, Porter, S., Couper, S.-L., & Rankin, C. (2012). The eyes don't have it: Lie detection and neuro-linguistic programming. *PLOS One*, *7*(7), e40259. https://doi.org/10.1371/journal.pone.0040259

Witkowski, T. (2010). Thirty-five years of research on neuro-linguistic programming. NLP research data base. State of the art or pseudoscientific decoration? *Polish Psychological Bulletin*, *41*(2), 58–66. https://doi.org/10.2478/v10059-010-0008-0

Yeh, L. C.-Y., Xi, L., & Zhang, J. (2013). Stereotypes of deceptive behaviors: A cross-cultural study between China and Japan. *Social Behavior and Personality: An International Journal*, *41*(2), 335–342.

Zuckerman, M., DePaulo, B. M., & Rosenthal, R. (1981). Verbal and nonverbal communication of deception. In L. Berkowitz (Ed.), *Advances in experimental social psychology* (Vol. 14, pp. 1–59). Academic Press. https://doi.org/10.1016/S0065-2601(08)60369-X

4 Making Lie-Truth Judgements

> **Box 4.1 Jessica Krug**
>
> An activist and African American history professor at George Washington University, Krug wrote a book, *Fugitive Modernities,* on the political and intellectual work on the resistance against the slave trade. She received financial support from cultural and financial institutions such as the National Endowment for the Humanities and the Schomburg Center for Research in Black Culture. Krug has said that she is Afro-Puerto Rican. But she has also claimed African Blackness and Bronx Blackness. A small number of Black Latina scholars recognised the inconsistencies in her ethnic claims and eventually discovered that she was, in fact, white Jewish and from Kansas City. Soon after this discovery became public, Krug resigned her academic post.

Given the clear application of lie detection research to, say, police interviewing, military deception, medical malingering, business negotiations, social welfare, cyber security, and so on, the field of deception detection has primarily focused on understanding how accurate people can be and what methods can be developed for improving accuracy. Relatively less work has been devoted to understanding the decision-making process that results in a judgement of 'lie' or 'truth' (see, e.g., Hartwig et al., 2014; Lane & Vieira, 2012). Understanding what information people select from the environment and memory, how they process this information, and how this comes to result in a lie-truth judgement will provide a strong footing for understanding how the decision process functions, where it may result in poor judgements, and how it may be changed or improved. This chapter focuses on developing that understanding.

Truth Bias

Thus far, the picture that has been painted in this book so far has been bleak. Cues to deception are rare and people seem to hold all the wrong beliefs about how a liar will behave in any case (see Chapter 3). The truth bias seemingly adds another layer of pessimism. When people decide if senders are lying or telling the truth, they judge that senders are telling the truth more often than there are truth-tellers present (C. F. Bond & DePaulo, 2006; Zuckerman et al., 1981). That is, when judging a set of senders of whom half are lying and half are telling the truth, receivers tend to make more than 50% of their judgements as one of 'truth'. This is referred to as the truth bias. In a meta-analysis, C. F. Bond and DePaulo (2006) estimate that 53% of deceptive statements and 61% of honest statements are judged as truths in studies where half of senders lie and half tell the truth. In a second meta-analysis, they report that receivers make 55.50% truth judgements (C. F. Bond & DePaulo, 2008). As the proportion of truth-tellers to liars increases in a given study, the accuracy also increases (Levine et al., 1999), reflecting that the tendency to judge a statement as 'truth' more frequently lines up with speakers who are actually telling the truth, thereby artefactually increasing accuracy.

Box 4.2 Implied Explanations

Consider the term 'truth bias'. Based on this terminology alone, one may get the impression that the lie-truth decision is skewed due to an in-built error or simplification in the decision-making process that tips the scales towards deciding that the person is telling the truth. That word 'bias' comes with some baggage, suggesting cognitive distortions or limitations in the process. Which of the following appear as reasonable *possible* explanations without yet having read what the evidence suggests? People judge others as truth-tellers because:

- cultural norms demand politeness, and so the person may hold a private view that the sender is lying but would only publicly claim that the sender is telling the truth.
- they are reluctant to engage in the social confrontation that results from calling another person a liar. The accusation could lead to aggression or relationship breakdown.
- they more readily perceive and guide their attention towards the available behaviours that both liars and truth-tellers present, namely behaviours that attempt to convey that the speaker is being truthful.
- in order to understand a statement, the person making the judgement first has to build a mental representation of the situation as though the statement is true so that they are able to comprehend the statement and then assess its validity. The initial representation of the message as true may bias further assessment.
- liars are typically successful in hiding any cues to deception, and so the lie detector has little choice other than to rely on their past

history of the world (e.g., that most people tend to tell the truth most of the time) in order to reach their judgement (that the sender is likely to be telling the truth).

Presumably, most if not all of these appear to you as reasonable potential explanations of why people judge others as truth-tellers, and yet a number of these accounts require no assumption about a cognitive bias existing. Each of these explanations has been put forward as potential account of the truth bias (C. F. Bond & DePaulo, 2008; B. M. DePaulo, 1992; Gilbert, 1991; Levine, 2014; O'Sullivan, 2003; Street, 2015). It can be rather tempting to read terminology such as 'bias' and allow our past experiences with this word to ascribe additional meaning to a phenomenon that need not be the case. Of course, that the truth bias is an error or simplification in the decision-making process is a reasonable potential explanation as well (see Vrij et al., 2010), but we must work hard to avoid ascribing additional meaning to terms that are chosen as shorthand for the phenomenon. In the case of the truth bias, remember that we are referring not to a psychological explanation, but to an *observation* that people tend to judge statements as truths more often than there are truths present in the environment. The truth bias is a phenomenon, not an explanation.

As a final example for you to work on by yourself, in Chapter 2 we came across the term 'pathological lying'. Does this phrase suggest to you the notion that there is a cognitive error occurring? Does 'pathological' suggest a medical diagnosis or a physiological abnormality? What is the phenomenon being described with this term, and are there other possible (non-medical) explanations as to why people may be pathological liars?

As seen in Box 4.2, there are a variety of possible explanations for the truth bias. In this chapter, we will explore public displays of belief (e.g., O'Sullivan, 2003), the Spinozan mind hypothesis (Gilbert, 1991), Truth Default Theory (TDT; Levine, 2014), and the Adaptive Lie Detector account (ALIED; Street, 2015) as possible explanations of why a truth bias is observed. It is certainly worth noting that the ALIED account was developed by the author of this book. I encourage you to take a sceptical view of all arguments, including my arguments, although this must be done in a reasoned and evidence-based way rather than relying on subjective preferences (see Box 1.4, Chapter 1).

Accounts of the Truth Bias

Public displays of belief. When we give gifts to others, it can be unpleasant to hear from the recipient that they did not like it. There are times when we may not want to learn the truth, and so may not actively seek it out (see O'Sullivan, 2003; Vrij et al., 2010, for anecdotes).[1] Vrij (2008) called this the ostrich effect, bringing to mind the image of sticking one's head in the sand to avoid learning the truth and to instead accept what is presented is, in fact, the truth. Such a position could reasonably lead to a truth bias. While there may be many anecdotes of the ostrich effect that one could imagine, accounts of this nature often present limited empirical evidence to support the position (see Box 4.3 for an exploration of an adjacent field considering an ostrich effect). Perhaps some evidence may be gleaned from a study showing that 49 criminal investigators considered a witness to be more credible and reliable when they gave an account that was consistent (versus inconsistent) with the favoured explanation of the case (Ask & Granhag, 2007), suggesting a preference to discredit unwanted information, although it is not clear if this is a result of wanting to not learn the truth or rather a separate desire to confirm and reaffirm one's already held belief.

Accusing others of deception may not only disrupt a person's preferred world view, but it may be interpreted as a socially aggressive act that may lead to hostility or relationship breakdown. As such, people may want to avoid labelling others as deceitful. O'Sullivan (2003) called this an 'accusatory reluctance'. Accusing others is an aggressive social act that breaks with societal rules and norms in some parts of the world (Vrij et al., 2010) and could potentially result in retaliation. Consistent with this view, people lie to the ones they feel close to in order to prevent relationship breakdown (e.g., Bell & DePaulo, 1996; Guthrie & Kunkel, 2013), but they are less accurate at detecting the lies of intimate partners compared with strangers (McCornack & Parks, 1986; although see Van Swol et al., 2012, for evidence of no effect of relationship closeness on detection accuracy) and are more truth biased (e.g., Van Swol et al., 2012). People from cultures that value honesty over social harmony should presumably have a reduced accusatory reluctance and be more inclined to label a sender as a liar. Some work shows that people from these cultures are more willing to rate people who are not forthcoming as liars (see Griffin & Bender, 2019). Note that this does not imply that they are able to *accurately* detect deception, but only that they are more willing to believe others are deceptive when social harmony is valued less than honesty.

If people are reluctant to make a public accusation, the implication is that they hold some private understanding that the person is lying but are not willing to share it. In Chapter 7, we will consider whether people can unconsciously detect deception with higher accuracy than they are capable of when making a conscious lie-truth judgement. In particular, see discussion of the research using the indirect lie detection method towards the start of Chapter 7. For a view that the unconscious does not improve lie detection ability, see Street and Vadillo (2016), but see Reinhard et al. (2013) for a more favourable view of unconscious lie detection.

The accusatory reluctance account also implies receivers should feel less comfortable when listening to a lie than when listening to a truth because of the apprehension associated with accusing another person. Work by B. M. DePaulo et al. (1997) found that there is greater discomfort and less confidence when listening to lies than when listening to truths.

> **Box 4.3 Ostrich Effect: Evaluating Information Across Disciplines**
>
> It is often useful to consider research in adjacent fields so that we can understand human psychology from a broader perspective. In the economics research literature on selective attention, Galai and Sade (2016) also coined the term 'ostrich effect' to refer to "avoiding apparently risk financial situations by pretending they do not exist". When we attempt to reach across disciplinary boundaries in this way, it is important to reflect on the validity of bridging the gap between the two. It may be tempting to assume that the use of the same word means that they are referring to the same psychological concept. But of course, the terminology is generated by a human being like you and I, and so they may not be aware that the term is being used in another field and may have no intention to imply that they are exploring the same phenomenon.
>
> What are the differences between these fields? Here we are specifically referring to differences that we think may have substantive psychological effect. Let us reflect first on some examples from the economics literature and consider how well they fit with our definition of the ostrich effect in the deception literature. In the context of economics research, the ostrich effect has been employed to argue that (i) people check their stock portfolios more often when the stock market is up compared to when it is down, suggesting a preference to avoid negative information (Karlsson et al., 2009), (ii) students see education as an imperative and so ignore information about the cost and debt of higher education (Elengold, 2019), and (iii) people avoid health screening in order to avoid receiving negative health information (Panidi, 2015; Webb et al., 2013). Which of the following links these three issues in economics in a way that is meaningful for our purposes of understanding deception detection?
>
> - This research does not come from the field of deception, but from the field of economics.
> - The economics research concerns itself with potentially substantive material losses (of health and wealth), while deception detection does not involve material loss.
> - In the contexts discussed in economics (stock markets, student debt, and health), the information that is needed to make an appropriate decision is readily available but is wilfully ignored, while in deception there are not clear reliable indicators of deception that can be wilfully ignored.
>
> *(Continued)*

The second option may lead us to reflect that deception detection can be relatively mundane and have little consequence. Naturally, this need not always be the case, so this option has limited applicability in contrasting the two fields. The third option is perhaps more relevant: we have seen in Chapter 3 that liars do not produce reliable cues to deception (B. M. DePaulo et al., 2003; Luke, 2019), whereas the opportunity to check the stock market or attend a health centre is readily available. Thus, we may question whether the ostrich effect as observed in economics truly extends into helping us understand the ostrich effect in deception detection because there may not be information readily available to the potential lie detector that one is ignoring and choosing to avoid learning about.[2]

That the research happens to appear in different fields does not de facto mean that they are incompatible with one another, however. It is often fruitful to understand how we can borrow from adjacent fields of research to better understand human thinking and behaviour. Doing so shows a capacity to synthesise information. However, we must always remind ourselves that being critical of one's own perspectives and ideas is an essential component of being a truly evaluative reasoner. I hope you can see that while we may not have gained a list of additional empirical studies that we can now rely on to substantiate the ostrich effect, we have engaged in an evaluation of potentially relevant literature and determined that it may not have direct relevance to us (and relevance of information is one of the most important criteria for producing cogent and coherent arguments). Perhaps most importantly of all, we have learnt *why* the two do not marry up. In the process, we made use of our understanding of other areas of deception research (cues to deception, Chapter 3) to develop a novel insight (that deception detection may be fundamentally distinct from other fields of research because the information in the deception environment is inherently noisy and unreliable). This insight may even lead you to consider whether the concept of an ostrich effect (that people choose to ignore highly diagnostic cues to deception in order to believe a preferred view of the world) is consonant with findings that suggest there are no highly diagnostic cues to deception (B. M. DePaulo et al., 2003).

A final note of caution: it is useful to explore related fields, but do not assume that similar terminology reflects the same construct. Doing so can lead you to wander down a path of research papers that are not relevant to the core research question you are trying to address. Always keep in mind what research question you want to answer when you read the literature and ensure that your reading is allowing you to reflect on that question directly. Students sometimes have difficulty finding this balance, either choosing to silo their views strictly to a single subdiscipline of research or else find themselves jumping from topic to topic to topic, getting lost in a myriad of seemingly related research findings that do not directly tie back to the question that they are trying to address.

The Spinozan mind hypothesis. The truth bias has long been conceptualised as an aberration in the cognitive system. For example, receivers have been proposed to be truth biased because of the lack of appropriate knowledge (Fiedler & Walka, 1993) or the use of mental shortcuts or 'heuristics' that lead to inappropriately overgeneralised beliefs (e.g., O'Sullivan et al., 1988). The Spinozan mind hypothesis (Gilbert, 1991) similarly views the truth bias as a form of mistaken and erroneous judgement. It claims that in order to comprehend a statement, it is necessary to first automatically believe that the statement is true. It is only after the initial acceptance that we can consider rejecting the idea that we initially automatically believed. Thus, comprehension is considered a two-step process where the 'unbelieving' stage is preceded by automatic belief. A lack of time or cognitive effort put into evaluating the information means that the information will be encoded as true because of the requirement to first automatically accept information as true. This view continues to impact work in philosophy (Burge, 1993; Mandelbaum, 2014) and psychological fields such as hypothetical reasoning (Moore et al., 2012), text comprehension (Hasson et al., 2005), persuasion (Green & Brock, 2000), religious belief (Pennycook et al., 2012), and more (Chen & Blanchard-Fields, 2000; Colwell et al., 2012; Knowles & Condon, 1999). This view may also explain the truth bias: people automatically believe the statement as delivered and may fail to engage in the more cognitively effortful stage of relabelling the information as potentially false.

One key strength of the Spinozan mind hypothesis is in its predictions: for example, it is predicted to be *impossible* to disbelieve faster than or equally as fast as believing. This ability to formulate clearly testable predictions (regardless of whether those predictions turn out to be supported by the data) gives the Spinozan mind a strong degree of credibility in advance of data collection.

In an early test of the Spinozan mind hypothesis, Gilbert et al. (1990) presented participants with a list of invented words that supposedly had English translations. After seeing the definition, participants were told if the definition was true or false. Importantly, during the initial encoding phase, participants were sometimes required to press spacebar when they heard a tone, a secondary task intended to limit the available cognitive resources. This account claims that under these circumstances, the automatic belief stage will label the definition as true, but the lack of resources will prevent a relabelling of it as false. After this encoding phase, participants would see the same definitions and judge whether they were true or false. The researchers found that during recall participants were biased to endorse definitions as true. This finding is consistent with the Spinozan mind hypothesis that the re-evaluation was interrupted, and the information remained incorrectly labelled as true.

Other evidence in favour of the Spinozan view comes from research showing that negated sentences, for example, 'the eagle was *not* in the sky', are slower to process than affirmed sentences, for example, 'the eagle was in the sky' (e.g., Clark & Chase, 1972; Zwaan et al., 2002). However, contrary to the Spinozan position, there are findings that suggest people can negate information just as quickly as they can affirm information is true. A negated statement such as 'the eagle is *not* in the sky' leaves open multiple possibilities that are to be represented (e.g., the eagle is on the floor or in the nest). The affirmed statement provides only a single representation. This may be confounding the research showing that affirmations are faster than negations: negations may be slower either because of a Spinozan effect of time being required to negate the information or because there is no Spinozan effect and the extra time to negate is a result of having to form multiple representations as compared to a single representation for the affirmed statement. Research has found that when negated statements also allow only a single possible representation, they are processed equally as quickly as affirmed statements (e.g., S. E. Anderson et al., 2010; Hasson et al., 2005).

Further work challenging the Spinozan account comes from meta-analyses on the effect of forewarnings. While Gilbert et al. (1990, Study 2) find that people are biased to believe even when they are forewarned about that they will receive false information (suggesting a Spinozan automatic belief that cannot be overcome), other research has found that forewarning does, in fact, increase the tendency to disbelieve information (Kiesler & Kiesler, 1964; Wood & Quinn, 2003).

Spinozans have shown that interrupting the processing of information results in a truth bias, which they argue reflects a judgement based on their initial automatic believing of information. In the context of lie detection, Street and Kingstone (2017) aimed to use the procedures of Gilbert et al. (1990) to test an alternative interpretation of the truth bias: that the cognitive load caused participants to be unsure about the veracity of the information but tended to guess that the information was true. That is, rather than automatically believing, people may have been unsure and using a guessing strategy that could appear as though they are automatically believing.

During an encoding phase, 82 participants watched short clips of people lying and telling the truth and were told after each clip whether the sender was lying or telling the truth. During some of the trials where participants were learning about the veracity of the statements, a tone sounded, and participants were instructed to respond as quickly as possible to this tone by pressing a keyboard key. This follows the procedure of Gilbert et al. (1990). In a later test phase, participants were shown images of the senders and were asked to recall back to the videos of these speakers and accompanying feedback to judge whether the statements were lies or truths. Street and Kingstone (2017) replicated the Spinozan effect of a truth bias for those statements where encoding of the veracity of the statement was accompanied by a cognitive load of pressing the keyboard key. But this Spinozan effect was only found when participants were forced to make a binary lie or truth judgement.

In a second condition, participants had three response options: to indicate that they believed the statement was the truth, a lie, or that they were unsure. If the cognitive load causes uncertainty and participants are merely guessing that information is true because they are forced into making either a lie or truth response, having a third 'unsure' option removes the need to guess. However, a Spinozan position argues that people are not unsure and will fully believe that the statement is the truth if cognitive load was applied during encoding. Given this unsure option, participants were no more likely to believe a statement that was accompanied with cognitive load at encoding compared to a statement not accompanied with cognitive load. Cognitive load did not induce a truth bias in this lie-truth-unsure response condition. The researchers argue on the basis of this evidence that people were not automatically believing information was true, but rather were made unsure by the cognitive load and only showed a bias to believe if they were forced into making a binary lie-truth judgement (see also Street & Richardson, 2015). This guessing phenomenon is explained by ALIED (Street, 2015), an account of lie-truth judgements that we shall encounter later in the chapter.

The Spinozan account continues to be an area of active research across psychology (e.g., Asp & Tranel, 2012; Bernhard et al., 2022; Nadarevic et al., 2021; Nadarevic & Erdfelder, 2013, 2019; Vorms et al., 2022) and philosophy (e.g., Peters, 2017). This is beyond the scope of this book. For our purposes, it suffices to note that limited research has tested the applicability of the Spinozan account of lie-truth judgements. However, more recently, Levine (2014) has put forward an account of lie-truth judgements that is consistent with the Spinozan model: TDT.

Truth-Default Theory (TDT). Akin to the Spinozan mind hypothesis, TDT (Levine, 2014) argues that people default to a state of believing that others are telling the truth. As we walk around our lives, we tend not to keep bringing to mind the possibility that someone is lying or telling the truth: TDT argues that we passively accept that, without reflection, what we hear is the truth. However, a 'trigger' may create suspicion of deception. According to Levine (2014), triggers include but are not limited to

i   a belief that the speaker has a motive for lying,
ii behaviour that holistically makes the speaker appear deceptive, known as a deceptive 'demeanour',
iii inconsistencies within statements or between a statement and reality, and
iv inconsistencies between the speaker's statement and the claims of another person (see Levine, 2022, for more examples of triggers). Note that any of these listed triggers may not be discovered for some time after the statement has been delivered (Park et al., 2002).

These triggers will vary in how 'potent' they are (Levine, 2014, p. 387), and if sufficiently potent will result in a threshold being crossed. If it is crossed, the truth-default state is left and a suspicion stage begins. During this stage, the person seeks evidence from the environment and their memory to assess the veracity of the statement. This evidence includes, but again is not limited to, their demeanour and logical inconsistencies (within the statement, between the statement and reality, or between the statement and another person's statement). If the evidence is not sufficiently evidentiary to make a determination, the person will either continue to be suspicious or else fall back to the default truth state. But if the evidence is sufficiently evidentiary, it may lead the person to decide the speaker is telling the truth (i.e., they have made an active 'truth' decision based on evidence rather than passively accepting it as true) or that the speaker is lying, depending on whether the evidence exonerates or incriminates the sender.

If people default to passively believing others, TDT argues that people will rarely mention deception or honesty when reflecting on statements. Consistent with this position, Clare and Levine (2019) asked participants to watch videos of people lying and telling the truth about topics that the researchers considered plausible (e.g., pizza is their favourite food) and implausible (e.g., Brussel sprouts is their favourite food). Afterwards, participants were to write a free text response to the question "what are your thoughts about that answer?". Importantly, participants were not made aware in advance that they were to take part in a lie detection study. TDT argues that lie detection experiments artificially inflate the likelihood of making lie-truth judgements because it acts as a trigger to raise suspicion of the possibility of deceit. By not making participants aware of the possibility of deception, the researchers aimed to gain an insight into people's thoughts while in the truth-default state that TDT argues exists. Comparing explicit lie-truth prompting to free text responses, the researchers found that people were more likely to consider deception in the former than in the latter case, consistent with a presumption of honesty when not prompted. The researchers have also similarly noted that participants in famous social psychology experiments such as those of Asch (1951, 1956) and Milgram (1969) rarely realise that confederates are lying about claiming to be a real and naïve participant (e.g., in Clare & Levine, 2019).

Further evidence for TDT comes from research exploring senders' motives. If a sender is perceived to have a motive for lying, the truth-default should be dropped. The motive acts as a trigger to abandon the truth-default and engage in suspicion and evaluation. As a result, the sender should be more likely to be judged as deceptive compared to senders who do not appear to have a motive for lying. For example, when an artist denies a painting is a forgery and is benefiting financially, the denial is more likely to be considered deceptive (by experts in the art community in Study 1 and by lay participants in Study 2) compared to an artist who denies that a painting that has been attributed to the artist by a national gallery is actually theirs

(J. Lee et al., 2021). The researchers reasoned that participants would consider that the latter artist does not appear to have a good motive for disowning the work if they actually do own it, and so would be less likely to make a judgement of deception because there would be no perceived motive. In interviews and surveys, participants who thought an artist lied stated that they thought so because the artist appeared to gain from lying. Those who believed the artists tended to mention that artists in general tend to be honest people.

Another potential trigger is the plausibility of the statement. Implausible statements should trigger suspicion and active consideration of the possibility of deception. In one study (Levine et al., 2021), participants were shown videos of (i) a TED talk about the now highly challenged claims (see, e.g., Elkjær et al., 2022; Simmons & Simonsohn, 2017) of the 'power pose' (a spread out bodily posture that supposedly makes people feel more powerful), (ii) a Neil deGrasse Tyson video that was largely plausible but included discussion of aliens that some may find implausible, (iii) corruption in an American supreme court (the topic of corruption may trigger thoughts of deception), (iv) videos of US Presidents Obama and Trump (who may be viewed sceptically by those of opposing political views), and (v) *The Onion* (a satirical online magazine presenting comedic articles as though they are news, but the video began with a claim that it has been the most trusted name in journalism for 250 years, potentially lending the video credibility). Participants were to freely report their thoughts as they watched the videos, with no mention to the participants of the possibility of deception. The researchers found that fewer than 20% of statements mentioned any form of suspicion when viewing any of the videos, with the exception of *The Onion* where more mentions of suspicion were indicated. They suggest that these findings show that the truth-default holds in most cases but that in extremely implausible videos such as *The Onion*, the default can be overcome.

Clare and Levine (2019) also explored the role of plausibility on lie-truth judgements. They found that when participants wrote unprompted free text statements in response to watching videos without being artificially informed of the possibility of deception, participants mentioned honesty and deception more for implausible messages ($M = 6.45\%$, $SD = 11.58\%$) compared to plausible messages ($M = 2.02\%$, $SD = 4.67\%$: Study 1). This effect was moderated by the speaker's actual veracity: people mentioned deception and honesty more when listening to an implausible lie ($M = 8.87\%$, $SD = 16.52\%$) compared to an implausible truth ($M = 4.03\%$, $SD = 9.34\%$). Similarly, in Study 2, they found that 1.52% ($SD = 6.06\%$) of people mentioned honesty or deception when listening to an implausible lie but no one mentioned veracity when listening to an implausible truth. For plausible statements, the effect reversed: people mentioned veracity when listening to plausible truths 0.76% of the time ($SD = 4.35\%$) while no one listening to a plausible lie mentioned veracity. They interpret these effects as demonstrating that people rarely consider deception when unprompted (consistent with a truth-default) and that, overall, plausible messages received fewer mentions of veracity than implausible messages[3] (consistent with the notion that implausible statements act as a trigger to abandon the truth-default).

TDT also claims that senders deceive with an intention and so are necessarily aware of their deceptions. Because TDT claims that receivers have a truth-default and so should often find themselves unaware of deception, people should report being aware of sending lies more frequently than receiving them (see Levine et al., 2022, for this prediction). Contrary to this position, research suggests that people report similar frequencies of sending and receiving lies (Levine et al., 2022; Markowitz & Hancock, 2018; Park et al., 2021).

Another potential prediction of TDT is that because lie judgements first require a stage of suspicion and evaluation, people should not report that the lie was detected unexpectedly. A study by Sánchez et al. (2021) aimed to learn how deception is detected in people's daily lives outside of the laboratory. To do this, participants were instructed to fill in an online survey each time they felt they had discovered a lie over a period of ten weeks. They found that a large percentage, between 61% and 64%, of the time, participants reported discovering a lie unexpectedly. Interestingly, the authors conclude in the discussion that:

> It might seem that unexpected lie discovery is inconsistent with TDT. ... However, rather than falsifying this [TDT] process, the current results suggest that sometimes triggers are so strong that they not only arouse suspicion but expose the lie altogether. ... the current findings *expand* the theory by suggesting additional ways lies are detected in real life.
> (Sánchez et al., 2021, p. 413, italics added)

This leads into perhaps the boldest critique of all, presented in Box 4.4.

Box 4.4 Revisiting the Conditions for a 'Good' Account

In Box 2.4 back in Chapter 2, it was suggested that a 'good' account is one that makes falsifiable and testable predictions. The account gains strength when it has potential to be shown to be wrong with data, but when the data are collected, they are found to be consistent with the predictions of the account. The more opportunities there are for data to falsify the account, the stronger the account is supported when data are found to be consistent with the predictions. While accounts do expand and develop as part of the scientific process (see Kuhn, 1962, on the philosophy of scientific progress), we must be careful not to be too flexible so as to allow an account to fit data that is inconsistent with its spirit and ethos or to undo the predictions of the account when the data contradict them. Doing so can undermine the potential for data to be able to falsify accounts in principle.

Developing this critique, one may question the degree to which TDT offers opportunities for the data to be inconsistent with its account. The definitions of a trigger (that leads to suspension of the truth-default and subsequent suspicion) and evidence (that is sought during the suspicion stage to evaluate the veracity of the statement) are based on examples rather than offering boundary conditions that define them. Those examples that are offered are not exhaustive. Some of them may even be considered by some as circular. For example, one trigger that leads to abandoning of a truth belief is that the receiver perceives the sender to be displaying behaviours that appear deceptive (called a deceptive or dishonest demeanour). Put another way, people stop believing a sender is telling the truth when the sender is perceived by the receiver to be lying. Put yet another way, people believe others are lying because they perceive them to be lying. A similar argument may be applied to the definition of triggers. Receivers may become suspicious of a sender because they perceive the sender to have a motive for lying. That is, they are suspicious because the sender has a good reason to lie. Put another way, they are suspicious because they believe there is a reason to be suspicious. This makes it difficult to test the account.

It may be argued by some to allow the account to fit with all data presented to it. Consider the findings of the study exploring the varying plausibility of videos such as news reports, political speeches, and satirical 'news' (Levine et al., 2021). They found that some videos led to an abandoning of the truth-default state. The researchers argue that the truth-default is abandoned for extremely implausible videos (namely the satirical news item) but is robust against other potentially implausible videos (e.g., Donald Trump speeches and rallies). Yet the researchers noted that, "Some might expect oratory by other-party politicians would prompt scepticism. Further, fact-checking consistently reveals a plethora of false and misleading statements at Trump rallies.... Thus it is conceivable that merely observing a politician speaking is a sufficient trigger" (Levine et al., 2021, p. 137). Contrary to this initial prediction that the truth-default would be abandoned when viewing such a video, the findings showed that this video did not result in a particularly high level of suspicion. TDT was nonetheless able to explain this after the data were observed: the interpretation was that the trigger was not sufficiently potent to leave the truth-default state. But had the findings shown that people frequently mentioned deception in response to Trump videos, could the account have claimed that a trigger was sufficiently potent and so the truth-default was abandoned? If so, this would indicate that regardless of what data was observed, TDT could have claimed to have been supported by the data (see Best et al., 2019).[4] I leave this for you to consider.

(Continued)

> The issue arises as a result of a lack of clarity on the boundary conditions of what is a sufficiently 'potent' trigger and what is not. It is difficult to determine what the threshold would be ahead of seeing the data, and instead requires that the threshold is set to fit the observed data. If receivers demonstrate suspicion, it must be interpreted that the threshold was crossed. If receivers continue to believe, it must be interpreted that the threshold was not crossed.
>
> The issue extends to the definition of the evidentiary threshold that is to be met in order to leave a state of suspicion and enter a state of disbelief. Because the point at which the evidentiary threshold is placed is undefined, the account can (and perhaps must) adapt to the data. Consider, for example, a situation that appears antithetical to the nature and ethos of having a truth-default: imagine that a participant judged 95% of all statements as deceptive and did so as quickly and easily as judging statements to be truthful. TDT can be made to readily explain such a finding: some behaviour or set of behaviours acted as triggers in the environment, the threshold for the potency of the trigger is set very low, and the evidentiary threshold is also set low. In these circumstances, it may be relatively effortless to make lie judgements and/or to make them with high frequency. Put another way, truth-defaulting receivers could readily demonstrate behaviour that may appear as lie-defaulting. This limits the opportunity to find data that could be inconsistent with the account.
>
> Remember, evidence that is consistent with an account may also be consistent with other accounts (see Box 2.3 in Chapter 2). It is important that we develop research that could in principle be inconsistent with the account and the account must offer opportunities to develop that research.

One final critique of the data supporting TDT is offered (and remember: the author of this book is the key proponent of a competitor account, and so you must make your own determinations as to the reasonableness of these critiques). Clare and Levine (2019) found that people rarely mention honesty or deception when they are not prompted, and interpreted this as an indication that people default to believe others. One may wonder whether the absence of data (participants *not* reporting information) may be taken as positive evidence of a default towards believing. For instance, one could equally conclude that people rarely mention honesty or deception and therefore this suggests that people default to *disbelieving* others. The data are consistent with this interpretation. Equally, we may find that participants in this study rarely mentioned the sex of the speaker, or the age of the speaker, or how attractive the speaker is. Could one claim on this basis that people default to believing speakers are transgendered, or old, or attractive? Testing for the presence of a truth-default is difficult because one must do so without triggering suspicion.[5]

In summary, TDT (Levine, 2014) argues that people default to believing others, but in the presence of a trigger will enter a state of suspicion and actively consider the possibility of deception. If sufficiently diagnostic evidence is found, an active lie or truth judgement is made. If the evidence does not meet the diagnostic threshold, the person may continue in a state of suspicion or revert to the truth-default. While there has been evidence offered that is consistent with the account, a potential critique of the account is that the data can usually be made to be consistent with TDT because elements of the account are unconstrained and can flex to fit the data. As noted in Box 2.3 in Chapter 2, data that are consistent with one account may also be consistent with other accounts. We now turn to another account: ALIED.

The Adaptive Lie Detector. Both TDT (Levine, 2014) and ALIED (Street, 2015) argue that the truth bias reflects the finding that most people tell the truth most of the time (see Chapter 2).[6] But whereas TDT (and the Spinozan mind hypothesis) sees the truth bias as resulting from a default in the mind, ALIED argues that the truth bias is a flexible and adaptive decision based on the nature of the information available to the receiver.

ALIED makes a distinction between two types of information. 'Individuating information' refers to any piece of information that causally and directly relates to the statement that was delivered by the sender. For instance, if I claim to have been to Murano, the glass-making island of Venice, individuating information could be my eye contact as I deliver that statement. We saw in Chapter 3 that eye contact is not a diagnostic cue to deception (i.e., liars and truth-tellers do not differ on the amount of eye contact they hold; B. M. De-Paulo et al., 2003), but whether or not I held eye contact while delivering that statement still causally relates to the statement. A more diagnostic indicator would be a picture of me being in Murano, for example, although of course this could be photoshopped and so may not be a perfect cue to my honesty. Receipts from a shop in Murano, or CCTV footage, may be even more diagnostic of my honesty. In contrast, a passport with no travel stamps in it may be a relatively diagnostic indicator of my deception, as may a statement from my partner that I have never visited Murano. Individuating information can vary in their diagnosticity and whether they indicate honesty or deception.

A second type of information is called 'context-general information'. This information does not causally and directly relate to the *current* statement, but rather generalises *across* numerous statements. For example, research shows that people tend to tell the truth more often than they lie (B. M. DePaulo et al., 1996; Halevy et al., 2014), and for language to be functional, it has to be believed to be truthful most of the time (Grice, 1975). A context-general piece of information, then, would be that 'most people tend to tell the truth most of the time'. In other contexts, we may find the opposite. For example, in the context of buying a used car we may believe that used-car salespeople tend to lie (e.g., P. J. DePaulo & DePaulo, 1989).

ALIED argues that these two forms of information are used in the decision-making process in an adaptive and functional way. When individuating information is highly diagnostic, ALIED argues that this information more heavily weighs in on the decision outcome relative to context-general information. In the extreme, a perfectly diagnostic cue, such as Pinocchio's nose, would result in context general information having no influence on the decision outcome. But as the individuating cues become less diagnostic, context-general information weighs more heavily into the decision. In the extreme, if there are no diagnostic cues to deception available in the statement at all (a situation that is rather probable, as we saw in Chapter 3; e.g., B. M. DePaulo et al., 2003; Luke, 2019), then context-general information will largely determine the lie-truth judgement. In a context such as our daily lives where most people are expected to tell the truth, the absence of diagnostic individuating information would lead to a truth bias. Thus, while TDT expects people to typically have a strong truth bias in their daily lives because of truth-defaulting, ALIED also predicts that people will have a strong truth bias in their daily lives, but according to ALIED this is because there are typically no diagnostic indicators of deception or honesty and the context-general information is such that most people tell the truth most of the time.

ALIED views the truth bias not as the result of an in-built error or bias, then, but as an attempt to make informed decisions, either by (i) using a highly diagnostic honesty cue (e.g., CCTV footage, DNA evidence, and Pinocchio's nose not growing would likely lead to a great many truth judgements) or (ii) in the absence of diagnostic cues, relying on context-general information that suggests most people will tell the truth. The ALIED view that context-general information more heavily weighs on the judgement outcome as the individuating information becomes less diagnostic is consistent with research in social psychology (e.g., Kunda et al., 2002; Lick & Johnson, 2014), judgement and decision-making (e.g., Barbey & Sloman, 2007; Kruglanski et al., 2007), memory research (e.g., Meiser et al., 2007), communication research (Mercier, 2020; Sperber et al., 2010), and developmental psychology (e.g., Brosseau-Liard et al., 2014; De Luca & Leventer, 2008). It is a sufficiently detailed account as to allow for computational models of it to be developed (Peebles & Street, 2023; Street et al., 2016).

ALIED makes a potentially controversial prediction: that people can be just as easily biased to judge lie (i.e., showing a lie-bias) as they can be biased towards judging truth (i.e., showing a truth-bias). It is the nature of the information that is available that matters. This prediction stands in contrast to other accounts which suggest there are in-built separate 'truth' and 'lie' processes, such as TDT (Levine, 2014) and the Spinozan mind (Gilbert, 1991).

To test this claim, one study told 80 participants that they were going to be judging the honesty of people who had taken part in an earlier trivia game experiment (Street et al., 2016). Supposedly, the trivia game players were given the opportunity to cheat and were later interviewed about whether they cheated. All the trivia game players in the study denied cheating. It was the participants' job to identify which denials were lies and which were truths. In an encoding stage, participants first saw a written description of a cue on the screen (e.g., 'Participant #170, when asked about cheating: scratched chin') and had to make a lie-truth judgement. By seeing this cue (and other cues) multiple times and being given feedback on the accuracy of their judgement, participants learned how diagnostic these individuating cues were. They were manipulated to be anywhere between 80% diagnostic of honesty (a highly diagnostic cue to honesty, present mostly when people tell the truth) and 50% diagnostic (a perfectly non-diagnostic and useless cue) and 80% diagnostic of deception (a highly diagnostic cue to deception, present mostly when people lie). Afterwards, participants were either told that the trivia game was easy, and so most people could score as well as they claimed without lying and thus most people would be telling the truth, or they were told the game was difficult, and so most people could not score as well as they claimed and thus most people would be lying when they denied cheating. This information constitutes context-general information because it gives information that generalises across statements.

In a test phase, participants were shown a single individuating cue and made a lie-truth judgement without any feedback. The researchers found that when the cue was 80% diagnostic of honesty, about 80% of judgements were truth judgements regardless of context (i.e., people were heavily truth-biased). When the cue was 80% diagnostic of deception, about 80% diagnostic of judgements were lie judgements regardless of context (i.e., people were heavily lie-biased). As the diagnosticity of the individuating cue became weaker (moving towards 50% diagnosticity), the effect of context on the judgement was greater. At 50% diagnosticity (where the individuating cue is entirely useless), people were truth-biased if they believed that most people would be telling the truth and lie-biased if they believed that most people would be lying. These findings show that the presence of a lie or truth bias depends on adaptively using the available information that the receiver holds.

Other work has found that people can be lie-biased in certain contexts. For example, people who are concerned about missing deceptions in general or are made to be suspicious of statements in the moment are lie-biased (e.g., Castillo & Mallard, 2012; Masip et al., 2009; Millar & Millar, 1997). Training people to detect deception (instead of detecting honesty) can create a lie bias (Blair, 2006; Masip et al., 2009). Jurors are sceptical of suspect alibis (Allison et al., 2014; Fawcett & Winstanley, 2018), although when a reliable individuating cue to honesty is presented such as strong evidence indicating innocence, people become truth-biased (see Olson & Wells, 2004, for a review; see also Wu & Cai, 2018). Prisoners show a lie bias (G. D. Bond, Malloy et al., 2005; G. D. Bond, Thompson et al., 2005; Hartwig et al., 2004), which has been argued to reflect the deceptive context in which they live. Similarly, police officers exhibit a lie bias (e.g., Alonso et al., 2009; Mann et al., 2008; Masip et al., 2005; Meissner & Kassin, 2002). This bias is specific to their working police context rather than a generalised distrust at both work and at home

(Masip et al., 2016; Masip & Herrero, 2017). There may also be cross-cultural effects on the tendency to judge statements as honest or deceptive (Park & Ahn, 2007), and behaviours that are unexpected can result in a lie bias (C. F. Bond et al., 1992; Burgoon et al., 2008; although see Levine et al., 2000). Such findings show that whether people are truth or lie biased depends on context, provided there are no reliable individuating cues available.

Thus, from the ALIED account emerges the view that situational influences impact the lie-truth judgement. Dovetailing with this view, a meta-analysis has found that there are greater individual differences (in terms of variance or spread of judgements) in lie-truth judgements than in a lie detection accuracy, with the variation in lie-truth judgements approximately six times greater than the variation in lie detection ability (a true standard deviation of 5.13% in lie-truth judgements compared to 0.80% in lie detection accuracy; C. F. Bond & DePaulo, 2008).[7]

While ALIED (Street, 2015) outlines a number of predictions, limitations are also noted. In particular, the definition of context-general information is problematic. Consider that the following may all pass for context-general information: 'Chris tends to lie', 'Academics generally tell the truth', and 'in our daily lives, people tend to tell the truth'. Notice that all three of these could be true simultaneously. ALIED is unable to explain how people manage multiple pieces of context-general information. Speculatively, because the ethos of ALIED is such that people attempt to use the more diagnostic information available to them, a viewpoint consistent with ALIED is that the more individuating the context-general information, the greater the weight it has on the decision. In these examples, knowledge of 'Chris' (one person's statements) is more individuating than that of 'academics' (statements from a small group of people) and more individuating again than 'the general public' (statements from a very large group of people). However, ALIED has not tied itself to this prediction, which may question whether the account is sufficiently well defined.

In summary, ALIED contends that two pieces of information are critical to understanding lie-truth judgements: individuating information (that which causally relates to the statement being evaluated, e.g., corroborating CCTV footage) and context-general information (that which generalises across statements, e.g., an understanding that most people tend to tell the truth most of the time). These cues are used adaptively and functionally, such that when individuating information is highly diagnostic, it more heavily weighs in the decision, but as it becomes less diagnostic, context-general information has the greater influence on the decision. Controversially, the account predicts that lie and truth biases arise from the same underlying processes. One drawback of the account is its lack of clarity over how people manage multiple context-general pieces of information.

Comparing TDT and ALIED. These accounts fundamentally differ in their ethos, viewing the receiver as either passively defaulting to believe (TDT) or else able to make functional and adaptive inferences based on the available information (ALIED). But the findings consistent with one account can often be explained by the other account (Best et al., 2019; Sánchez et al., 2021). One reason for this is that TDT can fit almost any experimental result (see Box 4.4), and so findings consistent with ALIED (or any other account) will be possible to fit into TDT's framework. But ALIED is also able to account for findings consistent with TDT. For instance, Clare and Levine's (2019) study finding people rarely spontaneously mention deception in response to watching senders' statements is expected under ALIED. People do not tend to produce highly diagnostic individuating cues to deception. In the absence of diagnostic individuating cues to deceit and being in a daily life context that most people tell the truth, a strong truth bias is to be anticipated. Thus, both TDT and ALIED predict a strong truth bias on most occasions. For TDT, this is seen when people passively rest in the truth-default state. For ALIED, this is when there is an absence of diagnostic indicators but working in a context that most senders will tell the truth most of the time.

Evidence of what may appear to be truth-defaulting does not falsify ALIED. Indeed, ALIED suggests that the reason the truth bias is observed so frequently in the literature (C. F. Bond & DePaulo, 2006) is because these studies tend to use student participants watching videos about typically trivial topics. As such, there is little to no diagnostic individuating information available in these studies and the context is such that most people tend to tell the truth in their daily lives. The magnitude of the truth bias is reduced by an understanding that in the setting of a deception experience, the rate of deception is likely to be greater than usual. ALIED argues that manipulating the diagnosticity of individuating information or context-general information can result in radically different judgements, even showing a lie bias (Street et al., 2016; see also Granhag & Strömwall, 2000).

Another example of work that supports TDT but can also be explained by ALIED comes from J. Lee et al. (2021) showing that people tend to believe an artist is telling the truth about their work. Interestingly, participants frequently reported that the reason they believed the artist was because "artists are generally honest people" (p. 544), what ALIED calls a context-general indicator of honesty. Finally, the findings of Sánchez et al. (2021) showed that people frequently detected deception unexpectedly. In the same study, they found that when people had detected deception, they most often report using individuating cues and rarely report context-general cues. This is consistent with ALIED's notion that if deception is to be detected then people need to make use of diagnostic individuating cues because they relate to the specific statement under evaluation. Thus, ALIED can largely account for the findings that are offered as evidence supporting TDT.

An important point of departure is ALIED's claim that people can be lie-biased. While TDT is sufficiently flexible to also allow this prediction (see Box 2.4), it is arguably inconsistent with the intention and ethos of a 'truth-default'. In describing ALIED, we noted that people can be lie biased in certain contexts, for example, police officers may be lie-biased against potential suspects (e.g., Alonso et al., 2009; Meissner & Kassin, 2002). T. R. Levine et al. (2014) have argued that the evidence for a lie bias is limited, noting that Bond and DePaulo's (2006) seminal meta-analysis of lie-truth judgement studies found that even experts show a truth bias, contrary to findings discussed earlier that police officers are lie-biased.[8] As an example, Hubbell et al. (2001) found that suspicion influences the strength of the truth bias but does not create a lie bias, consistent with the notion that there is a tendency towards believing.[9]

Another potential concern for ALIED is that if people are functional and making good use of the available information, why do they tend to report cues to deception that are not useful, such as avoiding eye contact (The Global Deception Research Team, 2006; see Chapter 3)? A meta-analysis may be able to offer insights (Hartwig & Bond, 2011). The researchers found a correlation between the actual cues to deception presented in the studies and the judgements made by participants in those studies. That is, participants tended to use the more diagnostic individuating cues available. The typically observed low lie detection accuracy rates (see Chapter 5) can be explained as a result of liars typically not producing reliable cues to deception (see Chapter 3), consistent with ALIED. Curiously, people seem to self-report the useless cues when asked to explicitly state their beliefs, but in practice when they make lie-truth judgements they appear not to use them and instead rely on more useful available indicators (Hartwig & Bond, 2011). Dovetailing with this finding, Bond et al. (2013) found that when a perfectly diagnostic individuating cue to deception was presented to receivers, they made near-perfect decisions, achieving approximately 98% lie detection accuracy.

Box 4.5 Critiquing Accounts through Their Similarities

When we evaluate two competing accounts, we often think to 'compare and contrast' them. This phrasing is often used in university exam questions in the UK. But one can gain insights into the issues with *both* accounts when we reflect on their similarities. Take a few moments to reflect on how ALIED and TDT are alike. This can be in terms of what phenomenon they are trying to explain, what psychological mechanisms are supposedly at play, or even the sources of literature that they rely upon. Once you have found the similarities, ask yourself "what if the assumptions being similarly made by both accounts are wrong?". What would need to change for the accounts to be able to explain the changed assumptions? Is a new account of the psychology of lie-truth judgements needed? Back in Chapter 1, we discussed that reflecting on and challenging the assumptions can lead to some of the most important breakthroughs and truly novel insights. These reflections may lead you to generate your own account of lie-truth judgements and offer an exciting place to start your dissertation or thesis research.

Both ALIED and TDT may be described as 'cold' accounts, focused on the mechanisms and pistons that work to produce lie-truth judgements based on a mechanical calculation of information (see Ask et al., 2020). Neither account reflects on the emotions of the receiver and how these may influence their lie-truth judgement (see Ask & Landström, 2010, on the importance of emotion of the receiver). Ask et al. (2020) have recently argued that a lie-truth judgement is fundamentally driven by an evaluation of whether the sender is someone that should be considered approachable or someone that should be avoided (see also Koch & Forgas, 2012, for evidence of an effect of emotive processing on lie-truth judgements).

Relatedly, neither account considers how the receiver's motivation to make a lie-truth judgement affects their decision-making (Best et al., 2019). In many lie detection studies, videos of liars and truth-tellers talking about trivial topics are presented to receivers with no stakes for the receiver to judge accurately or to engage. An important question, then, is how one's motivations affect the lie-truth judgement process. Might there be situations where people want to be especially sure that they are not lied to, and so be especially prone towards making lie judgements (see Hurst & Oswald, 2012)? Might such motivation result in an abandoning of the truth-default absent any triggers? Might it result in highly diagnostic individuating information being down weighted in the decision process?

In a study by Ask et al. (2008), 117 police trainees in Sweden read a homicide case that suggested a particular person was the perpetrator, but left other options open. Participants were either given DNA, photo, and witness testimony evidence that was consistent with this view or inconsistent with it. Participants rated the information that disconfirmed that the preferred suspect was the perpetrator as less reliable than evidence that confirmed the preferred suspect and found more reasons to question its reliability (see also Ask & Granhag, 2007). These findings suggest that motivation to believe a particular version of events may affect people's use of individuating information. As yet, neither ALIED nor TDT offers direct predictions about how motivation or engagement may affect the decision process.

Box 4.6 Which Account Should I Put More Faith In? Managing Contradictory Information in the Published Literature

Call me predictable, but I cannot answer that for you. However, I hope I can help guide your thinking on this issue, or at least give you a starting point from which to derive your own views and then in discussion with others or through self-reflection develop your views further. The points that follow are not evidence-based, but rather a reflection on my own view of conceptually managing contradictory viewpoints in the literature.

(Continued)

First, always remember that no one is forcing you to categorically believe one view over another. Science is probabilistic: we observe data and make inferences about the wider population with a particular degree of certainty. Naturally, this inference is scientifically grounded, but it will never provide guarantees no matter how robust our account. Therefore, it is entirely reasonable to take a view that one account is somewhat more probable than the other or that the jury is still out and you do not feel there is enough evidence yet to make a determination. That second option should be looking relatively attractive if you are a student new to the field. It is okay to be uncertain, and you should embrace it. Having a view that reflects your understanding of the literature is perfectly acceptable. High school often leads us to think that the answers are all known and now we just need to assimilate all that information. But the reality is that there is much that we (both as a scientific field and as individuals) do not know, and we should not be afraid to acknowledge that and have it reflected in our conclusions and our actions.

It is also important to keep in mind that our aim as scientists is to develop an understanding of the world that offers reliable and accurate predictions. As much as possible, we need to put to one side our preferences for particular viewpoints and evaluate the evidence as it is. This can be difficult, particularly if one has built a research career around a particular view! But doing so offers us the best chance to develop suitably useful accounts and explanations. Because psychological research is inherently noisy and probabilistic, we can expect to discover findings on both sides of an argument (e.g., for TDT and for ALIED).

Try to avoid jumping to the conclusion that 'the research is mixed' each time you find yourself in this position. The research may truly be rather inconclusive but be sure to take the time to more deeply examine the literature and consider the strength of the evidence on each side. We may do this by considering the robustness of the research: for example, was a power analysis conducted to determine the sample size? Is the research engaging in 'open science' practices (such as making the predictions public before collecting the data and sharing the data once it has been collected)? Does the methodology allow the researchers to make the conclusions they are reaching? Has the finding been replicated in other labs? As a starting point, you may find it helpful to seek out reviews and meta-analyses of the area, although keep in mind that their results will be in part determined by the particular approach they take. For example, if a review aims to determine whether training improves lie detection accuracy, it may (implicitly or explicitly) only review research that required immediate lie-truth judgements in the lab, and so may not offer an accurate insight into how people can be trained to detect deception outside of the lab because of the explicit decisions made by the reviewers or because the field of research being reviewed has confined itself to exploring lab-based lie detection.

As a final point, although you may be trying to distinguish which of two accounts to find more probable (notice that I did not say 'correct' or 'true'), there may be more accounts that require consideration and other accounts that have not yet been discovered. Ultimately, arbitrating between two (or more) accounts will involve an academic judgement. It is this capacity that higher education offers you, and it is a vital transferrable skill that you can take with you into your future career.

Chapter Summary

When making lie-truth judgements, a reliable finding across the literature is that people tend to make more judgements of truth than there are truth-tellers present. This phenomenon is called the truth bias. Explanations of the truth bias have been social (e.g., O'Sullivan, 2003; Vrij, 2008), psycholinguistic (e.g., Gilbert, 1991), communicative (e.g., Levine, 2014), and cognitive in nature (e.g., Street, 2015).

Accounts of accusatory reluctance (O'Sullivan, 2003) and the ostrich effect (Vrij, 2008) argue that people do not want to learn the truth either because it is damaging in its own right or may result in an aggressive social interaction or relationship breakdown. The Spinozan mind hypothesis (Gilbert, 1991) argues that in order to comprehend a statement, a person *must* automatically believe information is true initially. To disbelieve, either time or cognitive resources need to be available.

TDT (Levine, 2014) similarly argues that people default towards believing information is true. Triggers such as inconsistency may lead to suspicion and evidence is sought to make a lie-truth decision. If the evidence is sufficient, a lie judgement is made. Finally, ALIED (Street, 2015) claims that people make use of two sources of information: individuating cues that causally relate to the statement under consideration and context-general information about statements generally. When diagnostic individuating information is available (e.g., Pinocchio's nose), this information weighs most heavily in the judgement. As they become less and less diagnostic, context-general information has greater impact on the judgement. Because cues to deception are typically weak or non-diagnostic and because the context is such that most people tend to tell the truth most of the time, ALIED predicts a truth-bias.

Notes

1 Relatedly, there are also times where detecting deception is rather inconsequential, such as in laboratory experiments, and so here too people may not make an effort to try to detect deception (Miller et al., 1986).

2 While the first option is accurate, it is not clear how noting this difference offers us an insight into whether the findings can extend across fields.
3 It is unclear how TDT would explain that the plausible honest statements are among the statements generating the greater suspicion (and so must be more triggering).
4 Similarly, some cross-cultural studies find that the behaviours of speakers from another culture (such as holding eye contact) are suspicious (Vrij & Winkel, 1991) while others find that speakers from another culture are not judged with suspicion and as deceptive (Bond Jr. & Atoum, 2000). These apparently contradictory findings are readily made consistent with TDT if one defines the triggers in such a way as to allow certain behaviours in one of the studies to be considered potent triggers but do not allow behaviours in the other study are to be considered potent triggers. This can be done post hoc because there are no bounds on what may be considered a trigger or how to determine whether a trigger is sufficiently potent or not.
5 However, there may be ways to capture positive evidence of truth-defaulting without triggering suspicion by requiring participants to act on information they receive and constraining the situation such that acting one way indicates that they trust the information they have received and acting another way indicates that they disbelieve the information. In this way, we may be able to indirectly capture people's belief or disbelief of others based on the actions they take without needing to explicitly prompt thoughts of deception.
6 The idea that receivers are truth-biased because senders usually tell the truth has been around for some time (e.g., G. D. Bond, Thompson et al., 2005; Hurst & Oswald, 2012; O'Sullivan et al., 1988).
7 The variation in lie detection ability may even be as small as 0.64% (C. F. Bond & DePaulo, 2008), resulting in an eightfold difference between the variation in detection ability and lie-truth judgements.
8 Experts were defined as "police officers, detectives, judges, interrogators, criminals, customs officials, mental health professionals, polygraph examiners, job interviewers, federal agents, and auditors" (C. F. Bond & DePaulo, 2006, p. 230). As a proponent of ALIED, I would argue that combining the results of studies that may vary in how diagnostic the individuating cues are and what form of context-general information is available may lead to a noisy and misleading picture that does not reflect the predicted interaction of these important variables. For example, police officers may be lie-biased at work but truth-biased outside of work (Masip & Herrero, 2017). Accounting for variability in the context will be important to assessing this claim. However, you should be skeptical of post-hoc attempts to make the data fit the theory as I am attempting to do here (see Box 4.4).
9 Although it is important to note that showing a truth bias is not inconsistent with ALIED, it depends on how diagnostic the available individuating cues were and the nature of the context-general information in this study. This highlights a potential danger of attempting to post hoc explain past findings that were not designed to directly test an account's claims.

References

Allison, M., Jung, S., Sweeney, L., & Culhane, S. E. (2014). The impact of illegal alibi activities, corroborator involvement and corroborator certainty on mock juror perceptions. *Psychiatry, Psychology and Law, 21*(2), 191–204. https://doi.org/10.1080/13218719.2013.803275

Alonso, H., Masip, J., & Garrido, E. (2009). La capacidad de los policías para detectar mentiras [Police officers' ability to detect lies]. *Revista de Derecho Penal y Criminología, 2*, 159–196.

Anderson, S. E., Huette, S., Matlock, T., & Spivey, M. (2010). Comprehending negated sentences with binary states and locations. In S. Ohlsson & R. Catrambone (Eds.), *Proceedings of the 32nd annual conference of the cognitive science society*. Cognitive Science Society.

Asch, S. E. (1951). Effects of group pressure upon the modification and distortion of judgments. *Organizational Influence Processes, 58*, 295–303.

Asch, S. E. (1956). Studies of independence and conformity: I. A minority of one against a unanimous majority. *Psychological Monographs: General and Applied, 70*(9), 1–70. https://doi.org/10.1037/h0093718

Ask, K., Calderon, S., Giolla, E. M., & Reinhard, M.-A. (2020). Approach, avoidance, and the perception of credibility. *Open Psychology, 2*(1), 3–21. https://doi.org/10.1515/psych-2020-0002

Ask, K., & Granhag, P. A. (2007). Motivational bias in criminal investigators' judgments of witness reliability. *Journal of Applied Social Psychology, 37*(3), 561–591. https://doi.org/10.1111/j.1559-1816.2007.00175.x

Ask, K., & Landström, S. (2010). Why emotions matter: Expectancy violation and affective response mediate the emotional victim effect. *Law and Human Behavior, 34*(5), 392–401. https://doi.org/10.1007/s10979-009-9208-6

Ask, K., Rebelius, A., & Granhag, P. A. (2008). The 'elasticity' of criminal evidence: A moderator of investigator bias. *Applied Cognitive Psychology, 22*(9), 1245–1259. https://doi.org/10.1002/acp.1432

Asp, E. W., & Tranel, D. (2012). False tagging theory: Toward a unitary account of prefrontal cortex function. In D. T. Stuss & R. T. Knight (Eds.), *Principles of frontal lobe function* (pp. 383–416). Oxford University Press.

Barbey, A. K., & Sloman, S. A. (2007). Base-rate respect: From ecological rationality to dual processes. *Behavioral and Brain Sciences, 30*(3), 241–254.

Bell, K. L., & DePaulo, B. M. (1996). Liking and lying. *Basic and Applied Social Psychology, 18*(3), 243–266. https://doi.org/10.1207/s15324834basp1803_1

Bernhard, R. M., Frankland, S. M., Plunkett, D., Sievers, B., & Greene, J. D. (2022). Evidence for Spinozan 'unbelieving' in the inferior prefrontal cortex. PsyArXiv. https://doi.org/10.31234/osf.io/bs9tf

Best, G., Hodgeon, J., & Street, C. N. H. (2019). How contemporary theory informs lie detection accuracy and bias. *Crime Security and Society, 1*(2), Article 2. https://doi.org/10.5920/css.555

Blair, J. P. (2006). From the field: Can detection of deception response bias be manipulated? *Journal of Crime and Justice, 29*(2), 141–152.

Bond, C. F., & DePaulo, B. M. (2006). Accuracy of deception judgments. *Personality and Social Psychology Review, 10*(3), 214–234. https://doi.org/10.1207/s15327957pspr1003_2

Bond, C. F., & DePaulo, B. M. (2008). Individual differences in judging deception: Accuracy and bias. *Psychological Bulletin, 134*(4), 477–492. https://doi.org/10.1037/0033-2909.134.4.477

Bond, C. F., Howard, A. R., Hutchison, J. L., & Masip, J. (2013). Overlooking the obvious: Incentives to lie. *Basic and Applied Social Psychology, 35*(2), 212–221. https://doi.org/10.1080/01973533.2013.764302

Bond, C. F., Omar, A., Pitre, U., Lashley, B. R., Skaggs, L. M., & Kirk, C. T. (1992). Fishy-looking liars: Deception judgment from expectancy violation. *Journal of Personality and Social Psychology, 63*(6), 969–977. https://doi.org/10.1037//0022-3514.63.6.969

Bond, G. D., Malloy, D. M., Arias, E. A., Nunn, S. N., & Thompson, L. A. (2005). Lie-biased decision making in prison. *Communication Reports*, *18*(1–2), 9–19. https://doi.org/10.1080/08934210500084180

Bond, G. D., Thompson, L. A., & Malloy, D. M. (2005). Vulnerability of older adults to deception in prison and nonprison contexts. *Psychology and Aging*, *20*(1), 60–70. https://doi.org/10.1037/0882-7974.20.1.60

Bond Jr., C. F., & Atoum, A. O. (2000). International deception. *Personality and Social Psychology Bulletin*, *26*(3), 385–395. https://doi.org/10.1177/0146167200265010

Brosseau-Liard, P., Cassels, T., & Birch, S. (2014). You seem certain but you were wrong before: Developmental change in preschoolers' relative trust in accurate versus confident speakers. *PLOS ONE*, *9*(9), e108308. https://doi.org/10.1371/journal.pone.0108308

Burge, T. (1993). Content preservation. *The Philosophical Review*, *102*(4), 457–488.

Burgoon, J. K., Blair, J. P., & Strom, R. E. (2008). Cognitive biases and nonverbal cue availability in detecting deception. *Human Communication Research*, *34*(4), 572–599. https://doi.org/10.1111/j.1468-2958.2008.00333.x

Castillo, P. A., & Mallard, D. (2012). Preventing cross-cultural bias in deception judgments: The role of expectancies about nonverbal behavior. *Journal of Cross-Cultural Psychology*, *43*, 967–978. https://doi.org/10.1177/0022022111415672

Chen, Y., & Blanchard-Fields, F. (2000). Unwanted thought: Age differences in the correction of social judgments. *Psychology and Aging*, *15*(3), 475–482. https://doi.org/10.1037/0882-7974.15.3.475

Clare, D. D., & Levine, T. R. (2019). Documenting the truth-default: The low frequency of spontaneous unprompted veracity assessments in deception detection. *Human Communication Research*, *45*(3), 286–308. https://doi.org/10.1093/hcr/hqz001

Clark, H. H., & Chase, W. G. (1972). On the process of comparing sentences against pictures. *Cognitive Psychology*, *3*(3), 472–517. https://doi.org/10.1016/0010-0285(72)90019-9

Colwell, L. H., Colwell, K., Hiscock-Anisman, C., & Hartwig, M. (2012). Teaching professionals to detect deception: The efficacy of a brief training workshop. *Journal of Forensic Psychology Practice*, *12*(1), 68–80.

De Luca, C. R., & Leventer, R. J. (2008). Developmental trajectories of executive functions across the lifespan. In V. Anderson, R. Jacobs, & P. J. Anderson (Eds.), *Executive Functions and the Frontal Lobes* (pp. 3–21). Taylor & Francis.

DePaulo, B. M. (1992). Nonverbal behavior and self-presentation. *Psychological Bulletin*, *111*(2), 203–243. https://doi.org/10.1037/0033-2909.111.2.203

DePaulo, B. M., Charlton, K., Cooper, H., Lindsay, J. J., & Muhlenbruck, L. (1997). The accuracy-confidence correlation in the detection of deception. *Personality and Social Psychology Review: An Official Journal of the Society for Personality and Social Psychology, Inc*, *1*(4), 346–357. https://doi.org/10.1207/s15327957pspr0104_5

DePaulo, B. M., Kashy, D. A., Kirkendol, S. E., Wyer, M. M., & Epstein, J. A. (1996). Lying in everyday life. *Journal of Personality and Social Psychology*, *70*(5), 979–995. https://doi.org/10.1037/0022-3514.70.5.979

DePaulo, B. M., Lindsay, J. J., Malone, B. E., Muhlenbruck, L., Charlton, K., & Cooper, H. (2003). Cues to deception. *Psychological Bulletin*, *129*(1), 74–118.

DePaulo, P. J., & DePaulo, B. M. (1989). Can deception by salespersons and customers be detected through nonverbal behavioral cues? *Journal of Applied Social Psychology*, *19*(18), 1552–1577.

Elengold, K. (2019). The investment imperative. *Houston Law Review, 57*(1), 1–60. https://doi.org/10.2139/ssrn.3372381

Elkjær, E., Mikkelsen, M. B., Michalak, J., Mennin, D. S., & O'Toole, M. S. (2022). Expansive and contractive postures and movement: A systematic review and meta-analysis of the effect of motor displays on affective and behavioral responses. *Perspectives on Psychological Science: A Journal of the Association for Psychological Science, 17*(1), 276–304. https://doi.org/10.1177/1745691620919358

Fawcett, H., & Winstanley, K. (2018). Children as alibi witnesses: The effect of age and confidence on mock-juror decision making. *Psychiatry, Psychology and Law, 25*(6), 957–971. https://doi.org/10.1080/13218719.2018.1482573

Fiedler, K., & Walka, I. (1993). Training lie detectors to use nonverbal cues instead of global heuristics. *Human Communication Research, 20*(2), 199–223. https://doi.org/10.1111/j.1468-2958.1993.tb00321.x

Galai, D., & Sade, O. (2006). The "ostrich effect" and the relationship between the liquidity and the yields of financial assets. *The Journal of Business, 79*(5), 2741–2759. https://doi.org/10.1086/505250

Gilbert, D. T. (1991). How mental systems believe. *American Psychologist, 46*(2), 107–119. https://doi.org/10.1037/0003-066X.46.2.107

Gilbert, D. T., Krull, D. S., & Malone, P. S. (1990). Unbelieving the unbelievable: Some problems in the rejection of false information. *Journal of Personality and Social Psychology, 59*(4), 601–613. https://doi.org/10.1037/0022-3514.59.4.601

Granhag, P. A., & Strömwall, L. A. (2000). Effects of preconceptions on deception detection and new answers to why lie-catchers often fail. *Psychology, Crime & Law, 6*(3), 197–218.

Green, M. C., & Brock, T. C. (2000). The role of transportation in the persuasiveness of public narratives. *Journal of Personality and Social Psychology, 79*(5), 701–721. https://doi.org/10.1037/0022-3514.79.5.701

Grice, H. P. (1975). Logic and conversation. In P. Cole & J. L. Morgan (Eds.), *Syntax and semantics 3: Speech acts* (pp. 41–58). Academic Press.

Griffin, D. J., & Bender, C. (2019). Culture and deception: The influence of language and societies on lying. In T. Docan-Morgan (Ed.), *The palgrave handbook of deceptive communication* (pp. 67–89). Springer International Publishing. https://doi.org/10.1007/978-3-319-96334-1_4

Guthrie, J., & Kunkel, A. (2013). Tell me sweet (and not-so-sweet) little lies: Deception in romantic relationships. *Communication Studies, 64*(2), 141–157. https://doi.org/10.1080/10510974.2012.755637

Halevy, R., Shalvi, S., & Verschuere, B. (2014). Being honest about dishonesty: Correlating self-reports and actual lying. *Human Communication Research, 40*(1), 54–72. https://doi.org/10.1111/hcre.12019

Hartwig, M., & Bond, C. F. (2011). Why do lie-catchers fail? A lens model meta-analysis of human lie judgments. *Psychological Bulletin, 137*(4), 643–659. https://doi.org/10.1037/a0023589

Hartwig, M., Granhag, P. A., & Luke, T. (2014). Strategic use of evidence during investigative interviews: The state of the science. In D. C. Raskin, C. R. Honts, & J. C. Kircher (Eds.), *Credibility assessment: Scientific research and applications* (pp. 1–36). Academic Press. https://doi.org/10.1016/B978-0-12-394433-7.00001-4

Hartwig, M., Granhag, P. A., Strömwall, L. A., & Andersson, L. O. (2004). Suspicious minds: Criminals' ability to detect deception. *Psychology, Crime & Law, 10*(1), 83–95. https://doi.org/10.1080/1068316031000095485

Hasson, U., Simmons, J. P., & Todorov, A. (2005). Believe it or not: On the possibility of suspending belief. *Psychological Science*, *16*(7), 566–571. https://doi.org/10.1111/j.0956-7976.2005.01576.x

Hubbell, A. P., Mitchell, M. M., & Gee, J. C. (2001). The relative effects of timing of suspicion and outcome involvement on biased message processing. *Communication Monographs*, *68*(2), 115–132. https://doi.org/10.1080/03637750128056

Hurst, M., & Oswald, M. (2012). Mechanisms underlying response bias in deception detection. *Psychology, Crime & Law*, *18*(8), 759–778.

Karlsson, N., Loewenstein, G., & Seppi, D. (2009). The ostrich effect: Selective attention to information. *Journal of Risk and Uncertainty*, *38*(2), 95–115. https://doi.org/10.1007/s11166-009-9060-6

Kiesler, C. A., & Kiesler, S. B. (1964). Role of forewarning in persuasive communications. *The Journal of Abnormal and Social Psychology*, *68*(5), 547–549. https://doi.org/10.1037/h0042145

Knowles, E. S., & Condon, C. A. (1999). Why people say 'yes': A dual-process theory of acquiescence. *Journal of Personality and Social Psychology*, *77*(2), 379–386. https://doi.org/10.1037/0022-3514.77.2.379

Koch, A. S., & Forgas, J. P. (2012). Feeling good and feeling truth: The interactive effects of mood and processing fluency on truth judgments. *Journal of Experimental Social Psychology*, *48*(2), 481–485.

Kruglanski, A. W., Pierro, A., Mannetti, L., Erb, H., & Young Chun, W. (2007). On the parameters of human judgment. In *Advances in experimental social psychology* (Vol. 39, pp. 255–303). Academic Press. https://doi.org/10.1016/S0065-2601(06)39005-3

Kuhn, T. S. (1962). *The structure of scientific revolutions* (4th ed.). University of Chicago Press.

Kunda, Z., Davies, P. G., Adams, B. D., & Spencer, S. J. (2002). The dynamic time course of stereotype activation: Activation, dissipation, and resurrection. *Journal of Personality and Social Psychology*, *82*(3), 283–299. https://doi.org/10.1037/0022-3514.82.3.283

Lane, S. M., & Vieira, K. M. (2012). Steering a new course for deception detection research. *Journal of Applied Research in Memory and Cognition*, *1*(2), 136–138. https://doi.org/10.1016/j.jarmac.2012.04.001

Lee, J., Abe, G., Sato, K., & Itoh, M. (2021). Developing human-machine trust: Impacts of prior instruction and automation failure on driver trust in partially automated vehicles. *Transportation Research Part F: Traffic Psychology and Behaviour*, *81*, 384–395. https://doi.org/10.1016/j.trf.2021.06.013

Lee, S.-A., Park, H. S., & Levine, T. R. (2021). Judgments of honest and deceptive communication in art forgery controversies: Two field studies testing truth-default theory's projected motive model in Korea. *Asian Journal of Communication*, *31*(6), 536–549.

Levine, T. R. (2014). Truth-default theory (TDT): A theory of human deception and deception detection. *Journal of Language and Social Psychology*, *33*(4), 378–392. https://doi.org/10.1177/0261927X14535916

Levine, T. R. (2022). Truth-default theory and the psychology of lying and deception detection. *Current Opinion in Psychology*, *47*, 101380. https://doi.org/10.1016/j.copsyc.2022.101380

Levine, T. R., Anders, L. N., Banas, J., Baum, K. L., Endo, K., Hu, A. D. S., & Wong, N. C. H. (2000). Norms, expectations, and deception: A norm violation model of veracity judgments. *Communication Monographs, 67*(2), 123–137. https://doi.org/10.1080/03637750009376500

Levine, T. R., Clare, D. D., Blair, J. P., McCornack, S. A., Morrison, K., & Park, H. S. (2014). Expertise in deception detection involves actively prompting diagnostic information rather than passive behavioral observation. *Human Communication Research, 40*(4), 442–462. https://doi.org/10.1111/hcre.12032

Levine, T. R., Park, H. S., & McCornack, S. A. (1999). Accuracy in detecting truths and lies: Documenting the 'veracity effect.' *Communication Monographs, 66*(2), 125–144. https://doi.org/10.1080/03637759909376468

Levine, T. R., Punyanunt-Carter, N. M., & Moore, A. (2021). The truth-default and video clips: Testing the limits of credulity. *Communication Studies, 72*(2), 133–145. https://doi.org/10.1080/10510974.2020.1833357

Levine, T. R., Serota, K. B., & Punyanunt-Carter, N. M. (2022). Sender and receiver lie frequencies and motives: Testing predictions from truth-default theory. *Southern Communication Journal, 87*(3), 220–234. https://doi.org/10.1080/1041794X.2022.2052745

Lick, D. J., & Johnson, K. L. (2014). 'You can't tell just by looking!': Beliefs in the diagnosticity of visual cues explain response biases in social categorization. *Personality & Social Psychology Bulletin, 40*(11), 1494–1506. https://doi.org/10.1177/0146167214549323

Luke, T. J. (2019). Lessons from Pinocchio: Cues to deception may be highly exaggerated. *Perspectives on Psychological Science, 14*(4), 646–671. https://doi.org/10.1177/1745691619838258

Mandelbaum, E. (2014). Thinking is believing. *Inquiry: An Interdisciplinary Journal of Philosophy, 57*(1), 55–96.

Mann, S., A, Vrij, A., Fisher, R. P., & Robinson, M. (2008). See no lies, hear no lies: Differences in discrimination accuracy and response bias when watching or listening to police suspect interviews. *Applied Cognitive Psychology, 22*(8), 1062–1071. https://doi.org/10.1002/acp.1406

Markowitz, D. M., & Hancock, J. T. (2018). Deception in mobile dating conversations. *Journal of Communication, 68*(3), 547–569. https://doi.org/10.1093/joc/jqy019

Masip, J., Alonso, H., Garrido, E., & Antón, C. (2005). Generalized communicative suspicion (GCS) among police officers: Accounting for the investigator bias effect. *Journal of Applied Social Psychology, 35*(5), 1046–1066. https://doi.org/10.1111/j.1559-1816.2005.tb02159.x

Masip, J., Alonso, H., Garrido, E., & Herrero, C. (2009). Training to detect what? The biasing effects of training on veracity judgments. *Applied Cognitive Psychology, 23*(9), 1282–1296.

Masip, J., Alonso, H., Herrero, C., & Garrido, E. (2016). Experienced and novice officers' generalized communication suspicion and veracity judgments. *Law and Human Behavior, 40*(2), 169–181. https://doi.org/10.1037/lhb0000169

Masip, J., & Herrero, C. (2017). Examining police officers' response bias in judging veracity. *Psicothema, 29*(4), 490–495. https://doi.org/10.7334/psicothema2016.357

McCornack, S. A., & Parks, M. R. (1986). Deception detection and relationship development: The other side of trust. *Annals of the International Communication Association, 9*(1), 377–389. https://doi.org/10.1080/23808985.1986.11678616

Meiser, T., Sattler, C., & Von Hecker, U. (2007). Metacognitive inferences in source memory judgements: The role of perceived differences in item recognition. *Quarterly Journal of Experimental Psychology, 60*(7), 1015–1040. https://doi.org/10.1080/17470210600875215

Meissner, C. A., & Kassin, S. M. (2002). "He's guilty!": Investigator bias in judgments of truth and deception. *Law and Human Behavior, 26*(5), 469–480. https://doi.org/10.1023/A:1020278620751

Mercier, H. (2020). *Not born yesterday: The science of who we trust and what we believe.* Princeton University Press.

Milgram, S. (1969). *Obedience to authority.* Harper.

Millar, M. G., & Millar, K. U. (1997). The effects of cognitive capacity and suspicion on truth bias. *Communication Research, 24*(5), 556–570. https://doi.org/10.1177/009365097024005005

Miller, G. R., Mongeau, P. A., & Sleight, C. (1986). Fudging with friends and lying to lovers: Deceptive communication in personal relationships. *Journal of Social and Personal Relationships, 3*(4), 495–512.

Moore, S. G., Neal, D. T., Fitzsimons, G. J., & Shiv, B. (2012). Wolves in sheep's clothing: How and when hypothetical questions influence behavior. *Organizational Behavior and Human Decision Processes, 117*(1), 168–178. https://doi.org/10.1016/j.obhdp.2011.08.003

Nadarevic, L., & Erdfelder, E. (2013). Spinoza's error: Memory for truth and falsity. *Memory & Cognition, 41*(2), 176–186. https://doi.org/10.3758/s13421-012-0251-z

Nadarevic, L., & Erdfelder, E. (2019). More evidence against the Spinozan model: Cognitive load diminishes memory for "true" feedback. *Memory & Cognition, 47*(7), 1386–1400. https://doi.org/10.3758/s13421-019-00940-6

Nadarevic, L., Schnuerch, M., & Stegemann, M. J. (2021). Judging fast and slow: The truth effect does not increase under time-pressure conditions. *Judgment and Decision Making, 16*(5), 1234–1266.

Olson, E. A., & Wells, G. (2004). What makes a good alibi? A proposed taxonomy. *Law and Human Behavior.* https://doi.org/10.1023/B:LAHU.0000022320.47112.D3

O'Sullivan, M. (2003). The fundamental attribution error in detecting deception: The boy-who-cried-wolf effect. *Personality and Social Psychology Bulletin, 29*(10), 1316–1327. https://doi.org/10.1177/0146167203254610

O'Sullivan, M., Ekman, P., & Friesen, W. V. (1988). The effect of comparisons on detecting deceit. *Journal of Nonverbal Behavior, 12*(3, Pt 1), 203–215. https://doi.org/10.1007/BF00987488

Panidi, K. (2015). *Ostrich Effect in Health Care Decisions: Theory and Empirical Evidence* (SSRN Scholarly Paper No. 2932181). https://doi.org/10.2139/ssrn.2932181

Park, H. S., & Ahn, J. Y. (2007). Cultural differences in judgment of truthful and deceptive messages, *Western Journal of Communication, 71*(4), 294–315.

Park, H. S., Levine, T. R., McCornack, S. A., Morrison, K., & Ferrara, M. (2002). How people really detect lies. *Communication Monographs, 69*(2). https://www.tandfonline.com/doi/abs/10.1080/714041710

Park, H. S., Serota, K. B., & Levine, T. R. (2021). In search of Korean Outliars: "A few prolific liars" in South Korea. *Communication Research Reports, 38*(3), 206–215. https://doi.org/10.1080/08824096.2021.1922374

Peebles, D., & Street, C. N. H. (2023). An ACT-R instance-based learning theory model of lie detection. *Manuscript in Preparation*.

Pennycook, G., Cheyne, J. A., Seli, P., Koehler, D. J., & Fugelsang, J. A. (2012). Analytic cognitive style predicts religious and paranormal belief. *Cognition, 123*(3), 335–346. https://doi.org/10.1016/j.cognition.2012.03.003

Peters, U. (2017). On the automaticity and ethics of belief. *Teoria, 37*(2), 99–115.

Reinhard, M.-A., Greifeneder, R., & Scharmach, M. (2013). Unconscious processes improve lie detection. *Journal of Personality and Social Psychology, 105*(5), 721–739. https://doi.org/10.1037/a0034352

Sánchez, N., Masip, J., & Herrero, C. (2021). How people [try to] detect lies in everyday life. *TRAMES: A Journal of the Humanities & Social Sciences, 25*(4), 395–419.

Simmons, J. P., & Simonsohn, U. (2017). Power posing: P-curving the evidence. *Psychological Science, 28*(5), 687–693. https://doi.org/10.1177/0956797616658563

Sperber, D., Clément, F., Heintz, C., Mascaro, O., Mercier, H., Origgi, G., & Wilson, D. (2010). Epistemic vigilance. *Mind & Language, 25*(4), 359–393. https://doi.org/10.1111/j.1468-0017.2010.01394.x

Street, C. N. H. (2015). ALIED: Humans as adaptive lie detectors. *Journal of Applied Research in Memory and Cognition, 4*(4), 335–343. https://doi.org/10.1016/j.jarmac.2015.06.002

Street, C. N. H., Bischof, W. F., Vadillo, M. A., & Kingstone, A. (2016). Inferring others' hidden thoughts: Smart guesses in a low diagnostic world. *Journal of Behavioral Decision Making, 29*(5), 539–549. https://doi.org/10.1002/bdm.1904

Street, C. N. H., & Kingstone, A. (2017). Aligning Spinoza with Descartes: An informed Cartesian account of the truth bias. *British Journal of Psychology, 108*(3), 453–466. https://doi.org/10.1111/bjop.12210

Street, C. N. H., & Richardson, D. C. (2015). Descartes versus Spinoza: Truth, uncertainty, and bias. *Social Cognition, 33*(3), 227–239. https://doi.org/10.1521/soco.2015.33.2.2

Street, C. N. H., & Vadillo, M. A. (2016). Can the unconscious boost lie-detection accuracy? *Current Directions in Psychological Science, 25*(4), 246–250.

The Global Deception Research Team. (2006). A world of lies. *Journal of Cross-Cultural Psychology, 37*(1), 60–74.

Van Swol, L. M., Malhotra, D., & Braun, M. T. (2012). Deception and its detection: Effects of monetary incentives and personal relationship history. *Communication Research, 39*(2), 217–238. https://doi.org/10.1177/0093650210396868

Vorms, M., Harris, A. J. L., Topf, S., & Hahn, U. (2022). Plausibility matters: A challenge to Gilbert's "Spinozan" account of belief formation. *Cognition, 220*, 104990. https://doi.org/10.1016/j.cognition.2021.104990

Vrij, A. (2008). *Detecting lies and deceit: Pitfalls and opportunities* (2nd ed., pp. xiii, 488). John Wiley & Sons Ltd.

Vrij, A., Granhag, P. A., & Porter, S. (2010). Pitfalls and opportunities in nonverbal and verbal lie detection. *Psychological Science in the Public Interest, 11*(3), 89–121. https://doi.org/10.1177/1529100610390861

Vrij, A., & Winkel, F. W. (1991). Cultural patterns in Dutch and Surinam nonverbal behavior: An analysis of simulated police/citizen encounters. *Journal of Nonverbal Behavior, 15*(3), 169–184. https://doi.org/10.1007/BF01672219

Webb, T. L., Chang, B. P. I., & Benn, Y. (2013). 'The ostrich problem': Motivated avoidance or rejection of information about goal progress. *Social and Personality Psychology Compass, 7*(11), 794–807. https://doi.org/10.1111/spc3.12071

Wood, W., & Quinn, J. M. (2003). Forewarned and forearmed? Two meta-analysis syntheses of forewarnings of influence appeals. *Psychological Bulletin*, *129*(1), 119–138. https://doi.org/10.1037/0033-2909.129.1.119

Wu, S., & Cai, W. (2018). The role of the oath in credibility assessment. *Journal of Investigative Psychology and Offender Profiling*, *15*(2), 249–254. https://doi.org/10.1002/jip.1506

Zuckerman, M., DePaulo, B. M., & Rosenthal, R. (1981). Verbal and nonverbal communication of deception. In L. Berkowitz (Ed.), *Advances in experimental social psychology* (Vol. 14, pp. 1–59). Academic Press. https://doi.org/10.1016/S0065-2601(08)60369-X

Zwaan, R. A., Stanfield, R. A., & Yaxley, R. H. (2002). Language comprehenders mentally represent the shapes of objects. *Psychological Science*, *13*(2), 168–171. https://doi.org/10.1111/1467-9280.00430

5 Accurate Lie Detection

> **Box 5.1 Stanley Rifkin**
>
> In 1978, Stanley Rifkin committed the largest bank heist to that date, securing a $10.2 m wire transfer to a Swiss bank account. All this was achieved not with a weapon or threats, but with a simple phone call. By alternatingly posing as someone working in the wire room and someone working at the to-be-heisted bank, Rifkin was able to secure pieces of information that eventually provided enough detail to be able to place a wire transfer of the money to his Swiss bank account. It was only years later when Rifkin attempted to sell diamonds on the black market that the FBI caught up with him. Despite the high security, Rifkin was able to steal millions of dollars without his deception being spotted by anyone on the other end of his phone calls.

If you are reading these chapters in order, you may wonder why the discussion of lie detection accuracy has been pushed back to halfway through the book. Accuracy is a rather tricky issue, because it is inherently an interaction between the liar and the lie detector. It has been necessary to first understand how and when people lie, what indicators of deception may be available in the environment, and how it is that the person judging for deception carries out the decision-making process to arrive at a solution—whether or not they arrive at the correct solution. Understanding these foundations that deception detection must be built upon will allow us to develop a more informed, and hopefully theoretically driven, approach. A recent review of lie detection accuracy contended that "most research on deception is predominantly practical, but with little supporting theoretical work. This is problematic: often the theoretical premises of deception detection methods are rudimentary, and rely on dubious inferences, or are even unspecified" (Nortje & Tredoux, 2019, p. 492).

A second point that is also worth noting before we begin is that the issue of lie detection accuracy has been approached from far greater a range of perspectives and directions than has most other topics in this book. Given the breadth of this topic, Chapters 2 (process of deception), 6 (developmental psychology), and 7 (unconscious lie detection) will also touch on lie detection accuracy in their own ways. This is a broad topic area, one that will be difficult to distil into a single chapter. We will necessarily have to pass by entire research areas. However, on reading this chapter, you should be left with an understanding of core issues in the field.

As a final point, the chapter has been separated into passive and active lie detection techniques. Passive lie detection techniques are those that involve receiving the sender's statement and making a lie-truth judgement. Active techniques are those where the person receiving the statement is not merely an observer but instead becomes involved in the dialogue with an aim to produce cues to honesty or deception, such as through asking probing questions. After making this distinction, we will consider technologically aided approaches such as the polygraph or 'lie detector' and the concealed information test (CIT).

Passive Lie Detection

Across the years, a number of meta-analyses have been conducted to capture how accurate people are at detecting deception (e.g., Bond & DePaulo, 2006; Kraut, 1980; Zuckerman et al., 1981). What is consistently found is that accuracy is only marginally better than chance. People achieve 54% accuracy overall, with the Bond and DePaulo (2006) meta-analysis finding that people detect 47% of lies and 61% of truths correctly.[1] While some individual studies may find higher or lower detection rates than these, Levine et al. (2022) recently noted that a pattern emerged: the further away a given study's accuracy deviates away from this 54% value, the smaller the sample size was likely to be. That is, high-powered studies tended to converge on the 54% detection accuracy observed in meta-analyses.

There is a surprising stubbornness to this low accuracy. The receiver's confidence in their judgement, how old they are and their life experience, their biological sex (treated as binary), and personality factors such as extraversion and Machiavellianism (a manipulative personality trait) have no bearing on how accurate they will be, as shown in meta-analyses (Aamodt & Custer, 2006; Zuckerman et al., 1981). To make matters worse, people tend to be overconfident in their belief about their own lie detection ability (DePaulo et al., 1997). Police officers, secret service agents, judges, parole officers, and those academics studying deception also fair no better at lie detection than students and the wider public, and the number of years' experience in their professional capacity does not improve their ability either (Aamodt & Custer, 2006). Bond and DePaulo (2008) found that the standard deviation across lie detectors' accuracy is very small, less than 1%.

O'Sullivan (2008) notes that Bond and DePaulo's (2008) meta-analysis concentrated largely on university students in laboratory settings. One captivating suggestion made by O'Sullivan and Ekman (2004) is that there may be certain individuals or 'wizards' that are naturally superior human lie detectors. The researchers sent a set of videos to professional groups such as therapists and secret service agents. Those selected to receive the videos had achieved over 90% accuracy in an earlier unrelated lie detection study, a rate that the researchers argue would occur only 1% of the time when the high accuracy is a result of chance rather than systematic ability based on the binomial distribution. If they achieved 80% or above in the received videotapes, the researchers claim that the probability of observing such high accuracy by chance alone is 1 in 40,000. By using these accuracy thresholds, they discovered 14 lie detection wizards (and by other means found another 15, totalling 29 wizards). In their book chapter, O'Sullivan and Ekman (2004) speculate as to the many possible causes of this high lie detection ability, ranging from higher intelligence to being highly motivated to unusual childhood experiences.

The proposition of lie detection 'wizards' has been met with some scepticism. Bond and Uysal (2007) note that there are statistical problems with the claims of O'Sullivan and Ekman. For instance, while the chance of one person achieving unusually high scores is rather rare, over 12,000 people took the test. The probability that should be considered is not the chance of one person achieving such unusually high accuracy, but rather the probability that one of the 12,000 people who took the test would achieve such high accuracy. This pool has a fair possibility of finding some people who score rather high on the test due to chance alone. Bond and Uysal (2007) calculate that approximately 70 people would qualify as a lie detection 'wizard' by chance alone, greater than the 29 people that the original researchers discovered. They venture that the relatively low number of people scoring well on the lie detection tests (29 instead of 70) may be due to methodological or statistical issues (see Bond, 2008; Ekman et al., 2008; O'Sullivan, 2007, for further debate on the issue of 'wizards').

While there may not be much promise for the concept of naturally expert lie detectors, researchers have explored whether training can improve detection accuracy. An initial meta-analysis found that training may produce small gains in detection accuracy (Frank & Feeley, 2003), but the small number of studies in the meta-analysis and issues with the methodologies of those studies led the researchers to caution readers about the effect of training on lie detection performance. Driskell's (2012) later meta-analysis similarly found that accuracy can be slightly improved through training, and that training was more effective for lay people than for police officers, who believe they are more accurate than the wider public even before they receive training (Kassin et al., 2007). Similarly, Hauch et al. (2016) found a relatively small improvement effect for lie detection training when the training focused on training verbal cues to deception rather than nonverbal cues, the latter of which tend to be less diagnostic of deception. Hauch et al.'s (2016) meta-analysis found that training tended to result in around half a standard deviation improvement, or put another way, about 70% of trained participants achieved higher lie detection accuracy than the mean accuracy of the untrained group while 30% would be below or at the mean of the untrained group. Thus, while there appears to be an effect of training, it is important to bear in mind that it leads to only relatively small gains in accuracy.

Box 5.2 Reviewing Our Understanding of Deception

Let us briefly revisit what we have learnt in this book so far. Remember that lie detection accuracy is the interaction of how people deceive and how people make lie-truth judgements. Which of the following are defensible statements based on the arguments put forward in earlier chapters?

- Deceivers and truth-tellers have a similar aim: to be believed by the person they are speaking to (Chapter 2).
- There are highly diagnostic indicators of deception that can be observed in senders' behaviours (Chapter 3).
- People are biased to judge that others tend to tell the truth rather than judge that they are lying (Chapter 4).

Hopefully, you recall that the first point is argued by the self-presentational perspective of deception (DePaulo, 1992) and the third point has been observed in a meta-analysis of how people make lie and truth judgements (Bond & DePaulo, 2006). In Chapter 3, we discussed how cues to deception are typically not diagnostic of deception or honesty, and when they are diagnostic they appear highly infrequently. Reflecting particularly on this point, why might people be such poor lie detectors and why may training fail to achieve significant accuracy gains? Consider this for a few moments before continuing to read on.

Why is accuracy so stubbornly low? A clue to the answer may be found in Chapter 3. Recall that cues to deception are at best unreliable and at worst non-existent (DePaulo et al., 2003; Luke, 2019). No amount of training will improve detection accuracy if there is no information that shows if the sender is lying or telling the truth. Hartwig and Bond (2011) sought to determine whether low detection accuracy is caused by lie detectors having the wrong beliefs about what cues indicate deception or whether it is caused by liars and truth-tellers not systematically differing. Their meta-analysis found that the primary cause of low detection accuracy was the lack of difference between liars and truth-tellers. That is, receivers are not necessarily using the wrong strategies[2]: it is that the information is not available to reach a correct judgement.

It was noted earlier that variation in lie detection ability is less than 1% (Bond & DePaulo, 2008). Variation in how believable some people appear to others is around 14 times greater. Some people appear deceptive regardless of whether or not they are lying, which is to say that they have a deceptive 'demeanour'. This demeanour has been found in five studies to account for up to 98% of the variance in lie detection accuracy (Levine et al., 2011). Bond and DePaulo (2008) also note that some sender's lies are more readily detectable or 'transparent' than others, which Levine (2010) speculated may account for the 54% detection accuracy typically observed: a small number of people producing readily detectable lies and the remaining majority being undetectable would average out to the typically observed 54% detection accuracy.

In summary, passive lie detection in standard lie detection studies is marginally, but reliably, better than chance. There is a lack of individual variation in people's ability to detect lies, but this may not be too surprising in the context of research showing that there are no highly diagnostic cues to deception. Some people are more readily considered to be liars or truth-tellers, though, and this apparent credibility or demeanour is a larger determinant of lie detection accuracy than the receiver's lie detection ability.

Passive Lie Detection Techniques

Detecting deception in others is evidently a difficult task. But this has not precluded attempts to develop techniques that may improve accuracy. Later, we shall consider technologically aided methods, but this section will consider two passive lie detection techniques that are employed without the aid of such devices: Statement Validity Analysis (SVA) and Reality Monitoring (RM).

SVA was designed to assess the veracity of child interviewees, but it has been researched with both children and adults (Sporer et al., 2021; Vrij, 2015). It consists of four steps: understanding the criminal case file, a semi-structured interview with the interviewee, an analysis of the content of the interview using Criteria-Based Content Analysis (CBCA), and finally assessing, with use of a validity checklist, the possibility that CBCA may be biased in this particular application. Here, we will focus on CBCA because this is the more central aspect related to assessing the veracity of the sender's claim. For a review of SVA, see Volbert and Steller (2014).

CBCA involves coding the semi-structured interview with the interviewee to assess the strength of the presence of 19 criteria (Steller & Köhnken, 1989). Assessing the degree to which the criteria are present requires trained evaluators. The stronger the presence of each criterion, the more likely the statement is the truth, but this does not imply that the absence of criteria are indicators of deception. For example, a lack of detail may result from a deceptive statement or a lack of motivation on part of the truth-teller to deliver a convincing statement. Given the large number of criteria, they will not be individually listed here. Köhnken (2004) has described the criteria in detail and those interested in learning the details may wish to read his book chapter.

In brief, the criteria have been grouped into cognitive criteria (indicating thought processes) and motivational criteria (indicating how information is presented by the sender). The criteria may be further broken down into criteria that relate to the statement as a whole, specific contents of speech relevant to the incident, motivational criteria, and content specific to certain types of crime. Some of these criteria indicate that truthful statements are thought to be logical, detailed, providing information that contextualises elements of the statement. And liars are expected to be more concerned with self-presentation and with appearing credible to the receiver compared to truth-tellers. The theoretical underpinning is that liars may attempt to incorporate indicators of truth-telling into their statement but will not be as successful as truth-tellers in doing so (Köhnken, 2004; Maier et al., 2018).

Although the number of studies testing the validity of CBCA is somewhat limited, meta-analyses have found that the criteria are able to distinguish truths from lies (Amado et al., 2016; Hauch et al., 2017; Oberlader et al., 2016). Vrij (2008) has argued that CBCA has been shown to achieve approximately 70% lie and truth detection rates, which is a noticeable improvement on the 54% value seen so far, but perhaps not sufficiently accurate enough for us to feel comfortable having decisions about our incarceration being based solely upon a CBCA assessment.[3] Some researchers argue that SVA should not be used as substantive evidence in courts (Vrij, 2008). However, SVA is used as evidence in criminal courts in a number of European countries and in parts of North America.

There are a number of critiques of SVA. First, it is complex to administer, involving understanding the case in detail and developing a robust semi-structured interview that does not lead (or mislead) the interviewee. The interviewer also needs to be trained to assess the presence of CBCA criteria weighted by their natural frequency of occurrence, and then the interviewer needs to be able to interpret the results of CBCA based on possible mitigating factors using statistical and clinical expertise (see Sporer et al., 2021). CBCA was not designed to be used independently of the SVA in part because of this last factor, where a validity checklist can assess the degree to which factors undermine the applicability of CBCA to the situation under assessment. But researchers have studied CBCA independent of the broader SVA framework, and in some cases even removed some criteria from the CBCA (see Maier et al., 2018). Removing criteria may be problematic, given that a meta-analysis of CBCA has found that use of all criteria outperforms any incomplete combination of CBCA criteria (Oberlader et al., 2016; although see Amado et al., 2016, for a meta-analysis finding that some criteria do not separate truths from lies in the fashion predicted by SVA).

The validity checklist aims to assess whether CBCA criteria may have been affected by factors unrelated to deception. But Vrij (2015) notes that applying these factors to assess the validity of CBCA is potentially problematic. In one example, he notes that one such factor is to assess whether behavioural displays of affect are appropriate to child sexual abuse. While some victims of sexual abuse show visible signs of distress, others do not (Vrij & Fischer, 1996), which questions the potential for being able to systematically apply this criteria. Other factors may be difficult to measure.

Vrij (2015) has also argued that experts sometimes dismiss the validity checklist altogether,[4] but items on the checklist such as age of the interviewee will affect the CBCA score as children's cognitive maturity develops with age (Lamers-Winkelman & Buffing, 1996). Accounting for such factors will allow a more nuanced understanding of any resulting CBCA scores: low scores may be obtained even for truthful statements if the assessment is of a younger interviewee, for example. But it is not only use of the validity checklist that varies among SVA experts: one study found that some experts varied in how they assessed the presence of the criteria (Gumpert & Lindblad, 2000; see also Sporer et al., 2021, for discussion of variation in how criteria are defined by different researchers). However, application of SVA is subjective based on the decision-making of subject matter experts, given the intricacies of the many possible interacting factors, and so it may not be appropriate to apply broad generalisations to a tool that will vary in its application from case to case (see Hauch et al., 2017).

As a final point of consideration, Cacuci et al. (2021) highlight that it is unknown how the criteria of CBCA are affected by cultural differences because of a lack of research. But the authors posit that there are possible cultural factors that could affect CBCA scores. For instance, communication in Arab cultures is more repetitive and indirect compared to other languages (Feghali, 1997), with British interviewees offering more detail in their statements (one of the CBCA criteria) compared to Arab interviewees (Leal et al., 2018). Cultures also differ in how they use elements of language such as nouns (e.g., Fichman & Altman, 2019) and how they construct and retrieve autobiographical memories (Stanley et al., 2021; Wang et al., 2017). Cacuci et al. (2021) also reflect on other cultural differences related to how they refer to mental states in language and their motivational aspects. For example, East Asian cultures discourage sexual disclosure and encourage silence, which may affect how the interviewer interprets the 'appropriateness' of the affective response of the interviewee. The researchers call for more work to be done cross-culturally and promote a more culturally sensitive approach to using SVA, ensuring that doing so avoids any unintentional outcomes of creating or promoting culture-based biases and stereotypes.

SVA has not been specific about when and why differences between liars and truth-tellers occur (see Sporer, 1997). RM has more clearly explicated its theoretical assumptions explaining when and why differences are to be expected. The theoretical basis was put forward by Johnson and Raye (1981) to distinguish between memories of the experienced world differ from those that are imagined. The technique was not designed as a lie detection technique, but it has since been put to work in the detection of deception.

There is a lack of standardisation of the approach, with some researchers considering there to be a differing number of criteria with different conceptualisations resulting in differing classification accuracy rates (see Oberlader et al., 2016), but the differing conceptualisations share the premise that real memories should contain more sensory (visual and auditory), time-related, and spatial details than invented memories. RM has criteria not just for truth detection, as is the case for CBCA, but also for lie detection: invented memories should have more mentions of thinking and reasoning (e.g., "I must have arrived after 8 pm because the television show I was watching was scheduled to end at that time"). These criteria have been supported by empirical data, achieving detection rates of approximately 70% (see Masip et al., 2005; Oberlader et al., 2016). A review of the neuroimaging research has found that the anterior prefrontal cortex appears to play a role in distinguishing real from imagined memories (Simons et al., 2017). There has also been some success in applying RM to detecting children's lies with similar discrimination accuracy rates (Santtila et al., 1998; Stromwall & Granhag, 2005).

RM has been found to be easier to administer than CBCA. The content cues to be coded in RM are fewer and more clearly operationalised (Sporer, 1997). But there are potential issues with the application of RM. As with CBCA, RM requires training in order to code statements appropriately. Sporer et al. (2021) have found that coders do not necessarily agree with one another when coding statements for some criteria (i.e., they have low 'inter-rater reliability'), although inter-rater reliability is greater for RM than CBCA (Oberlader et al., 2016).

At a more theoretical level, a meta-analysis has recently found that while RM has significant ability to discriminate lies from truths when RM is considered as a whole, the discriminant ability of any given RM criterion varies from study to study. And to some degree, the discriminant ability depended on the age of the interviewee and the types of details being mentioned (Gancedo et al., 2021). This may suggest that the presence of cues is context dependent. For instance, a sender's self-consciousness and acting ability negatively affect RM scores (Vrij et al., 2001). Despite its more robust theoretical basis compared to SVA, RM has not been used in the courts (Vrij, 2015). It has also been pointed out that there may be an unsafe logical leap that statements of imagined memories are equivalent to deceptive statements. Deceptive statements may involve elements of truth as well as falsity and additionally have a component of intending to mislead the receiver (Masip et al., 2005). This may create important differences between imagined memories and deceptive statements.

Finally, both CBCA and RM techniques may find themselves vulnerable to countermeasures. When senders are aware of how the techniques work, they are able to adapt their speech to make their statements appear believable or at least difficult to distinguish from truthful accounts (Nahari & Pazuelo, 2015; Vrij et al., 2002). Additionally, both techniques may be affected by cultural variation, where in some cultures memory may be tied more to social relationships and actions rather than to the perceptual details that are coded with these techniques (Taylor et al., 2015).

Summary. In summary, CBCA and RM are two techniques used to code the statements of potential liars to assess their veracity. CBCA has a greater number of (less well-defined) criteria to be coded than RM. It also requires additional steps such as a post-CBCA stage that assesses the validity of the CBCA score. While RM is easier to apply and has a more robust theoretical basis, RM and CBCA both require training to conduct an appropriate assessment and both suffer the issue that while they may be capable of classifying statements with approximately 70% detection rates when used as a whole, the presence of any given criteria in a sender's delivery appears to vary from study to study.

Active Lie Detection Techniques

Behaviour analysis interview. The Behaviour Analysis Interview (BAI; Inbau et al., 2013; Inbau & Reid, 1962) is part of an interrogation technique used in over 150,000 criminal investigations worldwide (Blair & Kooi, 2004) to assess whether a suspect is lying or telling the truth. The BAI is to be employed as the first step of a broader interrogation method known as the Reid Technique which advocates for the interviewer to use accusation and other techniques to push the suspect to confess. The technique has changed very little since it was first published (Kassin, 2012). Unlike RM and CBCA, it encourages the interviewer to focus on the *nonverbal* behaviours of the sender that are produced in response to 15 behaviour-provoking questions that assess the suspect's knowledge, suspicions of who the true culprit is, and who might have the motive to commit the crime (for a full list of the questions, see the appendix of Masip et al., 2011). Truth-tellers ought to appear relaxed and engaged, while liars ought to appear frozen, withdrawn, and avoid eye contact.[5] The idea is that truth-tellers will want to aid the investigation and offer speculation about who committed the crime while liars will try to avoid unsubstantiated conjecture so that they do not incriminate themselves. Those who endorse the BAI suggest it can achieve detection rates of 80% accuracy (Buckley, 2012).

Box 5.3 Plausibility of the BAI

Reflecting on what you know about the cues to deception (see Box 5.2 and Chapter 3), how plausible is it that attending to the nonverbal behaviours of the potential liar will prove a useful method for detecting deception? What evidence leads you to that opinion?

However, it has been noted that there are methodological issues that may undermine this accuracy rate, such as the lack of a control condition and that the truth or deceptiveness of most of the statements in the study could not be verified (see Hartwig et al., 2014). This latter issue is known in the deception field as establishing 'ground truth'. In a study where the ground truth could be established and where a control condition was used, no support for the BAI was found (Vrij et al., 2006).

Earlier in this chapter as well as in Chapter 3, we encountered research that suggests that 'leakage' cues to deception unwittingly produced by the liar are, at best, rare and infrequent and at worst are non-existent (Brennen & Magnussen, 2020; DePaulo et al., 2003). Blair and Kooi (2004) reviewed the evidence for the nonverbal behaviours that BAI suggests interviewers should attend to and found limited support for the empirical validity of the behaviours as cues to deception. Masip et al. (2011, 2012) found that officers trained on the BAI held the same stereotypical and inaccurate beliefs about cues to deception as lay students (see Chapter 3, subsection 'Beliefs About Cues to Deception'), leading the researchers to argue that the BAI is little more than 'common sense'.[6]

In more recent years, the focus of lie detection research has shifted. The view that liars will spontaneously 'leak' cues to their deception has fallen out of favour. While it is difficult to put dates on broader paradigmatic shifts, in my opinion it is since the 2000s–2010s in particular that researchers have moved towards the view that the receiver of the message should take an active role in trying to elicit cues to honesty and deception (e.g., Hartwig & Bond, 2011; Kassin, 2012; Vrij & Granhag, 2012). A concurrent shift has also been noted by Masip and Herrero (2015): the hunt for a behavioural marker of deception has been replaced with an attempt to understand the context in which the statement sits, such as understanding the surrounding physical and testimonial evidence that may corroborate or contradict a statement.

Strategic use of evidence. One technique that exemplifies this shift is the strategic use of evidence (SUE) approach (Hartwig et al., 2005). To employ the approach, the receiver needs to have some form of independent evidence available to them that is relevant to assessing whether a particular statement may be true or false. For example, CCTV footage of the sender on top of the Eiffel Tower may serve as evidence relevant to a sender's claim that they have been to Paris. An assumption of SUE is that liars and truth-tellers have the goal of wanting to convince the receiver that they are telling the truth, akin to the self-presentational perspective seen in Chapter 2. While the liar is thought to be primarily concerned with the possibility that the receiver will discover the truth, the truth-teller's primary concern is that the receiver will *not* learn the truth and will not believe them. Thus, the truth-teller should be forthcoming with information, feeling that merely being innocent and having nothing to hide will be enough to be believed by the receiver (Kassin, 2005). The information offered by a truth-teller is thus expected to match the evidence that the receiver has.

At the heart of SUE is the question of when the evidence should be disclosed to the sender. Early disclosure may force liars to adapt their story so that it includes the evidence. If the evidence is strongly incriminating, it may lead the sender to feel that lying would be unsuccessful and so they may simply choose to confess (Softley et al., 1980). But late disclosure of evidence means that the liar would have to invent their account without being aware that there is evidence that could contradict what they invent. The question becomes whether evidence should be disclosed early or late.

In one of their earlier studies, Hartwig et al. (2005) tested whether telling the sender about the evidence before or after their statement led to higher lie detection rates. Fifty-eight participants were instructed to look for a DVD in a box partially covered by a briefcase with a wallet sticking out. Those in the truth-telling condition were told to search for a particular movie. Those in the lying condition were instructed to pretend to look for the DVD but to secretly steal the wallet. One week later, all participants were interviewed by someone using either the early or late disclosure method, with both honest and deceptive senders attempting to convince the receiver that they only looked for a DVD. The receivers in the early disclosure condition achieved 43% overall detection accuracy, while those in the late disclosure condition achieved 62% accuracy. Allowing the sender the opportunity to unknowingly contradict physical evidence with late disclosure of evidence is what makes the SUE approach effective. A meta-analysis has found that liars are more likely to contradict the evidence if it is disclosed late (Hartwig et al., 2014). The contradiction can then be used to directly confront the sender. Because the sender only learns of the interviewer's evidence after the contradiction, the SUE approach has the added benefit of leaving the sender with the perception that the interviewer may have further evidence that they are withholding, when in reality they may not (Tekin et al., 2015).

One of the key benefits of SUE is that liars cannot attempt to counteract its effectiveness because they do not know what evidence the receiver has. Some have argued that this technique is ready to be deployed in legal settings (Vrij & Fisher, 2016). When police trainees are given training to disclose evidence late, their lie detection accuracy rates increase (85%) relative to being given no training (56%; Hartwig et al., 2006).

Cognitive load approach. The cognitive load approach (Vrij, Fisher, et al., 2008), meanwhile, has been argued by these researchers to not yet be ready for deployment (Vrij & Fisher, 2016). The cognitive load approach to detecting deception rests on the assumption that deceiving is cognitively more demanding than truth-telling. This is because the liar needs to generate the lie, monitor their own and the receivers' behaviour, and inhibit truthful information (see Chapter 2). By adding additional cognitive load to the sender, liars should face greater difficulty in producing a convincing story, and as such their lies should be detectable through cues such as the statement being less plausible and detailed. This can be done by having the sender make their statement in reverse chronological order (Vrij, Mann, et al., 2008) or asking questions that the sender is not expecting (Vrij et al., 2009), which have been found to create greater difficulty in producing a convincing story. These methods of creating cognitive load should not impact truth-tellers, however, who do not have the varying demands that liars have to contend with. Truth-tellers should be able to manage the additional cognitive load without it impacting the plausibility of their story.

The unanticipated questions method of increasing cognitive load is considered to be especially effective because liars cannot counteract questions that they cannot anticipate (Vrij & Fisher, 2016). A meta-analysis has found that the cognitive load approach can result in an overall detection rate of 71% (Vrij et al., 2017), which offers promise for both cognitive load accounts of deception production (Chapter 2) and as an easy-to-implement method for detecting lies.

However, the cognitive load approach has not explained what processes or mechanisms are operating that result in the cognitive load effect (Blandón-Gitlin et al., 2014). This may lead to some inconsistencies with what is known about cognition. Lane and Vieira (2012), for instance, argue that increasing cognitive load should affect people's ability to recall truthful information: after all, memory recall is not merely a case of retrieving a laid-down fact, but rather a case of reconstructing and editing a partially remembered (and perhaps even falsely remembered) set of information (e.g., Hemmer & Steyvers, 2009). Thus, imposing cognitive load on truth-tellers should affect the ability to recall truthful information, but Lane and Vieira contend that studies using the cognitive load approach seem not to find this.[7] In favour of a cognitive load explanation, however, Dando et al. (2011) have found that the reverse order instruction may introduce errors into truthful statements. While this offers support to the theoretical account, that truth-tellers may become more error-prone questions its utility as a tool to apply in real-world cases.

As we saw in Chapter 2, deception may sometimes be easier than telling the truth, which may again question the underlying premise of cognitive load affecting only deceivers. That lying is *sometimes* easier may suggest that the effectiveness of the cognitive load approach may be context-dependent (Levine & McCornack, 2014). Mac Giolla and Luke (2021) recently conducted a meta-analysis finding that the cognitive load approach was only effective when receivers were instructed about which cues to attend to.

As a further critique, Lane and Vieira (2012) also contend that studies tend to assume that cognitive load is being experienced as a result of the manipulation, but they do not measure the degree to which participants are experiencing cognitive load. This leaves open the possibility that the differences between liars and truth-tellers are a result of some confounding factor that accompanies the cognitive load manipulation. Similarly, Giles et al. (2021) raise the point that this approach works by making liars appear less fluent in their delivery. But it may be difficult for people from other cultures to recognise when speech is or is not fluent. This potentially limits the cross-cultural application of the approach, but as yet there is no research to test if this is the case.

Verifiability approach. "The more pieces of information you tell me that I could go out and check with evidence, the more willing I am to believe you". This is a crude summary of the verifiability approach (Nahari et al., 2014). Verifiable details are perceptual (i.e., visual, auditory, olfactory, etc.) and contextual (i.e., space and time) details that can be substantiated with (i) physical evidence (such as CCTV footage or a time stamped receipt form a shop that one claims to have visited), (ii) be witnessed by another named person (i.e., someone that the receiver has the potential to identify), or (iii) be carried out with another named person (see Nahari, 2018, for more detail about each criteria). The more of these verifiable details that appear in the statement, the more likely the statement is truthful.

The logic is that truth-tellers will want to be forthcoming and offer detail that can corroborate their stories. This may be particularly true in a police interview setting where a truth-teller risks imprisonment if they are not believed (Granhag et al., 2015). But liars will be unable to be able to offer verifiable detail precisely because they are lying: their story is not true and so cannot be corroborated with evidence. Indeed, it may be in their interest to withhold details so that the police cannot learn the truth (Granhag et al., 2015).[8] But providing little detail may make the liar appear suspicious. One way to resolve the dilemma is to produce a detailed statement but with few verifiable details. Truth-tellers are thus expected to provide a detailed statement that includes verifiable details while liars should withhold verifiable details despite providing an otherwise detailed statement.

For the verifiability approach to function, the sender needs to believe that the receiver will check the claims being made. But it is not necessary for the receiver to actually conduct the checks: the sender merely needs to *believe* that the receiver will check the details. As a result, the verifiability of each criterion is determined not by objective reality, but by the sender's *beliefs* about their verifiability (Nahari, 2018). If the sender believes that a detail is not verifiable even though actually it is (e.g., they discuss walking down a street and believe it is not verifiable, but CCTV footage may be able to corroborate the claim), this is not considered a verifiable detail. Similarly, a detail that could not be verified in reality may be considered a verifiable detail if the sender intends to for their statement to be verifiable. For example, mentioning having carried out an activity with 'a friend' may be believed by the sender to be a detail that the receiver could check. If the receiver does not know who this friend is, it may be difficult or impossible to carry out the check. Coding of verifiable details is thus not necessarily as straightforward as determining whether a statement can be checked against reality, which may create some difficulties in applying the approach.

In an early study, Nahari et al. (2014) asked participants to engage in activities of their choice for 30 minutes before returning to the lab. Upon arriving back at the lab, they were told a wallet was stolen and that they were a suspect. Participants were assigned to one of two conditions: either they had to lie throughout or they had to tell the truth throughout their statement.

The statements were coded, and a statistical method called linear discriminant analysis was applied to attempt to classify who was lying and telling the truth on the basis of the number of verifiable details in the statement. The analysis was able to classify statements with 79% accuracy (see Palena et al., 2021; Verschuere et al., 2021, for meta-analyses supporting the verifiability approach's effectiveness).

The ratio of verifiable to unverifiable details within a single statement can also be used to distinguish liars and truth-tellers with around 71% accuracy. This point may seem mundane at first, but it represents an answer to an important question. In experiments, we have the luxury of being able to compare liars and truth-tellers using multiple participants' statements and determining which group produces the relatively higher score. In applied settings, the interviewer only has the statement from the person in front of them. How is it possible to determine if a single statement is a truth or a lie without having access to multiple statements to compare against?[9] The ratio of verifiable to non-verifiable details represents an interesting solution to this problem. The ratio is determined by dividing the number of verifiable details by the number of non-verifiable details. Liars should offer few verifiable details and pad out their statement with more unverifiable details. As such, liars should have a low ratio of verifiable to unverifiable details in their statement. Truth-tellers, meanwhile, should have a higher ratio because they will offer more verifiable details (see Nahari et al., 2019).[10] This is a promising first step in developing a technique that does not rely on group-based analysis and that can be applied in the field with a single statement. But it is not yet clear what constitutes a sufficiently high or low ratio to categorise the statements as either truthful or deceptive (Nahari, 2018), which leaves open the question of how the ratio should be interpreted in practical settings.

Another strength of the approach is its resistance to countermeasures. We saw earlier that both CBCA and RM can be counteracted when liars understand how the techniques work. Curiously, the opposite is true of the verifiability approach: when senders know how it works, the verifiability approach is even more effective in separating liars and truth-tellers. This is because truth-tellers typically assume that the truth will be readily apparent to the receiver (Kassin, 2005; see Gilovich et al., 1998, for more on this 'illusion of transparency'). By discovering that they need to include verifiable details in their statement to be believed, truth-tellers will be encouraged to offer as many verifiable details as possible, thereby creating further separation between the number of verifiable details in liars' and truth-tellers' statements (see Harvey et al., 2017; Nahari & Vrij, 2014, for empirical support). However, this does not mean the approach is immune to countermeasures. For instance, a liar may have monetary or other resources available to them to generate apparently verifiable details of their false claim, whether this is through producing false documents or producing corroborating 'witnesses' who lie in order to support the sender's statement.

Studies on the verifiability approach have included at least one of the three original researchers (see Verschuere et al., 2021). There can be concerns about the generalisability of findings when they are investigated in a limited number of labs, just as one may question the cross-cultural generalisability of findings when they are conducted only in select parts of the world. The verifiability approach's effectiveness may result from unintended or unreported practices within those labs. It is thus useful to replicate findings with independent researchers in different labs. Meta-analyses conducted on the verifiability approach have made calls for replication studies to be conducted using larger sample sizes than the original studies and in independent labs (Palena et al., 2021; Verschuere et al., 2021). Additionally, it is unknown how individual differences in statements may affect the applicability of the approach (Nahari, 2018; Verschuere et al., 2021). For example, embedding a single lie in an otherwise truthful statement is liable to increase the number of verifiable details in the statement overall because the liar could offer verifiable details about only the truthful elements of the statement.

Summary. In summary, the BAI continues to be used in some countries to train police officers, despite its questionable claims and empirical evidence that contradicts its core claims. The SUE has a stronger empirical backing, as indeed do all the other approaches listed so far. The SUE encourages a late disclosure of evidence so that a liar has the potential to contradict known evidence, revealing the potential deceit. The cognitive load approach also attempts to elicit cues to deception but does so by requiring more thinking effort by the sender as they deliver their statement, with the expectation that liars will be overwhelmed with the cognitive load and thus result in cues to their deception. There have been questions regarding the cognitive processes and mechanisms that are at work, however, given the limited theoretical discussion of the cognitive load approach. Finally, the verifiability approach argues that truth-tellers will provide more checkable details than liars. Making people aware of how the approach works does not make it open to being counteracted. Quite the opposite: truth-tellers learn what they need to do to be believed while liars cannot adjust their strategy to make themselves believable. In fact, it is now recommended that the sender is made aware of how the technique works before they deliver their statement (Nahari, 2019).

Technologically Aided Lie Detection

Some of the approaches discussed so far have strong potential for detecting deception, but they are not infallible. Technological approaches have been developed to try to uncover deception. In this section, we consider the control question test (CQT) that was developed to be employed with the polygraph or 'lie detector', and the CIT designed to reveal that the sender has a memory for certain information.

Control question test. The polygraph, more commonly referred to as the 'lie detector', continuously measures the physiological responses of a person. These responses typically include respiration rate, skin conductance (or 'palmar sweating'), and blood pressure and blood flow, which are interpreted by a trained polygraph examiner to assess veracity. The CQT (Reid, 1947) is the most commonly used polygraph approach for questioning the sender (Ben-Shakhar & Elaad, 2003). The method uses three types of questions. Relevant questions are those that pertain to the issue under investigation (e.g., 'did you steal a wallet from the office last Monday?'). Irrelevant questions are neutral questions that have no bearing on the case and should not evoke a strong physiological response (e.g., 'are you breathing oxygen?'). A third question type is the control question, which is designed to illicit a physiological response but is only indirectly related to the issue under investigation (e.g., 'have you ever stolen something when you were a child?'). The set of questions is repeated around three times across the interview procedure (Elaad, 2000). The expectation is that liars will show a stronger physiological response to the relevant (compared to control) questions as a result of fear of getting caught in a serious lie. Truth-tellers are expected to more strongly react to the control (compared to relevant) questions because they create embarrassment and thus a physiological response. Truth-tellers have no reason to be concerned about their responses to crime-relevant questions because of their innocence (British Psychological Society, 2004). For those interested in the history of the polygraph, see Grubin and Madsen (2005) or Bunn (2012).

Box 5.4 Assumptions of the CQT

Reflect on what we have discussed about the CQT so far. Which of the following is the basis for the technique?

- Liars and truth-tellers will experience different emotional reactions.
- Liars and truth-tellers will engage in differing cognitive processes.
- Liars and truth-tellers will experience different degrees of cognitive load.

The first option should stand out as the correct option: the physiology is expected to result from emotional reactions (fear) to the questions being asked. Reflecting on Chapters 2 (the process of deception) and 3 (cues to deception), how plausible does this assumption seem to you? For instance, have theories of deception production found that liars experience different underlying affects that drive their behaviour? Have emotional cues to deception been found? What is the predominant focus of the research?[11]

The CQT has been widely criticised. The CQT suffers from a lack of standardised questions, which makes it vulnerable to the biases of the question setter and polygraph examiner (Ben-Shakhar, 2002). For instance, in one study 44% of truth-tellers were incorrectly judged to be lying (Patrick & Iacono, 1989). Its low accuracy has led the National Research Council

(2003, p. 2) in the US to conclude that "[a]lmost a century of research in scientific psychology and physiologic provides little basis for the expectation that a polygraph test could have extremely high accuracy", and that its use may create a false sense of confidence in the investigator. Similarly, the British Psychological Society (2004, p. 29) reached the conclusion that "even in the most favourable circumstances polygraphic lie detection accuracy is not high". Even when the polygraph interpretation produces correct classifications, research has shown that subtle countermeasures such as biting one's tongue, pressing one's toes to the floor, or counting backwards in sevens can prevent accurate polygraphic results (Honts & Kircher, 1994).

The theoretical assumption of the polygraph is that liars experience heightened arousal when asked topic-relevant questions. However, the British Psychological Society (2004) noted that a given physiological response need not reflect deception. For instance, a truth-teller may show a heightened physiological response when asked about the murder of their partner due to the love and the strength of the emotional bond that the truth-teller has for their late partner. Or a truth-teller may respond with fear to crime-relevant questions merely because they find themselves in an interview situation being asked questions that are evidently pertinent to the crime. Their emotional reaction may reflect concern that they will not be believed. There is no single physiological response that is uniquely linked to deceiving (Lykken, 1998), and a response may reflect a number of underlying causes.

It may be for this reason that more recent attempts to find neurological patterns of activity that isolate deception using functional magnetic resonance imaging (fMRI) have also had limited success (e.g., Ganis et al., 2011; Kessler & Muckli, 2011; Spence, 2008). This has not prevented for-profit companies like No Lie MRI and Cephos Corporation from marketing fMRI as a lie detector. Perhaps ironically, this has led Cohen (2010) to claim that these companies have violated US deceptive trade practice laws and consumer protection law.[12] For further consideration of whether the fMRI makes for an effective lie detector, see Langleben (2008) and Spence (2008).

Concealed information test. This test is also sometimes called the guilty knowledge test (GKT; Lykken, 1960) or the concealed knowledge test (CKT; Elaad, 1998), but today is more commonly referred to as the CIT. This technique does not detect the presence of deception, but rather aims to detect whether there exists a memory for information. The CIT is not widely used worldwide but it is employed in practice settings in Japan (Osugi, 2018).

The test uses a multiple-choice format, with each question having one relevant 'probe' answer (e.g., an element of the crime being investigated such as the weapon that the suspect used) and multiple control answers that are indistinguishable from the relevant item to an innocent person (e.g., a set of other weapons). As with the CQT, the CIT has traditionally been used in concert with physiological measures such as skin conductance, respiration, and heart rate (klein Selle et al., 2018). Increased physiological response to relevant items compared to control items suggests that the person has knowledge about the item. Assuming only guilty people have access to the crime-relevant information, one can infer their guilt. However, this assumption should not be taken for granted, given that media sources may have discovered details of an event and published them publicly.

In a study of the CIT, Elaad and Ben-Shakhar (2006 Experiment 1) asked participants to enter an office and search for an envelope. They were to remove a small sum of money, jewellery, and a writing instrument from the envelope and hide these in their pocket. After carrying out the activities, participants had skin conductance electrodes attached to them along with a respiration belt and plethysmograph to measure skin conductance, respiration, and finger pulse. Eight questions about their activities were asked (e.g., what was the colour of the envelope) one at a time with the one relevant probe (e.g., red) and four control answers following (e.g., blue, green, white, black). The five possible answers were presented visually and auditorily by the computer for five seconds each, one at a time. The participants' task was to answer 'no' to each item as soon as it appeared. As a result, they would be lying when saying 'no' in response to the relevant probe item and telling the truth when responding to the control items. The researchers found that using respiration information alone resulted in a 60% correct detection rate, finger pulse resulted in a 64% correct detection rate, and skin conductance resulted in a 71% correct detection rate. Using a combination of all three measures to assess veracity resulted in a detection accuracy rate of 87.5%.

The theoretical basis for the CIT has traditionally been based on the concept of the orienting response (Sokolov, 1963). The orienting response is a reflexive behavioural (e.g., shifting gaze position) or physiological reaction (e.g., skin conductance change) in response to a novel stimulus, especially one that carries personal significance (e.g., crime-relevant details). According to the orienting perspective, the reflex reflects their knowledge for the item they have been presented with, and hence is considered to result from cognitive processes rather than emotional, deceptive, or motivational processes. In two surveys of members of the Society for Psychophysiological Research and the American Psychological Association, around 75% of members believed the CIT has a cogent scientific basis (Iacono & Lykken, 1997).

However, the orienting response may not be the only causal factor creating the CIT effect. Some have suggested that there may be emotional or motivational factors that influence how effective the CIT is (e.g., Ben-Shakhar & Elaad, 2003; Verschuere et al., 2007; Zvi et al., 2012). For example, Verschuere et al. (2007) suggest that the CIT effect may reflect attempts to inhibit arousal as well as being a result of the orienting response.

There is evidence consistent with the position that the CIT effect results from more than solely an orienting response. In a study by Zvi et al. (2012), some participants were instructed that they needed to cope with a polygraph test that was biased against them and so should be alert, attentive, and prepared. The instruction was intended to motivate participants to 'beat' the test. Other participants were told that the polygraph was biased in their favour and so they should relax and avoid interfering with the process. These 'relaxing' participants should have had low motivation to influence the test outcome. If the CIT effect has a motivational component, the prediction was that those with a motivation to appear credible should be more readily detectable than those with low motivation. The researchers' study supported this prediction, showing increased skin conductance response when given motivation to perform. This suggests that the CIT effect may in part result from motivation, rather than solely resulting from an orienting response.

To further explore the orienting explanation of the CIT effect, Ambach et al. (2008) aimed to decouple the orienting response of the CIT from the act of deception. After all, it is the liars who are expected to show the orienting response and truth-tellers who will not, and so the two are typically confounded. They separated veracity from the orienting reflex by having participants answer honestly or deceptively after a four-second delay. The reflexive and relatively fast orienting response should be unobservable after this long of a delay. They found that skin conductance information was able to determine which item was the relevant probe item and which were the controls regardless of honesty or deception, potentially suggesting that these physiological responses reflect orienting because they appear regardless of honesty or deception. But heart rate and respiration could only be used to determine which item was the probe and which were controls in the deception condition, suggesting that these components of the CIT effect may reflect a deceptive component. Thus the CIT effect may not solely be driven by an orienting response, but also by an additional independent component—a deceiving component.

Although the CIT has been traditionally deployed with the polygraph, other technologies have also found success using the CIT paradigm, such as (i) electroencephalography (EEG), which measures electrical activity distributed across the brain (Ben-Shakhar, 2012), (ii) an attentional blink paradigm where a stimulus (e.g., a famous face) captures attention and thus distracts attention from the relevant probe item presented briefly and immediately following it (Ganis & Patnaik, 2009), and (iii) replacing the physiological measures with a simple reaction time measurement (Varga et al., 2014).

The reaction time-based approach presents the multiple-choice options to participants and requires them to answer (as quickly as possible) that they do not recognise the item. With the traditional CIT employed with the polygraph, senders would answer 'no' to all questions.[13] In a task designed to assess reaction time, repetitively responding 'no' could lead the sender to repetitively press the same button response inattentively and to begin mind wandering. To capture accurate reaction times, the sender needs to be engaged with the task and to respond as quickly and accurately as possible. To mitigate against this attentional issue, a third item type is included in the reaction time-based CIT. These are called 'target' items. These items are explicitly learned ahead of the CIT test being conducted. During the CIT, when they are asked whether they recognise this item, all respondents should respond 'yes' (i.e., that they do recognise the item). Because the questions can no longer be answered accurately by simply responding 'no' to all items, senders will need to attend to the task to respond accurately. Deceptive denials have been shown to result in a longer reaction time (of approximately 60–200 ms longer) compared to truthful denials (Suchotzki et al., 2017; Varga et al., 2014), potentially reflecting that lying is more cognitively demanding than truth-telling (see Chapter 2).

Longer CIT tests increase the ability to determine who holds concealed information and who does not (Lukács, 2022). Relatedly, the CIT is most useful if multiple pieces of concealed information can be tested for so that the guilty knowledge can be linked to this specific crime. The CIT may have limited utility when relatively little evidence about the crime is uniquely available to the investigators (Koller et al., 2022) or when short versions of the test are used.

As alluded to previously, the CIT primarily aims to detect knowledge, not deception. As such, it is unable to distinguish between guilty people, eyewitnesses, or those who have learnt about the details of the case through third-party information such as the media (Bradley et al., 1996). Using this same logic, deceptive senders who fail to encode information about the crime (e.g., because of drug use or memory impairment) may not show evidence of knowledge about the relevant probe items, and so may be indistinguishable from honest and innocent senders.

Another potential limitation of the CIT is its vulnerability to countermeasures (Honts et al., 1996; Rosenfeld et al., 2004; Suchotzki et al., 2017). For example, as with the CQT, pressing one's toes to the floor or counting backwards in sevens reduce the accuracy of the CIT (Honts et al., 1996). To tackle this limitation, Elaad and Ben-Shakhar (2008) have shown that a covert method of measuring respiration (using transducers hidden in the sender's seat) produced similar accuracy rates compared to a more overt respiration belt placed around the chest. Senders may fail to consider the need to countermeasure respiration if they are unaware that it is being captured.

Box 5.5 The Implications of Covert Measurement

It is important for a functioning society and for the victims of crime to ensure that criminals are caught and justice is served. But as Elaad and Ben-Shakhar (2008) note, we must be sensitive to the ethical implications that arise from covert measurement. Is it ethical for police to monitor potentially innocent people without their consent? When we develop lie detection techniques or when we develop any technique intended for wider application, we must be sensitive to the potential ethical and societal implications of our work. But let us not simply abandon the idea of a covert CIT just yet: might there be a way to maintain ethical standards while also measuring covertly? An interesting mitigation

> that the researchers suggested in this particular instance is to obtain consent for a polygraph examination but not to provide detail of all the measurements being taken. In this way, senders are consenting to having their veracity assessed by polygraphic means while allowing for some components of the polygraphic measurements to remain covert.

Summary. In summary, the CQT is the traditional approach used with the polygraph. However, it has been challenged on both a theoretical and empirical front, with national agencies dismissing the approach as lacking practical utility. The CIT has a more scientific theoretical underpinning and has had success in detecting concealed information in laboratory settings. This contrast highlights the need to build applied techniques on a sound, theoretical base, a topic we have discussed in earlier chapters and that will reappear in later chapters. However, the CIT's vulnerability to countermeasures questions whether it is ready for broader application in practice (Vrij & Fisher, 2016). For a discussion of recent developments in detecting concealed information, see Rosenfeld (2018).

Chapter Summary

Receivers score only marginally above chance accuracy when trying to detect who is lying and who is not. Training, life experience, confidence, and other individual factors contribute little to improving detection rates. One possible reason is that liars do not produce reliable cues to deception (Chapter 3), which limits the capacity to improve receivers' lie detection abilities. However, techniques such as CBCA (one part of the SVA) and RM may offer scope for improved detection accuracy. These techniques code for the content of the sender's speech and can achieve accuracy rates of approximately 70%. However, they require training to use and are vulnerable to countermeasures if the liar is aware of how the techniques work.

Given that liars do not produce clear markers of their deception (see Chapter 3), a number of more recent techniques have been developed to try to elicit cues to honesty and deception. The strategic use of information technique proposes that lie detection rates can be improved if the receiver withholds independent evidence that could corroborate or contradict the sender's statement. This is because a liar would not be able to adapt their story to incorporate the known evidence and thus potentially contradict the evidence. This contradiction can then be used to challenge their account.

The cognitive load approach advocates for increasing the thinking effort of liars (e.g., by having to tell the story in reverse chronological order). The technique has had success in improving detection accuracy rates, but there are questions about its theoretical underpinnings and about whether it would also impair truth-tellers' recall. The verifiability approach elicits cues to honesty by encouraging the truth-teller to provide as many checkable details as possible. This method benefits from being difficult, but not impossible, to countermeasure. One final approach discussed here was the BAI which promotes the use of nonverbal behaviours to detect deception, but such an approach has been critiqued on methodological, empirical, and theoretical grounds.

We also reflected on technologically aided approaches. The traditional control question technique used with the polygraph has low accuracy and limited theoretical support, with the British Psychological Society (2004, p. 29) concluding that "even in the most favourable circumstances polygraphic lie detection accuracy is not high". The CIT can also be deployed with the polygraph, but it has broader scientific support and research shows it has the capacity to detect concealed knowledge by detecting a reflexive orienting response to the known information. A comparison of the controlled question test and the CIT highlights the need to build applied techniques on a sound, theoretical base.

The topic of deception detection is vast. There are a number of topics that were not covered in this chapter, such as (i) how to detect medical malingering (Puente-López et al., 2022; Walczyk et al., 2018), (ii) detecting fake news (Khan et al., 2022; Zhou & Zafarani, 2020), (iii) deception in military and intelligence settings (Moffett et al., 2022; Tan et al., 2022), (iv) interview techniques such as the Cognitive Interview (Köhnken et al., 1999), (v) more nascent approaches such as asymmetric information management (Porter et al., 2020), and other topics such as (vi) deterring deception (van't Veer et al., 2014; Yip & Schweitzer, 2015), (vii) detecting deception in groups (Driskell et al., 2012; Marett & George, 2004), and more. This is a fascinating and diverse field that I encourage you to explore more deeply.

Notes

1 Recall from Chapter 4 that people tend to be truth-biased, labelling statements as truths more often than there are truths. In a situation where a person was 100% truth biased, they would correctly judge 100% of truthful statements and 0% of deceptive statements. A less extreme truth bias would result in more truths than lies being correctly judged.
2 You may have noticed the overlap with the Adaptive Lie Detector perspective discussed in Chapter 4.
3 Vrij and Fisher (2016) suggest that lie-truth decisions are not used as evidence in their own right (e.g., as evidence to incarcerate people), but rather as a steer for the investigator to help make decisions about, for example, whether to continue to interview a particular suspect or to follow up on their claims. Nonetheless, one may question whether an almost one in three chance of the investigator being steered down the wrong path is desirable.
4 Hauch et al. (2017), however, conclude that they are unaware of any German experts who rely solely on the CBCA score without the validity checklist.
5 Note that these are a small number of examples rather than an exhaustive list of behaviours that may be taken as indicators of deception or honesty, according to the BAI.

6 While this term is often used to mean 'evidently true', in this instance it is used by the researchers to indicate that it does not differ from opinions that lack scientific data.
7 In a recent review, Wylie et al. (2022) argued that speaking in a non-native language should increase cognitive load and thus lies should be more detectable. However, out of the 13 studies reviewed, only four produced above chance detection rates, five produced below chance detection rates, and the remaining four did not differ from chance detection rate. They contend that these findings are not consistent with the notion that cognitive load increases lie detection accuracy. But it is not clear whether those who can fluently speak their non-native language experience heightened cognitive load compared to when those same people speak their native tongue.
8 Up to this point, the verifiability approach holds the same assumptions about deception as the RM approach.
9 See Nahari et al. (2019) and Vrij (2016) for further discussion of this question.
10 As a worked example, imagine that a liar and a truth-teller produce the same number of non-verifiable details. Let us say that number is ten. Now imagine that the truth-teller provides 15 verifiable details while the liar produces only five. The ratio of verifiable to non-verifiable details is determined by dividing the number of verifiable details by the number of non-verifiable, so the ratio for the truth-teller would be 15 divided by ten, giving a ratio of 1.5 (or 1.5 verifiable details for every one non-verifiable detail). For the liar, the ratio is five divided by ten, giving 0.5 (or 0.5 verifiable details for every one non-verifiable detail).
11 Naturally, we should not simply believe the majority simply because it is predominant, but we may want to consider whether there is a limited evidence base if one approach is rarely explored or whether a particular approach was once predominant but has now fallen out of favour because it has been the subject of extensive falsifying evidence.
12 However, it is worth noting that there has been research finding neurological associates of deception, as discussed in Chapter 2 (e.g., Christ et al., 2009).
13 The reason they would answer 'no' to all questions is because either they are innocent and so truly do not recognise any of the items or because they are guilty and are lying about not recognising them.

References

Aamodt, M. G., & Custer, H. (2006). Who can best catch a liar?: A meta-analysis of individual differences in detecting deception. *The Forensic Examiner, 15*(1), 6–11.

Amado, B. G., Arce, R., Fariña, F., & Vilariño, M. (2016). Criteria-Based Content Analysis (CBCA) reality criteria in adults: A meta-analytic review. *International Journal of Clinical and Health Psychology, 16*(2), 201–210. https://doi.org/10.1016/j.ijchp.2016.01.002

Ambach, W., Stark, R., Peper, M., & Vaitl, D. (2008). Separating deceptive and orienting components in a concealed information test. *International Journal of Psychophysiology, 70*(2), 95–104. https://doi.org/10.1016/j.ijpsycho.2008.07.002

Ben-Shakhar, G. (2002). A critical review of the Control Questions Test (CQT). In M. Kleiner (Ed.), *Handbook of polygraph testing* (pp. 103–126). Academic Press.

Ben-Shakhar, G. (2012). Current research and potential applications of the concealed information test: An overview. *Frontiers in Psychology, 3*, 342. https://doi.org/10.3389/fpsyg.2012.00342

Ben-Shakhar, G., & Elaad, E. (2003). The validity of psychophysiological detection of information with the guilty knowledge test: A meta-analytic review. *Journal of Applied Psychology, 88*(1), 131–151. https://doi.org/10.1037/0021-9010.88.1.131

Blair, J. P., & Kooi, B. (2004). The gap between training and research in the detection of deception. *International Journal of Police Science & Management, 6*(2), 77–83. https://doi.org/10.1350/ijps.6.2.77.34465

Blandón-Gitlin, I., Fenn, E., Masip, J., & Yoo, A. H. (2014). Cognitive-load approaches to detect deception: Searching for cognitive mechanisms. *Trends in Cognitive Sciences, 18*(9), 441–444. https://doi.org/10.1016/j.tics.2014.05.004

Bond, C. F. (2008). A few can catch a liar, sometimes: Comments on Ekman and O'sullivan (1991), As Well As Ekman, O'Sullivan, and Frank (1999). *Applied Cognitive Psychology, 22*, 1298–1300. https://doi.org/10.1002/acp.1475

Bond, C. F., & DePaulo, B. M. (2006). Accuracy of deception judgments. *Personality and Social Psychology Review, 10*(3), 214–234. https://doi.org/10.1207/s15327957pspr1003_2

Bond, C. F., & DePaulo, B. M. (2008). Individual differences in judging deception: Accuracy and bias. *Psychological Bulletin, 134*(4), 477–492. https://doi.org/10.1037/0033-2909.134.4.477

Bond, C. F., & Uysal, A. (2007). On lie detection 'Wizards.' *Law and Human Behavior, 31*(1), 109–115. https://doi.org/10.1007/s10979-006-9016-1

Bradley, M. T., MacLaren, V. V., & Carle, S. B. (1996). Deception and nondeception in guilty knowledge and guilty actions polygraph tests. *Journal of Applied Psychology, 81*(2), 153–160. https://doi.org/10.1037/0021-9010.81.2.153

Brennen, T., & Magnussen, S. (2020). Research on non-verbal signs of lies and deceit: A blind alley. *Frontiers in Psychology, 11*. https://www.frontiersin.org/articles/10.3389/fpsyg.2020.613410

British Psychological Society. (2004). *A review of the current scientific status and fields of application of polygraphic deception detection.* (Report (26 May 2004) from the BPS Working Party). www.bps.org.uk

Buckley, J. P. (2012). Detection of deception researchers needs to collaborate with experienced practitioners. *Journal of Applied Research in Memory and Cognition, 1*(2), 126–127. https://doi.org/10.1016/j.jarmac.2012.04.002

Bunn, G. C. (2012). *The truth machine: A social history of the lie detector* (Illustrated edition). Johns Hopkins University Press.

Cacuci, S.-A., Bull, R., Huang, C.-Y., & Visu-Petra, L. (2021). Criteria-based content analysis in child sexual abuse cases: A cross-cultural perspective. *Child Abuse Review, 30*(6), 520–535. https://doi.org/10.1002/car.2733

Christ, S. E., Van Essen, D. C., Watson, J. M., Brubaker, L. E., & McDermott, K. B. (2009). The contributions of prefrontal cortex and executive control to deception: Evidence from activation likelihood estimate meta-analyses. *Cerebral Cortex, 19*(7), 1557–1566. https://doi.org/10.1093/cercor/bhn189

Cohen, J. T. (2010). Merchants of deception: The deceptive advertising of FMRI lie detection technology note. *Seton Hall Legislative Journal, 35*(1), 158–197.

Dando, C. J., Ormerod, T. C., Wilcock, R., & Milne, R. (2011). When help becomes hindrance: Unexpected errors of omission and commission in eyewitness memory resulting from change temporal order at retrieval? *Cognition, 121*(3), 416–421. https://doi.org/10.1016/j.cognition.2011.06.015

DePaulo, B. M. (1992). Nonverbal behavior and self-presentation. *Psychological Bulletin, 111*(2), 203–243. https://doi.org/10.1037/0033-2909.111.2.203

DePaulo, B. M., Charlton, K., Cooper, H., Lindsay, J. J., & Muhlenbruck, L. (1997). The accuracy-confidence correlation in the detection of deception. *Personality and Social Psychology Review, 1*(4), 346–357. https://doi.org/10.1207/s15327957pspr0104_5

DePaulo, B. M., Lindsay, J. J., Malone, B. E., Muhlenbruck, L., Charlton, K., & Cooper, H. (2003). Cues to deception. *Psychological Bulletin, 129*(1), 74–118.

Driskell, J. E. (2012). Effectiveness of deception detection training: A meta-analysis. *Psychology, Crime & Law, 18*(8), 713–731. https://doi.org/10.1080/1068316X.2010.535820

Driskell, J. E., Salas, E., & Driskell, T. (2012). Social indicators of deception. *Human Factors, 54*(4), 577–588. https://doi.org/10.1177/0018720812446338

Ekman, P., O'Sullivan, M., & Frank, M. (2008). Scoring and reporting: A response to bond. *Applied Cognitive Psychology, 22*, 1315–1317. https://doi.org/10.1002/acp.1474

Elaad, E. (1998). The challenge of the concealed knowledge polygraph test. *Expert Evidence, 6*, 161–187. https://doi.org/10.1023/A:1008855511254

Elaad, E. (2000). Detection of deception. In J. A. Siegel (Ed.), *Encyclopedia of Forensic Sciences* (pp. 550–556). Elsevier. https://doi.org/10.1006/rwfs.2000.0466

Elaad, E., & Ben-Shakhar, G. (2006). Finger pulse waveform length in the detection of concealed information. *International Journal of Psychophysiology, 61*(2), 226–234. https://doi.org/10.1016/j.ijpsycho.2005.10.005

Elaad, E., & Ben-Shakhar, G. (2008). Covert respiration measures for the detection of concealed information. *Biological Psychology, 77*(3), 284–291. https://doi.org/10.1016/j.biopsycho.2007.11.001

Feghali, E. (1997). Arab cultural communication patterns. *International Journal of Intercultural Relations, 21*(3), 345–378. https://doi.org/10.1016/S0147-1767(97)00005-9

Fichman, S., & Altman, C. (2019). Referential cohesion in the narratives of bilingual and monolingual children with typically developing language and with specific language impairment. *Journal of Speech, Language, and Hearing Research, 62*(1), 123–142. https://doi.org/10.1044/2018_JSLHR-L-18-0054

Frank, M. G., & Feeley, T. H. (2003). To catch a liar: Challenges for research in lie detection training. *Journal of Applied Communication Research, 31*(1), 58–75. https://doi.org/10.1080/00909880305377

Gancedo, Y., Fariña, F., Seijo, D., Vilariño, M., Arce, R., Gancedo, Y., Fariña, F., Seijo, D., Vilariño, M., & Arce, R. (2021). Reality monitoring: Una revisión meta-analítica para la práctica forense. *The European Journal of Psychology Applied to Legal Context, 13*(2), 99–110. https://doi.org/10.5093/ejpalc2021a10

Ganis, G., & Patnaik, P. (2009). Detecting concealed knowledge using a novel attentional blink paradigm. *Applied Psychophysiology and Biofeedback, 34*(3), 189–196. https://doi.org/10.1007/s10484-009-9094-1

Ganis, G., Rosenfeld, J. P., Meixner, J., Kievit, R. A., & Schendan, H. E. (2011). Lying in the scanner: Covert countermeasures disrupt deception detection by functional magnetic resonance imaging. *NeuroImage, 55*(1), 312–319. https://doi.org/10.1016/j.neuroimage.2010.11.025

Giles, M., Hansia, M., Metzger, M., & Dunbar, N. E. (2021). The impact of culture in deception and deception detection. In *Detecting trust and deception in group interaction* (pp. 35–54). Springer. https://link.springer.com/chapter/10.1007/978-3-030-54383-9_3

Gilovich, T., Savitsky, K., & Medvec, V. H. (1998). The illusion of transparency: Biased assessments of others' ability to read one's emotional states. *Journal of Personality and Social Psychology*, 75, 332–346. https://doi.org/10.1037/0022-3514.75.2.332

Granhag, P. A., Hartwig, M., Giolla, E. M., & Clemens, F. (2015). Suspects' verbal counter-interrogation strategies: Towards an integrative model. In P. A. Granhag, A. Vrij, & B. Verschuere (Eds.), *Detecting deception: Current challenges and cognitive approaches* (pp. 293–313). Wiley-Blackwell.

Grubin, D., & Madsen, L. (2005). Lie detection and the polygraph: A historical review. *The Journal of Forensic Psychiatry & Psychology*, 16(2), 357–369. https://doi.org/10.1080/14789940412331337353

Gumpert, C. H., & Lindblad, F. (2000). Expert testimony on child sexual abuse: A qualitative study of the Swedish åpproach to statement analysis. *Expert Evidence*, 7(4), 279–314. https://doi.org/10.1023/A:1016657130623

Hartwig, M., & Bond, C. F. (2011). Why do lie-catchers fail? A lens model meta-analysis of human lie judgments. *Psychological Bulletin*, 137(4), 643–659. https://doi.org/10.1037/a0023589

Hartwig, M., Granhag, P. A., & Luke, T. (2014). Strategic use of evidence during investigative interviews: The state of the science. In D. C. Raskin, C. R. Honts, & J. C. Kircher (Eds.), *Credibility assessment: Scientific research and applications* (pp. 1–36). Academic Press. https://doi.org/10.1016/B978-0-12-394433-7.00001-4

Hartwig, M., Granhag, P. A., Strömwall, L. A., & Kronkvist, O. (2006). Strategic use of evidence during police interviews: When training to detect deception works. *Law and Human Behavior*, 30(5), 603–619. https://doi.org/10.1007/s10979-006-9053-9

Hartwig, M., Granhag, P. A., Strömwall, L. A., & Vrij, A. (2005). Detecting deception via strategic disclosure of evidence. *Law and Human Behavior*, 29(4), 469–484. https://doi.org/10.1007/s10979-005-5521-x

Harvey, A. C., Vrij, A., Nahari, G., & Ludwig, K. (2017). Applying the verifiability approach to insurance claims settings: Exploring the effect of the information protocol. *Legal and Criminological Psychology*, 22(1), 47–59. https://doi.org/10.1111/lcrp.12092

Hauch, V., Sporer, S. L., Masip, J., & Blandón-Gitlin, I. (2017). Can credibility criteria be assessed reliably? A meta-analysis of criteria-based content analysis. *Psychological Assessment*, 29, 819–834. https://doi.org/10.1037/pas0000426

Hauch, V., Sporer, S. L., Michael, S. W., & Meissner, C. A. (2016). Does training improve the detection of deception? A meta-analysis. *Communication Research*, 43(3), 283–343. https://doi.org/10.1177/0093650214534974

Hemmer, P., & Steyvers, M. (2009). A Bayesian account of reconstructive memory. *Topics in Cognitive Science*, 1(1), 189–202. https://doi.org/10.1111/j.1756-8765.2008.01010.x

Honts, C. R., Devitt, M. K., Winbush, M., & Kircher, J. C. (1996). Mental and physical countermeasures reduce the accuracy of the concealed knowledge test. *Psychophysiology*, 33(1), 84–92. https://doi.org/10.1111/j.1469-8986.1996.tb02111.x

Honts, C. R., & Kircher, J. C. (1994). Mental and physical countermeasures reduce the accuracy of polygraph tests. *Journal of Applied Psychology*, 79(2), 252–259. https://doi.org/10.1037/0021-9010.79.2.252

Iacono, W., & Lykken, D. (1997). The validity of the lie detector: Two surveys of scientific opinion. *Journal of Applied Psychology*, 82(3), 426–433. https://doi.org/10.1037/0021-9010.82.3.426

Inbau, F. E., & Reid, J. E. (1962). *Criminal interrogation and confessions*. Williams & Wilkins.

Inbau, F. E., Reid, J. E., Buckley, J. P., & Jayne, B. C. (2013). *Criminal interrogation and confessions* (5th ed.). Jones & Bartlett.

Johnson, M. K., & Raye, C. L. (1981). Reality monitoring. *Psychological Review*, 88(1), 67–85. https://doi.org/10.1037/0033-295X.88.1.67

Kassin, S. M. (2005). On the psychology of confessions: Does innocence put innocents at risk? *The American Psychologist*, 60(3), 215–228. https://doi.org/10.1037/0003-066X.60.3.215

Kassin, S. M. (2012). Paradigm shift in the study of human lie-detection: Bridging the gap between science and practice. *Journal of Applied Research in Memory and Cognition*, 1(2), 118–119. https://doi.org/10.1016/j.jarmac.2012.04.009

Kassin, S. M., Leo, R. A., Meissner, C. A., Richman, K. D., Colwell, L. H., Leach, A.-M., & La Fon, D. (2007). Police interviewing and interrogation: A self-report survey of police practices and beliefs. *Law and Human Behavior*, 4, 381–400. https://doi.org/10.1007/s10979-006-9073-5

Kessler, K., & Muckli, L. (2011). Reading others' minds by measuring their brains: Fascinating and challenging for science, but ready for use in court? *Cortex; A Journal Devoted to the Study of the Nervous System and Behavior*, 47(10), 1240–1242. https://doi.org/10.1016/j.cortex.2011.04.019

Khan, A., Brohman, K., & Addas, S. (2022). The anatomy of 'fake news': Studying false messages as digital objects. *Journal of Information Technology*, 37(2), 122–143. https://doi.org/10.1177/02683962211037693

klein Selle, N., Verschuere, B., & Ben-Shakhar, G. (2018). Concealed information test: Theoretical background. In *Detecting concealed information and deception: Recent developments* (pp. 35–57). Elsevier Academic Press. https://doi.org/10.1016/B978-0-12-812729-2.00002-1

Köhnken, G. (2004). Statement validity analysis and the 'detection of the truth'. In *The detection of deception in forensic contexts* (pp. 41–63). Cambridge University Press. https://doi.org/10.1017/CBO9780511490071.003

Köhnken, G., Milne, R., Memon, A., & Bull, R. (1999). The cognitive interview: A meta-analysis. *Psychology, Crime & Law*, 5(1–2), 3–27. https://doi.org/10.1080/10683169908414991

Koller, D., Hofer, F., & Verschuere, B. (2022). Different target modalities improve the single probe protocol of the response time-based concealed information test. *Journal of Applied Research in Memory and Cognition*, 11(1), 135–141. https://doi.org/10.1016/j.jarmac.2021.08.003

Kraut, R. (1980). Humans as lie detectors. *Journal of Communication*, 30(4), 209–218. https://doi.org/10.1111/j.1460-2466.1980.tb02030.x

Lamers-Winkelman, F., & Buffing, F. (1996). Children's testimony in the Netherlands: A study of statement validity analysis. *Criminal Justice and Behavior*, 23(2), 304–321. https://doi.org/10.1177/0093854896023002004

Lane, S. M., & Vieira, K. M. (2012). Steering a new course for deception detection research. *Journal of Applied Research in Memory and Cognition*, 1(2), 136–138. https://doi.org/10.1016/j.jarmac.2012.04.001

Langleben, D. D. (2008). Detection of deception with fMRI: Are we there yet? *Legal and Criminological Psychology*, 13(1), 1–9. https://doi.org/10.1348/135532507X251641

Leal, S., Vrij, A., Vernham, Z., Dalton, G., Jupe, L., Harvey, A., & Nahari, G. (2018). Cross-cultural verbal deception. *Legal and Criminological Psychology*, 23(2), 192–213. https://doi.org/10.1111/lcrp.12131

Levine, T. R. (2010). A few transparent liars explaining 54% accuracy in deception detection experiments. *Annals of the International Communication Association*, 34(1), 41–61. https://doi.org/10.1080/23808985.2010.11679095

Levine, T. R., Daiku, Y., & Masip, J. (2022). The number of senders and total judgments matter more than sample size in deception-detection experiments. *Perspectives on Psychological Science*, 17(1), 191–204. https://doi.org/10.1177/1745691621990369

Levine, T. R., & McCornack, S. A. (2014). Theorizing about deception. *Journal of Language and Social Psychology*, 33(4), 431–440. https://doi.org/10.1177/0261927X14536397

Levine, T. R., Serota, K. B., Shulman, H., Clare, D. D., Park, H. S., Shaw, A. S., Shim, J. C., & Lee, J. H. (2011). Sender demeanor: Individual differences in sender believability have a powerful impact on deception detection judgments. *Human Communication Research*, 37(3), 377–403. https://doi.org/10.1111/j.1468-2958.2011.01407.x

Lukács, G. (2022). Prolonged response time concealed information test decreases probe-control differences but increases classification accuracy. *Journal of Applied Research in Memory and Cognition*, 11(2), 188–199.

Luke, T. J. (2019). Lessons from Pinocchio: Cues to deception may be highly exaggerated. *Perspectives on Psychological Science*, 14(4), 646–671. https://doi.org/10.1177/1745691619838258

Lykken, D. T. (1960). The validity of the guilty knowledge technique: The effects of faking. *Journal of Applied Psychology*, 44(4), 258–262. https://doi.org/10.1037/h0044413

Lykken, D. T. (1998). *Tremor in the Blood—Uses and Abuses of the Lie Detector*. Plenum Press. https://www.ojp.gov/ncjrs/virtual-library/abstracts/tremor-blood-uses-and-abuses-lie-detector

Mac Giolla, E., & Luke, T. J. (2021). Does the cognitive approach to lie detection improve the accuracy of human observers? *Applied Cognitive Psychology*, 35(2), 385–392. https://doi.org/10.1002/acp.3777

Maier, B. G., Niehaus, S., Wachholz, S., & Volbert, R. (2018). The strategic meaning of CBCA criteria from the perspective of deceivers. *Frontiers in Psychology*, 9. https://www.frontiersin.org/articles/10.3389/fpsyg.2018.00855

Marett, L. K., & George, J. F. (2004). Deception in the case of one sender and multiple receivers. *Group Decision and Negotiation*, 13(1), 29–44. https://doi.org/10.1023/B:GRUP.0000011943.73672.9b

Masip, J., Barba, A., & Herrero, C. (2012). Behaviour analysis interview and common sense: A study with novice and experienced officers. *Psychiatry, Psychology and Law*, 19(1), 21–34. https://doi.org/10.1080/13218719.2010.543402

Masip, J., & Herrero, C. (2015). New approaches in deception detection I. Background and theoretical framework. *Papeles Del Psicólogo*, 36, 83–95.

Masip, J., Herrero, C., Garrido, E., & Barba, A. (2011). Is the behaviour analysis interview just common sense? *Applied Cognitive Psychology*, 25, 593–604. https://doi.org/10.1002/acp.1728

Masip, J., Sporer, S. L., Garrido, E., & Herrero, C. (2005). The detection of deception with the reality monitoring approach: A review of the empirical evidence. *Psychology, Crime & Law*, 11(1), 99–122. https://doi.org/10.1080/10683160410001726356

Moffett, L., Oxburgh, G. E., Dresser, P., Watson, S. J., & Gabbert, F. (2022). Inside the shadows: A survey of UK human source intelligence (HUMINT) practitioners, examining their considerations when handling a covert human intelligence source (CHIS). *Psychiatry, Psychology and Law, 29*(4), 487–505. https://doi.org/10.1 080/13218719.2021.1926367

Nahari, G. (2018). The applicability of the verifiability approach to the real world. In *Detecting concealed information and deception: Recent developments* (pp. 329–349). Elsevier Academic Press. https://doi.org/10.1016/B978-0-12-812729-2.00014-8

Nahari, G. (2019). Verifiability approach: Applications in different judgmental settings. In T. Docan-Morgan (Ed.), The Palgrave Handbook of Deceptive Communication (pp. 213–225). Palgrave Macmillan https://doi.org/10.1007/978-3-319-96334-1_11

Nahari, G., Ashkenazi, T., Fisher, R. P., Granhag, P., Hershkowitz, I., Masip, J., Meijer, E. H., Nisin, Z., Sarid, N., Taylor, P. J., Verschuere, B., & Vrij, A. (2019). 'Language of lies': Urgent issues and prospects in verbal lie detection research. *Legal and Criminological Psychology, 24*(1), 1–23. https://doi.org/10.1111/lcrp.12148

Nahari, G., & Pazuelo, M. (2015). Telling a convincing story: Richness in detail as a function of gender and information. *Journal of Applied Research in Memory and Cognition, 4*(4), 363–367. https://doi.org/10.1016/j.jarmac.2015.08.005

Nahari, G., & Vrij, A. (2014). Are you as good as me at telling a story? Individual differences in interpersonal reality monitoring. *Psychology, Crime & Law, 20*(6), 573–583. https://doi.org/10.1080/1068316X.2013.793771

Nahari, G., Vrij, A., & Fisher, R. P. (2014). Exploiting liars' verbal strategies by examining the verifiability of details. *Legal and Criminological Psychology, 19*(2), 227–239. https://doi.org/10.1111/j.2044-8333.2012.02069.x

National Research Council, Committe to Review the Scientific Evidence on the Polygraph, & Division of Behavioral and Social Sciences and Education. (2003). *The polygraph and lie detection*. National Academies Press. https://nap.nationalacademies.org/initiative/committee-to-review-the-scientific-evidence-on-the-polygraph

Nortje, A., & Tredoux, C. (2019). How good are we at detecting deception? A review of current techniques and theories. *South African Journal of Psychology, 49*(4), 491–504. https://doi.org/10.1177/0081246318822953

Oberlader, V. A., Naefgen, C., Koppehele-Gossel, J., Quinten, L., Banse, R., & Schmidt, A. F. (2016). Validity of content-based techniques to distinguish true and fabricated statements: A meta-analysis. *Law and Human Behavior, 40*(4), 440–457. https://doi.org/10.1037/lhb0000193

Osugi, A. (2018). Field findings from the concealed information test in Japan. In J. P. Rosenfeld (Ed.), Detecting Concealed Information and Deception *Detecting concealed information and deception: Recent developments* (pp. 97–121). Elsevier Academic Press. https://doi.org/10.1016/B978-0-12-812729-2.00005-7

O'Sullivan, M. (2007). Unicorns or tiger woods: Are lie detection experts myths or rarities? A response to on lie detection 'wizards' by Bond and Uysal. *Law and Human Behavior, 31*(1), 117–123. https://doi.org/10.1007/s10979-006-9058-4

O'Sullivan, M. (2008). Home runs and humbugs: Comment on Bond and DePaulo (2008). *Psychological Bulletin, 134*(4), 493–497. https://doi.org/10.1037/0033-2909.134.4.493

O'Sullivan, M., & Ekman, P. (2004). The wizards of deception detection. In *The detection of deception in forensic contexts* (pp. 269–286). Cambridge University Press. https://doi.org/10.1017/CBO9780511490071.012

Palena, N., Caso, L., Vrij, A., & Nahari, G. (2021). The verifiability approach: A meta-analysis. *Journal of Applied Research in Memory and Cognition*, *10*(1), 155–166. https://doi.org/10.1037/h0101785

Patrick, C. J., & Iacono, W. G. (1989). Psychopathy, threat, and polygraph test accuracy. *Journal of Applied Psychology*, *74*(2), 347–355. https://doi.org/10.1037/0021-9010.74.2.347

Porter, C. N., Morrison, E., Fitzgerald, R. J., Taylor, R., & Harvey, A. C. (2020). Lie-detection by strategy manipulation: Developing an asymmetric information management (AIM) technique. *Journal of Applied Research in Memory and Cognition*, *9*(2), 232–241. https://doi.org/10.1016/j.jarmac.2020.01.004

Puente-López, E., Pina, D., López-López, R., Ordi, H. G., Bošković, I., & Merten, T. (2022). Prevalence estimates of symptom feigning and malingering in Spain. *Psychological Injury and Law*. https://doi.org/10.1007/s12207-022-09458-w

Reid, R. E. (1947). A revised questioning technique in lie-detection tests. *The Journal of Criminal Law and Criminological Sciences*, *37*(6), 542–547.

Rosenfeld, J. P. (Ed.). (2018). *Detecting concealed information and deception*. Academic Press.

Rosenfeld, J. P., Soskins, M., Bosh, G., & Ryan, A. (2004). Simple, effective countermeasures to P300-based tests of detection of concealed information. *Psychophysiology*, *41*(2), 205–219. https://doi.org/10.1111/j.1469-8986.2004.00158.x

Santtila, P., Roppola, H., & Niemi, P. (1998). Assessing the truthfulness of witness statements made by children (Aged 7—8, 10—11, and 13—14) employing scales derived from Johnson and Raye's model of reality monitoring. *Expert Evidence*, *6*(4), 273–289. https://doi.org/10.1023/A:1008930821076

Simons, J. S., Garrison, J. R., & Johnson, M. K. (2017). Brain mechanisms of reality monitoring. *Trends in Cognitive Sciences*, *21*(6), 462–473. https://doi.org/10.1016/j.tics.2017.03.012

Softley, P., Brown, D., Forde, B., Mair, G., & Moxon, D. (1980). *Police Interrogation: An Observational Study in Four Police Stations*. HMSO. https://www.ojp.gov/ncjrs/virtual-library/abstracts/police-interrogation-observational-study-four-police-stations-0

Sokolov, E. N. (1963). *Perception and the conditioned reflex*. Macmillan.

Spence, S. A. (2008). Playing Devil's advocate†: The case against fMRI lie detection. *Legal and Criminological Psychology*, *13*(1), 11–25. https://doi.org/10.1348/135532507X251597

Sporer, S. L. (1997). The less travelled road to truth: Verbal cues in deception detection in accounts of fabricated and self-experienced events. *Applied Cognitive Psychology*, *11*, 373–397. https://doi.org/10.1002/(SICI)1099-0720(199710)11:5<373::AID-ACP461>3.0.CO;2-0

Sporer, S. L., Manzanero, A. L., & Masip, J. (2021). Optimizing CBCA and RM research: Recommendations for analyzing and reporting data on content cues to deception. *Psychology, Crime & Law*, *27*(1), 1–39. https://doi.org/10.1080/1068316X.2020.1757097

Stanley, M. L., Taylor, M. K., & Marsh, E. J. (2021). Cultural identity changes the accessibility of knowledge. *Journal of Applied Research in Memory and Cognition*, *10*(1), 44–54. https://doi.org/10.1016/j.jarmac.2020.07.008

Steller, M., & Köhnken, G. (1989). Criteria-based statement analysis: Credibility assessment of children's statements in sexual abuse cases. In D. C. Raskin (Ed.), *Psychological methods for investigation and evidence* (pp. 217–245). Springer.

Stromwall, L. A., & Granhag, P. A. (2005). Children's repeated lies and truths: Effects on adults' judgments and reality monitoring scores. *Psychiatry, Psychology and Law, 12*(2), 345–356. https://doi.org/10.1375/pplt.12.2.345

Suchotzki, K., Verschuere, B., Van Bockstaele, B., Ben-Shakhar, G., & Crombez, G. (2017). Lying takes time: A meta-analysis on reaction time measures of deception. *Psychological Bulletin, 143*(4), 428–453. https://doi.org/10.1037/bul0000087

Tan, Y., Liu, J., & Wang, J. (2022). How to protect key drones in unmanned aerial vehicle networks? An SDN-based topology deception scheme. *IEEE Transactions on Vehicular Technology*, 1–13. https://doi.org/10.1109/TVT.2022.3200339

Taylor, P. J., Larner, S., Conchie, S. M., & van der Zee, S. (2015). Cross-cultural deception detection. In P. A. Granhag, A. Vrij, & B. Verschuere (Eds.), *Detecting deception: Current challenges and cognitive approaches* (pp. 175–201). Wiley-Blackwell.

Tekin, S., Granhag, P. A., Strömwall, L., Giolla, E. M., Vrij, A., & Hartwig, M. (2015). Interviewing strategically to elicit admissions from guilty suspects. *Law and Human Behavior, 39*(3), 244–252. https://doi.org/10.1037/lhb0000131

van't Veer, A. E., Stel, M., & van Beest, I. (2014). Limited capacity to lie: Cognitive load interferes with being dishonest. *Judgment and Decision Making, 9*(3), 199–206.

Varga, M., Visu-Petra, G., Miclea, M., & Buş, I. (2014). The RT-based concealed information test: An overview of current research and future perspectives. *Procedia – Social and Behavioral Sciences, 127*, 681–685. https://doi.org/10.1016/j.sbspro.2014.03.335

Verschuere, B., Bogaard, G., & Meijer, E. (2021). Discriminating deceptive from truthful statements using the verifiability approach: A meta-analysis. *Applied Cognitive Psychology, 35*(2), 374–384. https://doi.org/10.1002/acp.3775

Verschuere, B., Crombez, G., Koster, E. H. W., & De Clercq, A. (2007). Antisociality, underarousal and the validity of the concealed information polygraph test. *Biological Psychology, 74*(3), 309–318. https://doi.org/10.1016/j.biopsycho.2006.08.002

Volbert, R., & Steller, M. (2014). Is this testimony truthful, fabricated, or based on false memory? Credibility assessment 25 years after Steller and Köhnken (1989). *European Psychologist, 19*(3), 207–220. https://doi.org/10.1027/1016-9040/a000200

Vrij, A. (2008). *Detecting lies and deceit: Pitfalls and opportunities*, 2nd ed (pp. xiii, 488). John Wiley & Sons Ltd.

Vrij, A. (2015). Verbal lie detection tools: Statement validity analysis, reality monitoring and scientific content analysis. In P. A. Granhag, A. Vrij, & B. Verschuere (Eds.), *Detecting deception: Current challenges and cognitive approaches* (pp. 3–35). Wiley-Blackwell.

Vrij, A. (2016). Baselining as a lie detection method. *Applied Cognitive Psychology, 30*(6), 1112–1119. https://doi.org/10.1002/acp.3288

Vrij, A., Akehurst, L., Soukara, S., & Bull, R. (2002). Will the truth come out? The effect of deception, age, status, coaching, and social skills on CBCA scores. *Law and Human Behavior, 26*(3), 261–283. https://doi.org/10.1023/A:1015313120905

Vrij, A., Edward, K., & Bull, R. (2001). Stereotypical verbal and nonverbal responses while deceiving others. *Personality and Social Psychology Bulletin, 27*(7), 899–909. https://doi.org/10.1177/0146167201277012

Vrij, A., & Fischer, A. (1996). The role of displays of emotions and ethnicity in judgments of rape victims. *International Review of Victimology, 4*(4), 255–265. https://doi.org/10.1177/026975809700400402

Vrij, A., Fisher, R., Mann, S. A., & Leal, S. (2008). A cognitive load approach to lie detection. *Journal of Investigative Psychology and Offender Profiling, 5*(1–2), 39–43. https://doi.org/10.1002/jip.82

Vrij, A., & Fisher, R. P. (2016). Which lie detection tools are ready for use in the criminal justice system? *Journal of Applied Research in Memory and Cognition, 5*(3), 302–307. https://doi.org/10.1016/j.jarmac.2016.06.014

Vrij, A., Fisher, R. P., & Blank, H. (2017). A cognitive approach to lie detection: A meta-analysis. *Legal and Criminological Psychology, 22*(1), 1–21. https://doi.org/10.1111/lcrp.12088

Vrij, A., & Granhag, P. A. (2012). Eliciting cues to deception and truth: What matters are the questions asked. *Journal of Applied Research in Memory and Cognition, 1*(2), 110–117. https://doi.org/10.1016/j.jarmac.2012.02.004

Vrij, A., Leal, S., Granhag, P. A., Mann, S., Fisher, R. P., Hillman, J., & Sperry, K. (2009). Outsmarting the liars: The benefit of asking unanticipated questions. *Law and Human Behavior, 33*(2), 159–166. https://doi.org/10.1007/s10979-008-9143-y

Vrij, A., Mann, S. A., Fisher, R. P., Leal, S., Milne, R., & Bull, R. (2008). Increasing cognitive load to facilitate lie detection: The benefit of recalling an event in reverse order. *Law and Human Behavior, 32*(3), 253–265. https://doi.org/10.1007/s10979-007-9103-y

Vrij, A., Mann, S., & Fisher, R. P. (2006). An empirical test of the behaviour analysis interview. *Law and Human Behavior, 30*(3), 329–345. https://doi.org/10.1007/s10979-006-9014-3

Walczyk, J. J., Sewell, N., & DiBenedetto, M. B. (2018). A review of approaches to detecting malingering in forensic contexts and promising cognitive load-inducing lie detection techniques. *Frontiers in Psychiatry, 9*. https://doi.org/10.3389/fpsyt.2018.00700

Wang, Q., Song, Q., & Kim Koh, J. B. (2017). Culture, memory, and narrative self-making. *Imagination, Cognition and Personality, 37*(2), 199–223. https://doi.org/10.1177/0276236617733827

Wylie, K., Pena, M. M., Miller, K. B., Palmer, M. E., & Tate, E. (2022). *Observers' accuracy in detecting deception in non-native speakers versus native speakers: A systematic review.* https://doi.org/10.1002/jip.1595

Yip, J. A., & Schweitzer, M. E. (2015). Trust promotes unethical behavior: Excessive trust, opportunistic exploitation, and strategic exploitation. *Current Opinion in Psychology, 6*, 216–220. https://doi.org/10.1016/j.copsyc.2015.09.017

Zhou, X., & Zafarani, R. (2020). A survey of fake news: fundamental theories, detection methods, and opportunities. *ACM Computing Surveys, 53*(5), 109:1–109:40. https://doi.org/10.1145/3395046

Zuckerman, M., DePaulo, B. M., & Rosenthal, R. (1981). Verbal and nonverbal communication of deception. In L. Berkowitz (Ed.), *Advances in experimental social psychology* (Vol. 14, pp. 1–59). Academic Press. https://doi.org/10.1016/S0065-2601(08)60369-X

Zvi, L., Nachson, I., & Elaad, E. (2012). Effects of coping and cooperative instructions on guilty and informed innocents' physiological responses to concealed information. *International Journal of Psychophysiology, 84*(2), 140–148. https://doi.org/10.1016/j.ijpsycho.2012.01.022

6 Developmental Factors in Deception and Lie Detection

> **Box 6.1 Adolescent False Confession**
>
> Michael Crowe was a 14-year-old who confessed to murdering his 12-year-old sister. In 1998, when the crime was committed, Michael was interrogated for 27 hours over a period of three days. Police coerced a confession from Michael using questionable interviewing techniques, including deceiving the suspect. Michael was later acquitted of the charge and another person, Richard Tuite, was convicted of manslaughter based on DNA evidence of blood found on Tuite's clothing. Research on exoneration cases such as this found that 75% of juveniles between ages 12 and 15 years falsely confessed (Gross et al., 2005). A film titled *The Interrogation of Michael Crowe* was released in 2002.

We do not like it when people lie to us: we feel emotional when we discover we have been lied to (McCornack & Levine, 1990) and we choose to retribute against those who lie to us even if that may create some financial loss for ourselves (e.g., Boles et al., 2000). Perhaps this is why we teach children that lying is wrong (Lavoie et al., 2016).[1] And yet, the capacity to lie is an important developmental marker signalling a capacity to manage complex ideas, inhibit information, and understand the minds and thoughts of others (e.g., Lee, 2013; Polak & Harris, 1999). How do children develop a capacity and understanding of when and how to lie?

First Lies

The first deceptions children employ are to hide something that they should not have done (a 'transgression') or to avoid being punished. These lies have been observed in preschool children as young as two years old (Evans & Lee, 2013; Sodian et al., 1991; Wilson et al., 2003). For example, Wilson et al. (2003) found that 65% of two-year-olds told a lie in an observational study of children at home. Two-year-olds have also been found to spontaneously

DOI: 10.4324/9781003045298-6

lie in experimental settings. In one study, 41 two-year-olds and 24 three-year-olds took part in a 'temptation-resistance paradigm', a commonly used method for eliciting deception from children (Evans & Lee, 2013). The temptation-resistance paradigm involves leaving the child alone in a room with an unknown toy and asking them not to peek at the toy while the experimenter has left the room. On the experimenter's return, the child is asked whether they had looked at the toy. Approximately 25% of two-year-olds lied about not peeking if they had in fact peeked, while the majority of three-year-olds lied (Evans & Lee, 2013).

By age four, lie-telling is reliably being used by children with an aim to avoid punishment (Foster et al., 2020; Reddy, 2007). Children begin to reliably lie at this age across cultures (see Talwar & Crossman, 2011), and lying to conceal wrongdoing is one of the most common types of lie among children (Wilson et al., 2003). As they reach age four to five, their lies become more complex. They develop a capacity to lie not only to hide something they have done wrong, but to begin to mislead others in order to keep a prize for themselves (i.e., their lies can be self-benefiting as well as cost-avoiding; Sodian et al., 1991). At age six and seven, lying becomes more persistent (Gervais et al., 2000). They are not only able to conceal the truth, but also produce outright lies such as claiming that they were lucky or unusually capable of determining the correct answer to hide their previous cheating (Hu et al., 2020). Before this age, children are more likely to simply let their true intentions slip by stating them explicitly (Talwar, Gordon, et al., 2007). That is, as children age, their lies become more plausible, with an ability to maintain their deception when questioned about it (Gongola et al., 2017; Talwar, Murphy, et al., 2007).

To test the ability to maintain deception, four-, six- and eight-year-old children privately viewed a playing card and then had to give a hint to the experimenter as to the card's colour (red or black) by pointing at one of two face-up cards placed on the table (Smith & LaFreniere, 2013). Four-year-olds readily revealed the truth more often than six-year-olds, who, in turn, were more likely to reveal the truth than eight-year-olds. The older groups (11 eight-year-olds and 16 six-year-olds) were more likely to give false clues to the experimenter than four-year-olds (only one four-year-old did so) and to vary their strategy in how they would try to deceive compared to four-year-olds.

But the change towards more complex lying is thankfully accompanied by another developmental change: as children get older, they shift from telling lies for selfish reasons towards lying for more prosocial reasons (Lavoie et al., 2017; Talwar et al., 2019). A longitudinal study—a study that involves observing or testing the same participants over a period of time—aimed to explore how children's deceptions evolved as they aged. One hundred and twenty-seven children aged three to six years were measured at the first time point of the study ('time 1') and were measured a second time (at 'time 2') approximately two years later (aged 5–8). There was a tendency to tell fewer antisocial lies as children got older and to tell more prosocial lies (Talwar et al., 2019). The shift towards prosocial lying may reflect the development of moral reasoning with age. As children get older, they shift from focusing on self-centred gains to other-centred benefits (Eisenberg et al., 2014).

> **Box 6.2 Alternative Interpretations of Findings**
>
> Reflect on the findings of Talwar et al. (2019) for a moment. The decrease in antisocial lying and increase in prosocial lying with age may reflect a more nuanced moral reasoning that develops with age. How else might we interpret these findings? Take a moment to consider alternative explanations. You may wish to consider other developmental changes that may be taking place, socialisation practices between adults and children that may adjust as the child becomes older, personality development, and more. Do not worry too much about whether your suggestions are plausible at this stage. Just come up with an idea for an alternative explanation.
>
> We will explore an alternative interpretation outside of this Box in just a moment. Taking the time to consider different viewpoints is what allows for cogent and robust arguments to be made with a full view of what the data may be telling us. That is, the data may be telling us that a moral development may be occurring, but there may be other explanations that need considering too. If you take the time to reflect on alternative interpretations in an assessment, you can expect that your grades will likely improve. After all, what your lecturers want to see in you is an ability to generate sound, novel arguments that move forward our understanding of human psychology.
>
> Hopefully you have now found a potentially alternative explanation, but do not stop your reasoning at this point. It is great to be able to generate these ideas and then propose them for future research to explore. But it is even better to find some existing research that has already explored the plausibility of your suggestion. Moving your idea that next step forward will likely see you rewarded in your grades. You will also be rewarding yourself in terms of developing your own capacity to reason ideas through to their full conclusion.

Talwar et al. (2019) considered an alternative explanation of the shift from selfish to prosocial lying: as children age, their social skills also develop (see Soto-Icaza et al., 2015, for a review of the neural and behavioural development of social skills). Being more capable of interacting with others may help children recognise the utility of lying for polite reasons or for sparing the feelings of others (e.g., DePaulo et al., 1996). Consistent with this social development interpretation, empathy plays a role in the production of prosocial lies (Nagar et al., 2020; L. Xu et al., 2019) as does being able to understand the causes, consequences, and nature of emotions (Demedardi et al., 2021). However, this is not to say that children choose never to tell lies to benefit themselves. Selfish lies peak in the teenage years and become less common with age (Talwar & Crossman, 2011).

A developmental model of lying has been put forward to unify these developmental shifts into a framework (Talwar & Lee, 2008). The model will act as a useful summary of this section. The model proposes three phases of lying. Primary lies are the earliest lies that children tell at around age two to three. They are relatively simple counterfactual statements that do not consider the beliefs and mental reasoning of the person they are lying to. While lying is infrequent at this age (Wilson et al., 2003), primary lies typically involve concealing a transgression (Polak & Harris, 1999). Secondary lies appear at around age three to four years and involve lies that require an understanding that another person may hold a different set of beliefs and understanding to themselves (Chandler et al., 1989). This understanding is known as a 'first-order belief'. Lying becomes more prevalent at this age, but they may have difficulty maintaining consistency with their initial lie when prompted for further detail, thereby giving away that they lied (Talwar & Lee, 2002). Finally, tertiary lies appear at around age seven to eight years. These lies are more sophisticated and plausible insofar as children of this age are able to maintain consistency with their initial lie (Evans & Lee, 2011; Talwar & Lee, 2008). Whereas secondary lies involve an understanding of another person's thoughts and beliefs being different to one's own, tertiary lies require an ability to comprehend 'second-order belief'. Children who are capable of this are able to understand what another person believes about the child's beliefs (Talwar & Lee, 2008).[2] As such, tertiary lies are difficult to distinguish from truthful statements (see Chapter 5 for more on the difficulty of detecting deception).

Developing a Capacity for Deception

As alluded to in Talwar and Lee's (2008) model of deception development, an ability to comprehend that other people may hold different thoughts from the liar is an important component of being able to lie. This is also required of our definition of deception, namely making others believe something different to what the liar believes (see Chapter 2). The capacity to reason about the mental states of others is known as 'theory of mind' (Baron-Cohen et al., 2000). In particular, it is the false belief component (that others can hold beliefs about the world that are wrong) which is especially important for deception. That this capacity is needed for deception aligns with research on children with autism spectrum disorder, who have been found to have difficulty with theory of mind (Baron-Cohen, 2000). These children could enjoy a game of hiding a penny from another person who was guessing which hand the penny was in, but had difficulty recognising that it was also a game of deception and hiding information (Baron-Cohen, 1992). They either kept both hands open so the guesser could see the coin, hid the coin in one hand while the guesser was watching, or verbally gave away the penny's location.

Additionally, given the requirement of our definition of deception in Chapter 2 that deception involves producing a statement that is known not to be true, cognitive skills that involve inhibiting truthful information and manipulating information in working memory are needed to deceive. That is, effective deception will require a developed executive functioning (i.e., the high-level cognitive processes that facilitate new ways of behaving and optimise one's approach to unfamiliar circumstances; Evans et al., 2011; Polak & Harris, 1999). Let us first consider the development of theory of mind and return to the issue of a developing executive function later.

Eighteen-month-olds have been shown in one study to have a primitive theory of mind (Moll & Tomasello, 2007). In their study, Moll and Tomasello (2007) had an experimenter experience two toys with the child. The experimenter came to learn the identity of these toys either by playing with the toy together with the child (joint engagement), by playing with the toy alone while the child watched (individual engagement), or by watching the child playing with the toy alone (onlooking). The three conditions represent increasing psychological distance between the child and the experimenter, which may require a more developed theory of mind to appropriately understand the mental states of the other person. The experimenter then left the room and the child played with a third toy on their own. This way, the experimenter would be unaware of the identity of the third toy, and an infant with theory of mind would be able to determine of which of the toys the experimenter knew the identity.

After playing with this third toy and it being placed on a tray with the other two toys, the experimenter returned and, gesturing broadly to the tray, excitedly said "Oh, look! Look there! Look at that there! Give it to me, please!". The researchers reasoned that if children could represent the experimenter's mental states and so be aware that the third toy was novel to the experimenter, this is the toy that they would choose to give to the experimenter. Before we explore the results, read Box 6.3.

Box 6.3 Considering Multiple Effects for a Given Cause

In Box 1.4 (Chapter 1) and Box 3.4 (Chapter 3) we reflected on why it is important to consider different possible interpretations of an effect. Doing so benefits yourself and the field. It develops your capacity to evaluatively reason. In the short term, this will improve your assessment grades and in the longer term will give you a unique insight into difficult problems that others have not yet been able to address (or to reinterpret the data to propose different solutions to a problem). The field is moved forward by academics who develop these novel

(Continued)

propositions, test them with past research and new data, and thereby offer new theoretical and/or practical insights. Let us extend our skills into seeking alternative outcomes from a given cause.

Imagine that Moll and Tomasello's (2007) study involves only two conditions: a condition where the experimenter and child jointly play with the toy (joint engagement) and one in which the experimenter only watches the child playing with the toy (onlooking). Let us assume for the moment that choosing to pass the novel third toy to the experimenter evidences that they understand that the experimenter wants the child to pass to them the toy they have not seen before, and so is a measure of theory of mind. Assume also that we are concerned only with whether the number of novel toy passes differs between the two conditions, ignoring the size of the difference between the conditions. What is the full range of possible results that could be observed? Take a moment to think about this.

There are three possible outcomes: the child passes the novel toy more often after joint play compared to onlooking, the child passes the novel toy more often after onlooking compared to joint play, and the child passes the novel toy equally often after onlooking and joint play. How might we interpret each of these three possible results in terms of whether 18-month-olds have developed a theory of mind? Remember that there is an increased psychological distance between the child and the experimenter for onlooking, while the joint engagement condition helps to scaffold theory of mind through joint attentional interaction.

Take a few moments just to briefly consider what we would learn about 18-month-old theory of mind if each of these three results were found. Engaging in this form of reasoning develops your capacity to examine the research methodologies of others and to assess whether and how each of the possible results would be consistent with or falsify a particular account. Recall in Box 2.4 (Chapter 2) we discussed that for an account to be useful, it needs to be falsifiable. If all the results would be consistent with a particular perspective (e.g., that 18-month-olds have a theory of mind), we can question whether this methodology is a good test of the research question. After all, if all the results give the same conclusion, why bother running the experiment? Taking the time to explore the interpretation of the range of possible outcomes helps us to evaluate whether the experiment is a good test of the account.

The first possible outcome (more passes of the novel object for joint engagement compared to onlooking) is likely the easiest for which to find a psychological explanation: 18-month-olds have a limited theory of mind such that they require it to be scaffolded by joint attentional interaction. The second outcome (more passes of the novel object in the onlooking condition) is perhaps the most unusual. Such a finding could suggest that infants have a theory of mind but are distracted by joint attentional activities. You may find alternative interpretations.

However, in both cases, we would want to consider the pattern of the data: if children rarely pass the novel object in one condition and never pass it in the other condition, it may be difficult to claim that any theory of mind is being evidenced here because regardless of the condition the number of novel passes was very low. If the children regularly pass the novel object in at least one of the conditions, the claim that they hold a theory of mind appears more defensible. This consideration will also hold for the third possible outcome (equal passing of the novel object): it will depend to some extent on the pattern of the data as to whether one would wish to claim that they have theory of mind (shown by equally high frequencies passing of the novel toy) or do not have theory of mind (shown by equally low frequencies of passing the novel toy). Deciding whether the number of passes is 'high' or 'low' may be somewhat a subjective academic judgement where different researchers may reach different conclusions.

After reading the introduction and method sections of a research paper, we have an understanding of what the research question is and how that was tested. It is useful at this point to reflect on what possible results could be generated. Would all the possible results support the account being tested? If so, the study is not a test of the account at all (see Box 2.4, Chapter 2). Would the results falsify one account if they showed X but falsify a different account if they showed not X? If so, they are only comparing those two accounts and not ruling out other alternatives. These are the easier cases to deal with, but more typically the situation is not so straightforward (as above).

These questions should not solely be directed at other researchers' work. Reflecting on how the results *could* look will be especially important when you are designing your own research (perhaps as part of a dissertation). Considering the full array of patterns that the results could possibly show will ensure that your study is not set up for failure from the outset. For example, a study where all possible results would be consistent with the theory is not a useful study. The data will not teach us anything because we know what the interpretations of the results are before we even collect the data, namely that the theory will be 'supported'.

You may also have discovered while reading this Box that thinking about the study at this level of detail gives insights into alternative psychological interpretations of the data (e.g., that the difference between the conditions may reflect that one condition is distracted and resulting in lower novel toy passing rates rather than that one condition is showing more cognitive maturity resulting in higher novel toy passing rates). Indeed, as you read the results outside of this Box, you may want to ask yourself whether a distraction explanation could be applied to the results to reach a rather different interpretation of the findings. This is another example of what I called concrete reasoning in Chapter 3 (Box 3.2), and I hope you can see how delving deeper into the issues can give interesting new insights.

The researchers found that 18-month-olds passed the novel toy to the experimenter (taken as an indicator of theory of mind) when the experimenter jointly engaged with the toddler or when the experimenter was seen by the toddler playing with the two other toys. But they were less likely to pass the novel third toy (suggesting difficulties with theory of mind) when the experimenter watched the toddler alone playing with the two other toys. This evidence suggests that toddlers may have a primitive form of theory of mind at this young age, provided that it is scaffolded by joint attentional engagement.

An elaborated theory of mind begins to appear at around age four,[3] where the child is capable of representing a false belief about reality alongside their own correct belief about reality (i.e., a first-order belief; Wimmer & Perner, 1983). In a study of first-order false belief, Klafka and Liszkowski (2022) found that four-year-olds who were able to pass a false belief task lied more often when the receiver held a true belief about reality than when they held a false belief. This suggests that children were using their theory of mind to mislead the receiver only when they understood that the receiver held true information about the world (and allowed receivers with false information about the world to continue with their incorrect belief). With training on the concept of theory of mind and others' mental states, children as young as three begin to use deception consistently (Ding et al., 2015).

But to be an effective liar and to be able to maintain the plausibility of a lie, children need to develop an ability to represent second-order false beliefs (see previous section) so that they can mentally represent the false belief that the receiver holds about the child's own beliefs. Understanding what it is the receiver thinks about the child's understanding of reality is needed in order to maintain a lie (Hsu & Cheung, 2013; Talwar, Gordon, et al., 2007). A review by Miller (2009) found that second-order false belief representation appears at around age five to six, but sometimes earlier or later than this depending on the experimental method used to assess its presence.

Box 6.4 How Might We Measure Second-Order False Belief?

If you had to design a method to test whether young children can hold second-order false beliefs, what might you try? Have a think about this before continuing. Begin with a basic idea and then tailor it to capture children's beliefs about other's beliefs. Perhaps telling a story to the child about other people who hold false beliefs about events may be a good starting point. Keeping the story simple and easy to understand is also likely to aid the child's understanding. The story could even be made tangible by acting it out.

Having a story play out that involves people holding false beliefs could then be followed by a question about what one or both of those people should believe. But young children may have difficulty answering questions about the beliefs of others despite being able to mentally represent those beliefs. They may struggle with the complexity and abstracted nature of the question. Perhaps simplifying the question by asking the child what the person in the story would do in a situation could be a simpler and more concrete way to capture their understanding of that person's beliefs.

Baron-Cohen et al. (1999) developed the 'second-order Sally-Anne task' based on a discussion with the Spanish psychologist Angel Revière. Two dolls, Sally and Anne, are used to depict a scene to the child. Sally puts her marble in a basket in full view of Anne. Sally then leaves. In her absence, Anne takes the marble from the basket and hides it in a box. Unbeknownst to Anne, Sally is watching this through the keyhole. With this setup, Sally can understand that Anne holds the false belief that Sally will mistakenly look in the basket for her marble (a second-order belief). The question is whether the child can also hold this second-order belief. To assess this, children are asked, "Where does Anne think that Sally will look for her marble?". If the child can engage in second-order false belief representation, they should answer that Anne will think that Sally will look in the basket, because Anne mistakenly believes that the last time Sally saw the marble was when Sally placed it in her basket.

This is not the only way to capture second-order beliefs: you may have come up with a different but equally valid idea (or maybe an even better idea). Thinking about these design issues gives you experience of how we might progress from a broad psychological concept into a practical research design that we could employ. We made this transition by (informally) considering the implications of possible design decisions on our ability to capture useful data. When designing research, there is an element of using one's academic expertise about the challenges of collecting data, but we need to ensure that this is based in your knowledge of the research literature and your understanding of robust research design.

It is at around age six that lies do indeed become more plausible and are difficult to distinguish from truths. This is consistent with the position that effective deception requires second-order false belief understanding (Talwar & Lee, 2002). Children who score higher on second-order false belief tasks are more effective at maintaining their lies (Talwar, Gordon, et al., 2007; Talwar et al., 2017). They may also be more likely to use prosocial lying (Broomfield et al., 2002), with antisocial lying being related to lower scores on theory of mind tasks (Lavoie et al., 2017).[4]

Executive function (e.g., inhibiting information, planning, managing multiple pieces of information in working memory) also plays an important role in the capacity to lie (see Chapters 2 and 5 for similar arguments regarding adults' deceptions). It develops in children from around the end of children's first year (Fiske & Holmboe, 2019). Inhibition, an element of executive function, is especially relevant to lying, given that lying involves the need to suppress knowledge of the truth. In a study by Carlson et al. (1998), three-year-olds were shown a ball placed in one of two boxes. The experimenter suggested playing a 'funny trick' on another person who was currently not in the room (which we will call the guesser) and to mislead them about where the ball was hidden. Participant children were assigned to one of two conditions. In one condition, the guesser entered the room and the child was asked to point at which box the ball was in. Children would have to inhibit the truth and choose to point at the incorrect box. In a second condition, the experimenter explained that a picture of a ball was similar to the one put in the box, and the child could affix the picture to one of the boxes to indicate that the ball was in that box while the guesser was out of the room. Because the deception happened both in isolation of and in advance of the guesser's presence, the difficulty of inhibiting information was reduced. Three-year-olds chose to lie more frequently in the picture-based low inhibition condition than in the pointing-based condition requiring a more developed capacity for inhibiting the truth. Similar evidence comes from research showing that children (M_{age} = 31.75 months, SD = 1.87) with higher scores on a measure of inhibitory control lied more frequently in a temptation resistance paradigm (Williams et al., 2017).

These findings show that both theory of mind and executive function are predictors of the emergence of deception. In a ten-session study with 2.5-year-old children playing a game against an adult to win treats, by the final session most children discovered and used deception to win (Ding et al., 2017). Both theory of mind and executive function skills were predictors of how early children would discover deception to be an effective strategy. Carlson and Moses (2001) found that the ability to inhibit information may have a causal effect on, and so may be a prerequisite of, the development of theory of mind. In another study, children aged between four and 11 years old created a gift for their caregiver as a secret for them (Lavoie & Talwar, 2020). Afterwards, the caregiver asked the child about what they had been doing. Those with lower theory of mind and working memory scores were less likely to be able to keep the secret.

In summary, the capacity to lie requires an ability to understand that others can hold false beliefs (theory of mind) and a capacity to inhibit true information while also manipulating information to develop a lie (making use of executive function). Executive function begins to emerge at around one year of age and may be required before a theory of mind begins to develop. A rudimentary theory of mind has been found in 18-month-olds, but it is not until around age four that children develop a matured first-order false belief understanding. At around age six, second-order false belief understanding develops, at which stage children are able to produce lies that they are able to maintain when further probed.

Why Children Lie

As we have seen, children begin to tell fewer antisocial lies and tell more prosocial lies as they enter primary education (Talwar et al., 2019; F. Xu et al., 2010). For instance, children at around age six and seven consider the feelings of other people when deciding whether to tell them a white lie by pretending to like a disappointing gift (Popliger et al., 2011). Western children come to view prosocial lying as more acceptable than lies that have no prosocial component to them (Heyman et al., 2009), while Cheung et al. (2015) found that Chinese children come to view prosocial lies as morally good at around age nine (see also Ma et al., 2011). Thus, there appears to be a moral component to children's decision to lie, as Talwar and Lee (2008) have shown in their work.

Such a position is consistent with findings showing that just like adults (see Chapter 2), teenagers show an aversion to lying. That is, children of age ten and above choose not to lie even when doing so would offer them the most gain, with the likelihood of lying decreasing as they get older (Glätzle-Rützler & Lergetporer, 2015). Younger children may also engage in moral reasoning when deciding whether to lie. Hays and Carver (2014) brought children from one room to another either with the truth or a lie. One hundred and eighty-six children aged three to seven participated. In one condition, children were told that there were sweets in the next room and asked the child if they wanted to get some. On arriving, the experimenter revealed their lie, explaining that there were no sweets and that they just wanted to coax the child into the room to play a game with them. In another condition, the children were told truthfully that there was a game to play next door and asked if they wanted to play, with no lie about sweets. Afterwards, the children were engaged in the temptation resistance paradigm. The older children who were lied to by the experimenter were more likely to peek and to lie about having peeked, which the researchers suggested may indicate that children can use social imitation to inform their moral judgements. Similar interpretations have been made of findings showing that observing others benefit from being honest promotes honesty in children (Ma et al., 2018).[5] For further discussion of a morality framework for understanding children's decisions to lie, see Foster et al. (2020).

Thus far, the implicit assumption is that there are universal standards that determine children's decision to lie (i.e., a moral code). But children's frequency of lie-telling is not consistent and can vary based on the situation or even change over time given the same situation (see Talwar et al., 2019). In a study by Thijssen et al. (2017), eight-year-old children took part in a prediction task while in a functional magnetic resonance imaging (fMRI) scanner. Their task was to predict which of two pictured dogs would be given a bone. Children made their prediction privately and only indicated whether they were correct or incorrect after seeing which dog received the bone. They were financially rewarded for each correct prediction they claimed to have made. This constituted the low-risk condition. In a high-risk version, children were told that the experimenters could determine if the child was lying using the fMRI scanner. Approximately 74% of children lied in the low-risk condition, but when they believed that their lies were readily detectable, this dropped to 43%. While there were still a substantial number of children lying in the high-risk condition, this was smaller than the low-risk condition. The findings suggest that children consider the context in which their claims are being made when deciding whether to lie (see Talwar et al., 2019, for comparable findings indicating that children consider the consequences of their lies).

One may imagine that chronic lying—that is, frequent antisocial lying—may be less situationally determined. Chronic lying may be a precursor to the development of problematic pathological lying where children may come not to care about the antisocial consequences of their lies (Mugno et al., 2019; Stouthamer-Loeber & Loeber, 1986).[6] Chronic lying may onset at around age seven (Gervais et al., 2000; Talwar & Crossman, 2011). There is a link between chronic lying in children and their disruptive behaviour (as rated by their teachers and mothers; Gervais et al., 2000), being less socially accepted by other children (Rotenberg et al., 2005), as well as fighting and stealing (Ostrov, 2006; Stouthamer-Loeber & Loeber, 1986), even among three-year-olds (Ostrov et al., 2008). And offenders convicted after age 21 have been found to be 10% more likely to have lied frequently in class as a teenager compared to non-offenders (Farrington et al., 2009). Children with behaviour disorders may lie for selfish gains more frequently than typically developing children (Lavoie et al., 2018; Mugno et al., 2019), but unfortunately frequent lying can lead to them being socially excluded (Tyler et al., 2006).

Talwar and Crossman (2011) proposed that chronic lying may in part be a result of cognitive immaturity.[7] By failing to learn prosocial behaviours that could resolve a situation, the child may rely on more impulsive and less considered behaviours such as lying. But they also acknowledge that this interacts with the child's disposition and social experiences. Regarding disposition, children with better social skills are more likely to lie for selfish reasons (Lavoie et al., 2017). And with regard to socialisation, being a child in a controlling family and excessive discipline may encourage deception as a solution to an otherwise socially dominating environment (Jensen et al., 2004; Talwar & Lee, 2011).

For example, Talwar and Lee (2011) studied three- and four-year-old children in two West African schools in the same neighbourhood: one that used an authoritarian, punitive form of discipline (e.g., slapping the child and using a stick to administer physical punishment) and one that used non-punitive scolding and timeouts as a form of discipline. Using the temptation-resistance paradigm—where children are instructed not to peek at a toy in the experimenter's absence and are later asked about whether they had peeked—it was found that children were not only approximately 12 times more likely to lie if they were attending the punitive school, but were also five times more likely to conceal their peeking by giving an incorrect but plausible answer when they then had to guess the identity of the toy once it was hidden under a cloth. That is, punitive environments do not discourage lying: they may have the ironic effect of increasing children's effectiveness at lying.

In summary, as children age, there is a shift away from lying for self-gain and towards more prosocial and altruistic lies. As with adults, young people also show an aversion to lying, suggesting a moral component to the decision. While the moral component may give the impression that there is a fixed threshold that determines whether a child will lie or not, there is an adaptive element to children's lying that is contingent on the situation. For instance, children will lie more frequently in situations with lower risk of getting caught, and children with greater social skills tend to lie more frequently. Lying frequently for antisocial reasons can become chronic, which may predict behaviour problems, and may be a result of a combination of the situation, the child's disposition, and an authoritarian environment that they are raised in. For discussion of why adults lie, see Chapter 2.

Box 6.5 Finding the Links

As you consider what you have read in this chapter and continue to read in the remainder of the chapter, reflect on what you already understand about why and how adults lie. Is there a developmental profile linking what is known about adult's lying and what we are seeing here regarding children's lying? Are there apparent inconsistencies? Evaluating our understanding of human thinking and behaviour in a more holistic sense, rather than treating each chapter in isolation, will provide a more informed understanding of the psychology of deception and lie detection.

Development of Children's Understanding of Deception

Children of age four are capable of recognising deception when clear evidence of falsity is presented (Bussey & Grimbeek, 2000). Although when it comes to understanding that people can hide less tangible and directly verifiable information like their internal mental states, a capability to recognise deception may not appear until as late as five years old (Wellman & Liu, 2004). These younger children tend to interpret truths as good and lies as bad (Bussey & Grimbeek, 2000), although they may interpret some prosocial lies more favourably than selfish lies (Bussey, 1999). By age seven, lies are more consistently considered good when the motive of the lie is prosocial (Heyman et al., 2009). This shift from interpreting all lies as bad to evaluating the goodness of lies depending on the motive is related to higher scores on second-order theory of mind tasks. This implies that the moral valuation of lies may involve reflecting on others' mental states (Cheung et al., 2015).

As with many other areas of deception detection that we have visited thus far in the book, there may be cultural differences in how children evaluate deception. In Taiwan and China, showing modesty for one's accomplishments is valued over promoting oneself. Across the course of development between ages seven and 11, Taiwanese and Chinese children come to positively value lying for reasons that conceal one's own achievements, but Canadian and American children viewed lying about one's own good deeds negatively regardless of age (Cameron et al., 2012; Fu et al., 2001, 2010; Lee et al., 1997, 2001). Cheung et al. (2015) found that children from Hong Kong aged seven to 11 years considered lies to be bad when the motive was selfish, but when it was prosocial the badness of the lie depended on what they lied about. Lies about reality were less favourably viewed by children than lies about opinion. Other cultural differences in the moral evaluation of lies between Russian, American, and Korean children have been observed (see Griffin & Bender, 2019).

In the studies of lie evaluation above, the experimental materials explicitly indicate that a lie was told. Are children capable of trusting those who tell the truth and distrusting those who do not when they are not explicitly informed of who is lying? Studies find that children as young as three keep track of who has previously given accurate and inaccurate information when learning from them (Birch et al., 2008; Brosseau-Liard et al., 2014; Eskritt et al., 2008; Rakoczy et al., 2009). For instance, in a study of 96 participants, four- and five-year-olds learned about the reliability of two adults: one who was accurate but lacking confidence and another who was inaccurate but confident in their response (Brosseau-Liard et al., 2014). On test trials, the two adults described an unusual animal (such as a lanternfish or a pygmy sloth) that the child had no prior experience with. The two adults then gave a name to the animal (e.g., the accurate adult claimed, "It's called a lanternfish", while the inaccurate adult claimed, "It's called a paddlefish"). Children were more likely to accept the answer of the accurate adult who had low confidence over the answer of the inaccurate adult who had high confidence. Such findings suggest that children are sensitive to the past reliability of others and are not easily duped by the apparent confidence of the sender. At this same age, they are also more willing to trust information from a kind puppet (one who strokes the experimenter) compared to a mean puppet (one who hits the experimenter) (Mascaro & Sperber, 2009).

Note, however, that these findings do not show an ability to detect deception: they show that children use past reliability to adaptively inform their decisions about what information is more likely to be correct. Using our understanding of the world to make informed decisions about what information to trust is known as 'epistemic vigilance' (Sperber et al., 2010). As Levy (2022) puts it, "Trust is ... very valuable. But in trusting, we expose ourselves to risks of harm and betrayal. It is therefore important to trust well". Epistemic vigilance is trusting well. At age four, children are able to understand that a character that has always lied should not be trusted when they claim which of two boxes a sweet is hidden inside (Mascaro & Sperber, 2009). And by age six, they are capable of inferring that a character may have a deceptive intent based on the character's disposition to be mean (Mascaro & Sperber, 2009). Indeed, children of five and six (but not of three or four) can use the plausibility of a claim (e.g., that a ghost jumped out of a book and broke a glass) based on their understanding of reality to infer that the sender was lying (Lee et al., 2002).

In summary, four-year-olds are capable of understanding the concept of lying when the statement is inconsistent with physical reality. While they tend to view lying as bad and truth-telling as good, as children develop second-order theory of mind they are more accepting of prosocial lying. Young children also have the capacity to make use of simple, generalised rules about the benevolence of the sender, for example, to decide what information to trust. By age six to seven, they may infer that a sender has a deceptive intent on the basis of their past behaviour and plausibility of the statement.

Detecting and Preventing Children's Lies

If you have read Chapter 5, you will be aware that adults are able to detect other adults' lies and truths with around 54% accuracy, where 50% would be achieved in the long run by random guessing (Bond & DePaulo, 2006). One might imagine that detecting a child's lie would be easier. After all, we have seen how children are still developing theory of mind and cognitive control. A recent meta-analysis found that adults were able to detect the youngest children's lies and truths (aged three to five: 60% accuracy) more accurately than six- to nine-year-olds (57%) and more accurately again than 10- to 15-year-olds (53%: Gongola et al., 2017), consistent with the position that children become more skilled liars as they age. But overall, adult's ability to detect children's lies and truths was at 54% (Gongola et al., 2017). It would seem that adults are not especially capable of detecting children's lies in comparison to adults' lies. Also aligning with what is seen in the judgement of adults' lies (see Chapter 4), Gongola et al.'s (2017) meta-analysis found that judgements of children's lies were truth-biased (i.e., adults made more 'truth' judgements than 'lie' judgements when rating children's statements).

Professionals are generally no more accurate than laypeople. Chahal and Cassidy (1994) found that social workers, teachers, and students did not differ in their ability to detect the lies of adolescents. Another study found that police officers, social workers, teachers, and students did not differ in their ability to detect the lies of five- to six-year-olds, with an accuracy of around 60% (Vrij et al., 2006). And police officers, customs officers, and students were unable to detect the lies of three- to 11-year-olds (Leach et al., 2004). In the Gongola et al. (2017) meta-analysis, professionals detected children's lies with 56% accuracy while laypeople achieved 54% accuracy. There is little evidence to suggest that professionals may be any better than laypeople, consonant with what is known about adult lie detection ability (e.g., Aamodt & Custer, 2006).

As was seen in Chapter 5, a number of techniques have been developed for detecting deception in adults, such as criteria-based content analysis (CBCA; Steller & Köhnken, 1989), reality monitoring (RM; Johnson & Raye, 1981), and the strategic use of evidence (SUE; Hartwig et al., 2005). See Chapter 5 for an overview of these methods.

CBCA has seen some success in distinguishing children's lies from truths. For example, a study of children between seven and 11 years old was able to distinguish with 70% accuracy between those who had told the truth about having taken part in a photography session and those who had lied about having taken part (Akehurst et al., 2001). But CBCA could not distinguish between those children who were telling the truth about having taken part in the session compared with those who had not taken part but had seen a video of the session. Others have found that CBCA can distinguish between lying and truth-telling children between the ages of five and 15 in limited circumstances (Vrij et al., 2002). CBCA failed to distinguish liars and truth-tellers across all but the youngest age group if the deceptive children were coached to provide CBCA criteria in order to appear honest (Vrij et al., 2002). Finally, given that there are differences in parenting styles, cognitions, and motivations across culture, the presence or absence of CBCA criteria in statements may also depend on the cultural background of the child (see Cacuci et al., 2021). Vrij et al. (2002) cautioned practitioners about employing CBCA with children.

RM has had some success in separating truthful from deceptive accounts, but only for older children. For instance, Strömwall and Granhag (2005) found that the presence of RM criteria could distinguish between 11-year-olds' lies and truths and Granhag et al. (2006) found that RM (but not CBCA) could distinguish 12–13-year-olds' lies and truths. In a direct comparison of younger (three to eight years old) and older children (nine to 16 years old), Roberts and Lamb (2010) found that older children's lies could be detected with RM, but not younger children's lies (see also Santtila et al., 1998, for similar findings with children aged seven to 14 years).

Johnson et al. (1979) have found that eight-year-olds are capable are distinguishing externally generated memories (resulting from experience, and thus should include relatively high levels of perceptual and spatial details) from internally generated memories (resulting from imagination, and so should have relatively fewer such details). Six-year-olds have greater difficulty making this distinction (Markham, 1991), which may explain why younger children's lies and truths are difficult to distinguish with RM. For further consideration of the role of RM in detecting children's lies, see Sporer (2004).

Similarly, SUE has also seen some success with older children. Lingwood and Bull (2013) found that disclosing evidence late in the interview (compared with towards the start of the interview) allowed better separation between the lies and truths of 12–14-year-olds about committing a mock crime. Truth-tellers gave more detail and liars gave less detail with late disclosure of evidence. Another study found that children in the same age range were more inconsistent with the evidence when lying compared to truth-telling but that this was amplified when the evidence was disclosed late in the interview (Clemens et al., 2010) as per the recommendations of the SUE technique. However, the research in this area appears somewhat limited both in terms of number of published studies and the span of ages explored. Further studies along with replications (see Chapter 8) would allow more confidence in the use of SUE with children.

Perhaps better than detection is prevention. As we have seen, strongly punitive and authoritarian environments (which one may expect could deter deception) have the effect of *increasing* the skill with which children lie (Talwar & Lee, 2011). Given that parenting styles differ across culture (e.g., collectivistic cultures tend towards teaching a respect for authority and rules; Cacuci et al., 2021), one may speculate that there may be cultural differences in children's deception skill. In any case, punishing children for lying does not appear to be a successful strategy for preventing lying.

Asking children to promise to tell the truth may be more effective in promoting honesty, though (Talwar et al., 2002, 2004). In one study, parents broke a puppet and children aged three to 11 years old were asked to not tell anyone (Talwar et al., 2004). Children who promised to tell the truth before they were questioned about what happened to the puppet were significantly more likely to tell the truth compared to those who did not make the same promise. Relatedly, listening to morality tales that show how being honest results in positive outcomes (e.g., a father's love for an honest child) may also promote honesty (Lee et al., 2014; see also Talwar et al., 2016), while seeing other children confess to cheating encourages five-year-olds to also confess to their wrongdoing (Ma et al., 2018; Sai et al., 2020).

In summary, adults achieve around 54% lie-truth detection accuracy when judging children and tend to judge that they are telling the truth rather than judge that they are lying (i.e., they show a truth bias). And professionals are no more adept than lay adults. These findings are consistent with experiments using adult senders (see Chapter 5). CBCA has seen limited success in detecting lying in 11-year-olds: some have warned that the technique may not be ready for deployment with children. RM and SUE have also seen some success with children of this age, but more research is needed to ensure that the findings thus far are replicable and to better understand the situations in which they are effective. Finally, asking children to promise not to lie has been shown to have some success in reducing lying and promoting honesty in children.

Chapter Summary

Children tell their first or primary lies at around two years of age with the intention to conceal wrongdoing. This is an age at which a primitive form of theory of mind may be observed. These primary lies tend to be simple counterfactuals. At around age four, they develop a first-order theory of mind that allows them to understand that the mental states of others can differ from one's own. These secondary lies are more complex, but children tend to have difficulty maintaining the lies when further questioned about them. By around age seven, lies become difficult to detect insofar as the child is able to maintain the lie with further probing. The developmental model of deception calls these tertiary lies. At around this same age, children develop second-order theory of mind or a capacity to represent another person's beliefs about the child's own beliefs. Their lies at this age tend to shift away from antisocial reasons that benefit themselves and towards more prosocial reasons that benefit others. To lie effectively, not only is a theory of mind required but so too is an executive function (a cognitive capacity to inhibit information, to develop plans, and to manipulate multiple pieces of information in working memory).

As with adults, children also show an aversion to lying and consider the morality of doing so before they choose to lie. But lying that becomes overly frequent and used for antisocial reasons, or chronic lying, can develop. Chronic lying has been found to be associated with behavioural problems. The causes may be a result of a combination of cognitive immaturity, the child's own disposition, and living in an authoritarian and overly strict environment. Adults' ability to detect children's lying is similar to their ability to detect other adults' lies, with accuracy only marginally above chance and exhibiting a truth bias. Techniques developed for detecting deception in adults, such as CBCA, RM, and SUE, have had some but limited success in detecting the lies of children, but further research is needed.

Finally, children may employ an epistemic vigilance from a young age to infer what information can be trusted. Friendly people are considered trustworthy sources at a young age, but as the child reaches around age six, they are capable of using the sender's past behaviour to infer deception.

Notes

1 While parents may discourage their children from lying, many parents (84% in the US and 98% in China) lie to their children (Heyman et al., 2013).
2 For example, the child may hold a belief that Stephen (person A) incorrectly believes that the child (person B) believes that the toy is hidden in the basket (but perhaps in reality the child has hidden the toy in the cupboard). That is, they are able to hold the belief that Stephen should be successfully deceived into believing that the child's claim of the location of the toy is where they are incorrectly claiming it is.
3 It is worth noting at this point that there are cultural effects that can influence the development of theory of mind and false belief understanding (e.g., Duh et al., 2016).
4 You may wish to consider whether there may be another explanation as to why antisocial lying is related to lower theory of mind, such as whether antisocial lying reflects a slower development more generally. This generalised underdevelopment could include both an underdeveloped moral understanding (which could be the true cause of more antisocial lying) as well as an underdeveloped theory of mind. That is, one need not be causing the other, but both may have a

common cause. The researchers consider such an explanation in the discussion of their research paper.
5 However, younger children's understanding that lying is wrong is unrelated to their decision to lie (Lee, 2013), suggesting that morality may only play a role in older children's lying behaviour.
6 See Chapter 2 for more on pathological lying.
7 For a suggestion that morality may instead be a causal force in chronic lying, see Foster et al. (2020).

References

Aamodt, M. G., & Custer, H. (2006). Who can best catch a liar?: A meta-analysis of individual differences in detecting deception. *The Forensic Examiner, 15*(1), 6–11.

Akehurst, L., Köhnken, G., & Höfer, E. (2001). Content credibility of accounts derived from live and video presentations. *Legal and Criminological Psychology, 6*, 65–83. https://doi.org/10.1348/135532501168208

Baron-Cohen, S. (1992). Out of sight or out of mind? Another look at deception in Autism. *Journal of Child Psychology and Psychiatry, 33*(7), 1141–1155. https://doi.org/10.1111/j.1469-7610.1992.tb00934.x

Baron-Cohen, S. (2000). Theory of mind and autism: A review. In *International Review of Research in Mental Retardation* (Vol. 23, pp. 169–184). Academic Press. https://doi.org/10.1016/S0074-7750(00)80010-5

Baron-Cohen, S., O'Riordan, M., Stone, V., Jones, R., & Plaisted, K. (1999). Recognition of faux pas by normally developing children and children with Asperger syndrome or high-functioning autism. *Journal of Autism and Developmental Disorders, 29*(5), 407–418. https://doi.org/10.1023/a:1023035012436

Baron-Cohen, S., Tager-Flusberg, H., & Cohen, D. J. (2000). *Understanding other minds: Perspectives from developmental cognitive neuroscience.* Oxford University Press.

Birch, S. A. J., Vauthier, S. A., & Bloom, P. (2008). Three- and four-year-olds spontaneously use others' past performance to guide their learning. *Cognition, 107*(3), 1018–1034. https://doi.org/10.1016/j.cognition.2007.12.008

Boles, T. L., Croson, R. T. A., & Murnighan, J. K. (2000). Deception and retribution in repeated ultimatum bargaining. *Organizational Behavior and Human Decision Processes, 83*(2), 235–259. https://doi.org/10.1006/obhd.2000.2908

Bond, C. F., & DePaulo, B. M. (2006). Accuracy of deception judgments. *Personality and Social Psychology Review, 10*(3), 214–234. https://doi.org/10.1207/s15327957pspr1003_2

Broomfield, K. A., Robinson, E. J., & Robinson, W. P. (2002). Children's understanding about white lies. *British Journal of Developmental Psychology, 20*, 47–65. https://doi.org/10.1348/026151002166316

Brosseau-Liard, P., Cassels, T., & Birch, S. (2014). You seem certain but you were wrong before: Developmental change in Preschoolers' relative trust in accurate versus confident speakers. *PLOS ONE, 9*(9), e108308. https://doi.org/10.1371/journal.pone.0108308

Bussey, K. (1999). Children's categorization and evaluation of different types of lies and truths. *Child Development, 70*, 1338–1347. https://doi.org/10.1111/1467-8624.00098

Bussey, K., & Grimbeek, E. J. (2000). Children's conceptions of lying and truth-telling: Implications for child witnesses. *Legal and Criminological Psychology, 5*, 187–199. https://doi.org/10.1348/135532500168083

Cacuci, S.-A., Bull, R., Huang, C.-Y., & Visu-Petra, L. (2021). Criteria-based content analysis in child sexual abuse cases: A cross-cultural perspective. *Child Abuse Review*, *30*(6), 520–535. https://doi.org/10.1002/car.2733

Cameron, C. A., Lau, C., Fu, G., & Lee, K. (2012). Development of children's moral evaluations of modesty and self-promotion in diverse cultural settings. *Journal of Moral Education*, *41*(1), 61–78. https://doi.org/10.1080/03057240.2011.617414

Carlson, S. M., & Moses, L. J. (2001). Individual differences in inhibitory control and children's theory of mind. *Child Development*, *72*(4), 1032–1053. https://doi.org/10.1111/1467-8624.00333

Carlson, S. M., Moses, L. J., & Hix, H. R. (1998). The role of inhibitory processes in young children's difficulties with deception and false belief. *Child Development*, *69*(3), 672–691.

Chahal, K., & Cassidy, T. (1994). Deception and its detection in children: A Study of adult accuracy. *Psychology, Crime & Law*, *1*(3), 237–245. https://doi.org/10.1080/10683169508411959

Chandler, M., Fritz, A. S., & Hala, S. (1989). Small-scale deceit: Deception as a marker of two-, three-, and four-year-olds' early theories of mind. *Child Development*, *60*, 1263–1277. https://doi.org/10.2307/1130919

Cheung, H., Siu, T.-S. C., & Chen, L. (2015). The roles of liar intention, lie content, and theory of mind in children's evaluation of lies. *Journal of Experimental Child Psychology*, *132*, 1–13. https://doi.org/10.1016/j.jecp.2014.12.002

Clemens, F., Granhag, P. A., Strömwall, L. A., Vrij, A., Landström, S., Hjelmsäter, E. R. af, & Hartwig, M. (2010). Skulking around the dinosaur: Eliciting cues to children's deception via strategic disclosure of evidence. *Applied Cognitive Psychology*, *24*(7), 925–940. https://doi.org/10.1002/acp.1597

Demedardi, M.-J., Brechet, C., Gentaz, E., & Monnier, C. (2021). Prosocial lying in children between 4 and 11 years of age: The role of emotional understanding and empathy. *Journal of Experimental Child Psychology*, *203*, 105045. https://doi.org/10.1016/j.jecp.2020.105045

DePaulo, B. M., Kashy, D. A., Kirkendol, S. E., Wyer, M. M., & Epstein, J. A. (1996). Lying in everyday life. *Journal of Personality and Social Psychology*, *70*(5), 979–995. https://doi.org/10.1037/0022-3514.70.5.979

Ding, X. P., Heyman, G. D., Fu, G., Zhu, B., & Lee, K. (2017). Young children discover how to deceive in 10 days: A microgenetic study. *Developmental Science*, *21*(3), e12566. https://doi.org/10.1111/desc.12566

Ding, X. P., Wellman, H. M., Wang, Y., Fu, G., & Lee, K. (2015). Theory-of-mind training causes honest young children to lie. *Psychological Science*, *26*(11), 1812–1821. https://doi.org/10.1177/0956797615604628

Duh, S., Paik, J., Miller, P., ChenWu Gluck, S., Li, H., & Himelfarb, I. (2016). Theory of mind and executive function in Chinese preschool children. *Developmental Psychology*, *52*. https://doi.org/10.1037/a0040068

Eisenberg, N., Hofer, C., Sulik, M. J., & Liew, J. (2014). The development of prosocial moral reasoning and a prosocial orientation in young adulthood: Concurrent and longitudinal correlates. *Developmental Psychology*, *50*, 58–70. https://doi.org/10.1037/a0032990

Eskritt, M., Whalen, J., & Lee, K. (2008). Preschoolers can recognize violations of the Gricean maxims. *The British Journal of Developmental Psychology*, *26*(3), 435–443. https://doi.org/10.1348/026151007X253260

Evans, A. D., & Lee, K. (2011). Verbal deception from late childhood to middle adolescence and its relation to executive functioning skills. *Developmental Psychology, 47*(4), 1108–1116. https://doi.org/10.1037/a0023425

Evans, A. D., & Lee, K. (2013). Emergence of lying in very young children. *Developmental Psychology, 49*(10), 1958–1963. https://doi.org/10.1037/a0031409

Evans, A. D., Xu, F., & Lee, K. (2011). When all signs point to you: Lies told in the face of evidence. *Developmental Psychology, 47*, 39–49. https://doi.org/10.1037/a0020787

Farrington, D. P., Ttofi, M. M., & Coid, J. W. (2009). Development of adolescence-limited, late-onset, and persistent offenders from age 8 to age 48. *Aggressive Behavior, 35*(2), 150–163. https://doi.org/10.1002/ab.20296

Fiske, A., & Holmboe, K. (2019). Neural substrates of early executive function development. *Developmental Review, 52*, 42–62. https://doi.org/10.1016/j.dr.2019.100866

Foster, I., Wyman, J., & Talwar, V. (2020). Moral disengagement: A new lens with which to examine children's justifications for lying. *Journal of Moral Education, 49*(2), 209–225. https://doi.org/10.1080/03057240.2019.1656057

Fu, G., Brunet, M. K., Lv, Y., Ding, X., Heyman, G. D., Cameron, C. A., & Lee, K. (2010). Chinese children's moral evaluation of lies and truths-roles of context and parental individualism-collectivism tendencies. *Infant and Child Development, 19*(5), 498–515. https://doi.org/10.1002/icd.680

Fu, G., Lee, K., Cameron, C. A., & Xu, F. (2001). Chinese and Canadian adults' categorization and evaluation of lie- and truth-telling about prosocial and antisocial behaviors. *Journal of Cross-Cultural Psychology, 32*, 720–727. https://doi.org/10.1177/0022022101032006005

Gervais, J., Tremblay, R. E., Desmarais-Gervais, L., & Vitaro, F. (2000). Children's persistent lying, gender differences, and disruptive behaviours: A longitudinal perspective. *International Journal of Behavioral Development, 24*, 213–221. https://doi.org/10.1080/016502500383340

Glätzle-Rützler, D., & Lergetporer, P. (2015). Lying and age: An experimental study. *Journal of Economic Psychology, 46*, 12–25. https://doi.org/10.1016/j.joep.2014.11.002

Gongola, J., Scurich, N., & Quas, J. A. (2017). Detecting deception in children: A meta-analysis. *Law and Human Behavior, 41*(1), 44–54. https://doi.org/10.1037/lhb0000211

Granhag, P. A., Strömwall, L. A., & Landström, S. (2006). Children recalling an event repeatedly: Effects on RM and CBCA scores. *Legal and Criminological Psychology, 11*(1), 81–98. https://doi.org/10.1348/135532505X49620

Griffin, D. J., & Bender, C. (2019). Culture and deception: The influence of language and societies on lying. In T. Docan-Morgan (Ed.), *The palgrave handbook of deceptive communication* (pp. 67–89). Springer International Publishing. https://doi.org/10.1007/978-3-319-96334-1_4

Gross, S. R., Jacoby, K., Matheson, D. J., Montgomery, N., & Patil, S. (2005). Exonerations in the United States, 1989 Through 2003. *Journal of Criminal Law and Criminology, 95*(2), 523–560.

Hartwig, M., Granhag, P. A., Strömwall, L. A., & Vrij, A. (2005). Detecting deception via strategic disclosure of evidence. *Law and Human Behavior, 29*(4), 469–484. https://doi.org/10.1007/s10979-005-5521-x

Hays, C., & Carver, L. J. (2014). Follow the liar: The effects of adult lies on children's honesty. *Developmental Science, 17*(6), 977–983. https://doi.org/10.1111/desc.12171

Heyman, G. D., Hsu, A. S., Fu, G., & Lee, K. (2013). Instrumental lying by parents in the US and China. *International Journal of Psychology, 48*, 1176–1184. https://doi.org/10.1080/00207594.2012.746463

Heyman, G. D., Sweet, M. A., & Lee, K. (2009). Children's reasoning about lie-telling and truth-telling in politeness contexts. *Social Development, 18*(3), 728–746. https://doi.org/10.1111/j.1467-9507.2008.00495.x

Hsu, Y. K., & Cheung, H. (2013). Two mentalizing capacities and the understanding of two types of lie telling in children. *Developmental Psychology, 49*, 1650–1659. https://doi.org/10.1037/a0031128

Hu, C., Huang, J., Wang, Q., Weare, E., & Fu, G. (2020). Truthful but misleading: Advanced linguistic strategies for lying among children. *Frontiers in Psychology, 11.* https://www.frontiersin.org/articles/10.3389/fpsyg.2020.00676

Jensen, L. A., Arnett, J. J., Feldman, S. S., & Cauffman, E. (2004). The right to do wrong: Lying to parents among adolescents and emerging adults. *Journal of Youth and Adolescence, 33*, 101–112. https://doi.org/10.1023/B:JOYO.0000013422.48100.5a

Johnson, M. K., & Raye, C. L. (1981). Reality monitoring. *Psychological Review, 88*(1), 67–85. https://doi.org/10.1037/0033-295X.88.1.67

Johnson, M. K., Raye, C. L., Hasher, L., & Chromiak, W. (1979). Are there developmental differences in reality-monitoring? *Journal of Experimental Child Psychology, 27*(1), 120–128. https://doi.org/10.1016/0022-0965(79)90064-X

Klafka, M., & Liszkowski, U. (2022). Four-year-olds adapt their deception to the epistemic states of others. *Cognitive Development, 64*, 101243. https://doi.org/10.1016/j.cogdev.2022.101243

Lavoie, J., Leduc, K., Crossman, A. M., & Talwar, V. (2016). Do as I say and not as I think: Parent socialisation of lie-telling behaviour. *Children & Society, 30*(4), 253–264. https://doi.org/10.1111/chso.12139

Lavoie, J., & Talwar, V. (2020). Care to share? Children's cognitive skills and concealing responses to a parent. *Topics in Cognitive Science, 12*(2), 485–503. https://doi.org/10.1111/tops.12390

Lavoie, J., Wyman, J., Crossman, A. M., & Talwar, V. (2018). Lie-telling as a mode of antisocial action: Children's lies and behavior problems. *Journal of Moral Education, 47*(4), 432–450. https://doi.org/10.1080/03057240.2017.1405343

Lavoie, J., Yachison, S., Crossman, A., & Talwar, V. (2017). Polite, instrumental, and dual liars: Relation to children's developing social skills and cognitive ability. *International Journal of Behavioral Development, 41*(2), 257–264. https://doi.org/10.1177/0165025415626518

Leach, A.-M., Talwar, V., Lee, K., Bala, N., & Lindsay, R. C. L. (2004). 'Intuitive' Lie detection of children's deception by law enforcement officials and university students. *Law and Human Behavior, 28*, 661–685. https://doi.org/10.1007/s10979-004-0793-0

Lee, K. (2013). Little liars: Development of verbal deception in children. *Child Development Perspectives, 7*(2), 91–96. https://doi.org/10.1111/cdep.12023

Lee, K., Cameron, C. A., Doucette, J., & Talwar, V. (2002). Phantoms and fabrications: Young children's detection of implausible lies. *Child Development, 73*(6), 1688–1702. https://doi.org/10.1111/1467-8624.t01-1-00499

Lee, K., Cameron, C. A., Xu, F., And, G. F., & Board, J. (1997). Chinese and Canadian children's evaluations of lying and truth telling: Similarities and dfferences in the context of pro-and antisocial behaviors. *Child Development, 68*(5), 924–934. https://doi.org/10.1111/j.1467-8624.1997.tb01971.x

Lee, K., Talwar, V., McCarthy, A., Ross, I., Evans, A., & Arruda, C. (2014). Can classic moral stories promote honesty in children? *Psychological Science, 25*(8), 1630–1636. https://doi.org/10.1177/0956797614536401

Lee, K., Xu, F., Fu, G., Cameron, C. A., & Chen, S. (2001). Taiwan and Mainland Chinese and Canadian children's categorization and evaluation of lie- and truth-telling: A modesty effect. *British Journal of Developmental Psychology, 19*, 525–542. https://doi.org/10.1348/026151001166236

Levy, N. (2022). In trust we trust: Epistemic vigilance and responsibility. *Social Epistemology, 36*(3), 283–298. https://doi.org/10.1080/02691728.2022.2042420

Lingwood, J., & Bull, R. (2013). Interviewing young adolescent suspects: When to reveal incriminating information? *The European Journal of Psychology Applied to Legal Context, 5*(2), 141–146. https://doi.org/10.5093/ejpalc2013a3

Ma, F., Heyman, G. D., Jing, C., Fu, Y., Compton, B. J., Xu, F., & Lee, K. (2018). Promoting honesty in young children through observational learning. *Journal of Experimental Child Psychology, 167*, 234–245. https://doi.org/10.1016/j.jecp.2017.11.003

Ma, F., Xu, F., Heyman, G. D., & Lee, K. (2011). Chinese children's evaluations of white lies: Weighing the consequences for recipients. *Journal of Experimental Child Psychology, 108*(2), 308–321. https://doi.org/10.1016/j.jecp.2010.08.015

Markham, R. (1991). Development of reality monitoring for performed and imagined actions. *Perceptual and Motor Skills, 72*(3), 1347–1354. https://doi.org/10.2466/pms.1991.72.3c.1347

Mascaro, O., & Sperber, D. (2009). The moral, epistemic, and mindreading components of children's vigilance towards deception. *Cognition, 112*(3), 367–380. https://doi.org/10.1016/j.cognition.2009.05.012

McCornack, S. A., & Levine, T. R. (1990). When lies are uncovered: Emotional and relational outcomes of discovered deception. *Communication Monographs, 57*(2), 119–138. https://doi.org/10.1080/03637759009376190

Miller, S. A. (2009). Children's understanding of second-order mental states. *Psychological Bulletin, 135*(5), 749–773. https://doi.org/10.1037/a0016854

Moll, H., & Tomasello, M. (2007). How 14- and 18-month-olds know what others have experienced. *Developmental Psychology, 43*(2), 309–317. https://doi.org/10.1037/0012-1649.43.2.309

Mugno, A. P., Malloy, L. C., Waschbusch, D. A., Pelham Jr., W. E., & Talwar, V. (2019). An experimental investigation of antisocial lie-telling among children with disruptive behavior disorders and typically developing children. *Child Development, 90*(3), 774–789. https://doi.org/10.1111/cdev.12985

Nagar, P. M., Caivano, O., & Talwar, V. (2020). The role of empathy in children's costly prosocial lie-telling behaviour. *Infant and Child Development, 29*(4), e2179. https://doi.org/10.1002/icd.2179

Ostrov, J. M. (2006). Deception and subtypes of aggression during early childhood. *Journal of Experimental Child Psychology, 93*, 322–336. https://doi.org/10.1016/j.jecp.2005.10.004

Ostrov, J. M., Ries, E. E., Stauffacher, K., Godleski, S. A., & Mullins, A. D. (2008). Relational aggression, physical aggression and deception during early childhood: A multimethod, multi-informant short-term longitudinal study. *Journal of Clinical Child and Adolescent Psychology, 37*, 664–675. https://doi.org/10.1080/15374410802148137

Polak, A., & Harris, P. L. (1999). Deception by young children following non-compliance. *Developmental Psychology*, *35*, 561–568. https://doi.org/10.1037/0012-1649.35.2.561

Popliger, M., Talwar, V., & Crossman, A. (2011). Predictors of children's prosocial lie-telling: Motivation, socialization variables, and moral understanding. *Journal of Experimental Child Psychology*, *110*(3), 373–392. https://doi.org/10.1016/j.jecp.2011.05.003

Rakoczy, H., Warneken, F., & Tomasello, M. (2009). Young children's selective learning of rule games from reliable and unreliable models. *Cognitive Development*, *24*, 61–69. https://doi.org/10.1016/j.cogdev.2008.07.004

Reddy, V. (2007). Getting back to the rough ground: Deception and 'social living'. In N. Emery, N. Clayton, & C. Frith (Eds.), *Social intelligence: From brain to culture* (pp. 219–244). Oxford University Press.

Roberts, K. P., & Lamb, M. E. (2010). Reality-monitoring characteristics in confirmed and doubtful allegations of child sexual abuse. *Applied Cognitive Psychology*, *24*, 1049–1079. https://doi.org/10.1002/acp.1600

Rotenberg, K. J., Boulton, M. J., & Fox, C. L. (2005). Cross-sectional and longitudinal relations among children's trust beliefs, psychological maladjustment and social relationships: Are very high as well as very low trusting children at risk? *Journal of Abnormal Child Psychology*, *33*(5), 595–610. https://doi.org/10.1007/s10802-005-6740-9

Sai, L., Liu, X., Li, H., Compton, B. J., & Heyman, G. D. (2020). Promoting honesty through overheard conversations. *Developmental Psychology*, *56*, 1073–1079. https://doi.org/10.1037/dev0000933

Santtila, P., Roppola, H., & Niemi, P. (1998). Assessing the truthfulness of witness statements made by children (Aged 7—8, 10—11, and 13—14) employing scales derived from Johnson and Raye's model of reality monitoring. *Expert Evidence*, *6*(4), 273–289. https://doi.org/10.1023/A:1008930821076

Smith, R. M., & LaFreniere, P. J. (2013). Development of tactical deception from 4 to 8 years of age. *The British Journal of Developmental Psychology*, *31*(1), 30–41. https://doi.org/10.1111/j.2044-835X.2011.02071.x

Sodian, B., Taylor, C., Harris, P. L., & Perner, J. (1991). Early deception and the child's theory of mind: False trails and genuine markers. *Child Development*, *62*, 468–483. https://doi.org/10.2307/1131124

Soto-Icaza, P., Aboitiz, F., & Billeke, P. (2015). Development of social skills in children: Neural and behavioral evidence for the elaboration of cognitive models. *Frontiers in Neuroscience*, *9*. https://www.frontiersin.org/articles/10.3389/fnins.2015.00333

Sperber, D., Clément, F., Heintz, C., Mascaro, O., Mercier, H., Origgi, G., & Wilson, D. (2010). Epistemic vigilance. *Mind & Language*, *25*(4), 359–393. https://doi.org/10.1111/j.1468-0017.2010.01394.x

Sporer, S. L. (2004). Reality monitoring and detection of deception. In *The detection of deception in forensic contexts* (pp. 64–101). Cambridge University Press. https://doi.org/10.1017/CBO9780511490071.004

Steller, M., & Köhnken, G. (1989). Criteria-based statement analysis: Credibility assessment of children's statements in sexual abuse cases. In D. C. Raskin (Ed.), *Psychological methods for investigation and evidence* (pp. 217–245). Springer.

Stouthamer-Loeber, M., & Loeber, R. (1986). Boys who lie. *Journal of Abnormal Child Psychology*, *14*(4), 551–564. https://doi.org/10.1007/BF01260523

Stromwall, L. A., & Granhag, P. A. (2005). Children's repeated lies and truths: Effects on adults' judgments and reality monitoring scores. *Psychiatry, Psychology and Law, 12*(2), 345–356. https://doi.org/10.1375/pplt.12.2.345

Talwar, V., & Crossman, A. (2011). From little white lies to filthy liars: The evolution of honesty and deception in young children. In J. B. Benson (Ed.), *Advances in Child Development and Behavior* (Vol. 40, pp. 139–179). JAI. https://doi.org/10.1016/B978-0-12-386491-8.00004-9

Talwar, V., Crossman, A., & Wyman, J. (2017). The role of executive functioning and theory of mind in children's lies for another and for themselves. *Early Childhood Research Quarterly, 41*, 126–135. https://doi.org/10.1016/j.ecresq.2017.07.003

Talwar, V., Gordon, H. M., & Lee, K. (2007). Lying in the elementary school years: Verbal deception and its relation to second-order belief understanding. *Developmental Psychology, 43*, 804–810. https://doi.org/10.1037/0012-1649.43.3.804

Talwar, V., Lavoie, J., & Crossman, A. M. (2019). Carving Pinocchio: Longitudinal examination of children's lying for different goals. *Journal of Experimental Child Psychology, 181*, 34–55. https://doi.org/10.1016/j.jecp.2018.12.003

Talwar, V., & Lee, K. (2002). Development of lying to conceal a transgression: Children's control of expressive behaviour during verbal deception. *International Journal of Behavioral Development, 26*(5), 436–444.

Talwar, V., & Lee, K. (2008). Social and cognitive correlates of children's lying behavior. *Child Development, 79*(4), 866–881. https://doi.org/10.1111/j.1467-8624.2008.01164.x

Talwar, V., & Lee, K. (2011). A punitive environment fosters children's dishonesty: A natural experiment. *Child Development, 82*(6). https://doi.org/10.1111/j.1467-8624.2011.01663.x

Talwar, V., Lee, K., Bala, N., & Lindsay, R. C. L. (2002). Children's conceptual knowledge of lying and its relation to their actual behaviors: Implications for court competence examinations. *Law and Human Behavior, 26*, 395–415. https://doi.org/10.1023/A:1016379104959

Talwar, V., Lee, K., Bala, N., & Lindsay, R. C. L. (2004). Children's lie-telling to conceal a parent's transgression: Legal implications. *Law and Human Behavior, 28*, 411–435. https://doi.org/10.1023/B:LAHU.0000039333.51399.f6

Talwar, V., Murphy, S. M., & Lee, K. (2007). White lie-telling in children for politeness purposes. *International Journal of Behavioral Development, 31*(1), 1-11. https://doi.org/10.1177/0165025406073530

Talwar, V., Yachison, S., & Leduc, K. (2016). Promoting honesty: the influence of stories on children's lie-telling behaviours and moral understanding. *Infant and Child Development, 25*(6), 484–501. https://doi.org/10.1002/icd.1949

Thijssen, S., Wildeboer, A., van IJzendoorn, M. H., Muetzel, R. L., Langeslag, S. J. E., Jaddoe, V. W. V., Verhulst, F. C., Tiemeier, H., Bakermans-Kranenburg, M. J., & White, T. (2017). The honest truth about deception: Demographic, cognitive, and neural correlates of child repeated deceptive behavior. *Journal of Experimental Child Psychology, 162*, 225–241. https://doi.org/10.1016/j.jecp.2017.05.009

Tyler, J. M., Feldman, R. S., & Reichert, A. (2006). The price of deceptive behavior: Disliking and lying to people who lie to us. *Journal of Experimental Social Psychology, 42*, 69–77. https://doi.org/10.1016/j.jesp.2005.02.003

Vrij, A., Akehurst, L., Brown, L., & Mann, S. (2006). Detecting lies in young children, adolescents and adults. *Applied Cognitive Psychology, 20*(9), 1225–1237. https://doi.org/10.1002/acp.1278

Vrij, A., Akehurst, L., Soukara, S., & Bull, R. (2002). Will the truth come out? The effect of deception, age, status, coaching, and social skills on CBCA scores. *Law and Human Behavior, 26*(3), 261–283. https://doi.org/10.1023/A:1015313120905

Wellman, H. M., & Liu, D. (2004). Scaling of theory-of-mind tasks. *Child Development, 75*(2), 523–541. https://doi.org/10.1111/j.1467-8624.2004.00691.x

Williams, S., Leduc, K., Crossman, A., & Talwar, V. (2017). Young deceivers: Executive functioning and antisocial lie-telling in preschool aged children. *Infant and Child Development, 26*(1), e1956. https://doi.org/10.1002/icd.1956

Wilson, A. E., Smith, M. D., & Ross, H. S. (2003). The nature and effects of young children's lies. *Social Development, 12*, 21–45. https://doi.org/10.1111/1467-9507.00220

Wimmer, H., & Perner, J. (1983). Beliefs about beliefs: Representation and constraining function of wrong beliefs in young children's understanding of deception. *Cognition, 13*(1), 103–128. https://doi.org/10.1016/0010-0277(83)90004-5

Xu, F., Bao, X., Fu, G., Talwar, V., & Lee, K. (2010). Lying and truth-telling in children: From concept to action. *Child Development, 81*(2), 581. https://doi.org/10.1111/j.1467-8624.2009.01417.x

Xu, L., Chen, G., & Li, B. (2019). Sadness empathy facilitates prosocial lying. *Social Behavior and Personality: An International Journal, 47*(9), 1–11.

7 Unconscious Lie Detection

Box 7.1 The Chengdu Twins

Pandas are an endangered species. Each new cub is an important lifeline for the longevity of the species. In Chengdu, the capital of Sichuan, China, a mother gave birth to twins. This is actually not unusual for pandas. Unfortunately, because of the limited milk and energy of pandas, a parent will more heavily invest in the caregiving of the stronger cub, meaning that other cubs which are part of the same litter tend not to survive. For 30 years, the Chengdu Research Base of Giant Panda Breeding has been looking for a way to increase the survival rate. They have now found one.

At birth, one of the twins is removed and cared for in an incubator and fed formula milk. The panda invests in the one remaining cub. But mother's milk has the nutrients and antibodies. Cubs need access to this milk to survive. The solution: deception. The mother is distracted with a honey feed a number of times across the day. Sufficiently distracted, the cub is taken from the mother and wrapped up in a towel, to be placed in the incubator to receive formula milk for a short period. The other cub, previously in the incubator, is switched into the enclosure with mother, giving the cub the opportunity to feed and connect with mother. This deception gives both cubs the potential to survive (Griffiths et al., 2015). The story is covered by Sir David Attenborough on BBC Earth: https://youtu.be/oSRv6znj-n8.

A Warning Note

Before we begin, I should explain that this chapter will read as rather critical. The intention here is not to disparage any of the researchers involved in this ongoing debate on a research topic that is intrinsically complex and difficult to test. Researchers aim to develop predictive and useful insights that can further our understanding of human thought and behaviour, and I am sure that all involved in this debate are earnestly trying to understand the role of the unconscious in lie detection. So, although this chapter may read somewhat critical of the research, the intent is to review the debate with an evaluative lens and reflect on whether the evidence to date allows us to conclude that we should leave lie-truth decisions to our unconscious. This aim is what we are all seeking to achieve regardless of our own perspectives on unconscious lie detection. With this final point in mind, let me briefly state my own perspective: I believe that the evidence is not sufficiently strong to provide robust evidence of an unconscious lie detection ability and that unconscious effects that have been observed may be equally or better explained as a result of conscious processing. You may find it especially beneficial to keep my perspective in mind as you read this chapter and consider whether there are interpretations that allow for unconscious processing accounts to be maintained in face of the critiques offered.

Indirect Lie Detection

If we are to understand how people detect lies and truths unconsciously, the first step may require us to ensure that participants are not consciously aware that they are in a lie detection study. After all, if participants are consciously aware of the possibility of deception in the study, it would be difficult to exclude the possibility that any judgements are not influenced by this conscious knowledge.

The indirect lie detection paradigm has sought to do just this. Participants sign up to an experiment that is supposedly unrelated to deception (perhaps a 'social judgement' experiment, for example). They are then shown a set of videos and are asked to judge how tense the speaker appears (DePaulo et al., 1982), whether the speaker has to think hard or not (Vrij et al., 2001), or some other behaviour that could be judged. The judgements are converted into lie-truth judgements. A judgement that the speaker has to think hard, for instance, is relabelled by the experimenter during data extraction as a lie judgement and a judgement that the speaker does not have to think hard is later relabelled as a truth judgement. These new *indirect* judgements are used to determine the participants' accuracy rates. In studies exploring indirect lie detection, it has been found that people can indirectly detect deception (e.g., DePaulo & Rosenthal, 1979). It is worth noting that these studies tend not to compare indirect lie detection accuracy with those making direct lie or truth judgements. Instead, they tend to address the question of whether indirect lie detection can result in above-chance accuracy (see DePaulo & Morris, 2004, for a review). Studies that have compared direct and indirect judgements are relatively few, but some find that indirect methods can achieve higher detection rates compared to people who, viewing the same videos, make direct lie or truth judgements (e.g., Vrij et al., 2001). This work, carried out since at least the late 1970s, has led some to conclude that "people know more about deception than it appears when experimenters ask them directly" (DePaulo, 1994, p. 85).

As an example, consider the study by Anderson et al. (2002), which asked people to judge how comfortable their friend felt (as well as a number of other measures) when their friend spoke a statement to them. Unbeknownst to the receiver, their friend was either lying or telling the truth. The receivers reported that their friend was more comfortable when delivering truths than when delivering lies, suggesting an implicit ability to detect deception via an implicit awareness of how comfortable the sender appeared.

Indirect lie detection studies have used a variety of behavioural cues as the focus of the indirect judgement. These may be how tense the sender appears (DePaulo et al., 1982), how comfortable they appear (Anderson et al., 2002), whether they are thinking hard (Vrij et al., 2001), the certainty that the speakers exhibit (e.g., Ulatowska, 2010), or how ambivalent the sender is in their message (DePaulo & Rosenthal, 1979). That is, it would appear that the causal effect is not the type of cue being rated, but rather that the indirect nature of rating speakers without conscious awareness of deception is what allows for above-chance detection accuracy.

Box 7.2 Potential Confounds in the Indirect Lie Detection Paradigm

If indirect lie detection results in greater accuracy than direct lie detection of the same senders, it seems unassailable that the only difference between the two conditions is that one is making a conscious and explicit judgement while the other makes an unconscious and implicit judgement. They watch and hear the same behaviours in both conditions, and yet an accuracy difference is observed. However, let us consider whether there may be other differences between these conditions. Which of the following differences are apparent between a direct lie-truth and an indirect (e.g., thinking hard versus not thinking hard) judgement condition?

- The behaviours of the senders in the video recordings between the two conditions may be different.
- One group is aware of the possibility of deception while the other is not.
- Participants receive different instructions from the experimenter.
- Participants in the indirect group are told to focus on a single cue (e.g., thinking hard), but those in the direct group are given no cues to consider.

The first option is relatively easy to dismiss: a good experimental design would ensure that the same senders' statements are presented to both conditions. The second option is true, and that is by design: this is the intended conscious versus unconscious manipulation. But the third

(*Continued*)

and fourth options, while differing between the conditions and so are also true, are not an intended element of the manipulation. They are required in order to allow the manipulation to exist, but in themselves are not manipulations of conscious versus unconscious thinking.

Reflecting on the complete set of differences between conditions is something we have done before under the guise of seeking alternative explanations. We are seeking out the inherent assumptions that are being made: in this case, that only one variable is being manipulated. If we find that others are also being manipulated, these may (or may not) explain the true cause of the differences observed. It is our job as scientists to reflect and evaluate on these possible alternative explanations and consider their a priori plausibility. If they have some plausibility (perhaps based on logical arguments or on the past literature), we can revisit the relevant literature and consider whether our alternative account can explain other findings. We could also design experiments that allow us to separate the accounts. We should be careful not jump to the conclusion that the alternative accounts are true or that the original account is false without first evaluating the evidence.

The focal account (Street & Richardson, 2015), however, takes a different perspective. It not only argues that the indirect lie detection method does not tell us about unconscious lie detection, but that it is incapable of answering whether unconscious processing affects lie-truth judgements. By way of example, imagine you are presented with a set of symbols that vary in their complexity, as shown below. I could ask you to sort them into two piles: ones that would be easy to draw and ones that would be difficult to draw. Give that a go:

(1) 공, (2) 球, (3) 드, (4) 牌, (5) 위, (6) 獮, (7) 鐘, (8) 벨

I would categorise items 1, 3, 5, and 8 as relatively easier to draw than items 2, 4, 6, and 7. For each item that you categorised in the same way as I did, give yourself one point. The symbols depict different characters in the Korean and Mandarin languages. Add up your points and divide by 8 to see what proportion of the characters you correctly categorised into their respective languages. If you scored greater than 0.50, then well done: you have correctly classified more than half of the items correctly. It would perhaps be a little silly for me to claim that you have unconscious knowledge of Korean and Mandarin characters,[1] and yet I suspect that even if you have never seen either language before, you would have been able to have achieved a relatively high accuracy on that task.[2] The reason is that I as the experimenter chose two languages where the complexity of the characters differs, broadly speaking. As such, I could be relatively confident that your indirect judgements would distinguish the two languages even if you have never encountered the languages before.

By analogy, Street and Richardson (2015) claim that the indirect lie detection method results in better-than-chance accuracy because the cue chosen by the experimenter (e.g., thinking hard) is known to be present more often when people lie than tell the truth (see Chapters 2 and 3 for more on the cognitive difficulty of lying). As a result, even someone who has never encountered the idea of deception would apparently distinguish the truth-tellers from the liars using the indirect method, provided that they are able to accurately tell who is thinking hard and who is not. As such, they argue that the method does not allow for claims about unconscious lie detection: one could achieve above-chance accuracy with no conscious or unconscious knowledge of deception.

One problem for the focal account perspective is that some studies find that indirect lie detection achieves higher detection accuracy than asking people to make direct lie-truth judgements. That is, not only can people classify deception with no experience of deception (if the focal account is correct), but they somehow do so even better than making an explicit lie-truth judgement. It is not clear why these indirect judgements should outperform people making an explicit lie-truth judgement, and one may argue that using additional unconscious knowledge could explain the improved accuracy.

Street and Richardson (2015) propose an alternative explanation. Indirect lie detectors only attend to a single cue, given that their sole job as a participant is to make judgements of that cue. Direct lie-truth judgements may use a myriad of cues, some of which may suggest honesty but some which may suggest deception. Combining these mixed cues leads to lower detection accuracy. They found that when two cues being rated using the indirect lie detection method both aligned with one another, indirect lie detection accuracy was higher than when the two cues contradicted, supporting this conclusion (Street & Richardson, 2015, Study 1).

If the focal account is correct, direct lie-truth judgements can also be influenced by focusing attention on a single cue. To test this, Street and Richardson (2015, Study 2) selected videos of senders who appeared tense but not thinking hard and vice versa. Sixty-two participants were shown the videos in an indirect lie detection study but were asked either to attend to how hard the speaker was thinking or how tense they appeared by pressing a key indicating the degree to which the behaviour was being shown as the video was played. At the end of the video, participants made a direct lie-truth judgement. The direct lie-truth judgements of the video depended on which cue they focused on. Participants who focused on a cue that was aligned with honesty (i.e., was not tense or was not thinking hard) made more truth judgements compared to participants viewing the same video but instead focused on a cue that was aligned with deception (i.e., was tense or thinking hard). The findings indicate that direct lie-truth judgements can be influenced by focusing attention on a single cue, consistent with the focal account's claim.

The focal account argues that indirect lie detection produces above-chance accuracy by focusing attention to a single diagnostic cue to deception. One implication of this is that having indirect judges attend to two cues at the same time should result in clashes (e.g., thinking hard which suggests deception but not appearing tense which suggests honesty), thereby lowering detection accuracy, which they found (Street & Richardson, 2015, Study 1). In short, they claim that the indirect method does not tap unconscious thinking, but rather forces participants to attend to a single cue to deception: one that the experimenter has selected ahead of time and that is known to be diagnostic of deception.

One prediction that arises from the focal account is that indirect lie detection should not affect detection accuracy rates if indirect judges are made conscious of the fact that they are in a lie detection experiment. While limited research has taken this approach, possibly because the indirect lie detection method is typically employed to assess unconscious thinking, studies that have informed participants that their indirect ratings will be converted to explicit lie-truth judgements find that it does not affect accuracy rates (Ulatowska, 2010, 2014).

The focal account also predicts that accuracy rates should be affected by how diagnostic the cues are of deception: if the experimenter selects a cue to deception that is not diagnostic, then the indirect lie detection method should not result in above-chance detection accuracy. In a meta-analysis, Bond et al. (2014) found that in 20 out of 24 studies reviewed, indirect lie detection was actually *lower* than direct lie detection accuracy. The studies achieving lower accuracy rates had indirect judges focus on cues such as whether or not the speaker was shielding their face, a cue that is not diagnostic of deception. Those studies that achieved the higher indirect lie detection accuracy rates were those that selected diagnostic cues to deception such as cooperativeness of the sender, although there are only a limited number of studies exploring these more promising cues (Bond et al., 2014). Recently, Verschuere et al. (2021) have found across seven experiments that instructing participants to attend to only the most diagnostic cue available in the study (how detailed the statements were) can result in increased detection accuracy relative to being given no instruction, as would be predicted by the focal account.

As a final point for consideration, Sporer and Ulatowska (2021) have recently argued that indirect lie detection studies have primarily used nonverbal cues as the focal cue that participants are instructed to rate. They contend that more work on indirect lie detection is needed using verbal cues, which are more diagnostic than nonverbal cues (e.g., DePaulo et al., 2003). However, they also note that the indirect lie detection methodology should be separated from the perspective that it tests unconscious thinking.

In summary, indirect lie detection has been argued to improve lie detection accuracy by accessing the unconscious. The focal account argues against this interpretation and instead argues the methodology is agnostic on this point: the unconscious may or may not improve lie detection accuracy, but the indirect method is unable to address this issue. For a review of indirect lie detection that offers a more favourable interpretation of evidencing unconscious thought, see DePaulo and Morris (2004).

Other Approaches to Unconscious Lie Detection

A number of other approaches have been taken to determine whether there is evidence that the unconscious can improve lie-truth judgements. 'Thin slicing' involves asking people to judge whether a sender is lying or telling the truth from only small segments of the sender's full statement. Albrechtsen et al. (2009) have argued that thin slicing may encourage more intuitive processing, based on the meta-analysis of thin slicing conducted by Ambady and Rosenthal (1992). Albrechtsen et al. (2009, Experiment 1) found that 80 participants viewing 15 thin slices were more accurate lie detectors than those who viewed the sender's entire three-minute statement. This method offers a novel approach to testing unconscious lie-truth judgements.

A second study with 120 participants found that distracting the conscious mind by engaging in a difficult secondary task (remembering the order of random letters of the alphabet presented sequentially and when a red letter showed, having to recall the letter that appeared three back) led to higher accuracy compared to those consciously seeking numerous reasons that the sender was lying or telling the truth. The findings of Albrechtsen et al.'s (2009) two studies suggest that unconscious thinking can improve lie detection accuracy.

While Ambady and Rosenthal's (1992) meta-analysis considers that automatic processing could be the cause of the thin slicing effect, they are unable to rule out other conscious explanations of the phenomenon (see Slepian et al., 2014, for a similar conclusion). One such explanation that they offer is akin to the focal account (Street & Richardson, 2015): it may be that thin slicing is removing information that is distracting and causing inaccuracy. Such an explanation does not require recourse to claims of unconscious processing. If such an interpretation were correct, one would expect thin slicing to cause accuracy to *decrease* in some studies, namely those where the speakers' behaviours do not contain useful clues to deception. Consistent with this, Street and Masip (2015) found that thin slicing caused lie detection accuracy to decrease relative to watching the full statement. However, it is worth remembering that psychology is a discipline reliant on statistics and probabilities, and so it is to be expected that some studies will find contradictory results. Unfortunately, there are very few published studies exploring thin slicing in the context of lie detection.

In contrast to the conscious perspective, Ambady (2010) considers thin slicing research in other domains to reflect intuitive and automatic processing. It is argued that thin slicing results in observers paying greater attention to nonverbal behaviours which are processed "outside awareness, without drawing on conscious, cognitive processing resources" (p. 271). Such an argument lends support to Albrechten et al.'s (2009) interpretation of unconscious lie detection. But recall from Chapter 3 that there are no known highly diagnostic cues to deception and that nonverbal behaviour in particular is less diagnostic than verbal behaviour (DePaulo et al., 2003; Luke, 2019; Sporer & Schwandt, 2006, 2007). Focusing attention to nonverbal cues is liable to reduce accuracy most of the time. Thus, if the improved lie detection reflects unconscious thinking, it may be argued that it is improving accuracy via means that do not relate to the nonverbal cues being produced by the sender.

However, note that Vrij and Fisher (2020) have recently contended that there may be some as-yet undiscovered cue or combination of nonverbal cues that may allow relatively high detection accuracy rates. Potentially, the participants in Albrechtsen et al.'s (2009) study may have been unconsciously attending to such cues. But given that it is not possible to rule out that thin slicing may be causing the conscious mind to focus on these particular cues (see Ambady & Rosenthal, 1992; Slepian et al., 2014), it is not possible to rule out a conscious explanation of their findings. Elucidating whether the increased lie detection resulting from thin slicing is the result of unconscious thinking (see Ambady, 2010) offers an intriguing opportunity to demonstrate the role of unconscious thought in lie-truth judgements.

Taking a different approach, ten Brinke et al. (2014) use two methods in two studies to show that unconscious lie detection outperforms conscious lie detection. In the first experiment, 72 participants were shown a pair of videos (one lie and one truth) with a pseudonym assigned to each sender (e.g., 'John') and were asked to make a conscious lie-truth judgement. Following this conscious judgement of the pair of videos, participants were shown a photograph of the sender and had to recall which of two pseudonyms was correctly associated with the pictured sender, repeating this procedure for both senders. Accompanying the names, but irrelevant to the name recall task, were words associated with either honesty or deception (e.g., 'John, Deceitful' and 'David, Genuine'). Given that the deceptive and honest words have no relevance to the conscious task being performed (matching the photo to the correct pseudonym), any effect of the presence of these words on people's judgements may reflect unconscious thinking. This setup is known as the implicit association test (see Nosek et al., 2007, for a review of this technique). Ten Brinke et al. (2014) found that people more often correctly associated the pseudonym with the pictured sender when the irrelevant word attached to the pseudonym reflected the sender's actual veracity (e.g., they more often selected 'John, Deceitful' when the pictured sender John had lied in the video).

In a second experiment, after viewing truthful and deceptive sender statements, 66 participants moved into a test phase where a still image of a sender was shown for 17 ms, or one frame of a screen refresh. After this extremely brief subliminal presentation that should not be consciously perceptible, participants had to classify words such as 'genuine' and 'invalid' as either belonging to the concept of 'truth' or 'lie'. They found that participants were faster to correctly classify words when the word to be classified was congruent with the subliminally presented sender's veracity (e.g., faster to classify the word 'genuine' when the sender that was shown subliminally had previously told the truth) compared to when it was incongruent (e.g., slower to classify the word 'invalid' for the same subliminally presented sender). These studies found that unconscious lie detection outperformed conscious lie-truth judgement accuracy.

Levine and Bond (2014) have argued that these findings do not show the benefits of unconscious lie detection. Instead, they note that those making conscious lie-truth judgements were performing at accuracy rates below what is typically observed (Bond & DePaulo, 2006). That is, they argue that the results of these studies show that conscious decision-makers in their study were particularly poor, and that unconscious decision-makers were performing no better than is observed in a meta-analysis of conscious judgements (Bond & DePaulo, 2006). Ten Brinke and Carney (2014) have replied to this critique, stating that it is not reasonable to compare detection accuracy in a single study using a particular set of senders with a conglomeration of studies in a meta-analysis that use a wide variety of different stimuli with different cues and content.[3]

Franz and von Luxburg (2014, 2015) also point out that the 'accuracy' differences observed in this work are based on reaction time differences. Reaction times can only show that people are either faster or slower for correct versus incorrect classification. That is, the size of the reaction time difference cannot be used as a measure of how *accurate* unconscious lie detection is. Using the original researchers' data, they conducted a number of analyses to attempt to estimate unconscious accuracy from reaction time data, such as using machine learning to try to predict whether a given decision would be correct or incorrect. The best unconscious detection accuracy that Franz and von Luxburg (2015) could achieve was 53.7%, which was below the 54% detection accuracy that ten Brinke et al. considered as 'deception-detection incompetence' (p. 1098).[4]

In summary, recent attempts to uncover an unconscious lie detection benefit have difficulty ruling out conscious explanations of the observed effects. Proponents of unconscious lie detection may see some promise in thin-slicing, although there are limited studies using this technique with mixed findings, and meta-analyses consider that conscious explanations of thin-slicing effects are plausible.

Unconscious Thought Theory

Box 7.3 Handling Abstract Psychological Concepts

Which of the following do you feel are defensible positions?

- Terms such as 'unconscious' do not need a precise definition that details all the criteria needed to define it. We all understand what

(*Continued*)

we mean by the term 'unconscious', and trying to define it would be too complex and time-consuming with little benefit.
- If we do not clearly define our terms, it will be difficult to subject them to experimental testing.

As psychologists, we are comfortable handling abstract conceptual ideas such as 'personality' and 'deception'. We are often required to rely on loosely defined terms when our field involves organisms as complex and as difficult to predict as human beings. But I would argue that we need to ensure that our terms are precise. If we cannot say whether unconscious thinking results in faster judgements than the conscious thinking, whether it is accessible or inaccessible to conscious thought, whether its processing capacity is limited or unlimited, and so on, we will have difficulty agreeing on what it is that we are testing. We may find ourselves in a position where different researchers are testing different psychological concepts because they hold different definitions. Worse yet, they may find themselves unable to test the concepts at all if it is unclear how unconscious processing is distinct from conscious processing.

Consider that, so far, the assumption we have worked with is that the unconscious is somehow smarter than conscious thinking. But what is meant by 'smart'?[5] Is it that it can handle complex information, that it can adapt flexibly to solve novel problems, or that it makes the best decisions for us (see Loftus & Klinger, 1992)? A lack of clear definition can lead to unconscious accounts that are logically incoherent (Stafford, 2014). Different methodologies that are all supposedly testing for the existence of smart unconscious lie detection may actually be testing different constructs. This may lead to conclusions that the findings on unconscious lie detection are mixed and thus fail to show evidence of its existence when actually evidence of the unconscious could be found if researchers agreed on how it is defined (see Rothkirch & Hesselmann, 2017, for discussion of this issue). That is, researchers may have different conceptions of what the 'unconscious' is, which may undermine our attempts to learn something about it (see Bowers, 1984).

I encourage you to reflect on the wording that we use in psychology. Consider the use of the word 'automatic' in Chapter 2 when discussing ADCAT's (Walczyk et al., 2014) activation of truthful information in memory, for example. What exactly does it mean to be automatic? Are we claiming that humans are operating like a machine, mechanistically churning the gears in a way that cannot be controlled or overridden? Is it merely shorthand for 'very fast', and if so, just how fast is that? (For an in-depth discussion of automaticity, see Moors & De Houwer, 2006. For a quick overview, see the glossary.) Similarly, defining phrases like 'costly' (when describing the high-stakes lies that ADCAT aims to explain in Chapter 2) may similarly leave you wondering how the cost is defined.

It is not uncommon to find that psychological terminology goes undefined, on the assumption that we all understand what it means. In fact, in Chapter 2, you will note that I rather quickly defined deception and moved on without a full discussion of the issue, and yet in Chapter 3 (Box 3.3) we found ourselves questioning whether the term 'deception' is meaningful.

One sign that a term needs better defining is when examples are used to explain concepts in order to avoid providing a clear and testable definition. Examples are sometimes used on the assumption that we can 'all see what is meant' on the basis of the examples. But as we have discussed in this Box, we cannot take for granted that we share the same definition. I encourage you to reflect on times where you have seen examples used in this book and consider whether they are being used as a means of avoiding a clear definition. If a term is not or cannot be clearly defined, we should stop and reflect on the usefulness of that concept and how (if at all) we can improve on it by offering a clear, testable definition.

Common to the approaches explored so far is an absence of a substantive accounting of what the unconscious is and how it operates.[6] This proves to be a rather difficult task (see Box 7.3), and has typically been missing from the unconscious lie detection literature (Sporer & Ulatowska, 2021; Street & Vadillo, 2016). Newell and Shanks (2014) reflect on the various ways in which a judgement could be considered to arise from unconscious processing. Definitions of the unconscious may consider (i) there being no conscious awareness that a cue is diagnostic of deception, (ii) there being no conscious detection of what cues are influencing their judgement, (iii) there being no conscious awareness of how they are processing and combining the cues into a judgement, or indeed (iv) there being no awareness that they are making a judgement at all.

Rather than try to resolve the complex and intricate issue of defining the unconscious here,[7] we will sidestep it by considering one account of unconscious thought known as unconscious thought theory (UTT; Dijksterhuis et al., 2006). The account has been subject to debate (e.g., Newell & Shanks, 2014), but proponents of the perspective continue to argue for its strengths (e.g., Dijksterhuis & Strick, 2016). UTT argues that the conscious mind is limited by the constraints of working memory. Unconscious thought, in comparison, is believed to be unlimited in its capacity. As a result, the unconscious is better placed to make decisions about complex tasks where multiple pieces of information need to be assessed before reaching a judgement.

Distracting the conscious mind when having to make complex decisions, then, should result in better performance because the distraction allows the unconscious mind to drive the judgement. Support for the account comes from work asking participants to decide which of four cars to buy based on 12 attributes (e.g., brand, mileage). Participants were asked to differentiate the best car (i.e., the car that scored highest when combining the 12 attributes) from the worst car on the basis of their subjective attitudes towards the overall quality of the cars. They better differentiated the cars if their conscious mind was distracted compared to when they were engaged in conscious deliberation for four minutes (e.g., Bos et al., 2008, Experiment 1; Dijksterhuis et al., 2006).

UTT has been challenged empirically and conceptually. Conceptually, González-Vallejo et al. (2008) argued that UTT has ignored research in cognitive and social psychology that has challenged the core components of UTT's claims, such as work suggesting that the unconscious is more primitive and less sophisticated than the more recently evolved higher cognition of conscious reasoning (see Loftus & Klinger, 1992). Empirically, meta-analyses of unconscious thought effects have found that when support for UTT is present, these findings tend to result from small sample sizes (Acker, 2008). When multiple studies are combined meta-analytically, the evidence suggests that there is no benefit of unconscious thought (see Acker, 2008; Newell & Rakow, 2011; Nieuwenstein et al., 2015; Vadillo et al., 2015, for meta-analyses).

One tangible benefit of UTT, whether it is considered empirically supported or not, is that it provides a means of testing its claims: distracting the conscious mind should lead to accuracy gains for complex, goal-directed tasks (see Chapter 2, Box 2.4, for more on why testability is a strength of a psychological account). Reinhard et al. (2013) set out to test whether unconscious thinking can be applied to improving deception detection performance. In five studies, they found that distracting the conscious mind was indeed able to boost lie detection accuracy. For example, in Experiment 1, approximately 22 participants[8] took part in one of three conditions in a study that they thought was about 'impression formation', with no mention of it being a lie detection study. After watching eight senders, participants in the unconscious thought condition were given a difficult word search puzzle to complete for three minutes that involved searching for invented words. In the conscious thought condition, participants were given three minutes to reflect on who had lied and who had told the truth. Afterwards, both conditions were asked to make lie-truth judgements. Those in the unconscious thought condition detected deception more accurately than those who consciously reflected on deception.

Moi and Shanks (2015) argued that the methodology of Reinhard et al. did not rule out the possibility that the instructions given to the different conditions may have influenced the results and that the difference between the conscious and unconscious thought conditions was relatively small. In their high-powered replication using a mixture of laboratory-based testing (where participants come into the lab) and online testing (where participants take part via the internet) to improve upon the methodology, they were unable to replicate the benefit of unconscious thought. Another recent high-powered replication using only laboratory-based testing, where participants may be more readily monitored for low engagement with the study, has similarly found evidence in support of the position that conscious and unconscious lie detection accuracy do not differ (Wu et al., 2019). Thus, there is some evidence to suggest that distracting the unconscious mind does not improve lie detection accuracy. Indeed, Street and Vadillo (2016) have noted that there are some lie detection studies showing that distracting conscious thinking has been shown to *reduce* lie detection accuracy rather than improve it (Feeley & Young, 2000; Street & Kingstone, 2017).

In summary, UTT has argued that the unconscious has unlimited capacity for processing and as such is better able to handle complex tasks to appropriately weigh multiple pieces of information to arrive at accurate outcomes. The account has been critiqued both empirically and on the basis of its conceptual claims, with meta-analyses failing to find evidence of unconscious thought benefits. Only recently has the account been explored in lie detection, with one study finding support for UTT (Reinhard et al., 2013). However, recent high-powered replications improving on the methodology have found evidence to support the position that unconscious thinking does not improve lie detection accuracy (Moi & Shanks, 2015; Wu et al., 2019).

The Tipping Point Account

An alternative unconscious account has been offered in the lie detection domain. Ten Brinke et al. (2016) have suggested that it is evolutionary beneficial to be able to detect lies that threaten us, but that the conscious mind is concerned with the reputational damage of confronting others and accusing them of deception. When people are threatened, their unconscious mind may be able to detect deception. Such a detection is kept out of conscious awareness because becoming conscious of deception could force them to confront the liar (ten Brinke et al., 2016). The account bears similarity to the accusatory reluctance account of conscious lie detection (O'Sullivan, 2003; see Chapter 4), which argues that people do not publicly accuse others of lying but privately are able to detect deception. The difference is that the tipping point account proposes that the private judgement is withheld even from the receiver's conscious thoughts: it is only the unconscious that is capable of making a correct determination. A potential strength of the account is that it is able to provide a list of predictions that arise from its claims.

In a test of the account, ten Brinke et al. (2019) suggested that the threat that the unconscious has evolved to detect will result in sympathetic nervous system responses of greater skin conductance (capturing general arousal) and reduced blood flow due to blood vessel constriction. Because these should be seen only in response to threat, it was predicted that these physiological responses would be observed when viewing footage of lies about real crimes (e.g., pleading for the safe return of a loved one when they were later convicted of being responsible for the loved one's disappearance) but not when observing footage of mock crimes that students are asked to act out as part of a psychology experiment because only the former should pose a threat. A series of five studies, typically using suitably large sample sizes, found evidence that people show physiological reactions to real (but not mock) crimes. Additionally, instructing participants to consciously attend to their own (unconscious) physiological responses resulted in improved conscious lie detection performance.

There are conceptual concerns for the tipping point account and its empirical test. In their multiple studies, the researchers find results that are somewhat inconsistent but are broadly claimed to support the general position of an unconscious effect. For instance, in Experiment 1 skin conductance and blood flow is not related to whether the receiver is viewing a lie or truth and whether it was a real or mock crime being viewed, but the unconscious perspective offered would claim that this relationship should have been observed. In Experiment 3, the threat experienced by pleas to return missing relatives resulted in reduced blood flow when viewing liars versus truth-tellers, as predicted by the unconscious account. But real high-stakes lies about unfairly taking large sums of cash—also expected by the tipping point account to be perceived as a threat that should be unconsciously detectable—did not result in the predicted physiological changes when viewing liars compared to truth-tellers.

Perhaps more difficult for the tipping point account to explain is the broad finding that when there are differences in skin conductance and blood flow, the effects are not in the direction predicted by the unconscious perspective. Recall that for real crimes, greater skin conductance (indicating physiological arousal) should be observed when listening to a lie relative to listening to a truth in the context of a real-life crime, signalling an unconscious detection of the deceit. Meanwhile, there should be no or relatively little physiological reaction to true versus deceptive *mock* crime stimuli. The findings show that there tends to be higher levels of arousal when viewing mock crime stimuli compared to real crime stimuli, although the results across the experiments are not meta-analysed to determine if this is reliably the case. Such a finding may be difficult to align with the view that arousal reflects an unconscious detection of a threat.

Relatedly, when exploring whether telling participants to consciously attend to their own physiological reactions will allow conscious detection accuracy to improve, the research design uses three conditions: a control condition given no instruction, the training condition given the instruction that increased arousal signals deception, and a bogus training condition given the instruction that increased arousal signals honesty. This latter condition should result in below-chance accuracy because participants are being instructed to consciously use their unconscious physiological reactions in a way that would result in systematically wrong answers, assuming the physiological arousal indicates accurate unconscious lie detection. However, the detection of lies in the bogus training did not differ from either the control or the training condition, the latter of which should have had a noticeably improved detection accuracy over the bogus training. When viewing truthful statements, the control condition was the most accurate and the unconscious condition was the least accurate. It is unclear how to align these findings with the tipping point perspective that physiological reactions indicate accurate unconscious lie detection.

Box 7.4 Researcher Degrees of Freedom

The worked example below is intended to develop your capacity to reason more abstractly. See if you can find the analogy between the discussion below and what might happen in an analysis of an unconscious lie detection study. In the main body of the chapter after this Box, we will marry the analogy with the practical psychological effect.

Imagine I am holding a bag of many marbles of different sizes, colours, and shapes. I throw them in the air and start looking for patterns scattered on the floor. Interestingly, I find that most of the red marbles seem to have landed near each other. This may lead me to claim that there is some force at work here: perhaps the red ink happens to be somewhat magnetic, for example. The reality, of course, is that I have capitalised on some randomness in my data that looks systematic and gives a statistically significant 'attraction' effect. How might we assess whether there really is a magnetic effect or whether the results are determined randomly but happen to look patterned on this occasion?

- Look at the data and see if other patterns emerge from the data, confirming the idea that random data sometimes appears patterned.
- Conduct another experiment that attempts to directly test this hypothesis.
- Run an analysis to determine whether the distance between the red marbles is significantly smaller than the distance between any other coloured marbles.

The original experiment was 'exploratory', meaning that I was looking at multiple patterns across the data without any pre-existing notions of what I may find with the hope of discovering something that looks potentially interesting. There was no a priori hypothesis that was being tested. There were many possibly interesting results that could have come about, and some of those 'interesting' results will occur by chance simply because there are so many possibilities. Put another way,

(*Continued*)

if you flipped a coin ten times, it is likely not to show heads on all ten flips. But if you flip one million coins ten times each, one of the coins has a good chance of coming up heads on all ten of its flips. Reporting only the one coin that came up heads ten times in a row is not evidence that this one coin is biased to always show heads: it is natural randomness that is to be expected. The problem comes when only this single coin result is reported and the remainder go unreported. If I repeat the coin toss in a 'confirmatory' study that directly tests the hypothesis that the coin is biased, I am unlikely to get the same result again if the original data was a chance finding. The same applies to the marble throwing example and the apparent attraction of the red marbles.

The problem with my interpretation of the marbles data was that I had many different ways to view the data: I could have focused on the yellow marbles, or only the large ones, or a combination of green and square marbles. I could have considered whether they attracted or repelled, whether they appeared on the north side of the room, and so on. The flexibility here gave me substantial opportunity to find a statistically significant result among one of the very many possibilities (in this case, the red marbles were close to each other), even though nothing systematic was occurring. Option 2 is a suitable approach to assess whether the effect is replicable and a genuine effect. See Simmons et al. (2011) for more on this fascinating issue called the researcher degrees of freedom problem and its effect on the replicability of psychological science.

Two other issues may also be considered. The first concerns the flexibility in analyses (see Box 7.4), while the second is a conceptual critique of the tipping point account. First, a wide range of analyses are employed to assess whether there are effects to be observed. This may be considered analogous to the coin flipping and marble tossing examples discussed in Box 7.4. For instance, in Experiment 3, the researchers begin by using an ANOVA test to explore whether skin conductance differs when viewing liars and truth-tellers, but only for real (versus mock) crimes. The analysis does not find evidence of this 'interaction' effect (i.e., that the combination of real versus mock crime and truth versus deceptive statement affects skin conductance, as would be predicted by the tipping point account), and so a combination of t-tests were then applied. These also do not provide results that are consistent with the tipping point account. Finally, a non-parametric version of the test is used, at which point the results are consistent with the tipping point account. This flexibility in analysis can be found in other sections of the work.[9]

Second, the tipping point has been considered to have some conceptual issues (Street & Vadillo, 2017). It has been argued that the predictions offered by the tipping point, while numerous, do not test whether the resulting effects arise from conscious or unconscious thinking. For instance, one prediction is that "individuals reporting high trait interoceptivity will be more sensitive to implicit threat signals occurring in their own bodies and detect deception at higher rates than those reporting low interoceptivity" (ten Brinke et al., 2016, p. 582). But it is possible that this prediction could hold true while participants are consciously aware of the threat signals and consciously making lie-truth judgements. Street and Vadillo (2017) argue that similar critiques can be levied at all predictions of the tipping point account. They also suggest that it is unclear what constitutes a sufficient 'threat' under the tipping point account to result in unconscious lie detection activity. For example, in ten Brinke et al.'s (2019) study, the researchers suggest that a video of someone making a false plea for the return of their child, which is unlikely to have a direct bearing on the participants' safety, is a sufficient threat to prompt unconscious detection.

In summary, the evidence for a tipping point perspective of unconscious lie detection has received only limited testing to date, and some have argued that there are empirical and conceptual questions the account cannot answer. Critics argue that a more clearly defined conception of unconscious lie detection is needed that specifies its mechanisms and processes while ruling out the possibility that conscious processing is operating. Proponents of the perspective, however, may argue that as more research is conducted to test the claims of the account, the data may converge to show an unconscious benefit.

Testing for Unconscious Thinking

The lack of a mechanistic and precise definition of the unconscious has led to some difficulties with testing it. Newell and Shanks (2014) offer four criteria that must be met in order to rule out the possibility that the results of a given study reflect conscious processes. First, the effect should be *reliable*, meaning that factors that are not intended to affect the results (such as social desirability) have been mitigated. This is a standard requirement for the experimental method to ensure the results are robust. Second, the test of whether conscious thinking is operating should be *relevant*. For example, if I attempt to measure whether your comprehension of this book is conscious or unconscious, it would not be relevant to ask you whether you were able to detect how often the passive voice was used. While you may be unable to consciously answer this question, it would not be appropriate to claim that your comprehension of the book relies on unconscious thinking: the question to assess conscious comprehension was not relevant to testing the aspect of conscious processing that is operating.

Third, the test of conscious awareness should occur with *immediacy*, meaning that it should happen as soon as the processing has been complete or possibly alongside it in order to ensure that the conscious processing of information is not simply forgotten or has not been subject to interference as a result of further conscious processing. Finally, the assessment of conscious awareness should be *sensitive*. It may be that one is consciously detecting deception in the moment by recognising a contradiction between a statement and evidence, but if the test of consciousness is to ask participants to select from a list which cue they were consciously aware of (one of them being the contradiction), the method of reporting of consciousness (select from a list) is rather different to the actual conscious process that was operating (conscious detection of a cue). This difference may make it difficult to retrieve the information that affected conscious processing.

Reviews of unconscious thinking in cognitive psychology have argued that studies tend to fail at least one of these criteria, making it difficult to claim that any observed effects are truly the result of unconscious thought (e.g., Shanks & St. John, 1994; Vadillo et al., 2015). While these criteria may appear difficult to achieve, Newell and Shanks (2014) review studies that do meet these criteria. The findings of such studies tend to find no unconscious advantage.

But such findings need not exclude the possibility that unconscious thinking is operating and could be used to improve lie detection. Some studies have found no benefit of unconscious lie detection and have used this as the basis on which to argue that there is no benefit of unconscious thought. While this appears reasonable, one may argue that these studies fail to find an unconscious benefit because the cues to deception typically have low or no diagnosticity to distinguish liars from truth-tellers (e.g., DePaulo et al., 2003). It may be that the unconscious can only outperform conscious lie detection only in situations where there are diagnostic cues available to be detected in the liar (or truth-teller). As we have seen, the indirect lie detection perspective implicitly takes the position that the cue being rated is not the critical factor to determining unconscious lie detection accuracy. But other unconscious perspectives could be bolstered by such an argument. Unfortunately, this could leave unconscious accounts in a position that is difficult to test because they may need to make explicit what cues are being used by the unconscious and why they are processed better by unconscious thought. Nonetheless, tests of unconscious thinking that explicitly manipulate the availability of highly diagnostic indicators of deception may offer fruitful routes for further developing unconscious lie detection accounts.

Chapter Summary

The modern view that unconscious thought may influence lie detection goes back to at least the late 1970s. Studies on indirect lie detection have found that, unaware of the possibility of deception, making an indirect judgement of another behaviour (such as whether the speaker is thinking hard or not) can distinguish between liars and truth-tellers better than making an explicit and direct lie-truth judgement. While these findings have classically been interpreted as an unconscious benefit, it has been recently claimed that the methodology is unable to test for unconscious knowledge. A meta-analysis of indirect lie detection effects has also found that the method more typically results in worse detection accuracy than direct lie-truth judgements, not better accuracy.

Other approaches have taken a more theoretically oriented perspective. This lends them an a priori credibility insofar as the approaches are based on a foundation of empirical evidence and, in turn, allows for testable predictions to be generated. UTT argues that the unconscious is capacity unlimited and so can better handle complex decisions like lie detection, provided the conscious mind is distracted. While some work has supported this perspective, recent high-powered replications have failed to replicate the effects. Another perspective, the tipping point account, argues that people may be able to unconsciously detect deception when a threat is potent but that this information is kept out of conscious awareness so that they do not feel impelled to engage in a social confrontation. There are arguably concerns about the empirical evidence used to support such a perspective along with conceptual concerns over how the account is defined and how it could be tested.

It will be important for future work to produce a clear definition of what exactly is meant by 'unconscious' thought by building on established theoretical perspectives and generating testable predictions that preclude the possibility that conscious thought is actually causing the effects. Until such time, it may be prudent to adopt the perspective of Occam's razor: let us not propose that there exist the two processing modes—conscious and unconscious thinking (or three or four processing modes, for that matter)—if there is no clear evidence that there exists more than one.

Notes

1 Unless of course you read either of those languages, in which case one might contend that you have used your conscious knowledge of the languages to make the decision.
2 If you can read Korean or Mandarin, imagine instead that the characters were the complex Tibetan script compared to the relatively easy-to-draw Greek characters. Please note that this is not a statement about the difficulty of learning any of these languages, nor is it intended to undermine their intricacies. The purpose is merely to highlight that different languages can potentially be distinguished based on an unrelated cue such as the difficulty someone with no prior experience of the languages may have in drawing the characters.
3 A similar argument has been made in Chapter 4 of this book when comparing the adaptive lie detector and truth default accounts of lie-truth judgements.
4 For a further critique of the subliminal priming approach, see Meyen et al. (2022) and Newell and Shanks (2014).
5 Hopefully this question has led you to query the assumption that the unconscious is smarter than conscious thinking. Greenwald (1992), for example, has argued that unconscious processes are rather simple and lack the sophistication of conscious processes.
6 We shall not be reflecting on the long outdated Freudian conception of the unconscious. For a description of the Freudian perspective, see Weber (2012).
7 Recently, Del Pin et al. (2021) contended that different research studies tend to select a different one of the multiple theoretical perspectives of the unconscious. They argue that the research comparing and testing different accounts of the

unconscious is lacking. In their paper, they offer suggestions on how to begin these comparisons, which could prove truly useful for researchers aiming to understand whether unconscious thinking improves lie detection accuracy.
8 The exact numbers are not known. The authors report that 66 participants took part in the study and that there were three conditions, but did not describe how many participants were in each condition. The approximation assumes that sample sizes were balanced across the three conditions.
9 Other analytical issues concern the variety of tests that are applied to the data, the use of marginally significant effects with $p > .050$, variation in what is considered an acceptable sample size from study to study, the capturing of data that is not reported in the results and variation in how accuracy is measured. I encourage you to read ten Brinke et al. (2019) to make your own determination of whether these concerns preclude interpretations that the data support an unconscious perspective.

References

Acker, F. (2008). New findings on unconscious versus conscious thought in decision making: Additional empirical data and meta-analysis. *Judgment and Decision Making*, *3*(4), 292–303.

Albrechtsen, J. S., Meissner, C. A., & Susa, K. J. (2009). Can intuition improve deception detection performance? *Journal of Experimental Social Psychology*, *45*(4), 1052–1055. https://doi.org/10.1016/j.jesp.2009.05.017

Ambady, N. (2010). The perils of pondering: Intuition and thin slice judgments. *Psychological Inquiry*, *21*(4), 271–278. https://doi.org/10.1080/1047840X.2010.524882

Ambady, N., & Rosenthal, R. (1992). Thin slices of expressive behavior as predictors of interpersonal consequences: A meta-analysis. *Psychological Bulletin*, *111*(2), 256–274. https://doi.org/10.1037/0033-2909.111.2.256

Anderson, D. E., DePaulo, B. M., & Ansfield, M. E. (2002). The development of deception detection skill: A longitudinal study of same-sex friends. *Personality and Social Psychology Bulletin*, *28*(4), 536–545. https://doi.org/10.1177/0146167202287010

Bond, C. F., & DePaulo, B. M. (2006). Accuracy of deception judgments. *Personality and Social Psychology Review*, *10*(3), 214–234. https://doi.org/10.1207/s15327957pspr1003_2

Bond, C. F., Levine, T. R., & Hartwig, M. (2014). New findings in non-verbal lie detection. In P. A. Granhag, A. Vrij, B. Verschuere (Eds.), *Detecting Deception: Current Challenges and Cognitive Approaches* (1st ed., pp. 37–58). John Wiley & Sons. https://doi.org/10.1002/9781118510001

Bos, M. W., Dijksterhuis, A., & Baaren, R. B. van. (2008). On the goal-dependency of unconscious thought. *Journal of Experimental Social Psychology*, *44*(4), 1114–1120. https://doi.org/10.1016/j.jesp.2008.01.001

Bowers, K. S. (1984). On being unconsciously influenced and informed. In K. S. Bowers & D. Meichenbaum (Eds.), *The unconscious reconsidered* (pp. 227–273). Wiley.

Del Pin, S. H., Skóra, Z., Sandberg, K., Overgaard, M., & Wierzchoń, M. (2021). Comparing theories of consciousness: Why it matters and how to do it. *Neuroscience of Consciousness*, *2021*(2), niab019. https://doi.org/10.1093/nc/niab019

DePaulo, B. M. (1994). Spotting lies: Can humans learn to do better? *Current Directions in Psychological Science*, *3*(3), 83–86. https://doi.org/10.1111/1467-8721.ep10770433

DePaulo, B. M., Lindsay, J. J., Malone, B. E., Muhlenbruck, L., Charlton, K., & Cooper, H. (2003). Cues to deception. *Psychological Bulletin*, *129*(1), 74–118.

DePaulo, B. M., & Morris, W. L. (2004). Discerning lies from truths: Behavioural cues to deception and the indirect pathway of intuition. In *The detection of deception in forensic contexts* (pp. 15–40). Cambridge University Press. https://doi.org/10.1017/CBO9780511490071.002

DePaulo, B. M., & Rosenthal, R. (1979). Telling lies. *Journal of Personality and Social Psychology*, 37(10), 1713–1722. https://doi.org/10.1037/0022-3514.37.10.1713

DePaulo, B. M., Rosenthal, R., Green, C. R., & Rosenkrantz, J. (1982). Diagnosing deceptive and mixed messages from verbal and nonverbal cues. *Journal of Experimental Social Psychology*, 18(5), 433–446. https://doi.org/10.1016/0022-1031(82)90064-6

Dijksterhuis, A., Bos, M. W., Nordgren, L. F., & Van Baaren, R. B. (2006). On making the right choice: The deliberation-without-attention effect. *Science*, 311(5763), 1005–1007. https://doi.org/10.1126/science.1121629

Dijksterhuis, A., & Strick, M. (2016). A case for thinking without consciousness. *Perspectives on Psychological Science*, 11(1), 117–132. https://doi.org/10.1177/1745691615615317

Feeley, T. H., & Young, M. J. (2000). Self-reported cues about deceptive and truthful communication: The effects of cognitive capacity and communicator veracity. *Communication Quarterly*, 48(2), 101–119. https://doi.org/10.1080/01463370009385585

Franz, V. H., & von Luxburg, U. (2014). *Unconscious lie detection as an example of a widespread fallacy in the Neurosciences* (arXiv:1407.4240). arXiv. https://doi.org/10.48550/arXiv.1407.4240

Franz, V. H., & von Luxburg, U. (2015). No evidence for unconscious lie detection: A significant difference does not imply accurate classification. *Psychological Science*, 26(10), 1646–1648. https://doi.org/10.1177/0956797615597333

González-Vallejo, C., Lassiter, G. D., Bellezza, F. S., & Lindberg, M. J. (2008). 'Save angels perhaps': A critical examination of unconscious thought theory and the deliberation-without-attention effect. *Review of General Psychology*, 12(3), 282–296. https://doi.org/10.1037/a0013134

Greenwald, A. G. (1992). New Look 3: Unconscious cognition reclaimed. *American Psychologist*, 47(6), 766–779. https://doi.org/10.1037/0003-066X.47.6.766

Griffiths, K., Hou, R., Wang, H., Zhang, Z., Zhang, L., Zhang, T., Watson, D. G., Burchmore, R. J. S., Loeffler, I. K., & Kennedy, M. W. (2015). Prolonged transition time between colostrum and mature milk in a bear, the giant panda, Ailuropoda melanoleuca. *Royal Society Open Science*, 2(10), 150395. https://doi.org/10.1098/rsos.150395

Levine, T. R., & Bond, C. F. (2014). Direct and indirect measures of lie detection tell the same story: A reply to ten Brinke, Stimson, and Carney (2014). *Psychological Science*, 25(10), 1960–1961. https://doi.org/10.1177/0956797614536740

Loftus, E. F., & Klinger, M. R. (1992). Is the unconscious smart or dumb? *American Psychologist*, 47(6), 761–765. https://doi.org/10.1037/0003-066X.47.6.761

Luke, T. J. (2019). Lessons from Pinocchio: Cues to deception may be highly exaggerated. *Perspectives on Psychological Science*, 14(4), 646–671. https://doi.org/10.1177/1745691619838258

Meyen, S., Zerweck, I. A., Amado, C., von Luxburg, U., & Franz, V. H. (2022). Advancing research on unconscious priming: When can scientists claim an indirect task advantage? *Journal of Experimental Psychology. General*, 151(1), 65–81. https://doi.org/10.1037/xge0001065

Moi, W. Y., & Shanks, D. R. (2015). Can lies be detected unconsciously? *Frontiers in Psychology* (6), Article 1221. https://doi.org/10.3389/fpsyg.2015.01221

Moors, A., & De Houwer, J. (2006). Automaticity: A theoretical and conceptual analysis. *Psychological Bulletin*, *132*(2), 297–326. https://doi.org/10.1037/0033-2909.132.2.297

Newell, B. R., & Rakow, T. (2011). Revising beliefs about the merit of unconscious thought: Evidence in favor of the null hypothesis. *Social Cognition*, *29*(6), 711–726. https://doi.org/10.1521/soco.2011.29.6.711

Newell, B. R., & Shanks, D. R. (2014). Unconscious influences on decision making: A critical review. *The Behavioral and Brain Sciences*, *37*(1), 1–19. https://doi.org/10.1017/S0140525X12003214

Nieuwenstein, M. R., Wierenga, T., Morey, R. D., Wicherts, J. M., Blom, T. N., Wagenmakers, E.-J., & van Rijn, H. (2015). On making the right choice: A meta-analysis and large-scale replication attempt of the unconscious thought advantage. *Judgment and Decision Making*, *10*(1), 1–17.

Nosek, B. A., Greenwald, A. G., & Banaji, M. R. (2007). The implicit association test at age 7: A methodological and conceptual review. In J. A. Bargh (Ed.), *Social psychology and the unconscious: The automaticity of higher mental processes* (pp. 265–292). Psychology Press.

O'Sullivan, M. (2003). The fundamental attribution error in detecting deception: The boy-who-cried-wolf effect. *Personality and Social Psychology Bulletin*, *29*(10), 1316–1327. https://doi.org/10.1177/0146167203254610

Reinhard, M.-A., Greifeneder, R., & Scharmach, M. (2013). Unconscious processes improve lie detection. *Journal of Personality and Social Psychology*, *105*(5), 721–739. https://doi.org/10.1037/a0034352

Rothkirch, M., & Hesselmann, G. (2017). What we talk about when we talk about unconscious processing – a plea for best practices. *Frontiers in Psychology*, *8*. https://www.frontiersin.org/articles/10.3389/fpsyg.2017.00835

Shanks, D. R., & St. John, M. F. (1994). Characteristics of dissociable human learning systems. *Behavioral and Brain Sciences*, *17*(3), 367–395. https://doi.org/10.1017/S0140525X00035032

Simmons, J. P., Nelson, L. D., & Simonsohn, U. (2011). False-positive psychology: Undisclosed flexibility in data collection and analysis allows presenting anything as significant. *Psychological Science*, *22*(11), 1359–1366.

Slepian, M. L., Bogart, K. R., & Ambady, N. (2014). Thin-slice judgments in the clinical context. *Annual Review of Clinical Psychology*, *10*, 131–153. https://doi.org/10.1146/annurev-clinpsy-090413-123522

Sporer, S. L., & Schwandt, B. (2006). Paraverbal indicators of deception: A meta-analytic synthesis. *Applied Cognitive Psychology*, *20*(4), 421–446. https://doi.org/10.1002/acp.1190

Sporer, S. L., & Schwandt, B. (2007). Moderators of nonverbal indicators of deception: A meta-analytic synthesis. *Psychology, Public Policy, and Law*, *13*(1), 1–34. https://doi.org/10.1037/1076-8971.13.1.1

Sporer, S. L., & Ulatowska, J. (2021). Indirect and unconscious deception detection: Too soon to give up? *Frontiers in Psychology*, *12*. https://doi.org/10.3389/fpsyg.2021.601852

Stafford, T. (2014). The perspectival shift: How experiments on unconscious processing don't justify the claims made for them. *Frontiers in Psychology*, *5*, 1067. https://doi.org/10.3389/fpsyg.2014.01067

Street, C. N. H., & Kingstone, A. (2017). Aligning Spinoza with Descartes: An informed Cartesian account of the truth bias. *British Journal of Psychology*, *108*(3), 453–466. https://doi.org/10.1111/bjop.12210

Street, C. N. H., & Masip, J. (2015). The source of the truth bias: Heuristic processing? *Scandinavian Journal of Psychology, 56*(3), 254–263. https://doi.org/10.1111/sjop.12204

Street, C. N. H., & Richardson, D. C. (2015). The focal account: Indirect lie detection need not access unconscious, implicit knowledge. *Journal of Experimental Psychology: Applied, 21*(4), 342–355. https://doi.org/10.1037/xap0000058

Street, C. N. H., & Vadillo, M. A. (2016). Can the unconscious boost lie-detection accuracy? *Current Directions in Psychological Science, 25*(4), 246–250.

Street, C. N. H., & Vadillo, M. A. (2017). Commentary: Can ordinary people detect deception after all? *Frontiers in Psychology, 8*, 1789. https://doi.org/10.3389/fpsyg.2017.01789

ten Brinke, L., & Carney, D. R. (2014). Wanted: Direct comparisons of unconscious and conscious lie detection. *Psychological Science, 25*(10), 1962–1963. https://doi.org/10.1177/0956797614544308

ten Brinke, L., Lee, J. J., & Carney, D. R. (2019). Different physiological reactions when observing lies versus truths: Initial evidence and an intervention to enhance accuracy. *Journal of Personality and Social Psychology, 117*(3), 560–578. https://doi.org/10.1037/pspi0000175

ten Brinke, L., Stimson, D., & Carney, D. R. (2014). Some evidence for unconscious lie detection. *Psychological Science, 25*(5), 1098–1105. https://doi.org/10.1177/0956797614524421

ten Brinke, L., Vohs, K. D., & Carney, D. R. (2016). Can ordinary people detect deception after all? *Trends in Cognitive Sciences, 20*(8), 579–588. https://doi.org/10.1016/j.tics.2016.05.012

Ulatowska, J. (2010). The influence of providing the context of the assessment on the accuracy of the indirect method of deception detection. *Problems of Forensic Sciences, 84*, 380–391.

Ulatowska, J. (2014). Different questions – different accuracy? The accuracy of various indirect question types in deception detection. *Psychiatry, Psychology and Law, 21*(2), 231–240. https://doi.org/10.1080/13218719.2013.803278

Vadillo, M. A., Kostopoulou, O., & Shanks, D. R. (2015). A critical review and meta-analysis of the unconscious thought effect in medical decision making. *Frontiers in Psychology, 6*. https://www.frontiersin.org/articles/10.3389/fpsyg.2015.00636

Verschuere, B., Lin, C.-C., Huismann, S., Kleinberg, B., & Meijer, E. (2021). *Use the best, ignore the rest: How heuristics allow to tell a lie from the truth.* PsyArXiv. https://doi.org/10.31234/osf.io/kdr6u

Vrij, A., Edward, K., & Bull, R. (2001). Police officers' ability to detect deceit: The benefit of indirect deception detection measures. *Legal and Criminological Psychology, 6*(2), 185–196. https://doi.org/10.1348/135532501168271

Vrij, A., & Fisher, R. P. (2020). Unraveling the misconception about deception and nervous behavior. *Frontiers in Psychology, 11*. https://www.frontiersin.org/articles/10.3389/fpsyg.2020.01377

Walczyk, J. J., Harris, L. L., Duck, T. K., & Mulay, D. (2014). A social-cognitive framework for understanding serious lies: Activation-decision-construction-action theory. *New Ideas in Psychology, 34*, 22–36. https://doi.org/10.1016/j.newideapsych.2014.03.001

Weber, E. T. (2012). James's critique of the Freudian unconscious – 25 years earlier. *William James Studies, 9*, 94–119.

Wu, S., Mei, H., & Yan, J. (2019). Do not think carefully? Re-examining the effect of unconscious thought on deception detection. *Frontiers in Psychology, 10*, 893. https://doi.org/10.3389/fpsyg.2019.00893

8 Challenges for Deception and Lie Detection Research

> **Box 8.1 Ukraine's Wooden Missile Systems**
>
> On 24 February 2022, Russia invaded Ukraine. On 30 August 2022, *The Washington Post* (Hudson, 2022) reported that Ukraine had found a novel approach to countering the cruise missile carriers of the Russians. Ukraine has been in receipt of advanced US rocket systems, which were reportedly considered by Russia to be high priority targets. In a successful attempt to lure the Russians into wasting their cruise missiles, Ukraine constructed wooden replicas of US artillery batteries, according to anonymous Ukrainian officials speaking to *The Washington Post*. These fake wooden rocket systems were indistinguishable from the real ones to an overhead drone, leading Russia to launch its naval cruise missiles on the dummy targets. Days later, *The Guardian* (Koshiw et al., 2022) reported that Ukraine carried out a successful disinformation campaign that led Russian forces to prepare for a southern offensive, allowing Ukraine to make significant gains in the north east.

This chapter is intended as an introduction to the evaluation of the field of deception and lie detection as a whole. It can often be difficult, as a student, to take a step back from the individual research papers that you are reading and to consider the broader context in which they sit. This chapter aims to help situate some of those considerations and encourage you to reflect on the broader issues. This chapter is not intended to spur academics into new directions of research or to highlight the understudied areas of our discipline, but rather to offer a first step towards understanding some of the broader concerns that have previously been raised in the literature or that require consideration.

Constraints of Laboratory Research Methods: Ecological Validity

A frequently cited question is whether laboratory research duplicates the important elements that would exist outside of the laboratory. This is a question of ecological validity. If laboratory lies do not mimic real-world lies, there is a question of whether the results of laboratory studies will generalise to the wider population and whether the findings will have value for practitioners.

To explore deception and to conduct lie detection studies, researchers typically video-record senders lying and telling the truth about a topic or event. These videos are the data set for those researching deception, but are the stimulus set to be shown to receiver participants for those researchers interested in lie detection. In a review, Semrad et al. (2019) noted that many of the lies collected in the laboratory may not be considered lies at all. This is because senders are lying not to achieve some goal that truth-telling would not allow, but instead are told just to follow the experimenter's instruction. One may question whether these deceptive statements are truly intended to mislead the person receiving them at the time of their delivery. The person who typically receives the statement is the experimenter, who the participant may believe already knows that they are going to lie. Thus, there is a question of whether these stimuli capture an *intention* to deceive. Intentionality is at the core of most definitions of deception. Levine (2017) also notes that many laboratory-generated lies involve producing explicitly false information, whereas real-world lies are more subtle, such as omitting key details from an otherwise truthful account. And when people are free to choose how they lie, they typically choose to embed their lie inside an otherwise truthful story (Leins et al., 2013).

Not only does this question whether laboratory lies are a good simulation of real-world lies, but when we use real-world lies in our research, it can be difficult to establish whether the statement should be considered a lie or a truth. Indeed, one of the benefits of laboratory-based lies is that ground truth can be established, meaning that it is known whether the sender is lying or telling the truth. In the real world, this has to be inferred on the basis of (potentially erroneous) physical evidence, court sentencing, or witness testimony. The difficulty of establishing the ground truth makes it difficult to determine how people lie outside of the lab and how accurate lie detection techniques may be in real settings (see Hartwig et al., 2014; Sternglanz et al., 2019; Vrij, 2015).

Researchers sensitive to these concerns of intentionality and qualitatively different speech content have sought to use real-world lies in their studies (e.g., Porter & ten Brinke, 2010) or create laboratory situations that allow senders the opportunity to spontaneously intend to mislead the receiver (e.g., Duran et al., 2013; Street & Richardson, 2015). For example, Street and Richardson (2015) used a stimulus set of liars and truth-tellers that were not recorded in the laboratory as part of a deception experiment. Instead, senders were recruited outside of a film recording studio and, because of a supposedly short deadline of the filming company, requested that the senders tell a lie as part of a tourism documentary. Those who agreed (and so chose to lie of their own volition) were taken into the filming studio and left alone with a film director who was supposedly unaware that the sender would be lying. In this way, the sender entered the situation with an intent to make the documentary director believe that their deceptive story about visiting a particular country was, in fact, the truth.

Another potential concern for laboratory-based deceptions is that they lack the emotion, arousal, and high stakes that real-world lies have and consequently may result in different behaviours produced by senders (Buckley, 2012; Porter & ten Brinke, 2010). As a result, lie detectors outside the lab may achieve higher accuracy rates than they do inside the lab (Burgoon, 2015; Levine et al., 2014). Counterarguments note that the stakes of the lie (or whether the liars are students or non-students) have not been found to affect the presence or diagnosticity of cues to deception (Hartwig & Bond, 2014). Hartwig and Bond (2014) suggest that there may not be an important distinction between laboratory and real-world lies because their meta-analysis found that lie detection was similar across a variety of settings. Another meta-analysis by Bond and DePaulo (2006) had earlier found that the stakes of the deception does not appear to affect detection accuracy.[1] Additionally, Leach et al. (2009) examined whether receivers' lie detection accuracy is consistent over time and found that the type of lie being judged—naturalistic or lab-based—did not affect their consistency over time.

How people detect lies may also be different inside versus outside the lab. It is typical for lab-based studies to present a participant with a sender's statement (perhaps as a video or transcript) and for the experimenter to request that the participant makes a lie or truth judgement immediately after receiving the statement. Then the next statement is delivered, and another judgement requested, and so on. Because of this, participants in these studies usually only have access to the speech and nonverbal behaviours of the sender, depending on the medium of presentation. In real-world lie detection, the situation is not the same. Park et al. (2002), in a paper entitled *How people really detect lies*, asked student participants to recall a time when they had been lied to and to explain how they had discovered the lie. Rather than mentioning verbal and nonverbal behaviours, 32% of participants mentioned that they detected a lie by having received contradictory information from a third party. Eighteen per cent mentioned physical evidence and 31% mentioned a combination of methods. The indicative evidence was sometimes not received for days or weeks after the lie was told. Only 2.1% of participants mentioned discovering deception by using the verbal or nonverbal behaviours of the sender at the time the lie was told. That is, lies in people's daily lives may be detected after a substantial period of delay and with the use of physical or testimonial evidence, whereas in the lab participants are constrained to respond immediately and on the basis of the verbal and nonverbal behaviours presented. Laboratory studies have found that when receivers have access to peripheral contextual details such as what the sender gains from lying and telling the truth (Bond et al., 2013) or whether a situation encouraged cheating and lying about it afterwards (Blair et al., 2010), higher lie detection accuracy rates can be achieved.

> **Box 8.2 Limitations Are Not Weaknesses**
>
> While the points considered so far may stand as a limitation of laboratory-based work, they do not prevent us from learning something about how people lie or detect lies. Instead, we must use our academic judgement to decide what are the boundary conditions or limits of what can be inferred on the basis of these studies. For example, we are still able to gain an insight into how people make lie-truth judgements when the cues available to them (verbal and nonverbal behaviours) have low diagnosticity and when they cannot seek out further evidence. We may also understand the cognitive processes that are involved in generating entirely fabricated statements on behest of another person's request. There are both theoretical and practical reasons why we may wish to study these seemingly 'artificial' settings. It is a mistake to think that a limitation is a weakness of the study. All research is necessarily limited in what it allows us to infer. It is our job to make *appropriate* interpretations of what can be learnt and when or how those findings can be applied in appropriate contexts.

In summary, there have been questions raised about whether laboratory-generated lies requested by the experimenter capture the true nature of deception, including an intention to mislead the receiver. Researchers have become aware of this issue and are designing studies to capture more naturalistic lies. The laboratory may also constrain the way in which lie detection is studied. Outside of the laboratory, people rarely report using the verbal and nonverbal behaviour of the sender to reach their judgement, and yet in the laboratory this is typically the only information receivers have available to them. Lab-based lie detection, for practicality's sake, asks participants to make immediate lie-truth judgements. But outside the lab, people may not detect deception for days or weeks. These issues may require a shift in the methodologies used to study deception and lie detection. However, it would be foolhardy to conclude that the scientific research into deception detection has taught us little because of these limitations. As interpreters and sense-makers of scientific enquiry, it is our job to appropriately interpret the limits and boundaries on our ability to apply the research to real-world settings. And experimentally controlled settings allow us to control and manipulate so that we may develop strong theoretical bases for applied research.

Constraints of Real-World Research Methods: Establishing Robust Theory

Experimental control. While ecological validity is a concern that should be considered in earnest, perhaps less often considered in the deception community are the difficulties that arise from real-world and more ecologically valid paradigms, as well as the strengths that laboratory-based methods hold. In naturalistic settings, it is difficult, if not impossible, to control and manipulate variables such as the emotional experience of the liar or the diagnosticity of the cues available to the lie detector. This can undermine an ability to establish or test causal relationships. The laboratory is well-situated for generating testable predictions, systematically manipulating variables, controlling variables that we do not want to affect the results, and determining whether effects are caused by particular forces. Thus, while it may seem reasonable to suggest that all research should be practitioner-led with a focus on developing novel applications, laboratory-based methods are important for developing our understanding of deception and its detection.

If one wishes to test whether senders decide whether to lie by calculating the pros and cons of lying and telling the truth (a prediction of the activation-decision-component-action theory of deception production; Walczyk et al., 2014), being able to tightly define the circumstances in which the sender finds themselves will allow the researchers to isolate this element of the account and attempt to falsify it (e.g., Masip et al., 2016). If one wishes to understand whether people make lie-truth decisions by using a combination of individuating and context-general information depending on how diagnostic the cues are (a prediction of the adaptive lie detector account; Street, 2015), being able to systematically control which cues are presented and how diagnostic they are offers a robust test of how people make lie-truth decisions (e.g., Street et al., 2016). And if one wishes to know whether distracting the conscious mind can improve lie detection accuracy (a prediction of unconscious thought theory: Dijksterhuis et al., 2006), presenting identical lies and truths to a conscious reflection and a conscious distraction condition will help ensure that no other influences are unintentionally causing the results (e.g., Moi & Shanks, 2015).

There is one area where experimental control may be difficult (and arguably impossible) to implement, and that is in the case of examining the influence of the sender's behaviour on lie detection accuracy. To determine if a receiver has made a correct or incorrect judgement, it must be possible to label a given sender's statement as the truth or a lie. If an experimenter were to artificially manipulate the behaviour of the sender (e.g., by providing senders with a scripted statement or by manipulating the senders' visual behaviours using video editing software), one may question whether these statements can be thought of as truths and lies. They are controlled and possibly even generated by the experimenter, and potentially the resulting behaviour no longer reflects an attempt by the sender to deliver a statement that the receiver believes to be true, nor may it reflect any intent to mislead the receiver. Taken to the extreme, if one were to programme a robot to produce verbal and nonverbal behaviours, which statements would be the truths and which the lies? An attempt to control the behaviour of a liar or truth-teller potentially leaves the researcher in a position of capturing statements that cannot be considered lies or truths. As a result, it would not be able to assess whether receivers are making accurate judgements.[2] Because the behaviours cannot be controlled, it may be difficult to assess whether there may be highly diagnostic cues to deception that are present in the senders' statements, for example, or even whether there are behaviours that systematically lead receivers to make the wrong judgement.

Another concern with lie detection experiments is that given the time and resource constraints along with the limits of participants' attention, studies tend to use a rather small sample of senders (Sporer & Ulatowska, 2021). Based on computer simulations, Levine et al. (2022) recommended that lie detection studies have at least 500 judgements in total (e.g., 50 receivers judging the statements of 10 senders), with the recommendation that if studies want to keep the deviance in their studies within the 55% ± 10% accuracy rate, *at least* 20 senders and 50 receivers should be used (giving a total of 1,000 judgements).

In short, experimental control offers the opportunity to manipulate, control, and draw causal relationships in a way that may not be possible in more realistic environments.

Replicability. Using more controlled laboratory procedures allow research methodologies to be reproduced in other research labs and, hopefully, for their findings to be replicated. However, replicability cannot be taken for granted. In a study of 100 important papers in the field of psychology, the Open Science Collaboration (2012) found that only 39% of the studies' results could be replicated. This 'replication crisis' has pervaded all of science, not just psychology. Naturally, the subfields of deception and lie detection are not free from the crisis.

There are a number of possible reasons why research may not replicate. Questionable research practices such as reporting only a selection of the collected variables (and concealing those that may not offer favourable results) or attempting multiple analyses on the data until one provides a positive outcome are thought to contribute to the crisis (Fiedler & Schwarz, 2016; John et al., 2012), along with cases of outright fraud (e.g., Levelt et al., 2012) all contribute. These problems may result from the poorly aligned incentive structure of academia (Nosek et al., 2012). Academics are rewarded individually (by promotion and with international reputation) for publishing in quantity, producing tantalising findings that are regularly cited by other researchers, and, in turn, generating research grant income. Researchers must balance these personal incentives with their desire to produce rigorous, high-quality work that is reproducible and replicable for the good of science and society.

Suggested solutions to the crisis are to encourage 'open science' practices (O. Klein et al., 2018). Open science involves making one's research materials and data freely available to other scientists via an online platform, such as the Open Science Framework (https://osf.io). This allows other researchers to scrutinise the data and analytical methods and allows them to reproduce the study to assess whether the findings can be replicated in other laboratories.

Another of the suggested solutions is to encourage researchers to more frequently conduct replication projects. The Many Labs projects (e.g., R. A. Klein et al., 2014, 2018) have brought together many researchers from multiple countries to assess whether important findings in psychology can be replicated. There are, however, some difficulties in clearly defining what a replication entails (see Brandt et al., 2014, for detailed guidance on what makes for a convincing replication). There are also questions about whether a failed replication attempt should lead us to believe that the original effect does not hold or whether, given the probabilistic nature of our field, the failed attempt should lead us to conclude that the original effect does hold but even a real effect will sometimes fail to replicate (Francis, 2012).[3]

A particularly influential proposal that has been taken up by psychologists is that of preregistration (J. Simmons et al., 2021). By preregistering one's hypotheses, methodology, and analytical plan in an immutable public record (i.e., a record that cannot be deleted or changed), the opportunity to engage in questionable research practices is reduced. Additionally, journals can commit to publishing a research study before the data are collected. One issue researchers face is that highly prestigious journals tend to publish only the most engaging and exciting findings that have broad reach. If a journal accepts a preregistered study before the data have been collected, there are reduced incentives for the researchers to find ways of creating tantalising findings in the data: the work will be published by the journal regardless of what story the data tell. For further discussion of research practices that may prevent false findings in the published literature, see Simmons et al. (2011) and Murayama et al. (2014).

Theoretical basis. Research on deception detection has primarily sought to develop methods and interventions designed to improve lie detection accuracy. This is certainly a worthwhile effort that deserves attention and financial support, given the broad range of positive applications to society (see Chapter 1). But this can lead to a neglect of developing and testing theoretical accounts that explain the phenomena (see Blandón-Gitlin et al., 2014). While research on deception has been driven by numerous theoretical accounts of how lies and truths are produced (see Chapter 2), theorising about how lie-truth judgements are made has been somewhat absent until recently (see Chapter 4). Understanding how people accurately detect deception will necessarily require an understanding of how they reach a judgement of 'lie' or 'truth'. This focus on phenomena over theory can be seen across other subdisciplines of psychology too (van Rooij & Baggio, 2021).

But is a theoretical understanding needed if a lie detection technique is shown to work? As klein Selle et al. (2018) point out when discussing the theoretical background of the concealed information test, a robust scientific theory can tell us how to apply a technique optimally, under what conditions it will work, what factors will undermine its utility, and what the technique's scope and boundaries are for application. And a lack of substantive theory can result in techniques being taken into practice too early (see Blandón-Gitlin et al., 2014; Denault et al., 2020, for a real-world example of the SPOT programme, or Chapter 5 for discussion of the lack of theoretical underpinning for the polygraph and the control question technique). Thus, there are real and practical implications for failing to ground a technique in a robust theoretical base.

Whether formal or informal, scientists use theory to develop their research plans and interpret their data. For example, the cognitive load approach to lie detection is based on the theory that liars experience greater cognitive load than truth-tellers. This acts not only as a steer as to what techniques can be developed (e.g., recalling statements in reverse order may increase lie detection accuracy because doing so would increase the cognitive load), but it is also the lens through which the results are interpreted (e.g., the increase in accuracy is because liars are cognitively overwhelmed). It may be tempting to believe that we can observe data objectively without the need for a theory, but ultimately those statistical results from our analyses have to be interpreted and made sense of by the researcher (Dennett, 1996). This researcher-contingent interpretation is most easily seen when different researchers hold different interpretations of the same empirical data (see Chapter 7, for example, for debates on whether unconscious thinking improves lie detection accuracy).

The absence of a robust theory will prevent a deeper understanding of the phenomenon. Farrell and Lewandowsky (2010) give the example of how, in early studies of planetary motion, the planets appeared to briefly loop back on their trajectory. It took more than 1,000 years to understand the phenomenon. This only came about when the Ptolemaic Earth-centred theory was replaced by the Copernican Sun-centred theory. Similarly, despite dissections of the human eye having been carried out since antiquity, it was not until Descartes's theory of the eye as a camera lens that the correct anatomical structure of the eye was described. Data is necessarily interpreted on the basis of theory. Developing techniques in the absence of a substantive theory risks misinterpreting the data or failing to understand the phenomenon that has been discovered.

We have previously considered that one element of a useful theory is its ability to formulate clearly testable, novel predictions (Box 2.4., Chapter 2). Ideally, accounts will reflect on the literature across the psychological discipline to form a more holistic view of human thinking and behaviour and to ensure that the subfields of deception and its detection are informed by relevant work being carried out in other subfields, such as judgement and decision-making, emotion, consciousness, cognition, and more. As van Rooij and Baggio (2021, p. 683) state, explanations should "offer a vantage point from which to ... explain known effects ... [and] guide inquiry into the discovery of new informative ones". Taking a more holistic perspective offers a stronger vantage point from which to integrate multiple phenomena into a unified psychological theory.

Summary. Laboratory research is not fundamentally problematic. By producing empirically informed accounts and testing them, researchers work from a bedrock of credibility on which to develop new techniques. This bedrock provides the understanding of when and how techniques may be best applied. Pseudo-scientific claims are being promoted to and employed by lie detection practitioners (Denault et al., 2020), making the call for theoretically informed practices all the more pressing. Establishing and testing these accounts will require systematic control of key variables. The experimental approach is the propelling force for the scientific discipline, and with good reason. Engaging with open science and preregistration practices will help ensure that the results of research are replicable and robust.

The WEIRD World of Psychology

Psychological research tends to be published by researchers from Western countries and based on samples of Western participants. Arnett (2008) found that 96% of participants in papers in six well-respected journals were WEIRD, which is to say, they were Westernised, educated, and from industrialised, rich, and democratic regions of the world. WEIRD populations tend to be more independent and individualistic, with an emphasis on each person being responsible for themselves (Schulz et al., 2018). We might compare this with more collectivistic cultures that value group connections, loyalty to the group and working together towards common goals. But it is not just our samples that are WEIRD. Researchers from WEIRD backgrounds receive privilege. Being on an editorial board for a journal is a prestigious position to hold, but the roles are predominantly occupied by researchers from the US and the UK, and who identify as male (Altman & Cohen, 2021).

Cheon et al. (2020) found that studies tended not to refer to their samples being American in the titles of their papers unless they also sampled from other non-WEIRD cultures, suggesting that there is an implied belief among US researchers that American participants are considered globally generalisable. It is only when researchers explicitly seek out other non-US samples that there is consideration that the findings may be culturally bound (This book is guilty of this issue, too). Similarly, Giles et al. (2021) argue that deception detection research has been largely conducted from the WEIRD perspective. This is, in part, due to greater research funding available in WEIRD countries (see funding information from UNESCO, 2021).

When research is overgeneralised across cultures, Brady et al. (2018) argue that the best outcome is that psychological interventions implemented in cultures other than the ones they were developed in will not work. At worse, the intervention may backfire and make the situation worse rather than providing benefit. Suggestions have been made for beginning to tackle the WEIRD problem in science. For example, the internet offers ready access to potentially diverse research participant samples (Bergman & Jean, 2016; Smith et al., 2015). However, it has been argued that online 'crowdsourcing' platforms for recruiting research participants tend to be WEIRD and that research conducted in the English language will place limits on the potential diversity of samples that can meaningfully take part (Keith & Harms, 2016). Others have suggested that the academic structures require change (Brady et al., 2018), such as adding sections to journal articles that highlight the 'Constraints on Generality' to make explicit the cultural assumptions of the researchers based on their sample (Simons et al., 2017). However, little change has been made to date (Thalmayer et al., 2021).

A novel perspective on this issue comes from Kanazawa (2020). The WEIRD problem may not necessarily be a problem that requires change in the more traditional sense. It may be possible to abstract beyond the level of culture in some instances. He gives the example of how the grammatical structures of two different languages may differ, but that this can be abstracted to state that languages, regardless of culture, have a grammatical system. Such abstraction may similarly be applied to psychological findings that differ between cultures, where an overarching abstracted explanation may account for the variation without requiring different cultural perspectives.

Where abstraction fails, explanation may substitute. Rather than describing differences between cultures, explaining why the differences exist removes the WEIRD/non-WEIRD distinction. For example, if a hypothetical study found that a sample from a more individualistic culture was more willing to accuse others of deception compared to a sample from a more collectivistic culture, this could be explained as an accusatory reluctance (i.e., a desire to avoid confronting others with their deception) that is more pronounced because of the differences in the groups' social norms. Explanations of cultural distinctions may not be informative when the phenomenon may be explained by social or psychological processes such as social norms.

Finally, Kanazawa (2020) reflects that in some cases a WEIRD population may offer a less constrained testing platform for research hypotheses. For instance, if one wishes to know what proportions of the population identify as gay, one may be able to more easily achieve an accurate count in a more liberal WEIRD culture. Equally, of course, one may find that non-WEIRD cultures open opportunities to address research questions that are less easily achieved by using WEIRD samples.

Chapter Summary

This chapter has started you on a journey to consider the challenges that face our field. There are questions about whether the laboratory sufficiently replicates the real-world situation of deceiving and detecting deceit. Researchers have sought to tackle this by co-developing research with practitioners and developing paradigms that capture the intentionality behind deception. However, there are benefits for conducting more artificial, laboratory-based studies. They allow more robust theory development and testing, which can form the scientific bedrock on which applied techniques are built. To do this effectively, we must be keen to considerations of how we can make our field more replicable. This may include preregistering our research, but making the field more replicable may extend more broadly into considerations of how our work is limited by the cultural lens that we as researchers bring to our work and how we may sample more diverse participants.

Closing Remarks

This book has set out to achieve two aims: to offer an introduction to the core contemporary issues in the science of deception and its detection, and to offer practical guidance for and hands-on experience with developing your evaluative reasoning. I hope you have engaged with the Boxes, which have been the primary means of encouraging reflection and analysis. We have discovered the processes that people engage with when deciding whether to lie or not and how both verbal and nonverbal behaviours may reflect these processes. Despite what much of the received wisdom of popular culture tells us, there are no clear-cut signs to deception.

When people make judgements about whether others are lying or not, they tend to be truth-biased: that is, they guess that others are telling the truth rather than consider that they are lying. Chapter 4 offers different explanations of this: either that people default to believing others or that they are engaged in adaptive, functional, and informed decision-making strategies. The accuracy of these judgements tends to be marginally better than chance. But more active techniques that are designed to elicit cues from the sender show potential, and it appears to be the direction that the field is heading towards. There is limited work exploring whether people can unconsciously detect deception, but there have been a number of critiques against work that has claimed to show an unconscious benefit.

We have also considered how people develop an understanding of deception and an ability to deceive. Being able to deceive requires establishing an ability to comprehend others' thoughts (theory of mind) and to manage multiple pieces of information (executive function). As children age, their lies become more convincing. They also tend to tell and be more forgiving of prosocial lies.

Finally, we have explored some of the core concerns and challenges for studying deception and detection. I hope this has offered you an opportunity to step back from the published literature in the fields of deception and lie detection and to reflect on how we can situate what we have learnt into the broader context of human psychology.

Notes

1 It is noteworthy that the studies in this meta-analysis were based on laboratory-generated lies.
2 Studying how people form lie-truth judgements (Chapter 4) need not suffer from this issue. One could study, for instance, whether a receiver perceives a robot to be lying or telling the truth without the experimenter having to determine whether or not the robot is lying.

3 In much the same way, a truly fair coin flipped 50 times will sometimes show heads more than half the time.

References

Altman, M., & Cohen, P. N. (2021). *Openness and Diversity in Journal Editorial Boards.* SocArXiv. https://doi.org/10.31235/osf.io/4nq97

Arnett, J. J. (2008). The neglected 95%: Why American psychology needs to become less American. *The American Psychologist, 63*(7), 602–614. https://doi.org/10.1037/0003-066X.63.7.602

Bergman, M. E., & Jean, V. A. (2016). Where have all the "workers" gone? A critical analysis of the unrepresentativeness of our samples relative to the labor market in the industrial–organizational psychology literature. *Industrial and Organizational Psychology, 9*(1), 84–113. https://doi.org/10.1017/iop.2015.70

Blair, J. P., Levine, T. R., & Shaw, A. S. (2010). Content in context improves deception detection accuracy. *Human Communication Research, 36*(3), 423–442. https://doi.org/10.1111/j.1468-2958.2010.01382.x

Blandón-Gitlin, I., Fenn, E., Masip, J., & Yoo, A. H. (2014). Cognitive-load approaches to detect deception: Searching for cognitive mechanisms. *Trends in Cognitive Sciences, 18*(9), 441–444. https://doi.org/10.1016/j.tics.2014.05.004

Bond, C. F., & DePaulo, B. M. (2006). Accuracy of deception judgments. *Personality and Social Psychology Review, 10*(3), 214–234. https://doi.org/10.1207/s15327957pspr1003_2

Bond, C. F., Howard, A. R., Hutchison, J. L., & Masip, J. (2013). Overlooking the obvious: Incentives to lie. *Basic and Applied Social Psychology, 35*(2), 212–221. https://doi.org/10.1080/01973533.2013.764302

Brady, L. M., Fryberg, S. A., & Shoda, Y. (2018). Expanding the interpretive power of psychological science by attending to culture. *Proceedings of the National Academy of Sciences, 115*(45), 11406–11413. https://doi.org/10.1073/pnas.1803526115

Brandt, M. J., IJzerman, H., Dijksterhuis, A., Farach, F. J., Geller, J., Giner-Sorolla, R., Grange, J. A., Perugini, M., Spies, J. R., & van 't Veer, A. (2014). The replication recipe: What makes for a convincing replication? *Journal of Experimental Social Psychology, 50,* 217–224. https://doi.org/10.1016/j.jesp.2013.10.005

Buckley, J. P. (2012). Detection of deception researchers needs to collaborate with experienced practitioners. *Journal of Applied Research in Memory and Cognition, 1*(2), 126–127. https://doi.org/10.1016/j.jarmac.2012.04.002

Burgoon, J. K. (2015). Rejoinder to Levine, Clare et al.'s comparison of the Park–Levine probability model versus interpersonal deception theory: Application to deception detection. *Human Communication Research, 41*(3), 327–349. https://doi.org/10.1111/hcre.12065

Cheon, B. K., Melani, I., & Hong, Y.-Y. (2020). How USA-centric is psychology? An archival study of implicit assumptions of generalizability of findings to human nature based on origins of study samples. *Social Psychological and Personality Science, 11*(7), 928–937. https://doi.org/10.1177/1948550620927269

Denault, V., Plusquellec, P., Jupe, L. M., St-Yves, M., Dunbar, N. E., Hartwig, M., Sporer, S. L., Rioux-Turcotte, J., Jarry, J., Walsh, D., Otgaar, H., Viziteu, A., Talwar, V., Keatley, D. A., Blandón-Gitlin, I., Townson, C., Deslauriers-Varin, N., Lilienfeld, S. O., Patterson, M. L., … Koppen, P. J. van. (2020). The analysis of nonverbal communication: The dangers of pseudoscience in security and justice contexts. *Anuario de Psicología Jurídica, 30*(1), 1–12. https://doi.org/10.5093/apj2019a9

Dennett, D. C. (1996). *Darwin's Dangerous Idea: Evolution and the Meanings of Life.* Simon & Schuster.

Dijksterhuis, A., Bos, M. W., Nordgren, L. F., & Van Baaren, R. B. (2006). On making the right choice: The deliberation-without-attention effect. *Science, 311*(5763), 1005–1007. https://doi.org/10.1126/science.1121629

Duran, N. D., Dale, R., Kello, C. T., Street, C. N. H., & Richardson, D. C. (2013). Exploring the movement dynamics of deception. *Frontiers in Psychology, 4.* https://doi.org/10.3389/fpsyg.2013.00140

Farrell, S., & Lewandowsky, S. (2010). *Computational Modeling in Cognition: Principles and Practice* (1st edition). SAGE Publications, Inc.

Fiedler, K., & Schwarz, N. (2016). Questionable research practices revisited. *Social Psychological and Personality Science, 7*(1), 45–52. https://doi.org/10.1177/1948550615612150

Francis, G. (2012). The psychology of replication and replication in psychology. *Perspectives on Psychological Science, 7*(6), 585–594. https://doi.org/10.1177/1745691612459520

Giles, M., Hansia, M., Metzger, M., & Dunbar, N. E. (2021). The impact of culture in deception and deception detection. In *Detecting trust and deception in group interaction* (pp. 35–54). Springer.

Hartwig, M., & Bond, C. F. (2014). Lie detection from multiple cues: A meta-analysis. *Applied Cognitive Psychology, 28*(5), 661–676. https://doi.org/10.1002/acp.3052

Hartwig, M., Granhag, P. A., & Luke, T. (2014). Strategic use of evidence during investigative interviews: The state of the science. In D. C. Raskin, C. R. Honts, & J. C. Kircher (Eds.), *Credibility assessment: scientific research and applications* (pp. 1–36). Academic Press. https://doi.org/10.1016/B978-0-12-394433-7.00001-4

Hudson, J. (2022, August 30). Ukraine lures Russian missiles with decoys of U.S. rocket system. *Washington Post.* https://www.washingtonpost.com/world/2022/08/30/ukraine-russia-himars-decoy-artillery/

John, L. K., Loewenstein, G., & Prelec, D. (2012). Measuring the prevalence of questionable research practices with incentives for truth telling. *Psychological Science, 23*(5), 524–532. https://doi.org/10.1177/0956797611430953

Kanazawa, S. (2020). What do we do with the WEIRD problem? *Evolutionary Behavioral Sciences, 14,* 342–346. https://doi.org/10.1037/ebs0000222

Keith, M. G., & Harms, P. D. (2016). Is mechanical Turk the answer to our sampling woes? *Industrial and Organizational Psychology, 9*(1), 162–167. https://doi.org/10.1017/iop.2015.130

Klein, O., Hardwicke, T. E., Aust, F., Breuer, J., Danielsson, H., Mohr, A. H., IJzerman, H., Nilsonne, G., Vanpaemel, W., & Frank, M. C. (2018). A practical guide for transparency in psychological science. *Collabra: Psychology, 4*(1), 20. https://doi.org/10.1525/collabra.158

Klein, R. A., Ratliff, K., Vianello, M., Jr, R. A., Bahník, S., Bernstein, M., Bocian, K., Brandt, M., Brooks, B., Brumbaugh, C., Cemalcilar, Z., Chandler, J., Cheong, W., Davis, W., Devos, T., Eisner, M., Frankowska, N., Furrow, D., Galliani, E., ... Nosek, B. (2014). Data from investigating variation in replicability: A "many labs" replication project. *Journal of Open Psychology Data, 2*(1), Article 1. https://doi.org/10.5334/jopd.ad

Klein, R. A., Vianello, M., Hasselman, F., Adams, B. G., Adams Jr., R. B., Alper, S., Aveyard, M., Axt, J. R., Babalola, M. T., Bahník, Š., Batra, R., Berkics, M., Bernstein, M. J., Berry, D. R., Bialobrzeska, O., Binan, E. D., Bocian, K., Brandt, M. J., Busching, R., ... et al. (2018). Many labs 2: Investigating variation in replicability across samples and settings. *Advances in Methods and Practices in Psychological Science*, *1*(4), 443–490. https://doi.org/10.1177/2515245918810225

klein Selle, N., Verschuere, B., & Ben-Shakhar, G. (2018). Concealed information test: Theoretical background. In *Detecting concealed information and deception: Recent developments* (pp. 35–57). Elsevier Academic Press. https://doi.org/10.1016/B978-0-12-812729-2.00002-1

Koshiw, I., Tondo, L., & Mazhulin, A. (2022, September 10). Ukraine's southern offensive 'was designed to trick Russia'. *The Guardian*. https://www.theguardian.com/world/2022/sep/10/ukraines-publicised-southern-offensive-was-disinformation-campaign

Leach, A.-M., Lindsay, R. C. L., Koehler, R., Beaudry, J. L., Bala, N. C., Lee, K., & Talwar, V. (2009). The reliability of lie detection performance. *Law and Human Behavior*, *33*(1), 96–109. https://doi.org/10.1007/s10979-008-9137-9

Leins, D. A., Fisher, R. P., & Ross, S. J. (2013). Exploring liars' strategies for creating deceptive reports. *Legal and Criminological Psychology*, *18*(1), 141–151. https://doi.org/10.1111/j.2044-8333.2011.02041.x

Levelt, P., Noort, E., & Drenth, P. (2012). *Flawed Science: The Fraudulent Research Practices of Social Psychologist Diederik Stapel.* https://pure.mpg.de/rest/items/item_1569964/component/file_1569966/content

Levine, T. R. (2017). Ecological validity and deception detection research design. *Comunication Methods and Measures*, *12*(1), 45–54. https://doi.org/10.1080/19312458.2017.1411471

Levine, T. R., Clare, D. D., Blair, J. P., McCornack, S. A., Morrison, K., & Park, H. S. (2014). Expertise in deception detection involves actively prompting diagnostic information rather than passive behavioral observation. *Human Communication Research*, *40*(4), 442–462. https://doi.org/10.1111/hcre.12032

Levine, T. R., Daiku, Y., & Masip, J. (2022). The number of senders and total judgments matter more than sample size in deception-detection experiments. *Perspectives on Psychological Science*, *17*(1), 191–204. https://doi.org/10.1177/1745691621990369

Masip, J., Blandón-Gitlin, I., de la Riva, C., & Herrero, C. (2016). An empirical test of the decision to lie component of the activation-decision-construction-action theory (ADCAT). *Acta Psychologica*, *169*, 45–55. https://doi.org/10.1016/j.actpsy.2016.05.004

Moi, W. Y., & Shanks, D. R. (2015). Can lies be detected unconsciously? *Frontiers in Psychology* (6), Article 1221. https://doi.org/10.3389/fpsyg.2015.01221

Murayama, K., Pekrun, R., & Fiedler, K. (2014). Research practices that can prevent an inflation of false-positive rates. *Personality and Social Psychology Review: An Official Journal of the Society for Personality and Social Psychology, Inc*, *18*(2), 107–118. https://doi.org/10.1177/1088868313496330

Nosek, B. A., Spies, J. R., & Motyl, M. (2012). Scientific Utopia: II. Restructuring incentives and practices to promote truth over publishability. *Perspectives on Psychological Science*, *7*(6), 615–631. https://doi.org/10.1177/1745691612459058

Open Science Collaboration. (2012). An open, large-scale, collaborative effort to estimate the reproducibility of psychological science. *Perspectives on Psychological Science*, *7*(6), 657–660. https://doi.org/10.1177/1745691612462588

Park, H. S., Levine, T. R., McCornack, S. A., Morrison, K., & Ferrara, M. (2002). How people really detect lies. *Communication Monographs*, *69*(2). https://www.tandfonline.com/doi/abs/10.1080/714041710

Porter, S., & ten Brinke, L. (2010). The truth about lies: What works in detecting high-stakes deception? *Legal and Criminological Psychology*, *15*(1), 57–75. https://doi.org/10.1348/135532509X433151

Schulz, J., Barahmi-Rad, D., Beauchamp, J., & Henrich, J. (2018). *The Origins of WEIRD Psychology*. PsyArXiv. https://doi.org/10.31234/osf.io/d6qhu

Semrad, M., Scott-Parker, B., & Nagel, M. (2019). Personality traits of a good liar: A systematic review of the literature. *Personality and Individual Differences*, *147*, 306–316. https://doi.org/10.1016/j.paid.2019.05.007

Simmons, J., Nelson, L. D., & Simonsohn, U. (2021). Pre-registration: Why and how. *Journal of Consumer Psychology*, *31*(1), 151–162. https://doi.org/10.1002/jcpy.1208

Simmons, J. P., Nelson, L. D., & Simonsohn, U. (2011). False-positive psychology: Undisclosed flexibility in data collection and analysis allows presenting anything as significant. *Psychological Science*, *22*(11), 1359–1366.

Simons, D. J., Shoda, Y., & Lindsay, D. S. (2017). Constraints on generality (COG): A proposed addition to all empirical papers. *Perspectives on Psychological Science*, *12*(6), 1123–1128. https://doi.org/10.1177/1745691617708630

Smith, N. A., Sabat, I. E., Martinez, L. R., Weaver, K., & Xu, S. (2015). A convenient solution: Using Mturk to sample from hard-to-reach populations. *Industrial and Organizational Psychology*, *8*(2), 220–228. https://doi.org/10.1017/iop.2015.29

Sporer, S. L., & Ulatowska, J. (2021). Indirect and unconscious deception detection: Too soon to give up? *Frontiers in Psychology*, *12*. https://doi.org/10.3389/fpsyg.2021.601852

Sternglanz, R. W., Morris, W. L., Morrow, M., & Braverman, J. (2019). A review of meta-analyses about deception detection. In T. Docan-Morgan (Ed.), *The palgrave handbook of deceptive communication* (pp. 303–326). Springer International Publishing. https://doi.org/10.1007/978-3-319-96334-1_16

Street, C. N. H. (2015). ALIED: Humans as adaptive lie detectors. *Journal of Applied Research in Memory and Cognition*, *4*(4), 335–343. https://doi.org/10.1016/j.jarmac.2015.06.002

Street, C. N. H., Bischof, W. F., Vadillo, M. A., & Kingstone, A. (2016). Inferring others' hidden thoughts: Smart guesses in a low diagnostic world. *Journal of Behavioral Decision Making*, *29*(5), 539–549. https://doi.org/10.1002/bdm.1904

Street, C. N. H., & Richardson, D. C. (2015). *Lies, Damn Lies, and Expectations: How Base Rates Inform Lie–Truth Judgments*. Applied Cognitive Psychology, 29(1), 149–155. https://doi.org/10.1002/acp.3085

Thalmayer, A. G., Toscanelli, C., & Arnett, J. J. (2021). The neglected 95% revisited: Is American psychology becoming less American? *American Psychologist*, *76*, 116–129. https://doi.org/10.1037/amp0000622

UNESCO. (2021). *UNESCO Science Report: The race against time for smarter development* (SC-2021/WS/7). UNESCO. https://unesdoc.unesco.org/ark:/48223/pf0000377250

van Rooij, I., & Baggio, G. (2021). Theory before the test: How to build high-verisimilitude explanatory theories in psychological science. *Perspectives on Psychological Science*, *16*(4), 682–697. https://doi.org/10.1177/1745691620970604

Vrij, A. (2015). Verbal lie detection tools: Statement validity analysis, reality monitoring and scientific content analysis. In P. A. Granhag, A. Vrij, & B. Verschuere

(Eds.), *Detecting deception: Current challenges and cognitive approaches* (pp. 3–35). Wiley-Blackwell.

Walczyk, J. J., Harris, L. L., Duck, T. K., & Mulay, D. (2014). A social-cognitive framework for understanding serious lies: Activation-decision-construction-action theory. *New Ideas in Psychology, 34*, 22–36. https://doi.org/10.1016/j.newideapsych.2014.03.001

Glossary

Accusatory reluctance: Accusing others of *deception* may be interpreted as a socially aggressive act that may lead to hostility or relationship breakdown. As such, people may want to avoid labelling others as deceitful.

Activation-Decision-Construction-Action Theory (ADCAT): ADCAT provides an explanation of how people lie in high-stakes situations (Walczyk et al., 2014). The account proposes that the truth is first activated in memory, and then a decision is made about whether or not to lie based on the expected outcomes of doing each. After deciding, a response is formulated or constructed and is then delivered.

Active lie detection: In contrast to *passive lie detection*, active lie detection is a broad categorical term that describes lie detection techniques designed to elicit cues to honesty and *deception* from the *sender*.

Adaptive lie detector account (ALIED): An account of how people form lie-truth judgements (Street, 2015). It claims that people make adaptive and functional lie-truth judgements, and controversially predicts that people can be biased to make lie judgements as well as being biased to make truth judgements. It argues that people rely on cues that causally relate to the statement being evaluated (e.g., CCTV footage, *nonverbal behaviour*), but that as these cues become less *diagnostic* of honesty or *deception*, information that generalises across statements (e.g., a belief that people tell the truth most of the time) has a heavier weighting in the lie-truth judgement.

Anecdote (i.e., anecdotal evidence): Anecdotes or anecdotal evidence refers to non-scientific claims, typically *consistent* with a particular argument being put forward. Because the anecdote does not provide evidence that results from applying the scientific method, they cannot be used as a form of reliable evidence to support an argument.

Anterior cingulate cortex (ACC): Located in the *medial* region of each hemisphere of the human brain, the ACC is involved in multiple cognitive functions such as impulse control, decision-making, attention allocation, emotional expression and more.

Anterior insular: Located in the *lateral* region of each hemisphere between the *temporal*, parietal, and frontal lobes of the human brain, a location where greater activation has been associated with a lower willingness to lie.

Application: In the context of *applied psychology*, application refers to the implementation of academic research in practical sectors outside of academia (such as with police forces or social services) such that knowledge is transferred from the former to the latter.

Applied psychology: A branch of psychology with the aim of tackling practical real-world problems.

Assumption: A part of an argument that is accepted without evidence as true.

Automatic: While different interpretations of automaticity exist, Moors and De Houwer (2006) argue that most definitions consider an automatic *process* to be independent of goals, acting without additional cognitive oversight, to be fast and efficient, and to be uncontrolled.

Bayesian analysis: A statistical framework for analysing data using probability theory to make inferences. The Bayesian framework proposes that one's beliefs about a hypothesis should be combined with the observed data to reach a new belief about the hypothesis. In doing so, one's beliefs about the hypothesis are formally captured and updated using probability theory.

Behaviour Analysis Interview (BAI): The BAI is to be employed as the first step of a broader interrogation method known as the Reid Technique which advocates for the interviewer to use accusation and other techniques to push the suspect to confess. It encourages the interviewer to focus on the *nonverbal behaviours* of the *sender* that are produced in response to 15 behaviour-provoking questions that assess the suspect's knowledge, suspicions of who the true culprit is, and who might have the motive to commit the crime. For a full list of the questions, see the appendix of Masip et al., 2011.

Behavioural research: An application of the scientific method to measure human behaviour and/or to understand the effect of interventions on human behaviour.

Behaviourism: A branch of psychology that views all behaviour as a learned association with a stimulus in the environment, such that the behaviour produced is rewarding to the person.

Blood oxygenation level, blood oxygenation level dependent (BOLD): Activation of brain cells results in an increase in blood flow to the surrounding area, which can be measured by *functional magnetic resonance imaging (fMRI)* to determine precise anatomical locations of brain activity. However, because BOLD is a response to cell activation rather than being present at the precise time of cell activation, it is a relatively poor measure of the timings of brain activity.

Blood pressure: The force exerted by blood on the walls of blood vessels.

Butler lie: A type of lie used as a way of maintaining positive relationships.

Cisgender: A person who self-identifies as one's determined birth sex.

Classical conditioning: A stimulus (e.g., food) that produces a response (e.g., salivation) can be unconditioned. But introducing a new stimulus (e.g., a bell) to co-occur alongside the food will lead to learning such that the new stimulus (the bell) will be capable of triggering the response (salivation). This introduction of a new stimulus to create a new stimulus-response pairing is known as classical conditioning.

Cognitive effort, cognitive load: The amount of information that is being manipulated in working memory at a given time. The greater the quantity of information, the greater the cognitive load and the resulting cognitive effort needed to *process* it.

Cognitive load approach: The cognitive load approach to detecting *deception* rests on the assumption that deceiving is more cognitively demanding than truth-telling due to the need to generate the lie, monitor one's own and the *receivers'* behaviour, and *inhibiting* truthful information (see Chapter 2). By adding additional *cognitive load* to the *sender* such as by having the *sender* make their statement in reverse chronological order (Vrij et al., 2008) or asking questions that the *sender* is not expecting (Vrij et al., 2009), liars should face greater difficulty in producing a convincing story, and as such, their lies should be detectable through cues such as the statement being less plausible and detailed.

Cognitive psychology: A branch of psychology concerned with understanding how humans think. Examples may include how judgements are formed, how learning occurs, or how attention is distributed to complete a task.

Cohen's *d*: A measure of *effect size*, Cohen's *d* allows for a standardised comparison of the difference between two groups (e.g., between liars and truth-tellers).

Collectivistic culture: Cultures are the collection of ideas, norms, and beliefs that make up a society. Cultures that value relationship and group goals over individual achievements are considered to be more collectivistic in their nature.

Communication research: A broad empirical discipline concerned with the many varied aspects of how humans share information with each other.

Concealed information test (CIT): The test uses a multiple-choice format, with each question having one relevant 'probe' answer (e.g., an element of the crime being investigated such as a weapon that the suspect used) and multiple control answers that are indistinguishable from the relevant item to an innocent *sender* (e.g., a set of other weapons). The CIT has traditionally been used in concert with physiological measures such as *skin conductance, respiration*, and heart rate (klein Selle et al., 2018). Increased physiological response to relevant items compared to control items suggests the person has knowledge about the item. This technique does not detect the presence of *deception*, but rather aims to detect whether there exists a memory for information.

Concealed knowledge test: See *Concealed information test*.

Concrete reasoning: A term I use to refer to a technique employed for the purpose of *evaluative reasoning*. It is often useful to imagine specific, concrete examples of a problem. Often, there is no singular way to concretely imagine the steps of a problem. In such cases, it is useful to consider the variety of possibilities that could be enacted. When these are very plentiful, working through concrete examples of the most extreme versions can help you gain an insight into the boundaries on the problem. Thinking in this way can help you ensure that you do not miss small but crucial parts of a problem and understand the full implications of any suggested solutions. For more on concrete reasoning, see Box 3.2 (Chapter 3).

Confederate: Someone, typically an experimenter, who acts as though they are a real participant with the aim of convincing one or more true participants that the confederate is as naïve to the situation as they are themselves.

Consistent (in the context of supportive findings): Empirical data that is consistent with a particular view or argument indicates that the argument is not contradicted or disproved by the data; however, it is important to keep in mind that this does not show that the data could *only* be explained by this view or argument.

Context-general information: A term used by the *adaptive lie detector account (ALIED)*, this information does not causally and directly relate to the current statement, but rather generalises *across* numerous statements. For example, research shows that people tend to tell the truth more often than they lie.

Contingent negative variation: An electrical signal that can be detected with *electroencephalography (EEG)*, a negative wave component that occurs between a warning (e.g., 'get ready....') and a signal indicating that a task that requires a quick response has begun (e.g., 'Go!').

Control question test (CQT): The CQT (Reid, 1947) is the most commonly used approach for questioning the *sender*. The method uses three types of questions. Relevant questions are those that pertain to the issue under investigation (e.g., 'did you steal a wallet from the office last Monday?'). Irrelevant questions are neutral questions that have no bearing on the case and should not evoke a strong physiological response (e.g., 'are you breathing oxygen?'). A third question type is the control question, which is designed to illicit a physiological response but is only indirectly related to the issue under investigation (e.g., 'have you ever stolen something when you were a child?'). The expectation is that liars will show a stronger physiological response to the relevant (compared to control) questions as a result of fear of getting caught in a lie. Truth-tellers are expected to more strongly react to the control (compared to relevant) questions because they create embarrassment and thus a physiological response, whereas truth-tellers have no reason to be concerned about their responses to crime-relevant questions.

Correlation (r): A statistical analysis that measures the relationship between two measures. For example, a correlation between age and height can be observed such that larger values of age are associated with larger values of height. Such a relationship is known as a positive correlation: high values for one measure are associated with high values on the other measure. Negative correlations can also be observed, such as may be the case with the number of hours revising for an exam and the number of incorrect answers. Higher values of revision hours should be associated with lower values of the number of incorrect answers.

Countermeasures: An action taken to overcome the effectiveness of a lie detection technique and thereby prevent or inhibit its ability to accurately classify lies and truths.

Criteria-Based Content Analysis (CBCA): CBCA involves coding the semi-structured interview with the interviewee to assess the strength of the presence of 19 criteria (Steller & Köhnken, 1989). Assessing the degree to which the criteria are present requires trained evaluators. The stronger the presence of each criterion, the more likely the statement is the truth, but this does not imply that the absence of criteria is an indicator of *deception*.

Cronbach's alpha: A statistical measure of how consistent a particular measurement has been made across multiple measurement opportunities. Values near 1.00 indicate high consistency while values near 0.00 indicate low consistency. A typical rule of thumb is to interpret values greater than or equal to 0.70 as indicating good consistency.

Crowdsourcing: The act of collecting human data from online platforms often using behavioural tasks or surveys, typically with participants being compensated financially.

Cyber security: The practice of ensuring that computer systems and digital data are safe from online malicious attacks designed to cause damage to or commit theft of the data.

Deception: Lying and deception are considered synonymous in the context of this book. To deceive or lie is to make a believed false statement (to another person) with the *intention* that that statement be believed to be true (by the other person) (Mahon, 2008). However, note that a more accurate interpretation of deception is any attempt to create a false belief in another with the *intention* that they believe the false information is true (e.g., animal camouflage), while lying is restricted only to delivering a statement (written or verbal).

Deceptive demeanour: Some people appear deceptive regardless of whether or not they are lying, which is to say that they have a deceptive 'demeanour'.

Defensible conclusions: *Evaluative reasoning* involves developing novel, robust arguments that reflect on the strengths and limitations of multiple alternative viewpoints to arrive at a logically and/or empirically defensible conclusion. Thus, a defensible conclusion is a deduction or induction made on the basis of rigorous evidence or logic such that it can stand up to scrutiny from a scientific audience.

Denial-induced forgetting: Repeating a (false) denial about engaging in an event can lead people to forgetting that they had, in fact, engaged in the event. That is, the act of lying may result in a forgetting of the truth.

Developmental psychology: A branch of psychology concerned with how human thinking and behaviour develops over the lifespan.

Diagnostic: How often an indicator or cue is present and absent when an individual lies and tells the truth. Cues with perfectly high diagnosticity are present only when a *sender* lies (i.e., on 100% of occasions) and never (i.e., 0% of occasions) when they tell the truth (or vice versa). Cues that are perfectly nondiagnostic appear equally as often (i.e., 50% of the time) when a *sender* lies as compared to when they tell the truth. Note that it is possible to distinguish the independent contributions of how diagnostic a cue is of honesty from how diagnostic a cue is of deception. For example, a cue could appear 100% of the time when a *sender* tells the truth but appear 60% of the time when the *sender* lies.

Dorsolateral: Relating to the back (dorsal) region and towards the side edge (lateral, i.e., towards the ears as compared with the brain centre) of the brain.

Dynamical systems theory: The mathematical study of how a system such as cognition or bodily movement changes over time.

Ecological validity: A study that demonstrates high ecological validity is one that demonstrates a high degree of similarity between the design of the research and the real-world context. It is often incorrectly argued that laboratory studies cannot be ecologically valid. For example, a study of playing video games in a laboratory that has a video game console set up would demonstrate a high degree of similarity to the real-world context of playing video games.

Effect size: When we engage in interventions (e.g., training participants, manipulating a variable), we want to be able to measure how much of a difference the intervention caused. This is an effect size. Typically, we wish to use standardised effect sizes. Imagine in one study that people detect two more lies on average as a result of the intervention. In another study, people detect four more lies on average as a result of the intervention. At face value, it looks like the second study found a higher effect of the intervention. But if the first study only had ten lies presented to participants as stimuli and the second study had 20 lies, then it becomes apparent that the size of the effect in both studies was comparable (i.e., 2/10 is equal to 4/20). By standardising the size of the effect, we can fairly compare across different studies that use different measurement scales. Cohen's *d* and Pearson's r are just two of the standardised effect sizes discussed in this book. The first attempts to explain how different two groups' scores are and the second how strongly associated two variables are with each other.

Electroencephalography (EEG): EEG measures brain electrical activity by recording from the scalp of the participant. As a result, it has difficulty localising activity to particular brain regions because the electrical signal conducts across the scalp, but the method can offer more precise timings of activity compared to *functional magnetic resonance imaging (fMRI)*, which measures the relatively slow changes in *blood oxygenation level* in the brain.

Epilepsy: A medical condition that causes physical seizures and uncontrollable bodily shaking.

Epistemic vigilance: Attending to information in the world and from one's past experience to determine what information can be trusted.

Evaluative reasoning: Developing novel and original arguments, considering the relative merits of alternative viewpoints, reflecting on the strengths and limitations of evidence and arguments, especially one's own arguments, and arriving at sound conclusions that can be cogently communicated to others.

Executive function: The high-level cognitive *processes* that facilitate new ways of behaving and optimise one's approach to unfamiliar circumstances (Gilbert & Burgess, 2008).

Expected value: The anticipated gain or loss as a result of an action (e.g., lying may persuade the jury to give a not-guilty verdict, which may have a relatively high value to the person compared to, say, the loss resulting from lying resulting in being caught and create a lengthier sentencing, which may have lower value) weighted by how likely that event is to occur (e.g., how likely it is the jury will give a not-guilty verdict as a result of lying or how likely the lie will be detected). Weighting is achieved by multiplying the outcome with the probability of that outcome occurring and summing across all possible outcome-probability pairs. The expected value of lying could be, for example, ([value of not-guilty verdict] × [probability of not-guilty verdict]) + ([value of being caught in a lie] × [probability of being caught]).

Extraversion: A personality trait where the individual obtains satisfaction from sources outside themselves and includes elements of being sociable and impulsive.

Fake news: Information presented in a news format, and so is lent an air of credibility, but which is actually factually inaccurate or misleading.

Falsifiable: An account that delineates which data would support the account and which data would show the account to be false is a falsifiable theory. It is falsifiable because it has the potential to be shown to be false. Accounts that do not allow for the possibility to be falsified are unscientific.

Few prolific liars, A: An argument that most people tell very few lies but that most of the lies being told are delivered by a small group of people. Diary studies tend to find that around 5% of people tell around 50% of all the lies told in that study.

Finger pulse: The rhythmic wave of blood passing through arteries in the finger.

First-order belief: In the context of *theory of mind*, first-order belief is the capacity to understand that another person's beliefs can be independent of one's own beliefs.

Focal account: The argument that *indirect lie detection* studies are unable to test for *unconscious lie detection*. The account proposes that the *indirect lie detection* allows higher lie detection accuracy because *receivers'* attention is focused to a single cue that the experimenter has selected. Provided the experimenter selects a cue *diagnostic* of honesty and deception, *receivers'* judgements of the cue should thereby result in a separation of liars and truth-tellers.

Forensic psychology: A branch of psychology that studies legal aspects of human thinking and behaviour. Some forensic psychologists research deception and its detection.

Four-factor theory: An account that aims to explain the elements that pertain to lying compared to truth-telling. Of particular note, the account is sometimes credited with being the turning point at which deception researchers more formally examine the cognitive difficulty associated with lying rather than exploring the emotional component of lying.

Functional magnetic resonance imaging (fMRI): A machine that uses large electromagnets to capture precise locations of brain activity. It does so by measuring the *blood oxygenation level*, which rises and falls in relation to brain function at specific sites of activity.

Ground truth: The veracity of a given statement. This is straightforward to determine in laboratory conditions where participants are explicitly assigned by the experimenter to either lie or tell the truth. In real-world settings, this is more challenging because there may be no evidence that definitively determines that the statement is a lie or truth. The ground truth may need to be inferred on the basis of whether a criminal was convicted for the crime, for instance.

Guilty Knowledge Test: See *Concealed information test*.

Heuristic: A decision rule that simplifies the decision-making *process* via overgeneralisations. Using heuristics may sometimes lead to poor outcomes but will typically provide satisfactory outcomes while also reducing the cognitive cost of processing a wide array of potentially relevant information.

Indirect lie detection: A method intended to examine whether *unconscious* thinking can improve lie detection accuracy. Participants are not made consciously aware that they are in a lie detection experiment but are instead asked to make judgements of the *senders* by rating a cue that may be related to deception or honesty, such as whether the *sender* is thinking hard or not. These indirect judgements have been found in some studies to better separate liars and truth-tellers compared to making explicit lie-truth judgements.

Individual differences: The difference between or variation in how different people think or behave.

Individualistic culture: Cultures are the collection of ideas, norms, and beliefs that make up a society. Cultures that value independence, individuality, and autonomy over the shared group goals and relationships are considered to be more individualistic in their nature.

Individuating information: Any piece of information that causally and directly relates to the statement that was delivered by the *sender*.

Infant: A child younger than approximately one year of age, typically characterised by being unable to yet walk.

Information manipulation theory 2 (IMT2): A theory of deception production that argues that people monitor and adapt their communication in-the-moment and on-the-fly in order to achieve the desired conversational goal.

Inhibitory control, inhibition: The ability to suppress a thought. In the context of deception, this may refer to inhibiting a memory of the truth when generating a lie.

Intentionality: A mental act that has the purpose of obtaining a particular outcome.

Interpersonal deception theory (IDT): An account of the *process* of deception which proposes that to understand deception, one must understand the dynamics of the interaction between the liar and the *receiver* of that lie.

Journal club: A group of people who read a given *scientific journal* article and come together to discuss the merits and limitations of the research contained in the article.

Journal, scientific: A reputable outlet for research carried out by academics. A journal will publish articles after two or more independent academics review the work to determine the *rigour* of the methods employed and the soundness of the conclusions reached on the basis of the data collected.

Leakage hypothesis: The claim that liars may experience emotions such as fear or guilt and that this may 'leak' from bodily behaviours and less so from facial behaviours because the face is readily observable and salient and so will be the subject of greater control.

Lie aversion: A preference to avoid lying, possibly due to an intrinsic desire to be honest, to avoid feelings of guilt associated with lying, or to avoid damaging their reputation.

Lie bias: The observation that participants make more 'lie' judgements than 'truth' judgements in a given study or situation.

Limbic system: A part of the brain associated with emotional behaviour and survival.

Linguistic Inquiry and Word Count (LIWC): Software used to analyse a transcript of speech to distinguish different parts and categories of speech (such as personal pronouns, emotion words, or words relating to community) with a view to understanding the speaker's psychological state.

Longitudinal study: A research design where the same participants are observed or tested on multiple occasions over an undefined but prolonged period of time.

Low attachment security: Holding fears of rejection, doubt about one's own value, and/or a disliking of close relationships.

Lying: see *Deception*.

Machiavellianism: A personality trait associated with manipulation and cunning.

Mean: The value that is the least distance from every observed data point. The mean, also called the average, can only be calculated for data that can be put on a scale with equal intervals between each value.

Mechanism: An element of a larger cognitive system that enables the *processes* of cognition to be performed. They are involved in transforming information. A series of cognitive mechanisms will allow for a broader cognitive *process* to be completed, such as how light reflecting from an object and hitting the retina requires the information is transformed for the object to be recognised and identified. The identification of the object involves a *process* that depends on multiple mechanisms. As such, a mechanism may refer to the anatomical instantiations that allow for cognition to occur.

Medial: The region of the brain nearest the centre as opposed to a lateral position of the brain that is located nearer the sides of the head.

Median: The 50th percentile in the data, meaning that half the observed data are higher than the median and half are lower than the median. The median can be determined by finding the value in a data set that can be ordered that, once put in order, is in the middle position.

Medical malingering: Appearing to show signs of an ailment that the person does not have or concealing signs of an ailment the person does actually have.

Meso level account: Psychological accounts that aim to describe or explain human behaviour at a relatively high level of abstraction.

Meta-analysis: A study that combines multiple past studies and analyses them together to see what can be learnt from the collection of past research.

Metabolic rate: The number of calories consumed over a given time.

Micro-expressions (ME): A fleeting facial expression that unintentionally conveys the *sender*'s true emotion that they are seeking to conceal.

Mock crime: An activity set up as part of a research study that aims to simulate the experience of committing a real crime.

Moral psychology account of deception: The position that people judge others' deceptions as morally deficient but view their own deceptions as a result of circumstance or as relatively innocuous.

Motivational impairment effect (MIE): The phenomenon that people who are motivated to succeed in their lies unintentionally give away their lie as a result of the high motivation to appear convincing. MIE may be the result of a greater emotional burden or the truthful information becoming more salient to the liar.

Neurolinguistic programming (NLP): An unscientific framework that makes multiple inaccurate claims about how people think, including how the direction the eyes are looking is an indicator of deception. Broader critiques of NLP as unscientific can be found in Witkowski (2010).

Neuroimaging: Techniques used to measure brain function such as *electroencephalography (EEG)* and *functional magnetic resonance imaging (fMRI)*.

Nonverbal behaviour: The collection of visible behaviours and behaviours that accompany speech (e.g., pitch, tone of voice) that a *sender* produces.

Normative hypothesis, The: A hypothesis that attempts to explain why people report that particular behaviours indicate deception when, in fact, they do not. It suggests that these stereotypes may be perpetuated by ourselves and the society we live in so that the younger generations are taught that their lies are detectable and lying is discouraged.

Open science: An approach to science which holds the principles of making data and resources available and transparent for others to openly review and assess.

Ostrich effect: There are times when we may not want to learn the truth, and so may not actively seek it out. The ostrich effect describes this phenomenon.

Overcommunication phenomenon: People communicate information about the true state of the world to another person even when the aims of the two people diverge. The degree to which the information is true is greater than would be expected if the *sender* aimed to achieve the highest possible gain for themselves over the *receiver*.

Paraverbal behaviour: Behaviours that accompany speech but are not the content of speech themselves, for example, *response latency*, pitch of voice.

Passive lie detection: In contrast to *active lie detection*, passive lie detection is a broad categorical term that describes lie detection techniques that involve observing the *sender's* behaviour without any attempt by the *receiver* to elicit cues to deception or honesty.

Pathological lying: Pathological lying has been defined by Healy and Healy (1926, p. 1) as "falsification entirely disproportionate to any discernible end in view, may be extensive and very complicated, manifesting over a period of years or even a lifetime, in the absence of definite insanity, feeble-mindedness or *epilepsy*". More succinctly, pathological lying is considered to be repeated and potentially compulsive in nature, told not as a means to some other goal but as a goal in its own right.

Peer review: When researchers submit articles for publication, the *journal* editor will send the submission out to two independent academics who review the soundness of the conclusions on the basis of the methods used. This process is known as peer review.

Phishing: An email scam that looks as though the email was sent from someone trustworthy in order to trick people into giving up sensitive information like credit card details and passwords.

Pinocchio's nose: The story of Pinocchio by Carlo Collodi tells the tale of a wooden puppet who wishes to one day be a real boy. Pinocchio is most famous for his nose that grows when he lies, which offers anyone speaking to Pinocchio a tell-tale sign of his deception (when it grows) and honesty (when it does not grow).

Polygraph: A device that measures the physiological reactions of a potential liar. It is used in combination with a questioning technique such as the *control question technique (CQT)* with an aim of separating liar from truth-tellers on the basis of their physiological reaction.

Positron Emission Tomography (PET): An imaging technique used to create a three-dimensional scan of the inside of the body.

Practitioner-led: Conducting research with, that begins from, and primarily focuses on the needs and goals of stakeholders.

Preregistration: The documenting of hypotheses and methods in an online, immutable repository that can be readily checked by others before the data is collected so that there is less room for questionable research practices such as adjusting hypotheses after the data have been analysed.

Prefrontal cortex: A region of the brain located at the front of the skull of both hemispheres. It is typically associated with higher level cognitive reasoning.

Primary lies: The first level of lying in Talwar and Lee's (2008) developmental model of lying. Primary lies are the earliest lies that children tell at around age two to three, and are relatively simple counterfactual statements that do not consider the beliefs and mental reasoning of the person they are lying to. While lying is infrequent at this age, primary lies typically involve concealing a *transgression*.

Principle of charity: While it can certainly be helpful to be critical of the work of others, one must also be willing to be charitable to the claims of others too. Hughes et al. (2015) refer to this latter point as the Principle of Charity. If a claim by a researcher is ambiguous or unclear, for instance, but you could provide an interpretation that is favourable to the researcher's claims, the Principle of Charity encourages us to offer that favourable opinion. This helps us not only generate a collegiate discussion in our writing, but also forces us to be more critical of our own perspective, which is a truly useful skill to have as both a consumer and producer of scientific research.

Process, psychological: A collection of *mechanisms* make up a broader psychological process. They involve multiple transformations of information to carry out a broader psychological task such as thinking or decision-making.

Psychiatric disorder: This term is synonymous with mental illness or mental health conditions, and describes the broad range of psychological difficulties that people may face emotionally, cognitively, or behaviourally.

Psychodynamic: A perspective that views behaviour and thought as a result of hidden *unconscious* forces outside of the person's awareness.

Psychopathy: A lack of empathy and detachment from others characterises psychopathy, although people with psychopathy may publicly display behaviours that conceal this detachment.

Reality monitoring (RM): The theoretical basis was put forward by Johnson and Raye (1981) to distinguish between memories of the experienced world differ from those that are imagined. As such, the technique was not designed as a lie detection technique, but it has since been put to work in the detection of deception.

Receiver: A term used to refer to the person who is listening to, reads, or otherwise receives a statement from another person. The other person is referred to as the *sender*.

Replication crisis: When researchers attempt to rerun an already published study, the findings often do not come out the same as the original study. With this happening so frequently, it has been dubbed the replication crisis.

Representativeness heuristic: A mental shortcut or rule of thumb that people use to estimate how likely an event occurs generally (e.g., that nervousness is associated with deception across the population) by drawing on one's memory of past 'representative' experiences (e.g., how often nervousness has been seen to occur with deception in one's limited experience).

Research seminar: A talk held at an academic institution that is typically delivered by a visiting academic who is not employed by that institution. The visiting academic will discuss their ongoing research, likely work that is not yet published. It is an opportunity to discover the latest in the field and be part of the discussion. Academics will ask questions at the end, and so should you, although there is no requirement to do so.

Researcher degrees of freedom: The number of ways in which data can be extracted, cleaned, and otherwise adjusted to reach a particular conclusion. To experience this for yourself, visit the interactive webpage https://projects.fivethirtyeight.com/p-hacking/.

Respiration rate: How frequently breaths are taken over a given period of time.

Response latency: The time taken from the *sender* being requested for a response and the time that the *sender* begins delivering their response.

Rigour: Scientific rigour requires that the best practices are followed and implemented. For example, was a power analysis conducted to determine the sample size? Is the research engaging in *open science* practices? Does the methodology allow the researchers to make the conclusions they are reaching? Has the finding been replicated in other labs? Answering these questions can help us assess whether a study has rigour.

Schema: Broad prototypes generated from multiple pieces of information that lack specific details but provide the gist of the situation (e.g., the schema for 'a restaurant' may include tables, chairs, mood lighting, and so on, even though this is not a memory of a specific restaurant).

Second-order belief: In the context of *theory of mind*, second-order belief is the capacity to hold a belief about what another person thinks of the child's (or a third party's) beliefs. For example, the child may hold a belief that Stephen (person A) incorrectly believes that the child (person B) believes that the toy is hidden in the basket (but perhaps, in reality, the child has hidden the toy in the cupboard). That is, they are able to hold the belief that Stephen should be successfully deceived into believing that the child's claim of the location of the toy is where they are incorrectly claiming it is.

Secondary lies: The second level of lying in Talwar and Lee's (2008) developmental model of lying. Secondary lies appear at around age three to four years and involve deceptions that require an understanding that another person may hold a different set of beliefs and understanding to themselves. Lying becomes more prevalent but may have difficulty maintaining consistency with their initial lie when prompted for further detail, thereby giving away that they lied.

Self-presentational perspective: The view that both liars and truth-tellers seek to strategically present themselves to appear credible and honest.

Seminal research: Work that is important to understand and has influenced the broad field of research and the many researchers working within that field, leading to streams of future research.

Sender-receiver game, The: Two participants take part in this incomplete information game. Two options are given to the *sender*: one option will financially benefit the *receiver* (option 1) and one will benefit the *sender* (option 2). The *receiver* knows nothing about how the options will pay out. This gives the *sender* the opportunity to lie (e.g., "choosing option 1 will pay out for you more than option 2"). The *receiver* is the person who has to choose which of the two options to select based solely on what the *sender* has said.

Sender: A person who delivers an honest or deceptive message. This may be through any medium (e.g., speech, writing). The person on the receiving end of the message is known as the *receiver*.

Skin conductance: The capacity to convey electrical activity across the skin.

Social engineering: Gaining unauthorised access to an organisation's sensitive data and assets, sometimes by means of deception.

Social psychology: A branch of psychology concerned with how humans think and behave with or around other people.

Socio-economic background: The social and financial background from which a person originates.

Spinozan mind: A psycholinguistic account of comprehension that has been used to explain how lie-truth judgements are formed. It claims that all information is automatically believed as true in the first instance, thereby explaining the *truth bias*. Only afterwards can information be tagged as false.

Standard deviation: A statistical description of the spread of data using the same scale that the original data was observed on.

Statement Validity Analysis (SVA): The SVA is an interviewing method that consists of four steps: understanding the criminal case file, a semi-structured interview with the interviewee, an analysis of the content of the interview using *Criteria-Based Content Analysis* (*CBCA*), and finally assessing the possibility that *CBCA* may be biased in this particular application using a validity checklist.

Statistically significant: Under a particular statistical framework known as NHST, we aim to understand whether the effect observed in a small sample of people will also be observed in the wider population. Statistical significance is a means of measuring that. The method assesses the probability with which an effect at least as big as the one that was observed in the small sample is likely to have been observed if, in the wider population, the effect does not actually exist. For example, we may ask what the probability is that 50 coins would show a bias towards coming up heads if, in the entire population of minted coins, there is no bias. If the coins in our sample were heavily biased, it may be quite improbable to see them all showing such a strong bias if minted coins are not really biased. Smaller probabilities, then, are what should be expected if we want to rule out the idea that there is no effect in the population. Statistical significance refers to a threshold (in psychology, we commonly use less than 5% probability) below which we consider an effect to be substantially unlikely to have been found in our sample if the effect does not exist in the wider population.

Strategic Use of Evidence (SUE): An *active lie detection* technique intended to create a contradiction between a liar's statement and known evidence. The *receiver* is encouraged to hold back the evidence they have so that the liar can potentially contradict the evidence and then be confronted with it.

Subdiscipline: A more specialised subset of research that is embedded within a wider research field. In our case, the wider research field is likely to refer to the field of psychology.

Taxonomy: A classification scheme intended to provide a conceptual overview of an issue. A taxonomy was used in Chapter 2 to try to understand how to classify different types of lies that people may tell.

Temporal lobe: The areas of the brain that are located nearest the ears, commonly associated with processing auditory information.

Temptation-resistance paradigm: An experimental design commonly used when exploring children's *deception*. An item is placed behind the child. The child is asked not to peek at the toy while the experimenter is out of the room. The experimenter then leaves the room and eventually returns. Children often peek during the experimenter's absence. Upon returning, the child is asked whether they peeked at the toy. Those who peeked but deny having peeked are considered to be lying.

Tertiary lies: The third level of lying in Talwar and Lee's (2008) developmental model of lying. These lies are sophisticated insofar as their plausibility can be maintained upon further questioning

Theory of mind: The capacity to reason about the mental state of others. See also *first-order belief* and *second-order belief*.

Thin slicing: An experimental design whereby a video recording of a statement is edited. The video is separated into a number of short segments. A small selection of those segments is edited together into a shorter version of the original statement. The method has been used to explore *unconscious lie detection*.

Tipping point account, The: An account of *unconscious lie detection* that argues that people are not able to consciously detect *deception* because of the social implications and potential to be excluded from groups when accusing others of *deception*. But, it argues, because it is evolutionarily prudent to detect when one is being lied to in situations where it could cause us harm, the *unconscious* has evolved to detect lies and to hide this from our conscious awareness.

Toddler: A child between the approximate age of one to six years old.

Transcranial direct current stimulation (tDCS): A brain stimulation method that uses direct current using electrodes placed on the scalp to modulate the excitability of neurons.

Transgression: A behaviour that is not condoned, such as peeking at a toy that an experimenter has instructed a child not to peek at.

Truth bias: The observation that participants make more 'truth' judgements than 'lie' judgements in a given study or situation.

Truth-default theory (TDT): An account of how people make lie-truth judgements. It argues that people default to believing everything that they comprehend is the truth without considering the possibility that it may be a lie. If a trigger is present (e.g., the *sender* is believed to have a motive to lie), a suspicion stage is entered in which evidence is sought (e.g., that the *sender* is displaying a range of behaviours that appear deceptive). If the evidence is sufficiently potent and indicative of dishonesty, it results in a lie judgement. If it is indicative of honesty or if the evidence is not sufficiently potent, a truth judgement results.

Unconscious lie detection: The perspective that bypassing awareness of *deception* (i.e., engaging the *unconscious*) will result in greater lie detection accuracy.

Unconscious thought theory (UTT): UTT argues that the conscious mind is limited by the constraints of working memory. Unconscious thought, in comparison, is believed to be unlimited in its capacity. As a result, the *unconscious* is better placed to make decisions about complex tasks where multiple pieces of information need to be assessed before reaching a judgement. Distracting the conscious mind when having to make complex decisions, then, should result in better performance because the distraction allows the unconscious mind to drive the judgement.

Unconscious: A cognitive process that is distinct from conscious processing. Definitions of the unconscious may consider (i) there being no conscious awareness that a cue is diagnostic of deception, (ii) there being no conscious detection of what cues are influencing their judgement, (iii) there being no conscious awareness of how they are processing and combining the cues into a judgement, or indeed (iv) there being no awareness that they are making a judgement at all.

Ventrolateral: A region of the brain that is located on the underside (ventral) and towards the skull (*lateral*).

Verbal behaviour: The content of speech delivered by the *sender*.

Verifiability approach: An *active lie detection* technique. Truth-tellers are thought to include more checkable details in their statements compared to liars. Checkable or verifiable details include those which are physically documented or are witnessed by another named person.

WEIRD: Short for Westernised, educated, industrialised, rich, and democratic. WEIRD samples tend to dominate the psychological literature, questioning the generalisability of the findings to other cultures.

Wizards: The name given to human lie detectors who are naturally capable of detecting *deception* at unusually high levels of accuracy.

Working memory model of deception: An account of *deception* formation and production that claims people rely on their memory for similar situations to develop their lies or rely on broader generalised *schema* when they do not hold specific memories for similar situations.

Working memory: Refers not only to temporary storage of visual and auditory information but also active manipulation of that information in memory.

Index

accusatory reluctance 86–87, 185
activation-decision-construction-action theory (ADCAT) 38–41, 43–44, 60, 68
active lie detection 4–5, 17, 116, 123–135
Adaptive Lie Detector account (ALIED) 4, 85, 91, 97–100, 101–103
Albrechtsen, J. S. 179
automatic: belief 4; processing 14, 39, 40, 89, 90, 91, 97

Behaviour Analysis Interview (BAI) 123–124
beliefs about deception cues 71–75, 124
Ben-Shakhar, G. 132, 134–145
Bond, C. F. 4, 30, 84, 116
Buller, D. B. 31, 60, 70
Burgoon, J. K. 31, 60, 70
butler lie 26

cognitive effort: lie-truth judgments 89–90, 91; lying 4, 32–35, 38, 40, 42, 43–44, 60, 68–71, 126
cognitive load approach 125–126
cognitive strain model of lie production 69–70
compulsive lying 23–24, 158
Concealed Information Test (CIT) 131–134
consistency 28, 60, 125
Control Question Test (CQT) 129–130
Criteria-Based Content Analysis (CBCA) 119–122, 162

denial-induced forgetting 41, 44
DePaulo, B. M. 4, 22, 24, 30, 40, 60, 61, 64, 66, 84, 116
detecting children's lies 161–163
developmental model of lying 150

ecological validity 196–198, 199–201
effective lying 44–46
Ekman, P. 4, 32, 59–60, 65, 117

Elaad, E. 121, 132, 134–135
embedded lie 40, 42, 45
evaluative reasoning: alternative explanations 34–35, 70, 72–73, 84–85, 102, 175–176; assumptions 25, 67–68, 95, 130, 181–183; concrete reasoning 62–64, 151–153; falsifiability 36–38, 197–198; overview 1, 17, 19–20, 27–28; reflection 2, 3, 5, 87–89, 100–105, 118, 159
executive function 29, 33, 39, 151, 155–156
expertise, lie detection 4–5, 17, 117

falsifiability 15–17, 36–38, 89, 94–96, 187–188
first lies, children's 147–150
Fisher, R. 125
focal account 176–179
four-factor theory 32

Gilbert, D. T. 4, 89
The Global Deception Research Team 71, 74, 102
ground truth 197

Hartwig, M. 124, 125
heuristics 4, 89

impression management 30–31, 44, 60, 66–67, 120
Inbau, F. E. 123
indirect lie detection 174–179
individual differences: accuracy 17, 116–119; decision to lie 27–30; prevalence of lying 25–26, 33
Information Manipulation Theory 2 (IMT2) 41–43, 60, 70
inhibition of the truth 32–33, 60, 155–156
Interpersonal Deception Theory (IDT) 30, 31–32, 42, 60, 66, 70

Johnson, M. K. 121

Kanazawa, S. 205
Köhnken, G. 119–120

leakage hypothesis 4, 32, 59–60, 63, 124
Levine, T. R. 4, 26, 91–92, 93, 100–103, 198
lie aversion 24–25, 157
lie bias 98–100, 101–102
lying: definition 21–22, 67–68, 197; emotional response 4, 24–25, 32, 44–45, 59–60, 64–66, 198; intentionality 21, 40–42, 94, 197; preparing 40, 46; prevention 163; motive 25, 26, 91–93, 95, 123, 160; reputational concerns 24, 26, 185; stakes 38–39, 42, 198; taxonomy 25–27, 46
Lykken, D. T. 131

Mahon, J. 21
McCornack, S. A. 41–44, 60, 70
memory 33, 38–39, 40, 41, 42, 44, 60; *see also* working memory model of deception
micro-expression 5, 32, 60, 65–66
moral psychology account 30
morality 28, 29, 30, 45, 148–149, 157
motivational impairment effect (MIE) 44–45

Nahari, G. 127–128
Newell, B. R. 189–190
nonverbal cues to deception 4, 61, 62, 63, 65, 69–70, 71, 74, 117, 123–124, 198–199

O'Sullivan, M. 86, 117
online lying 22, 25–26, 30, 31
open science 15, 104, 201–202, 204, 211
orienting response 132–133
ostrich effect 85–86, 87–89

Park, H. S. 198
passive lie detection 116–119, 161–163
pathological lying *see* compulsive lying
personal relationships 24–25, 26, 27, 28–29, 42, 67, 86
personality: extraversion 26, 116; Machiavellianism 26, 28, 45–46, 116 ; motive for lying 25–26; prevalence of lying 28; psychopathy 26
physiological arousal 42, 45; *see also* polygraph
polygraph *see* Control Question Test (CQT), Concealed Information Test (CIT)

prosocial lying 148–150, 155, 157, 159–160

reality monitoring (RM) 121–123, 162
Reid, R. E. 130
Repke, M. A. 69, 70
replication crisis 201–202, 204
response latency 33–34, 38, 42, 44, 45, 61, 65

self-deception 31, 45
self-presentational theory *see* impression management
Semrad, M. 197
social development, children 149–150, 158
Spinozan mind hypothesis 4, 85, 89–91
Sporer, S. L. 35, 38, 40, 41, 42, 60, 68
Statement Validity Analysis *see* Criteria Based Content Analysis (CBCA)
strategic model of lie production *see* cognitive strain model of lie production
Strategic Use of Evidence (SUE) 124–125, 162–163
Street, C. N. H. 4, 90–91, 97–99, 100–103, 176–178

Talwar, V. 148–149, 150, 158–159
temptation-resistance paradigm 148, 156, 157, 158
ten Brinke, L. 185–187, 188–189
theory of mind 28, 31, 38–39, 60, 150–155, 156, 159
thin slicing 179–180
time pressure 33–34, 89
tipping point account, the 185–189
training, lie detection 4–5, 73–74, 117–118
truth bias 4, 83–85, 161; *see also* Adaptive Lie Detector account (ALIED), Spinozan mind hypothesis; Truth-Default Theory (TDT)
Truth-Default Theory (TDT) 4, 85, 91–97, 100–103

unconscious 14, 189–190
unconscious thought theory 181–185

verifiability approach 127–128
Vrij, A. 30, 86, 125

Walczyk, J. J. 38–41, 42, 60, 68
wizards, lie detection *see* expertise, lie detection
working memory model of deception 35, 38, 40, 41, 60, 68

Zuckerman, M. 32, 116